Mary Coghill
**Semiotics and City Poetics**

# Semiotics, Communication and Cognition

Edited by
Paul Cobley and Kalevi Kull

# Volume 25

Mary Coghill

# Semiotics and City Poetics

Jakobson's Theory and Praxis

**DE GRUYTER**
MOUTON

ISBN 978-3-11-151866-4
e-ISBN (PDF) 978-3-11-061739-9
e-ISBN (EPUB) 978-3-11-061480-0
ISSN 1867-0873

**Library of Congress Control Number: 2022942857**

**Bibliographic information published by the Deutsche Nationalbibliothek**
The Deutsche Nationalbibliothek lists this publication in the Deutsche Nationalbibliografie; detailed bibliographic data are available on the internet at http://dnb.dnb.de.

© 2024 Walter de Gruyter GmbH, Berlin/Boston
This volume is text- and page-identical with the hardback published in 2023.
Cover design based on a design by Martin Zech, Bremen
Typesetting: Integra Software Services Pvt.

www.degruyter.com

# Acknowledgements

My grateful thanks go first to Professor Paul Cobley for his support and expertise over many years, commencing with the Directorship of my PhD and continuing throughout this project. He has been an invaluable editor. I also thank Professor Kalevi Kull for his editorial co-operation.

I warmly thank Professor Warwick Gould at The Institute of English Studies, School of Advanced Studies at the University of London for awarding me an Honorary Research Fellowship at the SAS (2014–2017), which was an opportunity to initiate research for this book. I also warmly thank Professor Katharine Hodgson, head of The Russian Language Department, the Department of Languages, University of Exeter, for her assistance in obtaining (2018) my continuing award of an Honorary Research Fellowship in The Department of Languages, University of Exeter. My thanks go also to Professor Linda Waugh, from the University of Arizona, whose lifelong interest in the work of Professor Roman Jakobson and her specialisms of Languages, Linguistics and Semiotics provided specialist support for this project. I thank Dr Yuliya Kostyuk, Lecturer in Russian at the University of Exeter, Department of Languages, who has, for the last three years, been my teacher of the Russian Language and provided translation assistance. Thanks also go to the excellent staff at Exeter University Library for assistance with references. I thank the translators Elena and Paul Richard (full details below), who have both supported this project with specialist subject material and translation expertise. And last, but not least, I thank De Gruyters for publishing this volume. If the book contains errors, these are acknowledged, with apologies, as my own.

Grateful acknowledgements are made to the publishers of the poetry quoted in this book which require copyright permission. Both they and the authors have been generous and obliging. In alphabetical order of the poet, these are: Elizabeth Bartlett: Bloodaxe Books; Hart Crane: W.W.Norton & Co; Carol Ann Duffy: Picador; Allen Fisher: Salt Publishing; Elena Guro translations: Jamie Bennett; David Jones: Faber and Faber; Velimir Khlebnikov (trans. Smith and Douglas) Harvard University Press; Professor Tony Lopez: Shearsman; Edwin Morgan: Carcanet; Max Nänny: Swiss Association of University Teachers of English; Stephen Rudy: the current author and the publisher were unsuccessful in ascertaining original copyright, any potential copyright holder is encouraged to contact the publisher; Rosemary Tonks: Bloodaxe Books; Sarah Wardle: Bloodaxe Books. The poems by Vladimir Mayakovsky, are reproduced here, with reference to Raduga Publishing, translation by Viktor Christyakov (1985). The author and the publisher were unsuccessful in ascertaining original copyright. Every effort has been made to contact the publishers and the translators. The poems are: "The City" (Chapter Two) and "Brooklyn Bridge" (Chapter Nine).

Elena Richard is a translator and editor who holds an M.A. in Russian Linguistics from the Department of Foreign Languages and Literatures at Bucharest State University, Romania, and a B.A. in Russian and English from the same university, where she taught Russian before relocating to the United States. She has translated from Russian into Romanian, works by Sergey Bulgakov and Leo Tolstoy, from English into Romanian, titles by Richard Dawkins and Edward O. Wilson, and from Russian into English, articles and theatre plays. She is a member of the Romanian Association of Literary Translators (Artlit), and currently resides in Bucharest, Romania. Together with Paul Jude Richard they translated the Roman Jakobson's articles in the Appendix of this book.

Paul Jude Richard is a former attorney, current teacher, translator and editor, and holds an M.A. in Russian Literature from the Department of Slavic Languages and Literature at University of Wisconsin-Madison, an M.A. in Russian Studies from Middlebury College, Vermont, an M.A. in German Studies from Middlebury College, Vermont and a law degree from Tulane University, New Orleans, Louisiana. He currently resides in Bucharest, Romania, where he teaches, translates and edits.

Three short notes on referencing:

Throughout the text, where the date of the original publication of a reference is significant in the study of the development of ideas, the original date is included in square brackets, supplementary to the actual reference used. With references that are originally written in Russian, the anglicised spelling can vary. In order to make these references easily accessible to the researcher, the standardised spelling has usually been used. However, in some cases, a more eclectic spelling is used where the reference indicates that this is the spelling that has been used for publication. All references to "The New Princeton Encyclopedia of Poetry and Poetics", is referred to as *NPEPP* throughout the text. The Oxford English Dictionary is referred to as *OED* and qualified, where relevant to the meaning in the text, with a date of publication or online referencing.

# List of figures

| | | |
|---|---|---|
| **Figure 1** | Jakobson's Theory of Communication —— 12 | |
| **Figure 2** | Jakobson's axial model, as developed by the author —— 44 | |
| **Figure 3** | Then and Now —— 65 | |
| **Figure 4** | Dirven's Jakobsonian Axial Diagram —— 86 | |
| **Figure 5** | Bühler's diagram of deictic relationships —— 115 | |
| **Figure 6** | Poem with diagonals —— 122 | |
| **Figure 7** | "Wrestle" without and with diagonals —— 126 | |
| **Figures 8 and 9** | Blake's illustration of "Infant Sorrow" and Jakobson's semiotic diagrammatic interpretation —— 225 | |
| **Figure 10** | Blake's poem "London" https://www.bl.uk/collection-items/william-blakes-songs-of-innocence-and-experience /page 43 in the digital reproduction —— 226 | |
| **Figure 11** | e e cummings: Grasshopper poem complete with drawing (Nänny 1985: 134, 135) —— 262 | |
| **Figure 12** | Baudelaire: poem as a cubist painting —— 269 | |
| **Figure 13** | Patterns of word usage: "usura" from Brooke-Rose (1976: 65) —— 274 | |
| **Figure 14** | Diagram of mood: "Frequency of primary stresses on the downbeats of the two versions" (1987: 238) —— 275 | |
| **Figure 15** | from Merrell Figure 10 (2000: 37) —— 293 | |

# List of tables

**Table 1**  (Bredin 1984: 48) —— 73
**Table 2**  Shifters —— 206
**Table 3**  Deictics —— 207
**Table 4**  Deictic analysis —— 208
**Table 5**  Deictic analysis —— 209
**Table 6**  Deixis and time —— 209
**Table 7**  Verbs – analysis —— 210
**Table 8**  Verb usage —— 221

# Introduction

The purpose of this book is firstly, to re-examine, and then develop, Jakobson's theories of Poetic Function and Communication (Chapters One and Two); secondly, to provide an increased range of examples of Formalist praxis; thirdly, to apply these theories to the analysis of city poetry with the intention of establishing a city poetic genre; and, lastly, to provide a basis for understanding Formalist praxis as a structural process which does not force the analyst to either use the full range of Formalist techniques, nor apply them to an entire poem. The current author's principal focus is semiotic rather than linguistic. Jakobson's legacy is extensive. The focus here is to take advantage of his research – to revisit, re-investigate, apply and develop it – adding to the body of knowledge in the fields of linguistics, semiotics and poetics. It is accepted throughout this book that Roman Jakobson's theory of Poetic Function combines semiotics, linguistics and poetics. An additional focus is the application of these theories and praxis to city poetry, with a specific emphasis on the woman narrator. These areas of research provide further material for the establishment of a city poetic genre.

Roman Jakobson's interest in linguistics, when considering poetry, was constantly super-imposed by the demands of the poetic text. From his early days he recognised that both pictorial art and, to a lesser extent, mathematics, played a part in enabling analysis of the text. From these two disciplines he derived his interest in the shape of poetry – its form and linked meanings; and from mathematics he derived his interest in the possibility of expressing those shapes in diagrammatic form. His interest in linguistics, especially phonemes, was largely shaped by his contemporary in Prague – Trubetzkoy (1939). His series of lectures "Six Lectures in Sound and Meaning" (1978[1942]) develop his links with Saussure and the axes of language. Jakobson continued to be inspired by Saussure's work throughout his life, adding to it, amongst others, an interest in the semiotic systems of Charles Sanders Peirce. But his linguistic interest was always placed within the context of the larger units of word, sentence and textual whole. His interest in poetry further pushed him towards analysis of the construction of the whole poem as a unit. His interest in phonemes, for example, was expressed through his interest in the bigger picture. He writes in his lecture: "Linguistics and Poetics":

> No doubt, verse is primarily a recurrent "figure of sound". Primarily always, but never uniquely. Any attempts to confine such poetic conventions as meters, alliteration, or rhyme to the sound level are speculative reasonings without any empirical justification. The projection of the equational principle into the sequence has a much deeper and wider significance. Valéry's view of poetry as "hesitation between the sound and the sense" is much

> more realistic and scientific than any bias of phonetic isolationism.//Although rhyme by definition is based on a regular recurrence of equivalent phonemes or phonemic groups, it would be an unsound oversimplification to treat rhyme merely from the standpoint of sound. Rhyme necessarily involves a semantic relationship between rhyming units ("rhyme-fellows" in Hopkins nomenclature). (1987: 81[1960])

Jakobson's engagement in poetry naturally included an interest in sound. In the same lecture, he also writes: "In poetry, any conspicuous similarity in sound is evaluated in respect to similarity and/or dissimilarity in meaning . . . [for example] Pope's alliterative precept to poets – 'the sound must seem an echo of the sense'." (1987: 87). He further states: "The analysis of a poetic sound texture must consistently take into account the phonological structure of the given language and, beside the overall code, the hierarchy of phonological distinctions in the given poetic convention as well." (1987: 88/9). Once again, he uses linguistics as a stepping stone to assist in analysing not only the larger unit of text but also the differing languages available to the poet.

Rhetoric had been the usual form of analysis of language construction but it was superseded by the emerging discipline of linguistics. Jakobson's Formalism is derived, not from this ancient art of rhetoric, but from his interest in linguistics. He made this clear in his reference to Mayakovsky's influence:

> When in 1919 the Moscow Linguistic Circle discussed how to define and delimit the range of *epithet ornantia*, the poet Majakovskij rebuked us by saying that for him any adjective appearing in a poem was thereby a poetic epithet, even "great" in the Great Bear of "big" and "little" in such names of Moscow streets . . . . "I live on the Big Presnja, 34, 24. Apparently it's not my business that somewhere in the stormy world people went and invented war". And the poem ends: "The war has killed one more, the poet from the Big Presnja" Briefly, poeticalness is not a supplementation of discourse with rhetorical adornments but a total reevaluation of the discourse and of all its components whatsoever. (1987: 93)

Formalism was not only an early major influence on Jakobson, it remained of primary importance for his lifelong research. He expressed his early commitment very clearly in his 1921 essay, "Novešaja russkaja poèzija. Nabtosok pervyi. Podstupy k Xlebnikovu." ["The Newest Russian Poetry. First draft with Viktor Khlebnikov"], which is, as yet, not fully translated into English. The paragraph below was translated for "Russian Formalism", 4. 1977: 17; trans. Ann Shukman and L.M.O'Toole):

> The subject of literary science is not literature, but literariness, i.e. that which makes a given work a literary work. Up till now, however, historians of literature have mostly behaved like the police who when they want to arrest someone take in everyone and everything found in the apartment and even chance passers-by. Historians of literature have in the same way

felt the need to take in everything – everyday life, psychology, politics, philosophy. Instead of a science of literature we have fetched up with a conglomeration of cottage industries.
(1979b [1921]: 299–354)

In another early lecture, "The Dominant" [1935], he writes: "With the further development of Formalism, there arose the accurate conception of a poetic work as a structured system, a regularly ordered hierarchical set of artistic devices." (1987: 44). He further indicates his linguistic interest in diachronic and synchronic methods. These are not confined to phonemes or linguistics but are used to understand how innovation is constructed in art forms:

The shifting, the transformation, of the relationship between individual artistic components became the central issue in Formalist investigations. This aspect of Formalist analysis in the field of poetic language had a pioneering significance for linguistic research in general, since it provided important impulses toward overcoming and bridging the gap between the diachronic historical method and the synchronic method of chronological cross section. It was the Formalist research which clearly demonstrated that shifting and change are not only historical statements . . . but that shift is also a directly experienced synchronic phenomenon, a relevant artistic value. The reader of a poem or the viewer of a painting has a vivid awareness of two orders: the traditional canon and the artistic novelty as a deviation from that canon. It is precisely against the background of the tradition that innovation is conceived.
(1987: 46)

Linda Waugh's chapter, "Roman Jakobson's work on semiotics and language", in *(Re)considering Jakobson* (eds. Sütiste, Grampigna, Griffin, Salupere. 2022: 15–32), provides an overview of the differing influences expressed by Jakobson in his work:

Since, for Jakobson, language is a pure system of signs, not only sound, but also grammar and syntax, [it] must be subjected to a semantic/semiotic analysis; the study of meaning cannot be excluded from linguistics, not from other semiotic systems such as music and non-representational painting . . . . That is, any formal analysis of signs necessitates a concomitant semantic analysis whether the object of study is phonological elements, morphological systems, syntactic structures, discursive aspects of texts, formal structure of poems, and so forth. Concomitantly, no semantic analysis can be done without close attention to form: e.g., the meaning/interpretation of a sentence or of a whole text depends crucially on how that meaning is interrelated with the formal elements.
(1922: 17)

Linguistic and semiotic theoretical research is now well-established. These disciplines are constantly developing in complexity and range. Fundamentally, it is generally accepted that linguistics is the scientific study of language (Cuddon 1999). The Introduction of *The Oxford Concise Dictionary of Linguistics* (Matthews 2005), states that linguistics is the study of grammar, syntax, sound systems, and the comparison of different language systems and their history and development. Semiotics is the 'science of signs', of which linguistics forms a part. Things and signs signify meaning, as well as words. Matthews (2005) gives examples of traffic lights, architectural features, the giving of presents. Cuddon (1999) explores more closely Peirce and Saussure's definitions, as originators of semiotics. Both subscribe to the fact that a word, in itself, does not carry its full meaning. Cobley also emphasises the process of semiology, by which the world is interpreted through the processing of all signs into systems of comprehension of the world (2010. Introduction: 3–13). Throughout this book, each poetic text demands that it is viewed as a whole – not just a series of lines, or tropes – rhyme for example – semiotics not linguistics, is the central basis for analysis.

Within the remit of this book the term "genre" also needs to be defined. Wales (2001) suggests that the theory of genre has developed and adapted to encompass the complexity of many differing styles of discourse. She favours the definition of a genre as a generic term (for example poetry) and the idea that within it, there are different specific registers – the sonnet or limerick for example. The register may include forms which become embedded within that form – for example a limerick is not considered to have a tragic register. Succinctly, Wales writes: "So any group of texts which show a similarity of register can be said to belong to the same genre." (2001: 178). Thus, for a city poetic genre, there are both content and different forms which become not only the expected register of the poet, but also the expected register of its content. Within the genre, the poet expresses a "vocabulary" or "idiom" which is both personal to the poet (the words and forms used are their particular choice), and also understood by the addressee – the message is therefore recognisable as one which has a register. In this instance the register arises from the city and constructs an ideation of the city – an "eidometropolis" or "eidopolis".

An early inspiration for this suggested genre was an essay by Gary Roberts: "London Here and Now: Walking, Streets, and Urban Environments in English Poetry from Donne to Gay" (1999: 33–54). Roberts demonstrates the importance of the ideation that the city might provide for poetry, and how it might be represented in a particular way. Roberts highlights the requirements for a city poetic: "When used in the context of a poetics that is self-consciously urbanizing itself, deictic adverbs, idiomatic verbs, and street names become primary devices for representing a practical and spatially productive knowledge of the city. These tactical linguistic moves are part of a complex metonymical system standing in place of a London that is in constant motion" (1999: 50). This quotation provides the keywords for a number of important themes for a city poetic. If it is decided that there is such a thing as an urban poetics, then this becomes self-conscious, that city-dwellers know that this is what they are (as opposed to, for example, rural dwellers) and that, as city dwellers, it is something to explore and express.

Deixis and shifters, or pronouns, are important if we, as humans, are to see ourselves in relation to the city. As will be discussed in various chapters, the deictic is an adverb which places everyone and everything in relation to each other in time, place and space. Roberts refers to idiomatic verbs as essential parts of a city poetic expression. The poem by Donne - Satire I, "Away, thou changeling motley humourist". Roberts analyses this poem in his essay, and it certainly provides a vocabulary which is only understood by those who are familiar with city life. He is perhaps using the idiomatic to mean a particular word-set, rather than indicating that there will be neologisms. Street names will definitely provide reference points, but if a city poetic seeks to provide a generalised interpretation, then a specific name will be omitted because it does not provide extra meaning to the poem. Robert's quote also includes the words 'in motion'. A city which is static, is dead, has ceased to exist. Mayakovsky's work includes this ideation. This could be said to be true for any environment, but the city exists because humans are propelled to interact with the city at every hour of the day. City-dwellers must go to work, study, take children to school, go shopping for food and so on – and all the time negotiating an environment which in itself is constantly changing: new buildings being constructed, shops which change their ownership, areas of cities which change their populations, people constantly on the move and always with a purpose. It is interesting to note that Roberts' understanding of 'walking, streets and urban environment' (1999: 33) is not an exploration of the flâneur – the idler who walks through the city with the sole aim of absorbing an "atmosphere" or impressions that come to his or even her attention. The themes of constant movement of both the humans and the development of structures in the city, mean that there is not much time for an idler. The relationship between the human and the city is expressed through activity, motivation for success, speed of stimulus, tension, all experiences which can be both rewarding and savage.

Roman Jakobson was a Russian Formalist from his early years. The Russian Formalist technique of studying the text "in itself" reveals the meaning of the text through its structure, its literariness, with the use of linguistics and semiotics. Roman Jakobson has also interpreted the tools of linguistics and semiotics to achieve his Formalist semiotic analysis. The emphasis is on the text, in itself, as a scientific construct and it is prioritised as the source of meaning. The use of semiotics allows a greater range of interpretation of the poetic text. While linguistics intends to perform this task, it often only deconstructs language within the syntactical structure of the sentence. Such emphasis does not always reveal the full interconnected semiotic meaning of the poetic text (the whole poem, or section of it) as a system of signs, this being more than a sentence, or sequence of lines within it.

The human brain is adroit at adapting its patterns of thinking and, having analysed a portion of a poem, the reader can adopt, and adapt, the Formalist analysis in order to all-the-more enjoy the meaning of other parts of it. At all times Formalist analysis enhances knowledge of the poet's skills. The semiotic aspect recognises that not only is the text itself being analysed, but also the structural patterns which the poem, as a whole, expresses. The Formalist specifically refuses to add to the semiosis, either the life of the poet or even the geographical and historical background to the text. However, as is demonstrated in the examples given, it is not always possible to adhere to these restrictions.

One of the truly exciting features of the poetic text is that, upon thorough investigation, no matter what rule system is used to analyse a poem, the poem often breaks the boundaries set by the selected rules. The poet is strongly attracted to the interpretation of the world through words, and analysis of poetry is enriched with the use of semiotic theory. These points are further ratified in the praxis which is developed in the following chapters, and demonstrates that poets can also use space on the page, punctuation and computer software to interpret meaning as part of the poem, providing further semiotic interpretation to their work.

The research developed in this book certainly demonstrates that Formalism is a very useful structure for analysis of the poetic text and, for this researcher, the primary conclusion is that the structural nature of the Formalist analytical process of poetry provides a strong set of techniques for understanding the aims and intentions of the text and that this may include the aims and intentions of both the poet and the reader. One area that would benefit from further research is Jakobson's axial model (Chapter Two). The axes can be represented diagrammatically. But, so often, it seems, the construction of a diagrammatic model falls short of the full meaning which the ideas demand. Yet, the impetus to design a diagram is always there. The complexity of language structure in poetry demands of the theorist some kind of semiotic representation of semiotic ideas. But can the various levels of theory be interpreted in one diagram with clarity? Jakobson produced two diagrams for his theory of communication which can, without too much difficulty, be amalgamated. The same cannot be said of his presentation of poetic function and the metaphoric and metonymic axes. This book suggests some variations, always in the hopes that the diagram is conclusive; but this area of research remains open for interpretation.

It is also not possible to explore Jakobson without reference to his contemporaries. The Russian influence is constantly felt. Several of the chapters refer to the Russian poet Vladimir Mayakovsky (including Chapters Eight and Nine). Mayakovsky was well known to Jakobson and his essays on him "About Mayakovsky's Later Lyrical Poems" and "Dostoyevsky Echoed In Mayakovsky's Work", have now been translated for the first time into English from the Russian, and are published here in the Appendix. The Russian poet and artist, Elena Guro's unique contribution, that of analogy, is also closely examined (Chapter Ten). But in the commitment to the provision of new examples of Jakobson's Formalist analysis, there is a need to demonstrate that Jakobson's Formalist techniques hold true for any poetic text. Contemporary poetry is also analysed throughout the book to provide examples. Every Formalist analysis of a poem is so detailed and requires such intricate dissection that long poems are realistically thought to be beyond this kind of analysis. However, extracts from longer poems have been attempted. The analysis of certain tropes has been highlighted in various chapters – metaphor and metonymy (Chapters Three, Four and Eleven), shifters and deictics (Chapters Five, Six and Twelve), idiom (Chapter Nine), and analogy (Chapter Ten). Hopkins' important contribution to parallels with reference to the city is explored in Chapter Seven. There is an emphasis on poetry which has the city as its subject matter. Analysis of the city poetry by the current author is also used, including in Chapter Twelve. Throughout, there is an attempt to demonstrate that city poetics may well contain certain constructions and patterns which are particularly relevant for a city poetic genre.

There is a history to Jakobson's development of his Formalist ideas. While living in America, a number of his essays were published, in English, in the book *Language in Literature* (1987) edited by Krystyna Pomorska and Stephen Rudy. This is a collection of key essays by Jakobson, in English. The original publication dates of these essays range from 1919 to 1975. It is a textbook which provides not only a great number of theoretical insights into semiotics and linguistics, but also, by looking at what lies behind the finished essays, the development of the theoretician himself. All too often, only one or two of these essays are referred to which has led to a repetition of very small parts of Jakobson's theories: his theory of Poetic Function, and the use of a small amount of material being used as part of "translation theory". It is important to remember that Jakobson wrote in a number of languages. He never expected his work to be constantly reduced to his model of communication and sometimes seemingly tireless references to his definition of Poetic Function. He would have expected his students to constantly investigate and develop his ideas.

Throughout the book each chapter seeks to extend the theoretical understanding of Jakobson's Formalism. Many chapters also provide the praxis which demonstrates the efficacy of Formalism. The results are not always predictable and fresh definitions emerge through the course of the research into the Formalist analysis of poetics. Use of Formalist techniques also provide the basis for the establishment of a city poetic genre. These chapters provide both a deeper understanding of how the text, in itself, achieves its impact and also a detailed understanding of poets' intentions. For Jakobson the text was all-important and the analyses that follow are all based on his fundamental premise. It is with this in mind that the first chapter provides an in-depth analysis of his Formalist theory of communication, the definition of Poetic Function.

# Chapter 1
# What is Roman Jakobson's "poetic function"?

Roman Jakobson sums up his theory of poetic function as follows: "The poetic function projects the principle of equivalence from the axis of selection into the axis of combination" (1987: 71). Analysis of this important theory originates from within the Russian Formalist tradition of the importance of function as communication. Close examination of the terms of reference within Jakobson's definition – "poetic function", "equivalence" and "projection" – give rise to an understanding of the sense of movement inherent in Jakobson's model which contributes to a semiotic structure. This is associated with iconicity and the interpretation of "similarity" in poetry. Jakobson's early essay "Realism in Art" (1987 [1921]) demonstrates his engagement with modern art and provides the basis for the connections with the semiotic, the grammar of poetry. It is therefore argued that "poetic function", within this definition, contains semiotic processes as well as linguistic ones. The importance of these semiotic characteristics is constantly highlighted and this demonstrates how they contribute to the construction of a city poetic genre. Analysis includes the use of linguistic, semiotic, structuralist, and stylistics methodology.

In "On Realism in Art" (1987), Jakobson indicates not only that his interest in poetic theory had a strong foundation in the theory of art, but also that his own theory of "Poetic Function", developed later in his life, was already in its earliest stages. He outlines the four different approaches to the analysis of painting which he later used to develop his methodology of poetic function. He looks for revolutionary realism in literature. He states that the words of "yesterday's narrative grow stale" (1987: 22). The adherence to a so-called "realism" and verisimilitude by traditionalists fixes the response to the artwork, in a framework of analysing two criteria which are non-essential details. Briefly, Jakobson provides three categories, each of which have sub-categories of definition:

1. Realism may refer to the aspiration and intent of the author; i.e. a work is understood to be realistic if it is conceived by its author as a display of verisimilitude, as true to life (meaning *A*).
2. A work may be called realistic if I, the person judging it, perceive it as true to life (meaning *B*) . . . [Then] one separate artistic movement, . . . was made the standard . . . Thus . . . a third meaning of the word 'realism' has crept in (meaning *C*), one which comprehends the sum total of the features characteristic of one specific artistic current of the nineteenth century (1987: 20).

The artist's life is Jakobson's category of meaning *A*, the emotional response of the viewer is Jakobson's category of meaning *B*. The presumed perception of realism is then completed by the viewer who has constructed a "standard" *C* for the artifact. None of these refers to how the artifact, in itself, is constructed. Even in this early essay Jakobson grasps the semiotic implication of the difference between the work of art and the work of literature. Verisimilitude may be possible in art as the pictorial representation of the object provides a clear and incontrovertible link between the object painted and its image. But there is no such direct link possible with the written word. This is further explored with reference to projection below.

What follows is an exploration of the understanding and application of Jakobson's theory rather than a detailed study of its sources and origins. Regrettably, therefore, an in-depth history of the development of Russian Formalism and ideas in the Prague Linguistic Circle (Erlich: 1981; Steiner: 1984, Todorov: 1985) and the contribution of Saussure's linguistic studies to Jakobson's theories, including the development of diachrony and synchrony, largely fall outside the scope of this research. One purpose of the following close analysis of Jakobson's "poetic function" and its interpretation is to demonstrate a formal structure for the construction of a city poetic genre.

Before moving on to consider Jakobson's "poetic function" in detail, the Formalist interpretation of "function" is explored. The interpretation, below, highlights the importance of poetic structure in itself and thus specifically provides an important basis for communication, as in a city poetic. Boris Èjxenbaum writes in "The Theory of the Formal Method" (in Matejka and Pomorska, 1978) that the Formalists wished to apply science to language, to construct "literariness", the science of poetics. He reveals both the historical derivation of the theory, and insight into Jakobson's definition of poetic function:

> The fact of the matter is that the Formalists' original endeavour to pin down some particular constructional device and trace its unity through voluminous material had given way to an endeavour to qualify further the generalized idea, to grasp the concrete *function* of the device in each given instance. This concept of functional value gradually moved out to the forefront and over-shadowed our original concept of the device. Such a process of making further qualifications of one's own general concepts and principles is characteristic of the entire evolution of the Formal method. We maintain no general, dogmatic positions that would bind our hands and keep us from getting at the facts . . . Work on concrete material is what started us talking about function and by that very fact led us to a new level of complexity in the concept of the device. Theory itself required our branching out into history.
> (1978: 29–30)

In a translation of Jakobson's and Tynjanov's article "Problems in the Study of Language and Literature" (1980) an Editor's note is added which succinctly explains some of the political background in defining "function":

> The modern science of language and literature abolishes this opposition between theory and history, and assumes that a theoretical analysis is impossible without a consideration of the dialectics of history (the flow and change of literary and linguistic values) and vice versa – historical research cannot be fruitful without a theoretical recognition of the specific aspects of its material.//Instead of the question posed by the old science 'why?' we find in the forefront the question 'what for?' (the problem of functionality). Research deals not merely with constructive functions (functions of elements constituting a literary fact), and not only with immanent literary functions of various genres, but also with the social function of the literary series in various periods.
>
> (1980: 31)

This quotation is interesting in that it also sheds light on how the early Formalists adopted a sense of historical development whilst continuing to preserve a distance between art and the biography of the artist. In *Dialogues* (Jakobson and Pomorska, 1983) Pomorska summarizes Jakobson's longstanding position: "The biographies of both poets [Mayakovsky and Pasternak], especially Pasternak's *Safe Conduct*, show that so-called real facts do not exist for the poet. Each detail of life is instantaneously transformed into a symbolic element and only in this form is it linked to the poet" (1983: 151). This validates Jakobson's own position of adherence to experimentation within the poetic message in and of itself, not as a representation of the real poet. His position enables an empirical study of poetry which, as will become clear below, provides a process of communication within a city poetic.

The main purpose for using this quotation here is to illustrate how the Formalists, with their interest in structure, understood that the artifact exists as something which has its own properties and that these are available, in themselves, for study and analysis. This is a fundamental precept which is derived from the Aristotelian empirical desire for observed knowledge and which has been used throughout the centuries to inform scientific observation. The Formalists wished to apply science to language through study of the text in itself and its language. This has been called into question especially by the post-structuralists with their emphasis on the reader's role in the control of the artefact's meanings (see Culler, 2002).

When considering the structure of poetry, any analysis of Jakobson's theory of "poetic function" must begin with his own central definition. Jakobson's essay "Linguistics and Poetics" (1987[1960]), includes this definition and analysis. Jakobson's own definition of "poetic function" includes the statement that the "focus on the message for its own sake, is the POETIC function of language" (1987: 69). The reference to "message" is part of the six-category structure that comprises Jakobson's structural model for the process of verbal and written communication: addresser, context, message, contact, code and the addressee. Of these six categories the central four (context, message, contact and code) describe the communication from the addresser to the addressee. Jakobson adds a further function to each of these categories. Emotive is added to the addresser, conative to the addressee. The communication itself is further described respectively as: referential, poetic, phatic and metalingual (1987: 71):

|             | Context/*Referential* |           |
|-------------|-----------------------|-----------|
| Addresser/  | Message/*Poetic*      | Addressee/|
| *Emotive*   | Contact/*Phatic*      | *Conative*|
|             | Code/*Metalingual*    |           |

**Figure 1:** Jakobson's Theory of Communication.

Jakobson refers to another important aspect of his understanding of poetics in the concept of the dominant: "The poetic function is not the sole function of verbal art but only its dominant, determining function, whereas in all other verbal activities it acts as a subsidiary, accessory constituent" (1987: 69). Jakobson's essay on "The Dominant", first given as a lecture in 1935 (1987: 41–46), reveals his early interest in the importance of both verbal sound and written patterns of meaning. This early essay demonstrates that Jakobson derived his theoretical inspiration from the Formalists and the Prague Circle. Saussure contributes to this theoretical development, though not without criticism from Jakobson in "A Glance at the Development of Semiotics" (1987: 436–454[1974]).

In "Linguistics and Poetics", Jakobson raises another central theme of his work: that "the linguistic study of the poetic function must overstep the limits of poetry, and, on the other hand, the linguistic scrutiny of poetry cannot limit itself to the poetic function" (1987: 70). The discussion, below, of Jakobson's "poetic function" will reveal that semiotic as well as linguistic elements are present in his theories from the earliest stages of their formation. Diagrammatic representation of this structure is an integral part of the interpretation of Jakobson's model.

There is a need for a detailed analysis of fundamental definitions. Firstly, here is Jakobson's central principle placed in its context:

> What is the empirical linguistic criterion of the poetic function? In particular, what is the indispensable feature inherent in any piece of poetry? To answer this question we must recall the two basic modes of arrangement used in verbal behavior, *selection* and *combination*. If 'child' is the topic of the message, the speaker selects one among the extant, more or less similar nouns like child, kid, youngster, tot; all of them **equivalent** [added emphasis in bold throughout quotations] in a certain respect, and then, to comment on this topic, he may select one of the semantically cognate verbs – sleeps, dozes, nods, naps. Both chosen words combine in the speech chain. The selection is produced on the basis of **equivalence, similarity and dissimilarity, synonymy and antonymy**, while the combination, the build-up

of the sequence, is based on contiguity. *The poetic function projects the principle of **equivalence** from the axis of selection into the axis of combination.* **Equivalence** is promoted to the constitutive device of the sequence. In poetry one syllable is **equalized** with any other syllable of the same sequence; word stress is assumed to **equal** word stress, as unstress **equals** unstress; prosodic long is matched with long, and short with short; word boundary **equals** word boundary, no boundary **equals** no boundary; syntactic pause **equals** syntactic pause, no pause **equals** no pause; syllables are converted into units of measure, and so are morae or stresses.  (Linguistics and Poetics. 1987:71)

Here "morae" can be understood as from *"mora"*, the Latin for "delay": "A unit of metrical time which denotes the duration of a short syllable ... The time occupied by a long syllable in quantitative verse is two *morae*." (Cuddon 1999: 518); see also Brogan's entry for "Duration" (*NPEPP* 1993: 312/313b).

For a more detailed understanding of the word "stresses" in the above quotation, consider also Jakobson's "Linguistics and Poetics": where he writes: "equivalence in sound, projected into the sequence as its constitutive principle, inevitably involves semantic equivalence, and on any linguistic level any constituent of such a sequence prompts one of the two correlative experiences which Hopkins neatly defines as "comparison for likeness' sake" and "comparison for unlikeness' sake" (Hopkins, 1959 [1865]: 85; also Jakobson, 1987: 83). In fact, this is not actually what Hopkins says. Hopkins wrote: "To the marked or abrupt kind of parallelism belong metaphor, simile, parable, and so on, where the effect is sought in likeness of things, and antithesis, contrast, and so on, where it is sought in unlikeness". Jakobson's version reflects the Hopkins text, although Hopkins uses different words.

Equivalence is clearly the key term, here; but, at this stage, it requires clarification, not least because, like much of Jakobson's theory of poetic function, it has been reinterpreted rather than fully understood (see Bradford 1994, below, for example) The entry on Equivalence in *NPEPP* (1993: 380,381b) indicates that Jakobson is using the classical definition of the term when he refers to the idea that one item **equals** another: "word stress is assumed to **equal** word stress" ("Linguistics and Poetics". 1987: 71). But the dictionary entry then goes on to say that Jakobson defines equivalence in a new way, quoting the key statement from "Linguistics and Poetics" reproduced above (1987: 71). The Dictionary entry, which is written by one of the overall Editors of the *NPEPP*, T.F.B Brogan, adds: "The principle of **equivalence** which **equates** the words in the vertical register of speech, can **equate** other features in poetry and thus become superimposed upon the horizontal sequence as well" (1993: 380b).

The next paragraph by Brogan is innovative in its interpretation of **equivalence**, not only because it interprets Jakobson without reference to other authors, but also because, whilst dependent on Jakobson's theory, it introduces an analysis of time which appears to go further than Jakobson himself does. (In Chapter Two, the importance of time as a property of the syntagmatic axis will be further explained):

> **Equivalence** is especially prominent in metrical verse, where one phonological feature is deployed (against its opposite) systematically. **Equivalence**, however, is not the meter but the system which *makes the meter possible*: the particular feature the meter will employ (stress, length, pitch) is determined by the language, and the specific pattern the meter will assume is mainly a convention. Meter, then, is a synecdoche for **equivalence**, but **equivalence** is a metonym for parallelism; indeed, Jakobson identifies parallelism as 'the fundamental problem of poetry'. As with the meter, so with all the other formal elements in the text – sound patterning, rhetorical figures, lexical echo and allusion, syntactic metaplasm: in every case '**Equation** is used to build up a sequence'. **Equivalence** is thus 'the indispensable feature inherent in any piece of poetry'. And since the syntagmatic axis presents the sequential unfolding of meaning in language, even as the paradigm represents the axis of simultaneity, [not to be confused with similarity] **equivalence** in poetry serves to embed the atemporal within the temporal: as the lines proceed through their sequent schemes of meaning, **equivalence** counterpoises a firm (if subliminal) sense of unchangingness, of the *re*-creation of the now which came before in the now which is now. (1993: 380b)

Jakobson's use of the word "equivalence" is central to his theory of poetry. It is as much a Jakobsonian term as "poetic function" (Nöth, 1990: 357; Wales, 2001: 133,134). He refers to it as the "principle of equivalence" ("Linguistics and Poetics". 1987: 71). Jakobson's key definition of poetic function: "The poetic function projects the principle of **equivalence** [added emphasis] from the axis of selection into the axis of combination" in itself reveals where Brogan finds his information on temporality and atemporality. The following is quoted from Brogan again: "**equivalence** in poetry serves to embed the atemporal within the temporal: as the lines proceed through their sequent schemes of meaning." (1993: 380b). That is, once selected, the lines proceed along the axis of combination – the temporal axis in effect.

This close analysis of Jakobson's terms allows the construction of an axial model based on his frames of reference. Jakobson is demonstrating that there are different attributes to the following: that "equivalence", and "equate" do not have the same meaning as is expressed by the word "equals" with respect to poetics. "Equivalent" indicates "corresponding significance", "something equal in value or worth"; "equate" indicates balance, average; but "equals" infers that two things are identical, very much the same (*OED online 2022*). In another paper, on the "Linguistic Aspects of Translation" (1987 [1959]), Jakobson makes this difference quite clear: "Equivalence in difference is the cardinal problem of language and the pivotal concern of linguistics" (1987: 430). The argument being made here is that an extension of this understanding of equivalence is made so that a semiotic dimension to Jakobson's poetic function is clearly revealed. "Equivalence in difference", as a part of the projective aspect of poetic function, is a crucial part of this, as will be further investigated and explained below.

The all important definition by Jakobson from "Linguistics and Poetics" above – "The selection is produced on the basis of **equivalence,** [added emphasis] similarity and dissimilarity, synonymy and antonymy" (1987: 71) – does, on close examination, indeed hold the key to the meaning of the words "equivalence in difference". Jakobson is referring to the words being equivalent (having the same or similar meaning) as each other and being equivalent in property or value rather than being equal in the sense of being the same or identical. The equivalence encompasses the sense that the words used are equivalent in value even though they might be dissimilar or apparently unconnected in meaning, as in a metaphor. Linda Waugh in her article "The Poetic Function in the Theory of Roman Jakobson" (1980) makes this meaning of equivalence clear: "equivalence is a *relational equivalence* based on sameness within system" and also when she identifies that the quality of "sameness is used as (the major) means of constructing the whole sequence." (1980: 64). As will be further argued, the "equivalence in difference" contributes to the semiotic structure of Jakobson's theory of "poetic function" when combined with a deeper understanding of projection. Within the axial model, the relational equivalence readily constructs a semiotic model of lines and layers and intersections. Jakobson highlighted the linguistic importance (1987: 71 above); the analysis of the present author proposes to highlight the pivotal importance of relational equivalence to a semiotic interpretation and construction of a city poetic genre.

There is context provided, not only from art, as mentioned above, but also from other art forms. Dinda Gorlée (2008) notes that: "One common feature shared by musical and poetic language alike is the role of repeated projection of paradigmatic (that is, structural) equivalences upon the syntagmatic (that is, serial) chain of signs. In music, the organic synthesis of synchronism and progression produces melody, harmony, as well as polyphony" (2008: 348). Music so readily contains more than one sound at a time that verbal and written language must envy the complex simultaneous combinations of sound.

In order to avoid any confusion, it should be noted, as is becoming clear from the above paragraphs, that there is a fundamental difference between linguistics and semiotics. Linguistics studies phonemes, lexis and the grammatical structure of language. It also has a strong emphasis on defining the structure of all languages with the view to establishing structural similarities between them (Matthews (2005); and Harris 2001: 118–133 (in Cobley. 2001c). Semiotics is wider in scope, in that it is not the grammar and structure of words alone but also the "general science of signs" (Petrilli in Cobley 2010: 322). It is also the "the theory or science and analysis of signs and sign systems and their meanings . . . involved with communication between human beings in different societies and cultures" (Wales 2001: 354). Thus it can be seen that, with reference to poetry, linguistics may provide analysis of grammar and choice of words and the implications arising from these choices; but that semiotics provides a wider definition of structure which can include line patterns and provide analysis of how different parts of a poem refer to each other without reference to linguistics as such. It is therefore semiotics which enables the iconicity which, as is argued below, enables a city poetic genre.

Gérard Genette and Thais Morgan (1989) note the differences in translation between the word "equivalence" in both French and English and its innate ambiguity in both languages. They note that Jakobson himself appears to understand that "equivalence" and "similarity" have the same meaning. Jakobson uses "similarity" in his "Linguistics and Poetics" where, earlier, he used the word "equivalence" in his definition of poetic function: "In poetry, where similarity is superinduced upon contiguity, any metonymy is lightly metaphorical and any metaphor has a metonymical tint" (1987: 85). The use of the word similarity does not appear to contradict "equivalence" as it is used to describe a similar function within the poetic function; but with reference to metaphor and metonymy, similarity is used in a different way, as an interpretation within its structure.

Balzer and Göttner's understanding of equivalence, is that a process of shifting is taking place: "in poetical texts the principle of equivalence is projected (shifted) from the axis of selection onto the axis of combination. 'Projection' here means a restriction of the principle of selection. Therefore, the equivalence in classes of words of similar meaning, are narrowed down by the principles of poetical combination. For example, by the principle of alliteration" (1983: 491). This example of interpretation of Jakobson's terms used in his definition of "poetic function" illustrates how subtle differences in interpretation can lead to large scale re-interpretation. Arguably, "shifting" is not a projection and poetic combination is not a "restriction".

Genette's understanding of the meaning of "equivalence" is broad in its application. He sums up Jakobson's model of poetic function:

> textual recurrence (formal similarities spread out over the space of the text) induces a sort of parallel recurrence at the level of the signified, which is metonymized metaphor, or similarities of meaning spread out over the space of the content. Ultimately, therefore, a veritable symbolic volume with three dimensions is established within the poem. In actuality, it constitutes the poem as a horizontal network of signifying equivalences (phonic, metrical, grammatical, intonational, prosodic) that refers to another horizontal network of equivalences signified by a series of (vertical) semantic equivalences between each form and each meaning (images) and between each group of forms and each group of meanings (diagrams) – a hyperbolic and flawless state of the Baudelairian 'forest of symbols'. (1989: 211)

It can be seen from the above, that the diagrammatic element of Jakobson's theory of poetic function is easily realised as including horizontal, vertical images and groups of meaning. There is an acceptance of "iconicity" here that contributes to construction of a city poetic. Iconicity is meant here as a semiotic interpretation of Peirce's definition of the "icon" and as understood by Jakobson in his "Quest for the Essence of Language" (1987: 413–435). Jakobson notes Peirce's interest in diagrams (1987: 419) and analyses a chapter heading of a novel by Ronsard entitled: "Le Rumeur de la rue Réaumur". The analysis is linguistic in principle but the representation of this analysis is diagrammatic (1987: 426). The diagram is iconic. The axial graph constructed and examined in Chapter Two illustrates how this iconicity can be represented.

Genette and Morgan refer to "Cratylism", deriving the term from Plato's *Cratylus*, where the student of Socrates wrestles with how most words bear no resemblance to their meaning, but there are some words which do, resulting in an understanding of iconicity in some words (Genette and Morgan (1989: 205 and 213 n. 6 and n. 7:). The structure of the city can be represented poetically and iconically by the sense of moving lines, intersections, verticals and horizontals. In a suggested change of metaphor, instead of Baudelaire's "forest of symbols", there is a densely written street map which is overlaid by time and movement.

Before moving on to a discussion of Jakobsonian projection, the apparent confusion over the use of the words "sameness" and "similar" or "similarity" with regard to Jakobson's theories and the description of metaphor should briefly be mentioned here. The confusion among critics about the meaning of these words in Jakobson's writings on poetry and their relation to metaphor can be problematic and has, perhaps, impeded the contribution that Jakobson has made to literary theory and analysis with his theory of poetic function. With reference to this possible confusion, interpretation rather than reinterpretation is more helpful in understanding Jakobson's contribution to a poetic. Does the word "similarity" really provide the mechanism for defining metaphor? Within Jakobson's definition of "poetic function" (1987: 71 quoted above) the word "similarity" is immediately followed by "dissimilarity". Metaphor is a trope where words stand in a combination that replaces a literal description. Within metaphoric use, the meanings of the individual words used are very different than when they are used in metaphoric combination. When used as less complex units or singly, they do not express the metaphoric trope in themselves. This raises interesting complexities in the use of the word "similarity" by Jakobson: "In poetry not only the phonological sequence but, in the same way, any sequence of semantic units strives to build an equation", and he writes. "Similarity superimposed on contiguity imparts to poetry its thoroughgoing symbolic, multiplex, polysemantic essence" (1987: 85).

What Jakobson writes next confuses things: "said more technically, anything sequent is a simile. In poetry, where similarity is superinduced upon contiguity, any metonymy is slightly metaphoric and any metaphor has a metonymic tint" (1987: 85). If a simile is sequent then surely it should belong to the combination syntagm. Once again Jakobson clarifies his position by pairing the word "simile" with "substitution". If one person/thing is someone/something else, then the simultaneity becomes a primary characteristic even though, in the text or speech, one part (word) occurs after the first part (word) (as "sequent"). Jakobson's understanding of the simultaneity of the metaphor, seems in effect, partly to extend to the simile, and his definition of "superinduced" makes clear that "similarity" and "simile" are not to be understood as simply similar. The simultaneity of the metaphor emerges as a fundamental attribute. What also therefore emerges is its position on the axis of selection from which it can be projected into the axis of combination. The simile is "sequent" and is therefore combinatory. The substitution of ideation in the simile does not have the property of simultaneity. It is only through a deeper understanding of Jakobson's use of the word "projection" as used in his definition of poetic function – and, in conjunction with this, his use of the model of axes – that this complexity becomes clear. The way Jakobson uses this word is not to be confused with the way it was interpreted by the projective poets. Theirs is a specific form of poetics: "A term coined by Charles Olsen in an influential 1950 essay on poetics to designate verse composed in open forms resulting from the poet's taking the stance of an object among other objects, rather than imposing himself upon content or materials" (Preminger and Brogan. 1993: 976). Projection as a term in poetics has been misunderstood by, for example, Andersen (1991 and see below), again hindering the kind of developments and interpretations that might have been made from Jakobson's theory. It may be easy to assume that this word is to be understood just as one would expect it to be, as no-one has sought to define or interpret it within the context that Jakobson has used it. However, his use of the word has a semiotic and poetic sense. In the paragraphs below, Jakobson's understanding of "projection" is examined in the context of his own early theory, especially in connection with the visual arts, ensuring that reinterpretation, or even misinterpretation, of Jakobson's theory, as has indeed occurred, is avoided.

Jakobson's theory of "poetic function" has been repeatedly "reinterpreted" so that its precision and potential are greatly weakened. The semiotic nature of Jakobson's theories is realised not only by aspects of this theory, as will be seen by the study of "projection", for example, but also by his construction of a graph that has two axes (see Chapter Two). Briefly, here, each axis has a pole of either metaphor (the paradigm) or metonymy (the syntagm). The construction of the axes arises from work done by Saussure (see Engler and Sanders 2008 [2006]: 237–240).

As can be seen from Chapter Two, below, this is not a straightforward derivation. The metaphoric pole is the axis of selection, similarity; the metonymic pole is the axis of combination, contiguity (Jakobson, 1971 [1956]: 90–96). These are simple definitions which provide the basis for the construction of the space between the axes; this space is found to be crucial to a city poetic genre.

Returning now to the process of assessing "projection", consider the basic definition of the verb "to project":

> To draw straight lines or 'rays' from a centre through every point of a given figure, so that they fall upon or intersect a surface and produce upon it a new figure of which each point corresponds to the point of the original, (with either the rays, the resulting figure, or the original figure as object). Hence, to represent or delineate (a figure) according to any system of correspondence between its points and the points of the surface on which it is delineated.
> 
> (*OED*, definition originating from 1679)

Bearing this definition in mind, Jakobson makes his own understanding of projection clear in his early essay "On Realism in Art" [1987 [1921]: 21]:

> Let us now analyze the concept of verisimilitude in art. While in painting and in the other visual arts the illusion of an objective and absolute faithfulness to reality is conceivable, 'natural' (in Plato's terminology), verisimilitude in a verbal expression or in a literary description obviously makes no sense whatever. Can the question be raised about a higher degree of verisimilitude of this or that poetic trope? Can one say that one metaphor or metonymy is conventional or, so to say, figurative? The methods of **projecting** [added emphasis] three-dimensional space onto a flat surface are established by convention; the use of color, the abstracting, the simplification, of the object depicted, and the choice of reproducible features are all based on convention. It is necessary to learn the conventional language of painting in order to 'see' a picture, just as it is impossible to understand what is said without knowing the language.
> (1987: 21)

The remainder of this paragraph is an analysis of the process whereby the artist makes strange something which is familiar (*ostranenie*) so that it can really, once again, be seen. Projection is a crucial aspect of *ostranenie* and also has a bearing on how "projected" is understood within a poetic framework. "Projected" has several properties here – firstly, that it describes a structure for poetic form as well as visual art form; secondly, it is a description of how an accepted code or convention is required in order for something to be seen and understood (it is within this property that *ostranenie* operates); thirdly, how the model proposed has a duality – verisimilitude and convention of technique; and lastly, how a sense of movement is demonstrated as a Formalist function within the suggested model. As a whole it suggests strongly that Jakobson's future model for the poetic function is expressed through his early theory of art with a structure arising from the visual arts which includes a visually-based image. Jakobson continues: "As tradition accumulates, the painted image becomes an ideogram, a formula, to which the object portrayed is linked by contiguity. Recognition becomes instantaneous. We no longer see a picture." (1987: 21). Perhaps the same could be argued with respect to letters and words – that is, how we come to accept their meaning, without any apparent connection between the words on the page and the meanings of the words.

Eco (1977: 43) notes that "Jakobson was semiotically biased from his early years". The axes and their poetic function are not simply a matter of linguistics tropes alone, but constitute a semiotic model which comprises theoretical and visual input, and "semiotic modelling" indicates a particular area of semiotic terminology. It would seem feasible that Jakobson's work would be more closely aligned to the Russian-based understanding of this (and see Ponzio in Cobley 2010: the entry on "Modelling": 267, 268). It is interesting that Jakobson's lifelong interest in parallelism is also manifested in this early essay, with his model explaining how the code or "conventional language" is established (or not) through the various modes of interaction between the artist (here this can also mean poet) and the perceiver. Jakobson wrote in *Selected Writings I* (1971a) in the "Retrospect": "Those of us who were concerned with language learned to apply . . . the pictorial theory and practice of cubism, where everything 'is based on relationship' and interaction between parts and wholes, between color and shape, between the representation and represented." (1971a: 632). Jakobson's lifelong interest in the variety of structure in communication between the art object and the perceiver produces the semiotic model of communication which is interpreted in his later theory of poetic function, and which adds another dimension to the proposed theory of a city poetic genre.

Bearing in mind how the basis for Jakobson's theory of poetic function was laid down clearly in his earliest essays, it is significant how his theories are reinterpreted by others without regard for this focused development by Jakobson. There is not space here to consider all such re-interpretations, some of which do not seem to be entirely accurate. The use of Jakobson's theories can only be used to derive a structure of a city poetic genre if there is a clear understanding of his theory. With this in mind, there follows a brief review of a selection of writers on Jakobson's theories, with respect to equivalence and projection which will demonstrate the necessity for investigation of Jakobson's key terms. It is suggested by referring to the articles below that: Jakobson's theories are more than "linguistic"; that they are defined as a grammar of poetry; and their construction interprets poetry as a "message", not only for its own sake but in terms of the poet as encoder of the message. That is, in terms of Jakobson's model of communication, whilst poetry is orientated toward the "message", the poet him/herself produces poetry with the use of the encoding function (see Osterwalder:1978, discussed below), i.e. from the point of the addresser (the emotive), rather than on the decoding function of the addressee (conative).

It might be expected, at this point, for reference to be made to more established works on Jakobson than are represented here. This research has arisen partly from a frustration that although Jakobson himself wrote a great deal, in a variety of languages and in different types of publication, analysis of his work tends towards a textbook level of representation, rather than interpretation (Bradford 1994, Chandler 2002, Chatman 1973, Hawkes 2003, Joseph 2001). In-depth analysis such as Steiner's (1984) are much rarer. Therefore, much of the in-depth analysis of Jakobson referred to here is from articles and conference papers rather than books. This position is echoed in Sütiste's article "Roman Jakobson and the topic of Translation: Reception in academic reference works" (2008), and is a review of how many times Jakobson has been mentioned in recent years and with reference to which aspect of his theories. It is remarkable that very many references allude to the same small part of his theories. Throughout the research on Jakobson, those who are favourable to Jakobson's analysis include:

> Andersen (1991); Armstrong and Schooneveld (1977) [collection of essays by different authors]; Barthes (1977); Bohn (1981); Bradford (1994); Cantor (2016); Chatman (1973); Cronan (2016); Daalder and Musolff (2011); Dalgård (1978); Daylight (2017); Denroche (2015); Dirven (1993); Durst-Andersen (2008); Durst-Andersen and Cobley (2018); Elleström (2016); Esh (1993); Gasparov (2014); Genette (1989); Hamacher (2019); Holenstein (1976); Jusdanis (1985); Kiparsky (1983); McLean (1983); Nänny (1985); Osimo (2008); Osterwalder (1978); Pomorska – several refs. inc. (1985), (1987), Rudy (1987); Silliman (1995); Stankiewicz (1982); Swann and Maybin (2007); Vallier, (1987); Waugh – several refs. inc. (1980), (1983), (1984); Wilson (1994).

These far outnumber those unfavourable to it:

> Balzer and Göttner (1983); Barsch and Hauptmeier (1983); Cureton (2000); Goodman (1981); Gorlée (2008); Joseph (2001); Kursell (2010); Surette (1987); T Turner (1977); Widdowson (2008).

And finally, there are those who are steadfastly against his ideas, briefly:

> Bredin (1984); Culler, (2001), (2002), (2002a); Drake, (1998 and 2002); Harris (2001); Merquior (1986); Riffaterre, (1966); Vickers (1988); Weststeijn (1983).

It is worth noting briefly, that communication theorists have asked questions about the origins and the nature of communication models, with respect to Jakobson's own theory. Daylight (2017) and Durst-Andersen (2008) both query Jakobson's acceptance of Saussure's binary model of language and suggest that this restricts Jakobson's own communication model. Daylight (2017) notes Jakobson's knowledge of Shannon and Weaver's (1998 [1943]) communication model and its American influence on Jakobson. Durst-Andersen (2008) highlights how Bühler's organon model needs to be re-interpreted and calls into question Jakobson's own model of communication. Durst-Andersen (2008), Denroche (2015), Elleström (2016), and Durst-Andersen and Cobley (2018) all propose new communication models which, although acknowledging the input from Jakobson (amongst others), seek to correct errors and gaps which they have perceived in his model.

Amongst the favourable responses to Jakobson's ideas, there are many different emphases. Paul Kiparsky (1983), stresses the semiotic (as opposed to strictly linguistic aspect) of Jakobson's poetic function. He briefly describes Jakobson's development from his early comparative linguistic theory, and addresses many of the questions regarding the criticism of Jakobson's theories that are frequently raised. He agrees that linguistics is a central part of Jakobson's theories, but that linguistics needs to broaden its scope in order to fully understand Jakobson. He quotes Jakobson's fundamental definition of "poetic function" (1983: 21) and adds: "That is to say, the *syntagmatic* recurrence of *paradigmatically* equivalent linguistic elements is the **constitutive** element of poetic form" (1983: 21). Kiparsky identifies Jakobson's interpretation of the metaphoric and metonymic axes in terms of a grammatical structure. His is not a linguistic analysis; this is a model that has semiotic scope. Kiparsky writes:

> An immediate consequence of this generalization is that principles like parallelism, the regular recurrence of syntactic patterns, which in traditional poetics stand out as exotic oddities, fall right into line as the predicted syntactic counterparts of metrical organization . . . . Thus, one corollary of Jakobson's idea is that it opens the way to an understanding of the *grammatical* texture of poetry, bringing to view a whole facet of poetic form of which traditional literary scholarship had only a dim and intuitive notion. (1983: 21)

He goes on to say that equivalence can also occur in any linguistic category, for example: syntax, morphology, lexicology. This point is important because it clarifies the difference between Jakobson's own understanding of relational similarity (see Waugh, 1980, and below) which is not to be confused with similarity established through simple categories such as identical parts of speech (prepositions for example). Jakobson uses the word "grammar" to denote the structure of poetry as well as in the conventional sense, the structure of a sentence. Kiparsky recognizes this in his article, he writes:

> Classical rhetoric . . . defined metaphor as based on the relation of similarity, and metonymy as based on 'material' relations. Jakobson interprets metaphor and metonymy in firmly grammatical terms as involving the two axes of selection among members of linguistic equivalence classes (the axis of similarity) and combination into syntactic units (the axis of contiguity). These axes can be equated with the paradigmatic and syntagmatic relations of Saussure. The opposition between metaphor and metonymy is of fundamental importance in Jakobson's poetic theory. (1983: 23)

Kiparsky suggests that grammar refers to the structure of poetry and is not just applicable in the linguistic sense – as in the construction of the structure of a sentence. In this sense, Kiparsky contributes to an understanding of the semiotic component of Jakobson's theory of poetic function. His semiotic analysis releases greater complexity from the Jakobsonian model. It is argued, by the current author, that a city poetic expresses an uneasy alliance between the city and human existence within it. This indicates that the balance of power is unstable and unequal between the two. Any poetic form which represents this imbalance, a projection of forces between two sources is bound, therefore, to be within a structural space which cannot be released by a linguistic analysis alone. Semiotics, which interprets both verbal and other indicative signs, therefore provides a structure to analyse the city. As an aside, if it can be suggested that a rural as well as an urban environment can be represented by the same imbalance of power and play of forces, then this model represents a structure for a rural poetic as well. Kiparsky's model provides an interpretation of the model which reflects the city structure iconically.

A different emphasis in interpretation of Jakobson is given by Waugh (1980) who frames her analysis of Jakobson's theory of "poetic function" with the use of the terms, *signans* and *signatum* in order to clarify the fact that a poem is a structure (1980: 60, 62). Waugh's use of these terms refers back to Jakobson's understanding of Saussure (see also his *Selected Writings I*, Retrospect, 1971a:629–660). The history of the terminology surrounding semiotics includes several terms which had specific meanings at the time of usage but are not necessarily included currently. A brief overview of these assists in clarifying their current meaning. The derivation of these terms and their associated words are as follows (not in chronological order or order of language of origin): signum, (sēmeion) – the whole sign; signifiant, signans, signifier, (sēmainon) – the sound image; signifié, signatum, signified, (sēmainomenon) – the concept; and St. Augustine wrote of sēmeiōsis – the action of signs. The Latin terms of *signans* and *signatum* were only adopted by Saussure in the middle of his last course (see Jakobson, "The Quest for the Essence of Language". 1987: 414). Then there is Peirce, whose classification of signs and understanding of the nature of signs leads to his use of the word "semiotic" (derived from the Greek: sēmeiōtikē) to describe the "doctrine of signs" (Jakobson, 1987: 414). Jakobson writes:

> From the end of the last century [19th] a similar discipline was fervently advocated by Saussure. Stimulated in turn by Greek impetus, he called it semiology and expected this new branch of learning to elucidate the essence and governing laws of signs. In his view, linguistics was to become but a part of this general science and would determine what properties made language a separate system in the totality of 'semiological facts' [no ref.].
> 
> (Jakobson, 1987: 414, 415)

Waugh also writes:

> since a poem is a sign, it is a combination of a *signans* and a *signatum*; it is *not*, as some studies of poetry have seemed to suggest a *signans* only. A poem is a *new intersubjective message-sign whose dominant function is an orientation toward the message-sign as a message-sign*. A poem is also a *system of systems of signs*, a complex and hierarchically ordered sign, made up of a variety of sign types, each with both a *signans* and a *signatum*, and in which the various signs are subordinated to the overall poetic function and coherence of the whole sign. As such, a poem is a *structure*. (Waugh, 1980: 62)

Accepting that a poem is a structure, reveals another aspect of the semiotic and iconic nature of poetry which informs a possible city poetic genre. It is not just the content or the meaning which is under consideration but how the poem, in its structure, reflects, for example the city, the content of the poem. She quotes Jakobson's central definition of poetic function and goes on to interpret "equivalence": "In poetry, the projection of the principle of equivalence from the axis of selection into the axis of combination means quite simply that such sameness is used as (the major) means of constructing the whole sequence. This projection is in fact the defining characteristic of poetry" (1980: 64). Waugh understands "equivalence", as "relational equivalence" (1980: 64): "Equivalence in difference is the cardinal problem of language and the pivotal concern of linguists (and see Jakobson, (1971[1956])), where the equivalence is a *relational equivalence* based on sameness within a system" (as quoted in Waugh,1980: 64). She also defines the linguistic aspect of "equivalence" that Jakobson highlights – stresses, pauses, long or short syllables in poetry. She continues, in the same article, with her analysis of combination: "the tendency is to invest such evident contiguity relations with similarity and equivalence. Thus, a preposition may become important not so much because it creates a contiguity relation between the two interrelated elements but rather because it is equated with another preposition. And the equivalence between one preposition and another as parts of speech may be as important as the interrelation between the given preposition and its context" (1980: 66). This explanation of equivalence reveals the two levels of analysis required to release the full complexity of the term. It is both a linguistic equivalence – word-on-word, or syntactical-position-to-syntactical position – and the more semiotic "relational equivalence", that is, one which eventually introduces the parallelism in poetry – that each component of words or form (grammatical or poetical) within a poem has a related expression. This is the basis for the structure of parallels in Jakobson's theories. These are semiotic in structure and are explored more fully in the next chapter (also Chapter Seven). Waugh's use of the word "similarity" here also provides a reason for the possible confusion between a definition of this word as "sameness" and Jakobson's use of it to indicate the structure of metaphor.

In the final section of her paper entitled "Sign vs. Object", Waugh (1980), with reference to Jakobson, further clarifies her understanding of relational equivalence: "In the poetic text, a given word may be chosen not only because of its paradigmatic associations with other words in the linguistic code, but also because of its equivalence relations with other words in the text itself. The choice of one word may dictate the rest of the poem" (see Jakobson, 1987 [1964]: 50–61 and 1980: 68). "Relational equivalence" is an understanding of how language works in a poetic dimension and can be further developed and understood with respect to the construction and definition of "similarity". For Waugh, similarity means not just the same, as in the choice between two words with similar meaning, for example: "mat" and "rug", but it also means similar in construction – that there are two subordinate clauses for example. The analysis is more strongly linguistic than semiotic. Similarity obtains another meaning when used to define the concept of metaphor. For Jakobson, metaphor is a trope that requires words that are used in combination to describe something other than their separate literal meanings. But the metaphoric words also have a similarity which is based on the relational equivalence as defined above. Other categories of similarity are identified – factual and imputed similarity. Waugh explains:

> If in the referential function the imputed contiguity relation is uppermost, in the poetic function it is closely combated both by factual similarity (iconicity) and by **imputed similarity** (artifice), thus creating a highly complex and hierarchized system of internal relations. Similarity proves to be not only the constructive device of the sequence but also of the internal relation within the sign as well as the relations between the signs as they occur contiguously in the sequence. In this fashion, the *signans* plays an active and constructive role in the creation and communication of meaning. (1980: 71)

Referring to Jakobson's theories, the iconic nature of poetry arises from this factual similarity; the artifice of poetry arises from the imputed similarity. For the purposes of definition here, and with regard to factual similarity, it is not accurate to assume that the "iconicity" derives from Peirce's category of iconic. For Jakobson the attribute of iconicity is specific to poetry. Jakobson refers to Peirce's definition of the icon in "Quest for the Essence of language" (1987 [1965]: 415): "The *icon* acts chiefly by a factual similarity between its signans [sound image] and signatum [concept], between the picture of an animal and the animal pictured; the former stands for the latter 'merely because it resembles it' [quoting from Peirce]". A decade later (1987 [1974]: 443) Jakobson refers to the icon as "effective similarity". His definition is further clarified with reference to Plato's *Cratylus* and is summarised by Nöth (1990: 121–127). The paragraphs on "Iconicity and the Origins of Language" (1990: 125) reveal how the relationship between meaning and actual shape or sound (see Jakobson and Waugh, 1979) of a word reflect each other or – as in most cases – do not. Iconicity, or factual similarity in poetry refers to poetry's form and structure rather than to the words used in the poem – though of course it is also possible to write poetry with sounds that closely echo it's intended meaning (see Khlebnikov's poem in Chapter Eight). The issue of how to interpret the "feel" of the words as well as their meaning, otherwise known as "imputed similarity", is a central concern of translators with regards to the rendition of a work from one language to another. The imputed similarity of translating with reference to Jakobson, for example, is the subject of an article by Bruno Osimo (2008). Osimo argues that "the notion of 'imputed similarity' was not covered by Peirce's triad . . . the notion of translation may be the missing link." (2008:315).

Parallels can form a part of this iconicity. For Waugh, the issue of central importance is that poetry interprets the word and meaning in very complex ways:

> One may say with Peirce, that in the referential or emotive use of language, the linguistic sign and the non-linguistic sign are in interpretive relation with one another. It is this status of interpretation which is broken in poetic discourse, for here it is the *interpretive relation between linguistic signs* which is important . . . Thus a 'literal' (i.e. referential) reading of a poem must be subordinated to a 'poetic' reading (just as the referential function is subordinated to the poetic). (1980: 67,68)

This leads to an understanding of imputed similarity. Waugh (1980: 71), again, also comments on the artifice of poetry and the tension between factual and imputed similarity in poetry.

Waugh's analysis of Jakobson's "poetic function" shows how this model comprehends more than the linguistic and she uses the term "grammar" to define her exploration of the poetic structure which Jakobson's model defines: "It is because there is a grammar of poetry that the focus on the message exists and because there is focus upon the message that the grammar of poetry exists." (1980: 78). Her analysis reveals that there is a semiotic interpretation of Jakobson's model as well as a linguistic one. The semiotic, "relational equivalence", constructs poetic grammar in a space that perhaps lies between the metaphoric and the metonymic poles.

The above paragraphs demonstrate that equivalence, projection and similarity, taken in conjunction with an understanding of iconicity will reveal a semiotic structure for poetics. Similarity has both a linguistic and a semiotic meaning. The semiotic meaning allows the iconicity which can be used to interpret a city poetic genre. In order to understand this construction, the factual or iconic similarity needs to be further defined. Nänny (1985) refers to "the trend for greater iconicity in poetry" through emphasis on Jakobson's "palpability of signs" (and see also Jakobson's "Linguistics and Poetics", 70: 1987). Nänny's study of a number of poems, through the use of Jakobson's interpretation of Peirce's definition of the "icon", reveals how iconicity is indeed an integral part of modernist and contemporary poetry which he concludes is manifested in three ways: "spatial configuration, sequential motion and successive change" (1985:133). Nänny's article (1985) is discussed further in Chapter Eleven.

The shape of the poem, the movement expressed by the poem, the constructed progression of the poem, are all part of iconicity. It should be noted that punctuation is also a part of a poem's iconicity. This is further referred to in Chapter Twelve. For the purposes of a city poetic genre, the attributes of the Jakobsonian axial model are an attempt at a comprehensive iconic structure of both factual and imputed similarity which reflects both the city itself and the life of those who live in it.

One further dimension of equivalence needs to be explored. Other theorists have combined "equivalence" with other aspects of Jakobson's theory of communication, in ways which establish an emphasis on strength of structure. Hans Osterwalder's exploration of poetic function (1978) links the principle of equivalence with the encoder (addresser) part of Jakobson's communication model. Osterwalder's main interest lies in the metaphoric and metonymic poles as forms of poetic and dramatic expression. The quotation below illustrates how this kind of equivalence arises, how it is used and to what effect. Osterwalder writes:

> I have come to the conclusion that there is an intrinsic link between the poetic function, the predominance of the metaphoric principle, and encoder-orientation. The encoder's point of departure when producing a message is the code, the storehouse of 'in absentia' paradigms. These are organized according to the similarity principle, which is projected into the axis of combination in an utterance dominated by the poetic function. In lyric poetry the poet very often uses an expanded, private code full of 'in absentia' associations which do not pertain to the common code of a language; in other words, he draws on an expanded range of similarity relationships. *The Waste Land* is a salient example. The notes Eliot added to this poem simply represent a key to his private code, an attempt to create 'a certain equivalence between the symbols used by the addresser and those known and interpreted by the addressee' without which 'the message is fruitless' [Jakobson, "Two Aspects of Language" 1987: 100].
> (Osterwalder 1978: 13,14)

His is an understanding of equivalence which is dependent on the projection – of poetic selection – into the combinatory text. Yet this projection is not just envisaged across the axes; it is also used in the sense that the equivalence is projected between the speaker (poet) and the reader (audience). In this sense, "equivalence" is not something that is inherent in the message – the poetry itself – but in the expression of communication between the addresser and receiver. Osterwalder's interpretation appears to be differ from Jakobson's. It clarifies that there is a particular Jakobsonian "communication equivalence" within the definition of "poetic function" and that this cannot be understood without accepting the addresser/message/addressee model devised by Jakobson.

This brief review of the work of theorists on Jakobson helps to identify three important areas in the construction of space within Jakobson's "poetic function" and, within the context of this research, a construction of a city poetic space. These are: equivalence, projection and similarity. From these examples the following three questions arise. Firstly, how does Jakobson's semiotic model of poetic function release a city poetic genre? Kiparsky (1983), who regrets the constriction of comprehension of Jakobson's theory of poetic function by linguistics, leads research towards the semiotic analysis. His approach releases greater complexity from the Jakobsonian model as well as providing a semiotic structure for a city poetic genre. It is argued by the current author that this must include the representation of the balance of forces exerted between the city and the human inhabitants and that this requires a structural space which cannot be released by a linguistic analysis alone. Semiotics, which interprets both verbal and other indicative signs therefore provides a model with which to analyse the city.

Secondly, how does a grammar of poetry – including relational equivalence – provide for a city poetic genre? Waugh's analysis of Jakobson's "poetic function" shows how this model comprehends more than linguistics and uses the term "grammar" to define her exploration of the poetic structure which Jakobson's model defines: "It is because there is a grammar of poetry that the focus on the message exists and because there is focus upon the message that the grammar of poetry exists" (Waugh, 1980: 78). Her analysis reveals that there is a semiotic interpretation of Jakobson's model as well as a linguistic one. The semiotic, "relational equivalence", constructs poetic grammar in a space that lies between the metaphoric and the metonymic poles. The complex nature of "similarity" is highlighted and, factual similarity is interpreted. The similarity releases both metaphor and metonymy into the space which, in this context, is used to construct a city poetic genre.

To develop Waugh's analysis, the conception of a grammar of poetry, rather than being just a linguistic analysis of its lexical or syntactical words, provides a structure which comprises the overall form of the poem rather than just the linguistically defined parts. If a city poem is written with a particular choice of words or form which reflects the city, then this form will be accepted as representing a "grammar of the city". "Relational equivalence" is a definition of the use of space between the two axes as suggested by Jakobson. It is not a linguistic definition. It is a definition that interprets iconicity. A further consideration is that the imbalance of forces between the city structure and the humans living within it is complemented and expressed by the play of poetic equivalences as suggested by the relational equivalence – in this instance either a factual similarity or an imputed similarity. If the subject matter of any poem can be represented with the use of axes as a central motivating structure, then this model is appropriate for more than city poetry.

Thirdly, how does the orientation towards the encoder, especially in modernist poetry, realise a city poetic genre? Osterwalder's work (1978) on T.S. Eliot concentrates on the metaphoric and metonymic poles rather than Jakobson's theory of poetic function and the construction of space between these two poles. But his work remains important because of his central emphasis on the encoder-orientation of this modernist poet. Osterwalder's emphasis on the poet's relationship with the poetic message as one whereby the poet provides a controlling force for the poetic message is crucial in accepting that not only does Jakobson's theory state that poetry is a message which concentrates on the message for its own sake, but also that the "Formalist" definition of "function" can include the role of the poet, where this role releases information about the structure and "literariness" of the text. This accepted emphasis describes the strength of the poetic function as a process of communication between the poet and the text, and within this, it produces a strong poetic space which can be realised by the space constructed by the axial model.

The notion that a city poetic space exists within this model arises because the reader is compelled to look to both the poet and the text for a scientific and structuralist form or grammar in the poetry which releases its meaning – that there is a structure of a city poetic genre. This is a central argument of this chapter. And is an antithesis to some leading theories of the practice of reading and reader response theory, and is a direct response to Culler's position in his *Structuralist Poetics*: "To say that a poem becomes an autonomous object once it leaves the author's pen is, in one sense, precisely the reverse of the structuralist position. The poem cannot be *created* except in relation to other poems and conventions of reading" (2002: 34). For Culler, when the text is analysed through linguistic structuralism even the role of the poet is a reflection of the poet as an individual without autonomy from any eventual meaning of the text:

> But though structuralism may always seek the system behind the event, the constitutive conventions behind any individual act, it cannot for all that dispense with the individual subject. He [the poet] may no longer be the origin of meaning, but meaning must move through him. Structures and relations are not objective properties of external objects; they emerge only in a structuring process. And though the individual may not originate or even control this process – he assimilates its rules as part of his culture – it takes place through him, and one can gain evidence about it only by considering his judgements and intuitions.
> (2002: 35)

For further clarification Culler defines the role of structuralist poetics:

> What is the role of structuralist poetics? In one sense its task is a humble one: to make as explicit as possible what is implicitly known by all those sufficiently concerned with literature to be interested in poetics. Viewed in this way it is not hermeneutic; it does not propose startling interpretations or resolve literary debates; it is the theory and practice of reading.
> (2002: 301)

Culler does accept the need for the study of the text itself but only in terms of what it releases for the benefit of the reader: "To read is to participate in the play of the text, to locate zones of resistance and transparency, to isolate forms and determine their content . . ." (2002: 302). The encoder orientation introduces the need for the poet's control of the message to be acknowledged and accepted as a necessary part of the construction of the poetic message. Again, the play of forces within the city, require an acceptance by the poet within the poetic function of the message otherwise the forces are not counterbalanced – the city structure would just override the human. The same would be true for poetry that covered subject areas other than the city – but would only be appropriate if the subject area included subject matter where the forces of the subject were overwhelming to the human.

Critics and theorists have variously interpreted Jakobson's theory of poetic function with regard to linguistics and semiotics, equivalence and similarity, encoder and decoder as can be seen from the above. This section now considers how Jakobson's use of the verb "to project" has been reinterpreted by some other critics and theorists. The Formalist insistence that "function", enables literary works to be understood and analysed with reference to the poet, only if such reference analyses the grammar and function of the poetry (see above), indicates that the quality of the "projection" is not primarily attached to the poet or encoder but rather to the poetry and the message (as within Jakobson's own model). Andersen (1991), in his desire to clarify what he sees as Jakobson's imprecision, defines a "projection principle" and a "projection thesis". It is important to note that these terms are not Jakobson's, but Andersen's definitions. Andersen has transferred the action of the verb "to project" into the noun phrases: "projection principle" and "projection thesis". This fundamentally subverts the action of the poetic function as defined by Jakobson. For example, Andersen ascribes the projection to the author/sender of a message, rather than understanding that the poetic function itself includes the action of projection. Andersen writes:

> Jakobson's formulation of the principle [of poetic function] . . . is tolerably clear, although in some respects it is not very precise. It is obviously not 'the principle' that is projected, but relations of equivalence. Nor is it 'the poetic function' that projects these relations of equivalence, but the author or sender of the aesthetically formed message. But such cavils aside, the principle and Jakobson's claim for it are clear enough: in verbal behaviour the operations of selection and combination may be executed in such a way that terms that are equivalent in the paradigmatic system of the code (grammar) enter contiguity relations in the syntagmatic chain of the message (text). This is the Projection Principle. Jakobson's thesis is that a predominance of precisely such selections and combinations will produce messages (texts) with such aesthetic qualities that they may serve a poetic function. I will refer to this as the Projection Thesis. (1991: 288,289)

He concludes that these are semiotic not linguistic structures (1991: 290). Although Andersen makes a number of interesting points, his definition of "equivalence" makes no reference to parallels and does not seem to coincide with Waugh's identified "relational equivalence" – that is, equivalence based on repeated combinations of grammatical structure rather than repeated syntax. He refers Jakobson's theory of "poetic function" back to Aristotle's three categories of language, rather than to Russian Formalism, and the source for his material is not quoted from Aristotle first hand. Andersen again:

> Perhaps the most generally interesting thing about the Projection Principle is the fact that it explicates properties of messages by referring to the processes of operations by which messages are produced in 'verbal behaviour' .... The principle, in point of fact, gives full recognition to all three modes of being of language: grammar (language as technique, Aristotle's *dýnamis*), speech (language as activity, *enérgeia*), and text (language as product, *érgon*); cf Coseriu (1974:37[Andersen's ref]). (1991: 290, 291)

In his summary Andersen demonstrates that he has not fully understood how Jakobson derived his understanding of "projection" and he falls back on his own redefinition of terms. In his conclusion he writes:

> The most serious difficulty with Jakobson's formulation of the Projection Principle arises from his use of the word *project*. This verb does not even begin to do justice to the creative process of poetic discourse, but rather begs the question of how an artist in fact contrives to perform the operations of selection and combination in such a way as to create an aesthetic object. What is worse, it fails to distinguish two crucially different kinds of equivalence relations in any poetic text, those that are generated by the Projection Principle, and which have no particular aesthetic value, and those which result from the poetic process properly speaking. (1991: 309)

His presentation of Jakobson highlights how Jakobson's apparently simple definition of "poetic function" can be seriously misunderstood. The root of the problem is that Andersen has not accepted the Formalist concept of "literariness" as primary within Jakobson's theory of poetic function. This means that the poetic text, perforce, becomes prioritised and the poetic text, or even perhaps the poet, does the projecting rather than the 'poetic function'. How, then, does the Formalist understanding facilitate a city poetic genre? Once again, if the balance of power between the city structure and the humans living within it is understood as central to city existence (a kind of "citiness"), then the requirement is that there must be a structure of poetry which will express it. Structure, as understood through the concept of "literariness" will potentially express two forces by virtue of the verb "to project" which describes the movement between selection and combination – all the properties of the paradigm (including simultaneity and metaphor) with the properties of the syntagm (including the passage of time, metonymy and contiguity) – thereby releasing the poetic and narrative forces. This process can only happen if the Formalist "literariness" is accepted as a primary process of understanding the poetic form of the text.

A similar failure to understand this point is characteristic of Richard Bradford (1994). Like Andersen, he formulates his own definitions and categorizations rather than exploring Jakobson's. He refers to the "Projection Principle" and though Andersen's paper precedes Bradford's, Bradford makes no mention of Andersen's paper. In his chapter on "The Poetic Function" (1994: 9–34), Bradford's listing of the attributes of the two axes – paradigm and syntagm, are identical to Dirven's (1993). Bradford does not refer to Dirven's work, however. Bradford writes: "Jakobson's projection principle consists of three interwoven elements: the syntagmatic and paradigmatic axes and the parallelism of the poetic line" (1994: 185).

Bradford (1994) devises other definitions: the double pattern, the sliding scale. He re-interprets Jakobson's model and refers to Chomsky: "To use a term made famous by Noam Chomsky, it is the deep structure, the abstract framework of rules and conventions, that allows us to encode and decode the specific and complex meanings of a chain of individual words, the surface structure" (1994: 37, 38). The double pattern appears to be a re-interpretation of parallelism. The sliding scale defines how poetic or prosaic the language of the text is. The double pattern is a model for poetic interlocking of selective and combinative elements of the poetic function. Bradford's interpretation of free verse in his section on "Space and Time" contributes to the continuing discussion between the proponents of formally devised poetry and those of free verse:

> The proversa modernists might have rejected the schema of metrical regularity, but by retaining the mysterious phenomenon of the line they maintained a crucial element of the versus tradition: the tension between the materiality and the signifying properties of the sign. Their reason for not abandoning the line is the same one that has motivated Jakobson's belief in the poem as the ultimate object language. (1994: 199)

But the line can, of course, be both significantly reworked and redesigned, and the elements of poetic function will remain operative. Combination and selection do not necessarily need a regular system of lines to operate. There is an attempt to demonstrate this, in the present author's poem *Shades of Light,* written with the aid of computer software, Adobe Indesign. In the "Fame" section of the poem, lines of poetry can be fluidly placed. Allen Fisher, Susan Howe and Ian Hamilton Finlay are examples of poets whose work calls into question the nature of the regular line as such with their experiments in poetic form. From the point of view of a city poetic, the suggested irregularity of lines constructs a poetic form as a more conceptual area, emphasising the scope of iconicity. It can be suggested that the system of lines as verticals, horizontals, angles, diagonals, axes represent aspects of city structure which impose themselves upon the inhabitant and the poetic form expresses this. Other sections of the poem express a sense of lines crossing, intersections, fragmentation, more from the point of view of how the subject matter of the poetry is arranged and the kind of poetic tropes used, than by the placing of the lines.

In this exploration of the fundamental nature of Jakobson's definition of "poetic function", it should be noted that Jakobson, according to some theorists, has a debt to Husserl. Bradford analyses Husserl's philosophical influence on Jakobson, as in Holenstein (1976) and (1983) and Steiner (1984). Peter Steiner describes Jakobson as Husserl's "most faithful follower" (1984: 257). Jakobson's Formalism goes beyond both OPOJAZ ideas on transrational language and the pre-Formalist conception of the poet's work as necessarily unfiltered personal expression (Steiner 1984: 208–10 and 254–57). The analysis is much more fully explored by Steiner (1984: 33–35). He criticises Erlich (1981) for leaving Bakhtin out of the Formalist Movement. A movement which contained a number of groupings and which developed over time. Husserl is recognised as a prominent influence on the thinking of the early Formalists. The history of the Formalist movement is complicated, crosses the boundaries of countries and is split by the events of the Russian Revolution in the early 20th century. But a simple summary is found in Erlich:

> Edmund Husserl, a philosopher who had a considerable impact on some of the Formalist theoreticians, made a fruitful distinction when he differentiated between the 'object' (*Gegenstand*), the non-verbal phenomenon denoted by the word, and the 'meaning' (*Bedeutung*), i.e. the way in which the 'object' is presented. In other words, to Husserl the meaning is not an element of extra-linguistic realism, but a part and parcel of the verbal sign. But if this is the case, the Futurist watchword becomes an absurdity or at least a misnomer.
> (1981: 185)

Erlich's definition of this "Futurist watchword" is on the previous page: "The futurist could talk glibly about liberating the word from its meaning because he tended to reduce the verbal sign to its sensory texture – or what is perhaps the same thing – because he confused the meaning of the word with its referent" (1981: 184,185). This is, it seems, a root of supraconscious poetry or *zaum*, which promoted the formulation of new words that previously held no meaning but which, with revised usage, produced new meaning. Erlich explains:

> Indeed, as the Formalist spokesmen could not help but recognize, no poetry, however non-objective, can dispense with meaning. Even in the most experimental poem of, say, Edith Sitwell or Ezra Pound, even in the most bewildering passage from *Finnigan's Wake*, replete as it is with quasi-words, coined *ad hoc* from familiar morphemes, the meaning is

> always present somehow, even if in an 'approximate' potential form. The impact of the context, as well as analogies with cognate 'real' words, endow these bizarre products of the poet's linguistic fancy with a certain semantic aura.
> (Erlich, 1981: 185)

Steiner interprets the same principle of Husserl – the split between the object and the meaning – to include the importance that Formalists and Jakobson attribute to essence and context. Steiner, quoting Holenstein, identifies Jakobson's early commitment to "literariness" arising from his commitment to Husserl's eidetic phenomenology [consciousness – the mind can conceive of the body] which "is concerned with the grasp of the essential features common to objects of the same category" (quoted from Holenstein in Steiner 1984: 201).

Jakobson pursues Husserl's ideas when he investigates the three functions of verbal art: "showing forth, naming, and meaning – [which] correspond [to] Jakobson's three goal-oriented verbal activities, or more precisely, functional dialects – the emotive, the practical, and the poetic" (1984: 203). Steiner states that Husserl's influence on the Formalists, along with Saussure, was profound. How does this help to interpret Jakobson's theory of poetic function? Steiner analyses the different factions of Formalism and its development over a passage of time. He concludes that: "Jakobson's conversion of the Husserlian expression from a logical to an aesthetic category was unorthodox to say the least, and generated certain problems that had to be solved as his expressionist model developed." (Steiner, 1984: 205). And: "With the expressionist model Jakobson could deny that the artwork was a mere psychological or sociological document without implying that it was therefore devoid of meaning." (Steiner, 1984: 205). Steiner then writes: "Jakobson believed that poetic works are intersubjective signs involving some form of rationality which he conceptualized as the (imperfect) sharing of cognitive meanings. The OPOJAZ theorists who emphasized the transrational components of poetic language (the emotive and so forth) had in Jakobson's opinion lost sight of the social nature of verbal art" (Steiner, 1984: 207). Bradford adds that Husserl is the basis for Jakobson's theory of communication, using the Kantian theory of apperception: "If, as Husserl argues, the apperceptive set involves the creator, the act of communication and the recipient as co-dependent elements, it follows that each will also depend upon contextual conditions." (Bradford, 1994: 33).

It would seem, with reference to Erlich (1981), Steiner (1984) and Holenstein (1976), that Jakobson's theory of poetic function (which Waugh 1980 examined in detail without significant reference to Husserl) is grounded in communication – addresser/message/addressee – with careful acknowledgement of the importance of context and meaning. Two observations are of particular importance in this respect: firstly, language is empirical, according to Jakobson, and can be analysed logically (as object); secondly, language is emotive and interpreted, through the "impact of the context" (Erlich 1981: 185). As Holenstein states: language "is concerned with the grasp of the essential features common to objects of the same category" (quoted from Holenstein in Steiner 1984: 201). This provides a structure from which a city poetic can be derived: the city is empirical and can be analysed logically (object); the poetic is emotive and provides the "impact of the context", with reference to essential features that are common to the city's inhabitants.

Bradford goes on to define the primary position of the encoder in formulating the poetic message when he highlights the importance of selection *into* combination in Jakobson's "poetic function" (Bradford, 1994: 34, 35). This introduces one last possible development of Jakobson's theory of "poetic function". Any in-depth investigation into the use of the verb "to project" in Jakobson's definition of "poetic function" raises another possibility, as demonstrated by Turner (1977). His paper attempts to discover a system of universal narrative (cf. Lévi-Strauss), suggesting, departing from Jakobson's model of a single model of projection, projection from the axis of combination upwards into the axis of selection as well: "In Jakobsonian terms, the point might be formulated as follows: the poetic function projects the principle of equivalence from the axis of selection to the axis of combination [thus much is pure Jakobson], in such a way that the principle of combination is reciprocally projected onto the axis of selection ... Combination, in other words, is infused with a paradigmatic quality" (1977: 145). If this is accepted it would mean that equivalence has a double movement of projection. Jakobson's equivalence projects from the axis of selection, and therefore this axis has a controlling influence, although Jakobson insists that the message is the dominant part of the model. Turner describes this double movement as provoking "tension" between the two axes (1977: 145). If the projection takes place from the axis of combination into the axis of selection, then this would enable a poetic which delivered its message primarily from within a prose construction and with all the attributes of metonymic combination. Jakobson's model of projection within poetic function does not comprise this reciprocal movement. Although, perhaps he does suggest it, where he says that there is metaphor in metonymy and vice versa (1987: 85). Perhaps it can only be interpreted as projecting meaning onto (or into) the reader? Turner seems to suggest that it can project meaning into the text or consider a perception of something arising from the perceived two-dimensional horizontal plane of the page – namely a projection of, for example, metonymy into selection (lyric), rather than metaphor into combination (narrative). Such a model, at first sight, might seem difficult to accept; but Jakobson makes his own position very clear: his model for poetic function is focussed on the message and this is the dominant aspect of the poetic form (see essays on "The Dominant" [1935] and "Linguistics and Poetics" [1960] (both in 1987).

However, if it is accepted that projection can take place from the axis of combination into the axis of selection then this would presuppose the possibility of a dominant combinatory metonymic form which touches on the simultaneous or similarity axis of selection. This would be a model for contemporary poetry which abandons metaphor and even simile and relies on contiguity and its related aspects – metonymy, meronymy for example. (This is a model which has in fact been used in the current author's poem: *Shades of Light* – "Wrestle"). The model also provides a double movement within the iconic space which, it is proposed, provides a space for a city poetic genre. It can certainly be suggested that it interprets an upward projection of the kind suggested by Turner.

Jakobson's definition of Poetic Function introduces a theory which can be applied to all poetry, by nature of its definition of function rather than poetic form. Poetic Function incorporates semiotics within its definition in that it defines poetic structure as a whole not just poetic sentence structure, that is, a linguistic structure, of poetry. Linguistics is the scientific analysis of language through its grammatical construction (Matthews 2005). In "The Framework of Language" (1980c) Jakobson explores his interest in linguistics as a part of semiotics. He acknowledges that signs can extend beyond the linguistic study of language:

> Those who consider the system of language signs as the only set worthy of being the object of the science of signs engage in circular reasoning . . . The egocentrism of linguists who insist on excluding from the sphere of semiotics signs which are organized in a different manner than those of language, in fact reduced semiotics to a simple synonym for linguistics
> (1980c: 19)

Jakobson, in his essay: "Quest for the Essence of Language", quoting from Peirce, urged students to understand the nature of the word – to understand its meaning as a symbol:

> How many futile and trivial polemics could have been avoided among students of language if they had mastered Peirce's *Speculative Grammar*, and particularly its thesis that 'a genuine symbol is a symbol that has a general meaning' and that this meaning in turn 'can only be a symbol' . . . A symbol is not only incapable of indicating any particular thing and necessarily 'denotes a kind of thing,' but 'it is itself a kind and not a single thing.' A symbol, for instance a word, is a 'general rule' which signifies only through the different instances of its application, namely the pronounced or written – thinglike – *replicas*. (1987: 427)

Semiotics, defined as the science of signs, is the acknowledgement of the importance of the meaning of words in relation to text and environment, rather than just the words themselves. As is explained in the entry on "Semiotics" (Petrilli in Cobley: 2010: 322,323). Within the context of Formalism, semiotic analysis of poetry applies the "science of signs" in an analysis of how meaning arises *within* poetry in ways that are not only syntactical, but are also a result of the constructed form and the meanings arising from this form.

The chapter has argued that the model of poetic function is a Formalist model, a semiotic one, rather than a linguistic one. The chapter has discussed in detail the definitions and understandings of the terms of "equivalence", "similarity" and "projection" within Jakobson's "poetic function". A city poetic genre can be understood as comprising: semiotics; a grammar of poetry; the encoder as part of the poetic message; and projection, which includes the function of movement, from both axes – the axis of selection and the axis of combination – in the search for a balance between the message, the poet and the subject, the city. It has been found that the Formalist definition of "function" is vital in interpreting the emphasis on the communication of the message within the poetic form. This is essential Jakobson. Both this, and the axial model, based on Jakobson's understanding of the axes are fully explored in the next chapter.

# Chapter 2
# Jakobson's semiotic axial model of poetic function, and a Formalist analysis and praxis of Mayakovsky's poem "The City"

## Part I

Russian Formalists understood that the artefact, in this instance, the poetic text, was something to be studied, in itself. They wished to apply science to language and with the use of linguistics and semiotics, construct a "science of poetics". Eikenbaum wrote:

> The question is not about the methods of studying literature, but about the principles for constructing a science of literature, – about its content, its basic subject, about the problems which organize it into a special science. It has at last become clear that a science of literature, inasmuch as it is not merely a part of the history of culture, must be an independent and specific science with its own field of specific problems. (1924: 2)

The definition arises from an analysis where Jakobson states that the "focus on the message for its own sake, is the POETIC [sic] function of language" (1987: 69). The reference to "message" is part of six categories that comprises Jakobson's structural model for the process of verbal and written communication. For definitions of these terms, please see Chapter One.

Hans Osterwalder's analysis in "T.S.Eliot: Between Metaphor and Metonymy" (1978) emphasises the poet's relationship with the poetic message, as one whereby the poet provides a controlling force. This is crucial in accepting that, not only does Jakobson's theory state that poetry is a message which concentrates on the message for its own sake, but also that the "Formalist" definition of "function" includes the communication role of the poet – where this role releases information about the structure and "literariness" of the text. Osterwalder's emphasis does two things: firstly, it describes how the strength of the poetic function is a process of communication from the poet and the text to the reader; and secondly, it produces a strong poetic space which can be realised by a model based on the poles of language.

Jakobson developed his communication theory, extending it into an axial model based on the poles of language, and he explores it in his essay: "Two Aspects of Language and Two Types of Aphasic Disturbances" in "Language in Literature" (1987 [1956]). Briefly, here, metaphor is defined as on the axis of selection or simultaneity (that is, without time) and metonymy as on the axis of combination or contiguity (that is, sequential and therefore having the property of time). The axes have an inherent semiotic rather than linguistic structure. Jakobson's theory of poetic function should be analysed from within the Russian Formalist tradition of the importance of function as communication. The close examination of Jakobson's terms of reference: "poetic function", "equivalence" and "projection" (Chapter One) gives rise to an understanding of the sense of movement in Jakobson's model and which contributes to a semiotic structure. Jakobson's work on aphasia is the most often quoted source for this aspect of his Formalist theory. His poetic function refers to the projection of metaphoric poetic language into metonymic, often more prosaic combinations of language. He explores the model through the use of axes which give rise to the metonymic pole (syntagm, horizontal axis) and the metaphoric pole (paradigm, vertical axis). As indicated below, these poles can be developed beyond Jakobson's original structure and this development can provide a space which interprets a city poetic genre.

It is generally accepted that Jakobson's use of the paradigm and syntagm, the axis of selection and the axis of combination, can be traced from work done by Saussure. But Saussure's ideas are not identical to Jakobson's. In *Six Lectures on Sound and Meaning* Jakobson writes about the importance of accuracy with respect to the axes and their value:

> Saussure on many occasions warned that linguistics, and all sciences which are concerned with values, must be very careful to ascertain the axes on which the entities under consideration are located. He rigorously distinguished two axes: (1) *the axis of simultaneity* (AB) which concerns relations between coexisting things, and from which any intervention by time is excluded, and (2) *the axis of succession* (CD). (1978: 100)

Jakobson follows this paragraph with a diagram of the axes: (AB) as the paradigm and (CD) as the syntagm. However, it is worth quoting the paragraph in Baskin in full:

> Certainly all sciences would profit by indicating more precisely the co-ordinates along which their subject matter is aligned. Everywhere distinctions should be made, according to the following illustration, between (1) *the axis of simultaneities* (AB), which stands for the relations of coexisting things and from which the intervention of time is excluded; and (2) *the axis of successions* (CD), on which only one thing can be considered at a time but upon which are located all the things on the first axis together with their changes. (1966:79/80)

However, this paragraph is followed with a diagram of the axes where (AB) is the syntagm and (CD) is the paradigm. This is either a confusion introduced by Saussure himself, or, given, that these lecture notes are very much edited (sometimes with good reason), perhaps the model has not been correctly understood. The customary placing of axes is to construct time (the successive events that take place over a period of time) as the syntagm (horizontal) and the values which do not have time expressed within them as the paradigm (vertical).

It is important to note that Saussure in Engler (2008: 237, 240) depicts these axes as medially intersecting each other. In Saussure's own diagram (2008: 237), which Engler reproduces, he labels one axis as the "axis of contemporaneity (in which the Time factor can be made to *disappear*) and axis of succession (things x Time)". It is not clear in his diagram which axis refers to which value. What is made clear from the later diagram (Engler: 240) is that when considering the development of word usage he places words horizontally along the page ("simile") in succession and the word "Dissimile", is placed above the line of words, where change in the word meaning occurs. The vertical axis is therefore the "axis of contemporaneity" and the horizontal axis is the axis of succession. Saussure's axes are used for linguistic analysis only. As Jakobson explains:

> Whether it is a matter of words within a syntactical unit, of morphemes within a word, or of phonemes within a morpheme, it is always a matter of things ranged in succession to one another, i.e., on the axis of succession. On the other hand, in language each of these units necessarily belongs to a system of similar and opposable values. These series of interdependent values are ranged on the axis of simultaneity. Thus, on the axis of succession, *amō* might be linked with *patriam* [I love my country], or more accurately the transitive verb combines with the accusative of the noun; and, on the axis of simultaneity, *amō* is connected on the one hand with *amās, amāmus, amābam* etc. [you love, we love, I loved].
> (1978: 101)

Saussure's analysis explores the dichotomy between the spoken and the written word. In Chapter V of his *Course in General Linguistics* (1966) Saussure writes of his theory regarding syntagmatic and associative relations, that: "words acquire relations based on the linear nature of language because they are chained together. This rules out the possibility of pronouncing two elements simultaneously . . . The elements are arranged in sequence on the chain of speaking. Combinations supported by linearity are *syntagms*." (1966: 123).

It would seem from this, that the syntagm therefore represents the sequential combinatory meaning and the paradigm that of simultaneity. He is not, however, being fully binary in his analysis when he acknowledges that: "Whereas a syntagm immediately suggests an order of succession and a fixed number of elements, terms in an associative family occur neither in fixed numbers nor in a definite order" (1966: 126). His example is the French word: *enseignement*. Saussure, in Baskin, however also describes paradigms emerging in associative groupings: "But of the two characteristics of the associative series – indeterminate order and indefinite number – only the first can always be verified; the second may fail to meet the test. This happens in the case of inflectional paradigms, which are typical of associative groupings." (1966: 126)

Saussure's theory of syntagmatic and associative relations is a prototype for Jakobson's axial model with its paradigm of simultaneity and syntagm of combination. But care needs to be taken with the interpretation of his work. It is Saussure's theory combined with Jakobson's "poetic function" that produces further development of the axes. The debt to Saussure, and the development of his ideas, is acknowledged by others, for example Ladislav Matejka, once a member of The Prague Linguistic Circle. Matejka wrote: "Both the Formalists and Structuralists paid close attention to Saussure's observations about the paradigmatic and syntagmatic usage of verbal signs, although they did not apply it without modifications. Eventually, the concept had to be substantially redefined, so that Saussure's syntagmatic procedure could embrace two varieties of combination, concurrence and concatenation, both distinguishable from the selection characterizing Saussure's paradigmatic procedure." (1978: 293).

In Jakobson's studies, the opposition between a paradigmatic and a syntagmatic procedure was early recognized as being connected with the two fundamental poles dominating the verbal operation: the metaphoric pole, making use of similarity, and the metonymic pole, making use of contiguity. In his study of Pasternak's prose (1987) [1927]), Jakobson applied the binary concept of the metaphoric and metonymic poles as a classificatory device of two profoundly different types of poetic creation. The opposition of the metaphoric and the metonymic, exemplified in the domain of verbal art, was linked in Jakobson's subsequent investigation with the very foundations of human capacity in using verbal signs (1978: 293,294).

It should also be noted from Matejka's article "Jakobson's Response to Saussure's Cours" (1997) where Jakobson's critical approach to Saussure is analysed and acknowledged, that when Matejka uses the word "similarity", when referring to the metaphoric pole, the meaning here is similarity in terms of its simultaneity not similarity in terms of similar meaning – as in simile. Jakobson's own definition of the word "similarity", also refers to the principle of parallelism in poetry. He gives the word a semiotic poetic meaning rather than a syntactic one.

Jakobson's criticism of Saussure's definition of synchrony and diachrony is central to the former's development of Saussure's ideas. In his *Six Lectures on Sound and Meaning* (1978), Jakobson explains his objections to Saussure's definition of synchrony and diachrony with reference to axes. He is critical of Saussure's understanding of time. For Jakobson, time is, in itself, a value: "In postulating that the science of language has values as its object, the Saussurian doctrine failed to take cognisance of the fact that in a system of values the time factor itself becomes a value" (1978: 106).

Once time is included as a value, the axes contain diachrony as an attribute of the combination syntagm, and synchrony as an attribute of the simultaneity paradigm. The word "value" should be carefully understood here. To quote from Saussure himself: "the idea of value, as defined, shows that to consider a term as simply the union of a certain sound with a certain concept is grossly misleading. To define it in this way would isolate the term from its system" (1966: 113). Or to sum up: "The *value* [current author's emphasis] of a term is not its **"meaning"**, although this equation, which Saussure explicitly rejects, is nowadays commonplace" (Cobley 2001b: 284). Jakobson's argument is lodged with respect to the nature of phonemes and their values and relations; with whether a letter must indicate links to another in the same word; or whether the letter is regarded as freely available to be linked with any other in the usual combination in the language. Saussure's use of the axes and Jakobson's development of them, which, as demonstrated above, includes time as a value, are crucial to constructing a space from which an axial poetic model can be delineated. The form is both iconic and, in terms of the Formalist use of "function", contains movement. It should be noted that his model relies upon both linguistic and semiotic construction.

There is also a debt to Alexander Belyj's contribution to this metaphoric and metonymic categorization. Belyj, a member of the Symbolist movement, anticipated the Formalists with his ideas, which were also acknowledged by Eichenbaum in 1923 (Helle 1994: 41). He was a contemporary of Jakobson and his interest in poetry "so clearly isolates metaphor and metonymy and arranges them in a relation of opposition as two different types of connections" (Helle 1994: 42). His work, which is mathematically inspired, provides a context for Jakobson's theory of the poles of language which otherwise might seem to be solely original. Helle quotes from Belyj's *O Simvolizme* (1912) where Belyj defines the metaphor as a trope in which there is a "total fusion (слияние, sliarnie) of two signs into one: … This implies that the metaphoric image is a union of maximal extremes or contrasts (слияние противоборствующаго, sliarnie protivoborstvyuschavo) based on a common ground of similarity" (1994: 42). Belyj's definition of the metonym, however, depends upon a different principle: that of proximity – or, as Jakobson says, contiguity (Helle 1994: 42). Thus the metaphor has an organic or internal structural requirement, whereas the metonym arises from an accidental and/or proximal relationships (1994:43). Unlike Jakobson, Belyj's ideas on metaphor and metonymy do not rely on analysis of speech defects, but on a categorisation of different qualities of poetic language. Helle compares Belyj and Ejchenbaum:

> For Ejchenbaum, metonymy becomes more valuable than metaphor because metonymy does not detach the sign from its semantic series, but only results in a certain displacement of meaning, for example from part to whole, without any pretence of creating qualitatively new semantic dimensions, as does the metaphor. According to Ejchenbaum, metaphor thus leads us away from the sign and "over to the idea" … while poetic metonymy to a greater degree focuses on the intrinsic value of the poetic word. The word's concrete side is thus crucial, and not it's transferred or symbolic meaning. For Belyj, on the other hand, the strength of poetry lies in the metaphor … This is because Belyj, in accordance with the

basic conception of symbolism, in which art is supposed to create new syntheses and new symbolic universes, considers metaphor as the unique way of bringing together different spheres of thought. (1994: 43)

Unfortunately, only parts of Beyj's *O Simvolizme* have been translated from Russian into English (Cassedy 1985). For Jakobson, metonymy is subject to the principle of contiguity and metaphor to the principle of similarity. This would seem to be a divergence from Belyj's definitions as there is an organic structure implied for both tropes. Jakobson's essay: "Linguistics and Communication Theory" (1961) reveals his interest in the scientific and mathematical analysis of language. Referring to Tomashevsky's statistical investigation of verse Jakobson suggested that: "a linguistic analysis of the verse structure . . . theory of verse based on the calculus of its conditional probabilities and of the tensions between anticipation and unexpectedness as the measurable rhythmical values, and the computation of these tensions . . . 'frustrated expectations', gave surprising clues for descriptive, historical, comparative, and general metrics on a scientific basis." (1961: 252).

For Jakobson, therefore, the poles of language as explored in his essay, "Two Aspects of Language" (1987[1954]), define metaphor as having the property of simultaneity and the metonym as having the property of contiguity. Within his structure of language analysis, his poles of language can be arranged as a graph with the property of timelessness on the perpendicular axis, providing for the simultaneity to be in the metaphoric trope. The syntagm or horizontal axis therefore gives the property of progress through time and this provides contiguity in the metonymic trope. That is, the poetic trope of the metonym is a succession of words placed one after the other, some of which may portray an aspect of the metonym, for example, the synecdoche. The Axial Model below (see Figure 2) provides a further development of the model. It has been suggested by the present author that there are developments to the Saussurean and Jakobsonian models which would allow an expanded Axial Model. The model was open to placing various qualities within its scope. It was a project first undertaken in Coghill (2011). Some additions have been made since then to the qualities placed on the model; but the overall design has not changed.

The qualities attributed to the axes in the diagram need some detailed explication, especially where the terms used are not those of Jakobson himself. The mathematical component of the graph indicates that the paradigm is the dependent variable (Simultaneity) and the syntagm is the independent variable (Time). The experimental component of the graph indicates that it is the attributes of simultaneity which are the potentially unexpected variables as against the attributes of time which are understood as sequential and proportioned. In a literary

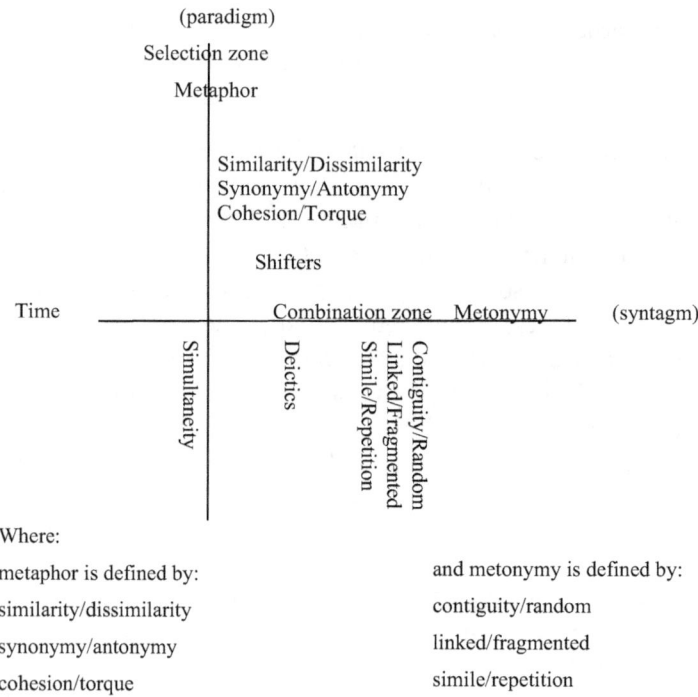

**Figure 2:** Jakobson's axial model, as developed by the author.

context, what is indicated is a progression of narrative. In the following paragraphs the qualities of the attributes of the axes are closely defined. It is important to bear in mind, at all times, Jakobson's own definition of these terms. The function of the model in the construction of a city poetic genre will be explored once the attributes have been explained.

The words paradigm and syntagm merely describe the axes themselves. The categories of selection and combination have been moved to the furthermost edges of the axes because they represent the categorisation of the other attributes. Metaphor governs the Simultaneity axis and metonymy governs the Time axis. The other forms of equivalence mentioned by Jakobson are also placed on the Metaphor axis: synonymy/antonymy and similarity/dissimilarity (1987: 71 and 99). It could be suggested that there is a gradation of complexity in these attributes, so that simile (metonymic), for example, is more complex than a simpler contiguity. Jakobson suggests this in his discussion of linguistic units:

> In order to comprehend the overwhelming majority of word groups, we need be familiar only with the constituent words and with the syntactical rules of their combination. Within these limitations we are free to put words in new contexts. Of course, this freedom is rela-

tive, and the pressure of current clichés upon our choice of combinations is considerable ... in the combination of linguistic units, there is an ascending scale of freedom. In the combination of distinctive features into phonemes, the freedom of the individual speaker is zero: the code has already established all the possibilities which may be utilized in the given language. Freedom to combine phonemes into words is circumscribed; it is limited to the marginal situation of word coinage. In forming sentences with words, the speaker is less constrained. And finally, in the combination of sentences into utterances, the action of compulsory syntactical rules ceases, and the freedom of any individual speaker to create novel contexts increases substantially. (1987: 98)

There is the possibility that other poetic qualities could be mentioned here. The graphic diagram (above) is proposed as a basis for discussion rather than as a definitive structure. It would seem appropriate, for example, that shifters should be on the Simultaneity axis and deictics on the Time axis. Shifters (pronouns) are placed on the metaphoric axis because they denominate the same people in different ways depending on the person who uses them, without reference to time. Deictics are on the metonymic axis because they register a sense of place (which cannot be simultaneous) and time (e.g. before and after). These terms are more fully discussed in Chapters Five and Six.

As mentioned above, the Time axis is governed by combination and metonymy. Other designations, which Jakobson does not include in his analysis, are included on the graph. It would be a mistake to consider metonymy as being less complex than metaphor. It is, as identified by Jakobson, only less well understood and analysed. His own analysis is more restricted than that of the metaphor. The axial model must be considered as still under consideration – theorists advocate that the metonym can be both as poetic and complex as metaphor, as in, for example, metonymic allegory (see Dirven: 1993; Silliman: 1995; Wilson, R: 1994). On the graph above, categories are included on the combination syntagm which correspond to the categories placed on the selection paradigm. Jakobson has itemized the metaphoric attributes clearly but the metonymic attributes are here named and explored for the first time as part of the graph. This is not to say that there have not been significant attempts to delineate the nature and extent of the metonym. Dirven defines the metonymic forms in increasing levels of complexity. It is worth quoting his summary in full:

There are not only different degrees in metaphoricity – as has already often been discussed in the literature – but there are also different degrees in metonymicity. The lowest degree of metonymicity is at the level of a linear metonym already discussed for the phrase *different parts of the country*, a next higher degree is at the level of a conjunctive metonym of the type *tea* for a "large meal", which is non-figurative; a further type is at the level of a figurative conjunctive metonym as in *the Crown* for the (British) Monarch or Queen; still more complex is the inclusive metonym, which is always figurative as (*have*) *a good head* for "intelligence"; the end of the continuum is taken up by metaphor, which is always figurative and which has a non-contiguous, contrastive conceptual basis. (1993: 16)

The suggestion is that metonymy has attributes, just as metaphor has, and that these have balancing attributes which can include their opposites: contiguity/random (cf. similarity/dissimilarity); linked/fragmented (cf. synonymy/antonymy), and simile/repetition (cf. cohesion/torque). And this is understood as within the context:

> where the addressee perceives that the given utterance (message) is a *combination* of constituent parts (sentences, words, phonemes) *selected* from the repository of all possible constituent parts (the code). The constituents of a context are in a state of *contiguity*, while in a substitution set signs are linked by various degrees of *similarity* which fluctuate between the equivalence of synonyms and the common core of antonyms. (Jakobson: 1987: 99)

An interpolation to the model is suggested by the Matejka (1978: 293) quotation above on Saussure's syntagmatic observations. He argued that "concurrence and concatenation" were properties which should be included as two varieties of combination. The rhetorical device of concatenation is also appropriate as an aspect of metonymy and should be inserted into the combination zone/syntagm, perhaps under the heading of "repetition". This device is used in the Old English poem "Pearl" (Anon) with great effect and thus demonstrates that metonymy in poetry is not a new aspect of poetic form. It is defined as the repetition of an important word or phrase from one stanza to the next, as well as the repetition of word rhyme, alliteration and sound echoes between stanzas (*NPEPP*. 1993: 231a/231b). The term "concurrence" is also metonymic and is an aspect of the designation "linked". It is not recognised as a poetic term or trope but its meaning is that of "running together in time or place" (*OED*: 1968: 363b). This makes it a sequential term. It is interesting to note that the more recent online *OED* interprets the word as harbouring a sense of simultaneous time included in it which would remove the term from the metonymic syntagm. That concurrence is therefore not sequential or accumulative, rather one that includes occurrence at one time (*OED online* 2022). For the purposes of this research, it remains metonymic.

The properties of metonymy are not yet fully understood. Other categories, suggested on the graph, have yet to be defined and understood poetically. These terms are: random (as paired with contiguity); and linked/fragmented. On the metaphoric axis the term "torque" is a term introduced, used and defined by Ron Silliman (1995). "Torque", is a term originally used in physics and engineering:

> Torque (moment of force or couple): The product of a force and its perpendicular distance from a point about which it causes rotation or torsion. The unit of torque is the newton metre, a vector product, unlike the joule, also equal to a newton metre, which is a scalar product. A turbine produces a torque on its central rotating shaft. (Daintith (2005: 823)

Silliman defines this term with reference to both prose and poetry. He explores its dislocative effect on prose and then defines it as a quality of poetry, with reference to the impact of line breaks: "continual torquing of sentences is a traditional quality of poetry, but in poetry it is most often accomplished by line breaks, or by other devices such as rhyme. Here [where Silliman is considering a prose example by Perelman] poetic form has moved into the interiors of prose." (1995: 89). Line breaks in poetry can delineate quantity and measure. Silliman, in his own words, goes on to elaborate his definition of torque: "But the torquing which is normally triggered by line breaks, the function of which is to enhance ambiguity and polysemy, has moved directly into the grammar of the sentence" (1995: 90). This, for Silliman, results in a "new sentence, that is, a sentence with an interior poetic structure in addition to interior ordinary grammatical structure" (1995: 90).

For city poetry, Silliman's contribution defines double force – rotation and vertical or horizontal pressure not only accurately delineates the movement implied by Jakobson's axes but it also provides a structure for certain kinds of pressured response to life in the city. It may not be fragmented or random as such but twisted and pushed apart (or pulled together) into certain verbal structures and meanings. The term therefore provides a tool for analyzing and understanding how a city poetic genre may be constructed and may also provide a tool for a poet to interpret city existence. The original link of torque to prose by Silliman, indicates its affinity with combination. However, it is placed on the graph on the selection/metaphoric axis, paired with cohesion. This metaphoric placing highlights the way in which its characteristic method of operation includes simultaneity. Torque also constantly breaks the combined and habitual apart and is counterbalanced with a quality which is dependent on the customary and habitual: cohesion.

An expressed thought may well be coherent, but if it is not a habitual expression, well known to ourselves, then it is difficult or even impossible to understand its meaning. The cohesion is the quality of the expressed thought and habit is the quality of the reader/perceiver. Therefore, the quality of cohesion is the one that should be inserted onto the graph. Cohesion can occupy several levels within the text: semantic, grammatical, and semiotic – patterns of customary spelling, the formation of the patterns of words and punctuation, and the arrangement of the sentences in a certain order within the text – this exists for both prose and poetry. Torque breaks this apart. Cohesion is expressed through usual and customary form – the habit with which we perceive the text. Thus, a metaphor "my love is a red rose" is customary, a coherent metaphor, one that is well known and has a standardised usage – both in word order and in the emotion it designates. Other metaphors can be understood with reference to this habitual device when they fall into the same structure (Lakoff: 2003). Cohesion is placed on the metaphoric axis because it also enables instant comprehension of the text.

Returning to the metonymic axis, repetition would seem to be an odd choice for a poetic device. It has a resistance to consecutive narrative, although by its very nature it absorbs a timeline. In other words, repetition is, or seems, purely sequential, apparently incapable of change, including through force and governed by the passage of time. It is paired with simile. It might, in a very fundamental form, result in a word which is repeated throughout a poem, either in conjunction with other words, or just simple repetition, for example in the use of a refrain, or the use of "found" elements in a poem (random or deliberate choice of text from other documents which are repeatedly inserted into a poem). A poem that consists of one word or phrase only, can result in a more metaphoric impact than might at first seem possible. The present author, for example, has written two poems (both unpublished sonnets): one is entitled, "please" and the second, "thank you". The poems consist solely of these words, which are repeated, with attention paid to the variations in intonation and comprehension of how and when these two words can be spoken, and the resulting variations of meaning and impact. Jakobson's reference to Stanislavskij in "Linguistics and Poetics" (1987: 67) where the phrase "This evening" could be said in forty different ways depending on the emotive context, is relevant here. City poetry may well include the use of repetition as an important device since much of city life is repetitive. The repetition is one of both place and time. Much of the nature of the city itself is also repetitive – streets, rows of houses, working five days a week for example. Dennis Cronan (2016), in his analysis of 'Beowulf', adds an interesting dimension to the quality of repetition, where "overlapping synonyms" in a poetic text can break through the syntagmatic and paradigmatic axial structure to form a poetic grammar which is governed by the text itself. His argument is, in part, based on Jakobson's theory of "poetic function" and he suggests that poetry written in Old English with its very large numbers of "alliterative collocations" (2016: 262) reveals a particular form.

The other two pairings contiguity/random and linked/fragmented are now considered. That which is contiguous is determined by that which abuts it (on any side). The opposite is therefore (cf. Jakobson's linkage of similarity/dissimilarity) random. This is an attribute which is not determined by what is on either side of it – or indeed by what is above or below. Perhaps the poetry of Jack Spicer and Barrett Watten can be understood to illustrate such a structure. Silliman, in *The New Sentence* (1995), discusses both these poets. "Found" poetry – where random texts are pulled together to construct a poem, is an extreme example of this (Lopez 2000). Silliman indicates that although the construction of both Spicer's and Watten's poetry may appear to be random collocations of words and sentences; there are "torque", tropes to be found within the text despite this. It might be asked why these categories are placed in the combination zone and are seen to be part of metonymy. It is because that which is combined can also be split apart, and that which uses parts of a whole are easily recognizable as aspects of the metonymic – as for example in the accepted term "synecdoche" which is a type of metonym. In city poetry it can be readily accepted that life contains much which is both a part of life – contiguous – and much which appears also to be random – the drunk on the street, the mugging, the chance encounter, the job termination email. Torque, where there is deliberate twisting of syntax or semantics to construct a sequence which is perhaps rich in sound and rhythm, is metaphoric because it has destroyed the original logical progression of meaning in such a way that the original meaning can only be guessed at. Repetition, where words and phrases may be repeated without attention to logical meaning, is obviously a combinatory form rather than a metaphoric one.

The terms linked/fragmented on the metonymic axis are balanced on the above graph by synonymy/antonymy on the metaphoric one. It has been suggested above that these may be less complex attributes than either similarity/dissimilarity or contiguity/random. Within the metaphoric paradigm, synonymy (two words which are different but mean the same, (Wales, 2001) and antonymy (two words which designate opposite characteristics (Wales, 2001); for example: "old heart/young love" describes a form of metaphoric construction. They define how selection occurs in the construction of the metaphor. Within the metonymic syntagm the attributes of linkage and fragmentation can be seen to define how combination occurs in the construction of the full metonymic: porch and shadow may be linked as meaning shelter, and because they are listed one after the other, may represent fragmentation of a physical environment. The linkage and fragmentation are a combination and therefore metonymic not metaphoric in the context. The speed and complexity of events within the city can be accurately recalled and interpreted through the use of these two devices within the poetic.

How does the graph construct a space which demonstrates a proposed city poetic genre? How is the city space represented as poetic space in the graph? Jakobson's definition of poetic function is, as Culler (2001) understands it, almost irritatingly simple; but it does, however, provide a useful and definitive structure which releases scope for clearly understanding the attributes of poetic structure. The structure, as a whole, is a semiotic structure and cannot be fully understood within only either a linguistic or a literary discipline. This justifies the representation of Jakobson's definition of poetic function as a graph. Any graph constructs a space between its two axes. The axes generate intersections of the independent variable (in this case combination/metonymy), and the dependent variable (in this case selection/metaphor). These intersections or interstices measure a doubly defined quality which takes place in the space provided by the graph. There is a suggestion that these spaces could be both positive and negative. This chapter argues that these sequences of intersections provide the iconic and grammatical poetic space to record the city in poetry. Or to argue backwards – the city is represented and recorded by intersections of selection and combination; time and simultaneity, torque and repetition for example.

As a poet it would be preferable to state that any selection/combination can be used together and each interstice will give rise to a particular poetic structure and content. Jakobson uses the term "equivalence" as the defining quality of the space between the axes (see Chapter One, above). "Equivalence" is further described and defined by the definition and use of "parallels" (for more on both of these terms, see also Chapter Seven, below). However, the construction of qualities within the axial space is developed by using the terms suggested above and it can result in a complex and new understanding of how poetry interprets its subject. Additionally, the construction provides a framework with which to understand interaction with the city. It has provided a source for understanding the Modernist poetic and artistic inspiration. The city gives rise to poetry of realisation rather than description and "Poets develop collage techniques for intensifying that sense of productive immediacy: it becomes the spaces between images that offer the audience its access to the mode of spirit defined by the work. Thus, Eliot's 'The Waste Land' [describes] the failure to integrate the multiple layers" (*NPEPP.* 1993: 793).

Jakobson does not seem to have extensively defined the metonym. He wrote that:

> nothing comparable to the rich literature on metaphor can be cited for the theory of metonymy . . . The principle of similarity underlies poetry; the metrical parallelism of lines or the phonic equivalence of rhyming words prompts the question of semantic similarity and contrast . . . Prose on the contrary, is forwarded essentially by contiguity. Thus for poetry, metaphor – and for prose, metonymy – is the line of least resistance and consequently the study of poetical tropes is directed chiefly toward metaphor. (1987: 113/4)

The historical analysis of the metonym includes several schools of study, including its rhetorical and classical origins, or more contemporaneously, through cognitive linguistics. These provide a number of categorisations and few conclusions. A number of other linguistic-based academic disciplines have grappled with the difficult issue of defining the metonym. Definitions of this poetic trope originating with classical rhetoric have been further investigated with varying degrees of success by semantics, stylistics, cognitive linguists and corpus linguists, for example: Allen (2008); Dancygier and Sweetser (Eds. 2014); Deignan (2005); Denroche (2015); Dirven and Pörings (Eds. 2003); Geeraerts (2010) (see Chapter Three for a fuller discussion).

The contemporary position is that metonyms cannot be altogether classified as separate from metaphor. However, for the purposes of this chapter, the terms metaphor and metonym are defined with reference to Jakobson's own definitions of these tropes. There is a definition of the relationship between the two in his essay "Linguistics and Poetics", written in 1960 (see Jakobson 1987). Here, he discusses Slavic folk poetry with allusion to Goethe:

> In poetry not only the phonological sequence but, in the same way, any sequence of semantic units strives to build an equation. Similarity superimposed on contiguity imparts to poetry its thoroughgoing symbolic, multiplex, polysemantic essence . . . Said more technically, anything sequent is a simile. In poetry, where similarity is superinduced upon contiguity, any metonymy is slightly metaphoric and any metaphor has a metonymic tint.
> (1987: 85)

The complexity inherent in this condensed statement requires much analysis of terms and their connections in order to fully understand it. It is beyond the scope of the current chapter to examine developing theories of the relationship of metaphor and metonym (see Chapter Three, below), but Jakobson's definitions, which identify the inter-relationship of the two terms, predate the subsequent work on the relationship between the two defined by Cognitive Linguists.

As mentioned above, Jakobson's Formalist techniques focus on the function of the poetic text, with the full and detailed analysis of linguistic, grammatical and semiotic parts as a scientific study. The end result of the Formalist approach was intended as a semiotic analysis of the whole of the poem as an artefact in its own right. For Jakobson, this is defined by its factual similarity (the text in itself) and its imputed similarity (the grammar and patterning of the text in itself). Jakobson explains his terms in his essays "Grammatical Parallelism" (1987:145–179) and "The Development of Semiotics" (1987: 436–454). Briefly, in poetic construction – where words, sounds, themes, patterns are repeated within the poem – the factual similarity produces the parallels. With regards to imputed similarity, he uses terms which derive from the work of the semiotician Charles Sanders Peirce – the icon, the index, the symbol. Jakobson also refers to Saussure's ground-breaking work on ancient poetry and then again to his own development of the work of the semiotician Peirce, where he (Jakobson) proposes that a fourth mode to be added to Peirce's index-symbol-icon triad – "artifice":

> The 'artifice' is to be added to the triad of semiotic modes established by Peirce. This triad is based on two binary oppositions: contiguous/similar and factual/imputed. The contiguity of the two components of the sign is factual in the *index* but imputed in the *symbol*. Now, the factual similarity which typifies *icon* finds its logically foreseeable correlative in the imputed similarity which specifies the *artifice*, and it is precisely for this reason that the latter fits into the whole which is now forever a four-part entity of semiotic modes.
> (1987: 451/2)

That is to say (with reference to Merrell 2000: 12) that a picture of a horse is factual (an icon), the word horse designates "horse" but is imputed, for the word "horse" is not at all like a horse (an index); the representation of the horse in a poem (a symbol) gives rise to imputed similarity through combinations of poetic devices and these construct poetic artifice. This develops Peirce's triadic semiotic structure into a quadripartite one.

The grammar of "similarity", either factual or imputed, can then be interpreted as an aspect of city poetry. The similarity releases both metaphor and metonymy into the space. This is the space which can be used to construct a city poetic genre. The conception of a "grammar of poetry" rather than a linguistic analysis of its lexical or syntactical words, releases a structure which comprises the overall form of the poem rather than just its linguistically defined parts. If a city poem is written in a particular way, then it's form can be understood to represent an aspect of the city, as, for example, a poem that revolves around a particular form, as an expression of its meaning. "Relational equivalence" is a definition of the use of space between the two axes as suggested by Jakobson. It is not a linguistic definition. Again, the imbalance of forces between the city structure and the humans living within it, is complemented and expressed by the play of poetic equivalences as suggested by the relational equivalence – in this instance, factual similarity and imputed similarity.

## Part II

The second part of the chapter illustrates the theory posited above, based on the axial diagram, and which includes defining metaphor and metonymy as the two categories of tropes. The above discussion enables metonymy to be understood as a poetic trope. Within the generic term there are types of metaphor or metonym – a variety of species as it were. Therefore, when the poem "City" by Mayakovsky, is analysed with reference to the axial model, the outcome is achieved through the analysis of tropes rather than through meter, rhyme, verse structure or grammar, linguistic observations and features such as onomatopoeia/assonance. As will become apparent throughout the book, each poem is analyzed with reference to Jakobson's definition that the "focus on the message for its own sake, is the POETIC function of language" (1987: 69). The Formalist brief is that the text in itself is the focus. However, the focus is with reference to the poem's own specific characteristics, rather than a formulaic Formalist technique. Bearing this in mind, Jakobson's own approach to Mayakovsky's poetry is now also considered.

The poem written by Vladimir Mayakovsky (1893–1930) entitled "The City" (1925) is about the city of Paris. Please see below for the two versions discussed.

"The City", in the English Raduga Publishers' translation, comprises 100 lines. The online literal translation (see www.v.mayakovsky.ru) splits the lines in a different way and is comprised of 121 lines. Historically the locations are very significant. Briefly, the Place de la Vendôme, at the time, was the location of the Ritz Hotel, the headquarters of Chanel and other wealthy businesses. The Place de la Concorde was the location of the guillotine in the French Revolution and, as mentioned below, more recent political events. Both of these locations are in close proximity to each other in central Paris.

The poem has been analysed in conjunction with two of Jakobson's essays on Mayakovsky which were written as a commentary to previously unpublished texts by Mayakovsky for an edition of his work *Russkij literaturnyi arxiv* ("The Russian Literary Archive") (1956) published in New York by Harvard University. These essays were published in a volume of Jakobson's *Selected Writings*, but in keeping with a number of his other essays in various languages, it was published in Russian, in the English edition: *Selected Writings, Vol. 5* (1979). The full details are as follows: К ПОЗДНЕЙ ЛИРИКЕ МАЯКОВСКОГО (382–405), translated as: "About Mayakovsky's Later Lyrical Poems" [AMLLP]; and ДОСТОЕВСКИЙ В ОТГОЛОСКАХ МАЯКОВСКОГО (406–412), translated as: "Dostoyevsky Echoed In Mayakovsky's Work" [DEMW]. Enquiries were made as to where an English translation of the essay might be found and none was located. These two essays were translated as part of the present author's Visiting Research Fellowship at the Institute of English Studies, School of Advanced Studies, University of London. The translation is reproduced in full in the Appendix of this volume. They are both also available online at: https://sas-space.ac.uk.

Jakobson's analysis, in these essays, of Mayakovsky as a poet and his poetic work is much more biographical than Formalist techniques would usually allow. Osip Brik made the Formalist position very clear when he wrote in 1923: "The social role of the poet cannot be understood by an analysis of his individual qualities and habits. It is essential to study on a mass scale the devices of poetic craft, what distinguishes them from adjacent domains of human labour, and to study the laws of their historical development." (Shukman and O'Toole 2013-12-05) Kindle locs. 2723–2725). However, the strong use of the personal pronoun or shifter, the "I" poet/narrator, makes "The City", a personal poem although, as demonstrated below, Mayakovsky's use of the metonym in his poem constructs a poem which is very much about world events.

Jakobson provides a personal overview of Mayakovsky's life and approach to his work in these essays. Crucially, Jakobson, quoting David Burlyuk, writes in the opening paragraph: "In Mayakovsky's literary works, love poems and lyrical cycles befittingly alternate with lyrical epic poems about world events". Jakobson sums up Mayakovsky's early poetic development: "Then again "the lyrics of the heart" are replaced by poetry ruled by reason" (AMLLP: 313–314). [All page references refer to the translation; see Appendix – AMLLP – not the original published text]. To use Mayakovsky's own poetic summary from his poem "Jubilee": "We repeatedly attack/lyrical verses/with bayonets" [AMLLP: 316]. On the same page, Jakobson's commentary provides a personal biographical story about Mayakovsky: "One evening in April 1927, in the restaurant Nezdara in Prague, famous for its vintage Tokay wine, Mayakovsky assured me that his rhythm of alternating genres was unchanged, and real lyrical poems are going to follow the "October" poem." [AMLLP: 316].

Both this essay and the earlier one written by Jakobson, "On a Generation that Squandered its Poets" (1987[1937]: 273–300), contain a mood of prescience in their interpretation of Mayakovsky's impending suicide. His approach reveals two things: firstly, that Jakobson has a strong emotional response to the poet that he had known for many years; secondly, that the emotional response sidelined Jakobson's commitment to Formalism.

The second essay on Mayakovsky's poetry, "Dostoyevsky Echoed in Mayakovsky's Work", was originally published in 1959. It was also specially translated for the current author's Fellowship. It contains extensive analysis of Shklovsky's interpretation of Dostoyevsky's work. Jakobson analyses Mayakovsky's use of star motifs and imagery to interpret both this and the function of the poet's life (DEMW: 337). The analysis of Dostoyevsky's work concentrates on how various Russian writers interact with each other's ideas and themes. Towards the conclusion of his essay, Jakobson returns to Mayakovsky's work within the context of how Russian authors used other writers' themes and ideas, including the idea of constructing "doubles".

Jakobson demonstrates Mayakovsky's ability to treat the same subjects throughout his work in both epic and parodic manner. Jakobson uses the example of Mayakovsky's poem "About This": "The other double of the autobiographical hero of the older poem 'A Man', who calls from the past to 'stop the suffering', while the younger double doesn't find a premise for an exchange in the "time being". Furthermore, the lyrical "I" of the poem 'About This' has a third and insufferable bedbug double." (DEMW: 340). Mayakovsky wrote a vicious and comic play entitled "The Bedbug" (1929). He described it "as being a caricature of his own poem ('About This') right after he finished it and it was performed" (DEMW: 340).

Finally, Jakobson picks up the central theme of analysis of Mayakovsky's poetic works when he refers back to his earlier essay, "About a Generation that Squandered its Poets", and insists that Mayakovsky's work contained the two themes which are always developed. Mayakovsky's poetic creation, from his first poems: "to his last lines is unitary and indivisible. There is a dialectic development of a unitary theme. There is an unusual unity of symbols. A Symbol that was alluded to in passing is developed and offered from a different angle . . . . Everything that Mayakovsky wrote is unitary inseparable and inextricable."

(DEMW: 341). It is of interest that the full quote from the original essay in the translation used in *Language in Literature* (1987) is as follows:

> The poetry of Mayakovskij from his first verses, in "A Slap in the Face of Public Taste", to his last lines is one and indivisible. It represents the dialectical development of a single theme. It is an extraordinarily unified symbolic system. A symbol once thrown out as a hint will later be developed and presented in a totally new perspective. (1987: 275/6)

Jakobson goes on to argue that Mayakovsky's social poems all end in the future, whereas his love poems end with "personal love tragedy, inescapable loneliness, and martyrdom" [DEMW: 341–342]. This is not a dichotomy of themes imposed by history but rather, as Jakobson wrote:

> The polyphonic character of Mayakovsky's poetry consists in the interruption of both unmerged genres. This is not a theory imposed from the outside and backdated to form the literary inheritance of a dead poet. Mayakovsky wrote many times in his poems and letters, and made oral declarations about the alternation of genres and their dramatic collisions; about the fight between the lyrical and anti-lyrical inspiration. This was not a fight imposed upon the poet. No one could have imposed anything upon such a stubborn poet.
> [DEMW: 342]

Jakobson's conclusion to his essay, where he refers back to Shklovsky's analysis, reveals his own deep fascination for form. Jakobson is a Formalist after all:

> It is not coincidental that these notes about Mayakovsky's poetry serve as a background for the notes about Dostoyevsky in Shklovsky's book "Pro and Contra". The researcher calls upon us not to confuse the polyphonic structure of confrontational lines [i.e. form] with the discord and gibberish of contradictory declarations [i.e. content], rather he prompts us to meditate on the polyphonic character of the opposing genres [i.e. forms], which shouldn't be confused with the silly chaos of discordant dissonance [i.e. meaning].
> (DEMW: 342) [interpretive comments in square brackets]

How does this fit with what actually happens in his short poem "The City"? It is not a love poem, it is not written to a woman in Mayakovsky's life – unless it be The Place de la Vendôme. However, the poem is often lyrical as well as reflecting life events. A significant poetic device is the use of animal imagery; these are similes, used as a means for the poet to interpret the city. It is interesting to note that the animal imagery is largely lost in the Russian-to-English translation of the poem by Raduga Publishers (1985). The literal translation of the poem, which is available on www.vmayakovsky.ru, provides all the similes – the camel, beetles, bison and lapdogs. The poem's length would seem to preclude it being defined as an epic poem; however, an examination of its structure and form indicates otherwise. The poem in three versions is reproduced below: the literal Russian-to-English translation from the Russian website (as above); the original Russian and the Raduga translation, including notes.

CITY

One Paris –
lawyers,
barracks,
other –
no barracks and no
Herriot.
Do not tear
the second
eyes –
this gray city.
From the walls of
promise:
"Un verre de koto
donne de l'energie"
Wine Love
What
and who
excite my life?
Maybe
criticism
They know better.
Maybe
their
and listen to the right.
But who I am, to the
devil, a fellow traveler!
Not a soul
no steps
beside.
Like before,
his
rock the hump
ahead
poetovyh carts –
Carry,
one
and joy,
and sorrow,
and other
Human belongings.
I'm bored
here
one
ahead –
poet
It does not need much –
let
only
time
soon give birth
such as I,
swift.
We are near
go
road pollen.
One
Desire
puchit:
I"m bored –
I wish
to see in person,
who is
I
companion ?!
"Je suis un chameau",
in the poster are
letters,
each – foot.
Quite true:
"Je suis", –
this
"I",
and "chameau" – is
"I'm a camel."
Purple cloud
probably stoop down,
me
Paris and fields,
so only
probably
bloom lights
length
Champs-Elysees.
During all fire –
and the sky in darkness
and drenched in black
dust.
In the fire
beetles
All systems
buzz
automobiles.
Steady water
the earth is burning,
lights
asphalt
before burning,
as if
bison
lights
multiplication table.
Area
handsomer
thousands
Dame lapdogs.
This area
b justified
each city.
If I was
Vendome Column,
I'd married
at the Place la concorde

ГОРОД

Один Париж –
адвокатов,
казарм,
другой –
без казарм и без Эррио.
Не оторвать
от второго
глаза –
от этого города серого.
Со стен обещают:
"Un verre de koto
donne de l'energie"
Вином любви
каким
и кто
мою взбудоражит
жизнь?
Может,
критики
знают лучше.
Может,
их
и слушать надо.
Но кому я, к черту,
попутчик!
Ни души
не шагает
рядом.
Как раньше,
свой
раскачивай горб
впереди
поэтовых арб –
неси,
один,
и радость,
и скорбь,
и прочий
людской скарб.
Мне скучно
здесь
одному
впереди,–
поэту
не надо многого,–
пусть
только
время
скорей родит
такого, как я,
быстроногого.
Мы рядом
пойдем
дорожной пыльцой.
Одно
желанье
пучит:
мне скучно –
желаю
видеть в лицо,
кому это
я
попутчик?!
"Je suis un chameau",
в плакате стоят
литеры,
каждая – фут.
Совершенно верно:
"Je suis",–
это
"я",
а "chameau" – это
"я верблюд".
Лиловая туча,
скорей нагнись,
меня
и Париж полей,
чтоб только
скорей
зацвели огни
длиной
Елисейских полей.
Во все огонь –
и небу в темь
и в чернь промокшей
пыли.
В огне
жуками
всех систем
жужжат
автомобили.
Горит вода,
земля горит,
горит
асфальт
до жжения,
как будто
зубрят
фонари
таблицу умножения.
Площадь
красивей
и тысяч
дам-болонок.
Эта площадь
оправдала б
каждый город.
Если б был я
Вандомская колонна,
я б женился
на Place la concorde

THE CITY (1925)

Two cities it is –
one of lawyers and barracks,
the other –
no barracks
and no Herriot.(1)
This other
brings up a lump in my larynx;
grey city –
sets my heart aglow.
From the walls          10
they promise:
*"Un verre de Koto
donne de l'energie"*...(2)
With what wine of love,
I'd like to know,
could anyone
stir up the life in me?
Maybe critics know better,
I won't deny,
yes, maybe –          20
it's hard to decide.
But whose
in hell
fellow-traveller (3) am I?
Not a soul
strides along
at my side.
As ever,
trudge on,
swinging your hump          30
in front of
Poetry's
waggon.
Alone
carry joy and grief
in a lump
and suchlike
human baggage.

It's lonesome –
forever alone here,          40
in front.
Not much does a poet need:
quick,
time,
give birth
to another one
like me,
with feet just as fleet.
We'd go side-by-side
on our dusty ways.          50
One wish eats my heart,
by the devil! –
it's lonesome.
I wish I could look in the face
of whoever's my fellow-traveller!
*"Je suis un chameau,"*
on a poster stand
say letters
each a foot.
*"Je suis"* means "I" –          60
that I understand;
*"chameau"* –
"I'm a camel" –
well put!
Purple-tinged cloud,
be quick
and pour down
on Paris and me
your spray,
so that lights          70
should go blossoming
all along
through the length
of Champs-Elysées.
Let the lights fill up all –
the dark of the sky
and the black
of the rain-soaked dust.

| | | |
|---|---|---|
| In the light | | the multiplication table. 90 |
| like beetles of diverse design 80 | | The square |
| automobiles | | looks more swell |
| buzz. | | than any dame. |
| The very asphalt burns, | | Any city'd be proud of it, |
| no, scorches, | | 'pon my word. |
| water and earth | | I swear, |
| burn as hard as they're able | | if I were |
| as if the streetlamps | | the Colonne de la Vendôme, |
| that stand like torches | | I'd go and marry |
| were cramming | | Place de la Concorde! 100 |

Vladimir Mayakovsky; taken from the Raduga Publishers USSR edition (1985) translated by Victor Christyakov

(1) ... *and no Herriot* ... -Eduard Herriot in 1924–1925 headed the French Government
(2) "Un verre de Koto donne de l'"energie" – "One sip of Koto brings new energy".
(3) *fellow-traveller* – reference to writers of non-proletarian origin who nevertheless accepted the Revolution. In the conditions of the ideological and aesthetic battles and literary polemics of the period, the term was often applied rather arbitrarily.

In the *NPEPP*, the entry on the epic opens with the following definition: "An epic is a long narrative poem that treats a single heroic figure or a group of such figures and concerns an historical event, such as a war or conquest, or an heroic quest or some other significant mythic or legendary achievement that is central to the traditions and belief of its culture" (1993: 361b). Cuddon in his *Literary Terms and Literary Theory* (1999) summarizes definitions of the epic poem as having the characteristics outlined below. These can be illustrated with reference to "The City" which, as a result, emerges as an epic on a very small scale. Cuddon's definitions are reproduced here and are used to provide specific interpretations of this poem. All line references used here refer to the Raduga translation):

**the grand scale, about the deeds of warriors and heroes** – this is depicted in the description of the city as bi-faceted: "Two cities it is -/one of lawyers and barracks," [lines 1/2] and the poet as a giant and grand figure on his journey of the poet through Paris – "whose/in hell/fellow-traveller am I?/Not a soul/strides along/at my side." [lines 22–27].

**of national significance, in a lofty or grandiose manner** – again this can be seen in the opening lines as above and in the metaphoric lines: "pour down/on Paris and me/your spray,/so that lights/should go blossoming" [lines 67–71].

**a central figure of superhuman calibre** – the poem, unlike some poems by Mayakovsky, for example "Brooklyn Bridge" written later that same year, has a strong narrator; there is no shift in the personal narrator, no other persona used. The central figure therefore attaches to himself, all the personal characteristics detailed in the poem. He describes himself as the poet, the interpreter of his environment in archetypal terms: "quick,/time, give birth/to another one/like me,/with feet just as fleet." [lines 43–47].

**a perilous journey** – "Alone/carry joy and grief/in a lump/and suchlike/human baggage./It's lonesome – forever here alone,/in front" [lines 34–41].

**there are various misadventures** – "Purple-tinged cloud,/be quick/and pour down/on Paris and me,/your spray" [lines 65–69]. There is also a sense of misadventure when he describes having trouble interpreting the French advertisement *"Je suis"* means "I" -/that I understand;/*"chameau"* -/ "I'm a camel" -/"well put!" [lines 60/61].

**an element of the supernatural** – see references to "hell" [line 23], "soul" [line 25], "One wishes to eat my heart,/by the devil!/It's lonesome." [lines 51/2], "we'd go side-by-side/on our dusty ways", and see other references to the heavens [lines 65 et seq.] and the stars "Let lights fill up all -/the dark of the sky" [lines 75/6].

**there are repeated passages of narrative or dialogue** – this takes place with the advertisements which he describes as "From the walls" [line10], this makes them separate or even remote from him – upwards and/or distant. See also the reference to "Koto" [line 12] and the *"je suis chameau"* [line 56] and his conversation with the advertisement: ""*je suis*" means "I" -/that I understand;/ "chameau"-/ "I'm a camel" -/well put!"" [lines 60–64].

**and there are elaborate greetings** – he interprets the message of the advertisement as an invitation to "the wine of love" and it becomes an address to the very central drive for life "From the walls they promise:/*"Un verre de Koto/donne de l'energie"* . . . /With what wine of love,/I'd like to know,/could anyone stir up the life in me?" [lines 10–17].

**digressions take place** – the poem takes the reader on a night journey where the weather has an impact on the city which is seen as separate from the poet/narrator [lines 65–90]: "Purple-tinged cloud" to "the multiplication table". This, in effect, becomes a speech or address to the city – another epic characteristic.

**and there are epic similes** – the poem contains a number of animal similes: the camel is repeatedly both evoked [lines 27–36] and directly referred to [lines 56–63], the cars are described as "beetles" [line 80] and other animal similes are lost in the Raduga Press translation (compare the online translation): "torches"/ "bison", [line 88], and "dame"/ "lapdogs", [line 93]. The "bisons" are a reference to the heavy iron lamp-posts which surround the Place de la Concorde. They are constructed with a massive central column which branches, midway up on each side, each branch carrying a large lamp. Their shape very much resembles a silhouette of a bison, black against the sky.

With reference to the original Russian, there is no first person until line 16, where Mayakovsky refers to his life being agitated or "excited" (in the English translation). But, here, the word for life has connotations of "soul" and it is followed in line 24 by his use of the first-person pronoun as a fellow traveller with the devil. This is not lyric, but epic language. In line 40, he refers to how the small trappings of life bore him. It's the littleness of life which he wants to transcend. This is rapidly followed by the first-person pronoun with reference to giving birth (lines 49 and 50). Then in line 58 the phrase "I'm bored" (Мне скучно/mne skychno), is repeated. The first occurrence is subsequent to a full stop and the capital letter is expected, but the second one also has a capital letter when it is placed after a colon. Here, the Russian grammatical habit of capitalising a pronoun- "Вы" (Vwi/You) in a sentence to be polite and give importance, is carried over to the first person. There are connotations here which are therefore more than personal. The second one is followed by "I wish" as an expressed strong desire to see his companion "мне скучно – /желаю/видеть в лицо,/кому это/я/попутчик?!" (I'm bored -/I wish/to see in person,/who is/I/companion?!) This cluster is placed at the centre of the poem (lines 58–63) and serves as a pivot. It is closely followed by another cluster of first-person pronouns (lines 64–76). The original is: " ""Je suis un chameau",/в плакате стоят/литеры,/каждая – фут./Совершенно верно:/"Je suis",- /"это/ "я",/а "chameau" – это/ "я верблю"".Лиловая туча, скорей нагнись, меня."); and in translation: ""Je suis un chameau" [I am a camel],/in the poster are/letters,/each – foot./Quite true:/"je suis" [I am], -/ this/"I",/and "chameau" – is/"I'm a camel."/ Purple cloud/ probably stoop down,/me""").

""Je suis", – /this/"I"/and "chameau – is": Here the first person is highlighted by the multiple use of inverted commas. Mayakovsky is indicating that the personal pronoun is not the same as himself. He is indicating an ulterior self who is acted upon by the text, its vocalisation, one who is linked to the French advertisement. It is correct to say that this seems to be a more personal expression of the poet. But Mayakovsky has already described himself as the poet/camel. He is the poet with a heavy hump or epic burden of necessary tasks. There is an association here to Jakobson's analysis of the "zero sign". Additionally, this is also relevant to the possible negative space on the axes analysed above. Jakobson in his essay "Poetry and Grammar" in *Dialogues* (1983) writes that:

> the opposition between the speaking subject and the forms of the third person (in linguistic terms the "zero" person, the unmarked term) is one of the central oppositions among grammatical categories. It is precisely this opposition that underlies the traditional definition of lyric poetry as the poetry of the first person, and epic poetry as the poetry of the third [person]. (1983: 120)

In fact, this was a criticism made by Culler in his misinterpretation of Jakobson's analysis of *"Les Chats"*; but the point has a broader application. The zero sign is indicated by the masculine nominative in Russian (or any language with words that take gendered endings). ("Zero Sign". Jakobson in *Russian and Slavic Grammar* (1984: 151–160). The use of the lyric in Mayakovsky's poem is obviously flagged by his use of the first-person pronoun (with reference to Russian). The use occurs in more than one grammatical case. It is here that the Raduga translation is very unhelpful. The Russian original contains twelve uses of the personal pronoun, plus two in French – "je suis". In terms of the original Russian, the lyric personal pronoun adds to the lyricism of the poem. In the analysis below, based on the Raduga translation, the line references are quite different from the original Russian. Any contra-indications with the analysis developed with the use of the English translation will be highlighted in a separate analysis which follows the analysis of the English version. Jakobson comments on the lyrical versus the "world event" poems. But, here, in the poem "The City", the lyrical, if one accepts that this is best represented by the personal pronoun (the poet/narrator) and the metaphor, alternate with the metonymic tropes of world events throughout the poem. The poem concludes with a strong metaphor which has been, perhaps, poorly translated. Also, the way in which the metaphor and metonym are used indicates that the poem contains the episodic characteristic of the epic. The subject matter is also epic – the city of Paris, world events and the impact of the great city on (in this instance) the poet and his beleaguered journey through it.

Close analysis of the poem, with an emphasis on Formalism as a semiotic rather than a linguistic tool, reveals how the metonym alternates with the metaphor throughout the poem. Jakobson's definition of the metonym as on the syntagmatic axis and the metaphor as on the paradigmatic axis of the poles of language is the theoretical basis for analysis here. The following designations for the poem are suggested as:

Lines 1–5 metonymic

Lines 6/7 – is this metonymic "it's as if I have a lump in my throat" or metaphoric "a sense of blocked speech"? It is certainly the beginning of the construction of the "camel" as archetype – but camels carry burdens they do not speak and therefore, as the lump in the throat is transposed later in the poem as a burden – the lump in the throat has the sense of a burden – and is therefore metaphoric.

Lines 8/9 metaphoric.

Lines 10–13 metonymic, or is it a metaphor as in the literal translation: "the walls of promise" so that it is the walls that have the quality of promise, not the advertisements which carry the message of promise.

Lines 14–17 metaphoric.

Lines 18–21 metonymic.

Lines 22–24 is metonymic, line 24 – "fellow-traveller" is a translation of a Rusword which describes those non-proletarian writers who supported the revolution, this gives the lines a metonymic expression, a simile.

Lines 25–27 metaphoric.

Lines 28–30 the use of the pronoun "your" – this, and the full phrase – "swinging your hump" previews the camel advertisement later in the poem. The lines are metaphoric in the sense that Mayakovsky does not literally have a hump – he *is* the "poet/camel". But the metonymic archetype is reflected back onto these lines by the camel references later in the poem.

Lines 32/33 metaphoric "poetry's waggon" [sic].

Lines 34–36 metaphoric – see "lump in my larynx" in line 7 which gives the metonymic image a metaphoric tint.

Lines 37/38 metonymic.

Lines 39–41 metonymic.

Lines 42–47 metaphoric – but: line 44 the word "time", is not an archetype just a reference to speed, in which case these lines are metonymic – "only time/ soon give birth/such as I" (see literal translation).

Line 48 metonymic (synecdoche) "with feet just as fleet" [as time – suggested interpretation].

Lines 49/50 metonymic.

Lines 51–53 metaphoric see "puchit" in the literal translation, meaning "a little gassy", but also see reference to cartoon (of which more below) where it becomes a political point – to become swollen and self absorbed and not useful.

Lines 54/55 metonymic.

Lines 56–64 camel (advertisement persona) as archetype (metonymic). But the meaning of these lines also contains the poet's effort to translate the meaning literally from the French – this is an epic dialogue. Therefore, the sentence "I am a camel" is not Mayakovsky saying he *is* a camel (metaphoric) but indicates that the advertisement is saying "I am a camel" and that he understands the message. However, he has already developed the simile of the "camel" as an archetype and "I am a camel" is therefore "I am as a camel" (metonymic).

Lines 65–69 metonymic – "spray" is a synecdoche.
Lines 70/71 metaphoric.
Lines 72–74 metonymic.
Lines 75–78 two metaphors – or are they metonyms – is the meaning virtual or literal? "fill up" in the sense of "take away, blot out, banish"? The literal translation seems to indicate a metaphoric interpretation: "During all fire -/and the sky in darkness/and drenched in black dust". The image perhaps becomes a heaven and hell confrontation.
Lines 79–82 metonymic (simile – cars/beetles).
Lines 83–86 metaphoric.
Lines 87–90 metonymic (simile – lights/bison) "multiplication table" is an extension of the simile.
Lines 91–93 metaphoric, the animal image of the lapdogs (see literal translation) would imply a simile but the meaning is "the square **is** more swell than any [pampered] dame").
Lines 94–100 (see analysis of conclusion below) is this expressed wish metaphoric – the Mayakovsky *is* the column, or an expressed wish for metonymic epic action – the column as simile for Mayakovsky?

In the closing lines of the poem, Mayakovsky has used a blending of both metonym and metaphor which cements the poem as an illustration of Jakobson's view that Mayakovsky uses the lyric for personal love poems and the metonymic device for the description of world events. Here it is posited that Mayakovsky has combined both in the same poem. It can be interpreted from the point of view of a metonymic trope, the interpretation of a world event and, from the point of view of a metaphoric one, a personal lyric response to the city of Paris and its potential for revolution.

Referring now to the two English translations of the poem: if the final fourteen lines of the poem are translated using the animal similes, then these lines are metonymic. If the animal similes are omitted from the poem then the final lines become influenced by a more metaphoric use of language. As in the examples: if the animal similes are included, as in lines 87/88 – "as if the streetlamps/that stand like torches" [bisons] and "The square [Concorde]/looks more swell [wealthy/handsome]/than any dame [Vendôme]" [lapdogs] [lines 91–93] – the overall effect is metonymic. As described earlier, the lights that stand at the Place de la Concorde actually look like bison heads and, by association, the description of the Place de la Vendôme with (fat pampered) lapdogs because it houses the offices of luxury brands such as Chanel and The Ritz Hotel, can therefore be interpreted as similarly metonymic. This is a complex image and illustrates Jakobson's theory of the "grammar of poetry" – that poetry is a semiotic sum of its poetic parts, not just an analysis of its individual linguistic and poetic components.

The metaphoric interpretation of the image "The square/looks more swell/ than any dame" creates the metaphoric requirement of simultaneity, expanded as: "the [Concorde] square is "greater than the swell" [Vendôme] dame". This results in the concluding lines of the poem also being interpreted as more metaphoric, for example, as in line 97: "if I were ... etc" becoming expanded as "I am the Colonne .... marrying/uniting with the Place de la Concorde".

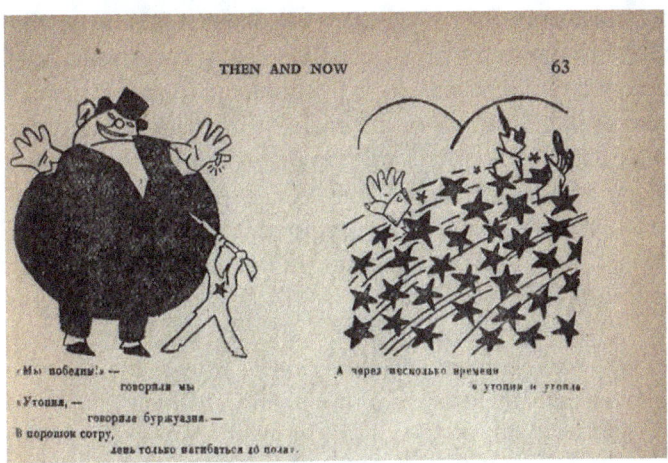

**Figure 3:** Then and Now.

The cartoon (see Figure 3), from a poster designed by Mayakovsky in 1921 (Marshall: 63), indicates that the pricking by the Vendôme column may not metaphoric but literal and metonymic. The cartoon demonstrates that gross (or swell) individual wealth can be released (pricked) by the individual revolutionary in order to empower the many – Mayakovsky *as* the colonne/bayonet. There was a strike of bank clerks who have been photographed, demonstrating in the Place de la Concorde in 1925, which Mayakovsky may have witnessed. In order to carry the image through, the wealth of the Place de la Vendôme, with its "colonne", is used by Mayakovsky to provide an image of how he would abandon the wealth of the Vendôme and join with the political history and current protest activity in the Place de la Concorde. As a column/bayonet, he will strengthen, team up with (marry), the workers in the Place de la Concorde, who would be empowered. The Russian words, if the grammatical meaning is taken into account, are specifically male: "я б женился/на Place la Concorde" – "женился/на" is "to marry a woman/the Place de la Concorde". In Russian "place" or "square" – "Площадь" (ploshad) is a female noun. The Russian grammatical language requirements enable this engendering. Mayakovsky has therefore used the linguistic requirement to construct an image which describes uniting male power against a female location. This is about political unification, the control of wealth, empowering political struggle.

Mayakovsky has alternated metaphoric and metonymic expressions throughout his poem. And in a final layer of extra skill, he combined the tropes, enabling two interpretations within the one conclusion. He used the metonymic to interpret world events and the metaphoric as a lyrical form to interpret the more personal emotions, his commitment to revolution. As a final point, his metaphoric expressed wish in the final lines ("I swear/if I were", lines 96/97) allows the concurrent metonymic revolutionary action. It is also a heroic image which also provides an epic conclusion to the poem – he *is* the uprooted column marching to the Place de la Concorde, and he acts *as* the enabler. This refers back to the requirements of the epic listed by Cuddon earlier in the paper: Mayakovsky is a central figure of superhuman calibre and performs the deed of a warrior or hero.

The use of the zero sign corresponds with the epic and lyric interpretation of the poem. Perhaps the last lines of the poem provide the best example with which to explore this. Mayakovsky ends with a prophetic "I": "'I'd go and marry the Place de la Concorde'". This is epic in intention; it cannot be literal and it combines with the desire of the poet (personified as the camel earlier in the poem) to travel through difficult terrain to achieve a goal. The unalloyed direct "I", placed within an almost allegorical context, makes an epic not a lyric poetic statement. In Russian, the zero sign may well be the lack of ending on the masculine nouns, as described by Jakobson; but the "I" ("Я") is not gendered; it is therefore either not a zero sign or it is a zero sign with both of Jakobson's meanings. It has neither a gendered ending nor is it the epic third person. It is therefore very easy to supersede the zero sign analysis and make it readily interpretable as both a personal "I" and an epic "I". Mayakovsky strides through the poem, facing down burdens and foreign languages. He uses the images of the advertisements to personify a hero, constructed by him as a conqueror of wealthy Paris. He combines both a lyric and an epic "I" to do this.

From the point of view of the development of Jakobson's axes, a zero sign would appear to be, by its very name, on the negative side of the axial space. The non-gendered pronoun is metaphoric in quality, the "I" represents that which *is*. But the masculine word without gendered ending is metonymic. The word is *as* it indicates. For Mayakovsky, after his struggles with the city, he is both zero signs. In the last four lines, his "Я" is doubly zero indicated. It is not admixed with a foreign language (French: "je suis") or with quotation marks or with a grammatical case ending: this is what he, the poet, prophetically intends to achieve.

The clarity of the Formalist analysis is made very complex by the fact that the poem was originally written in Russian not English. However, the literal translation is very helpful. Jakobson's Formalist theory has been developed, and with the aid of a diagram of the axes of language, has provided insight into the structure of metonymy in poetry. Jakobson's observation concerning the epic and the lyric with regard to Mayakovsky's poetry, when linked to his definition of the zero sign, has provided a theoretical structure which enables a development of his theories. Mayakovsky's poem is concerned with the city of Paris. The epic struggle of the poet, the evidence of lyric – his personal response to the city – and knowledge of the zero sign have all provided a nexus of poetic forms which enable a city poetic. Mayakovsky has constructed a balance of the three forms – epic, lyric and zero signs – which reveal the city at the time of his visit, both to him and us.

Jakobson suggested that metonymy is the province of prose (1987: 114 [1956]). However, he qualifies this in his later essay, "Toward a linguistic classification of aphasic impairments":

> Now that we have discussed, on the one hand, selection, based on similarity, as the first stage of the encoding process, and, on the other hand, combination, based on contiguity, as the start of the decoding operation, let us confront two kinds of poetry: lyric, which as a rule is built primarily on similarity; and epic, which operates chiefly with contiguity. We recall that metaphor is the inherent trope in lyric poetry, and that metonymy is the leading trope in epic poetry. In this connection, the lyric poet, we note, endeavors to present himself as the speaker, whereas the epic poet takes on the role of a listener who is supposed to recount deeds learned by hearsay. Here again, on another level, we observe the parallel relationship of encoding with similarity, and of decoding with contiguity; and this corresponds perfectly to the evidence provided by aphasia about the higher stability of similarity relations in encoding and of contiguity relations in decoding. (1971c: 297 [1963])

The epic form has been found to be both innovative and extensively used in this city poem. A complex structure of poetics has been achieved, providing an epic interpretation of both the "world event" and the personal lyric expression of emotions in poetry, and which has the city as its subject. Analysis of this poem is now developed by returning to the axial diagram (see Figure 2) and using the analysis of metaphoric and metonymic tropes. The use of the qualities within these tropes, reveals an analysis of the poem which looks somewhat different to that demonstrated above. As described above the qualities looked for are:

   metaphoric as defined by:
      similarity/dissimilarity
      synonymy/antonymy
      cohesion/torque
   and metonymic as defined by:
      contiguity/random
      linked/fragmented
      simile/repetition

It would, perhaps, not be realistic to find all of these qualities in one poem; but examination of the poem will reveal at least, some of the most apparent examples. It is, however, suggested that the qualities are all present. It is perhaps best to begin with the poem itself, in the order in which the qualities occur. The opening line illustrates the quality of contiguity of imagery: "Two cities it is – ". Antonymy is used in the lines: "grey city/sets my heart aglow" (lines 8,9). Synonymy follows with: "With what wine of love,/I'd like to know,/could anyone stir up the life in me?" (lines 14–17). The synonymy arises from understanding wine as an aphrodisiac. Wine therefore becomes synonymous with love. Lines 18–24 demonstrate cohesion, albeit through questioning – because the self "I" is overlaid with what others perceive as the more powerful ideation: "Maybe critics know better,/I won't deny,/yes maybe – /it's hard to decide./But whose/ in hell/fellow traveller am I?". The coherence of the first-person shifter pronoun is discussed in detail in Chapter Six. The lines 39–49 demonstrate a loss of a sense of identity. This would be satisfactorily interpreted as a torquing of identity. Lines 54–57 illustrate the quality of random as Mayakovsky's reported response to a problem just seems to be a repetition of the words in the advertisement, which are in fact written in a language that Mayakovsky does not really know – "I wish I could look in the face/ of whoever's my fellow traveller!/"*Je suis un chameau*,"".

He demonstrates the quality of linkage where he continues to explore his identity and positioning in the poem: ""*Je suis*" means "I" – /that I understand;/"-*chameau*" – /well put!" (lines 60–64). This is immediately followed by what feels to the reader to be the quality of the random: "Purple-tinged cloud," (line 65). This is followed by an extensive sequence which expresses the contiguity of himself and the city (lines: 66–90). The final lines of the poem indicate the dual qualities of similarity/dissimilarity. They are almost metaphoric. "Almost", because they contain an expressed wish transference of identity which is physically impossible – the ideation is metaphoric but the two ideations can never really happen – "I swear,/If I were/the Colonne de la Vendôme,/I'd go and marry/Place de la Concorde" (lines 96–100). This provides an interesting additional analysis to the above discussion as to whether the conclusion of the poem is metaphoric or metonymic in character. The role of the subjunctive (expressed wish) is to provide a quality which has a particular impact in poetry. Here, it causes the metonymic and the metaphoric to hang in the balance – a torque-ing of both the emotions and of tropes perhaps?

The French quotations, which are originally from a contemporaneous advertisement, provide both linked and fragmented qualities throughout the poem. They provide a linkage of similar language and through Mayakovsky's questioning of who he is, and indeed which creature he is. The poem includes the passage of time. In lines 48 and 49: "with feet just as fleet./We'd go side-by-side"; and in lines 65–67: "Purple-tinged cloud,/be quick/and pour down". The grammar and punctuation do not contain torque, but there is some fragmentation of language, which, as it is linked to Mayakovsky questioning his nature (both human and creature), provides some torque. There is a simile which is very important to the meaning of the poem: "Not a soul/strides along/at my side." (lines 25–27). With the level of questioning which the poet has introduced into the text, including a reference to hell (line 23), the soul becomes a simile – a fellow traveller, alongside the poet. This is therefore not metaphoric. Mayakovsky is not the soul itself, he is alongside it. In theory there is some repetition – of the words of the French advertisement – but these are superseded by the use of a time sequence in the poem which indicates that there is sequential interpretation of the words, and that therefore the repetition is overlaid by a stronger quality, that of the passage of time. This is made apparent by the lines "with feet just as fleet./We'd go side by side/on our dusty ways." (lines 48–50); and "Purple-tinged cloud, be quick/and pour down" (lines 65,66).

The above analysis of the poetic text which arises from the axial model, as posited by the present author. It has been adopted as praxis with reference to a specific poem. The poetic trope of metonymy is the generic quality which contains several of the qualities used in the analysis above. But as metonymy is still not fully understood as a poetic trope, the theory and history of the development of definitions of metonymy in the next chapter provides insight into its role in poetry.

# Chapter 3
# Roman Jakobson and metonymy: Linguistics and semiotics

This is the first of two chapters dedicated to the study of metonymy. In this chapter the emphasis is on the origins of the term and whether linguistics can provide a full interpretation of it. Jakobson's Formalist definition of the term provides further complexity – or indeed, perhaps, simplicity. Metonymy, especially in poetry, is one of the lesser studied tropes. This is a trope which functions through substitution. The roles of metonymy in both poetry and prose are explored. The other three major tropes are metaphor, synecdoche and irony (*NPEPP*. 1993. 1261a). Tropes can also be classified as having various more specific characteristics. Following Jakobson, others state that there are only two tropes – metaphor and metonymy, where synecdoche is an aspect of metonymy (*NPEPP*. 1993.1261a). What is a trope? It was used originally to describe certain forms of cadence or embellishment in church music. More generally, within literary criticism, it is: "a figure of speech which consists in the use of a word or phrase in a sense other than that which is proper to it; also, in casual use, a figure of speech; figurative language" (*OED* 1968: 2252c).

With regard to poetry, does metonymy form an appropriate poetic trope? Jakobson himself ascribed it to prose rather than to poetry. It is, however, hard to find a clear definition of metonymy. The word is from the Greek and means "change of name". It is, as stated in the *NPEPP*: "A figure in which one word is substituted for another on the basis of some material, causal, or conceptual relation" (1993: 783b). The fundamental characteristic of the metonym is that of substitution. "A proper term is substituted for another for the sake of ornament" (Cicero: "De Oratore 3.42".167/8). For St Augustine, the term "Metonymy" is not used as such; but he discusses in his "De Dialectica" (1975: 10) how words can mean more than one thing, which he calls "equivocal ambiguity".

The three categories of the definition of metonymy, now explored in this chapter, are provided here. It can be seen at a glance that a linguistic definition of metonymy will miss the more complex metonymic structures:
1. A semantic example: to substitute the word "tea" for the word "wine" would not be a metonym because there is no established usage which accepts that the two words can mean the same thing. However, if the word "crown" is substituted for the word "queen" or "king" then this is a metonym.
2. A syntactic example: The metonym also has the quality, as does metaphor, of existing in more than the form of a single word. So if the phrase "I'll have

a glass" is substituted for the phrase "I'll have a glass of wine" then this is a metonymic phrase.
3. A semiotic example: "Nelson" can refer to a statue, a historical admiral or an arm lock. It is one word substituted for another in a way which affects the meaning. Now, a corollary to this is that it must be a substitution which is clear to the listener or the reader; it cannot be a substitution which is not clear to the addressee.

There are other possible attributes of the metonym which arise from the fundamental attribute of substitution. These are: condensation, euphemism and idiom. The example above of "I'll have a glass", meaning "I'll have a glass of wine", demonstrates the attribute of condensation. Euphemism is where one word is substituted for another, perhaps for reasons of politeness. For example, one might use the term "passed away" instead of "dead". Again, it might be said "he's out of the office at the moment" instead of saying "he's gone home early". Within this category there are also metonymic phrases which are classified as proverbs and aphorisms. A proverb often substitutes one word or phrase for another, indicating a transfer of meaning, as in "money talks", meaning that money has the power to make things happen though material purchase. An aphorism is only sometimes metonymic. An example of an aphorism ("a principle or precept expressed shortly or pithily, a maxim" *OED*. 1968) is: "The proof of the pudding is in the eating". Here, the principle of substitution provides condensation of meaning. The *NPEPP* combines the aphorism with the epigram. This indicates a different emphasis in the analysis of the aphorism to the one indicated here.

Idiom is prevalent in any language, and for any student of a foreign language it is one of the most difficult aspects to absorb. For example, one could say: "this job is not a bed of roses" meaning that the job does not feature the best conditions. Another example could be "he sleep-walked his way to the top" meaning that, because of his skills (which may not be work related), he was easily promoted. Within the idiom, the substitution is so extensive that it is almost impossible to gauge the source of the term. Nevertheless, the substitution is not metaphoric in character. Within the category of "idiom" is the term "collocation", which is used to describe a pattern of word usage, which is usual but not as remote from the original meaning of the words as idiom. The *Oxford Collocations Dictionary* (McIntosh, 2020) defines collocations as a knowledge of language that readily releases the poetic from the literal use of language: "language that is collocationally rich is also more precise. This is because most single words . . . especially the more common words – embrace a whole range of meaning, some quite distinct, and some that shade into each other by degrees. The precise meaning in any context is determined by that context: by the words that surround and combine with the core word – by collocation." (2020: v). Examples are the expressions "broadly speaking" or "raining heavily". One does not say "widely speaking" or "raining weightily". Definitions of the term are hard to find. Even within the speciality of Translation Studies, the term is not commonly referred to. It is fully metonymic in nature and provides a useful category between the literal and the idiomatic.

Macey refers to collocation as a linguistic term coined by the linguist John Firth in 1951: "to describe the habitual co-occurrence of individual words such as 'spick and span'" (2000: 66). Wales (2001: 67/68) provides a broader definition which includes reference to literary language and poetry. The word encompasses both the sense of positioning of words – their selection – and their combined meaning – combination. The effect of a collocation can break established meaning if the selection is unexpected. Where an idiom provides a more metaphoric expression, the words, if separated, do not mean what the whole expression does, as in "raining cats and dogs". But the collocation as a whole is solely metonymic – the words are placed together in a habitual pattern. In poetry the words can be broken apart to realise new or startling meanings or uncharted meanings. Wales quotes Eliot's poem "Morning at the Window": "I am aware of the damp souls of housemaids/Sprouting despondently at area gates." (from "Prufrock and Other Observations" [1917]). The word "collocation" is also connected, in origin, with "collocatio", the rhetorical term where words of differing styles are juxtaposed.

These examples demonstrate how, in different ways, common language usage both permits – and often encourages – the substitution of words: a word which replaces the literal one with one which is perhaps felt to be more modern, colourful or incorporating wider connotative meaning. As a short note, it is possible to argue that there is a particular aspect of metonymy which has the quality of humour. The kind of jokes that it inspires are the kind that are often found in Christmas crackers: "Why does the stick move?"; "Because it is a walking stick". Here the fundamental quality of substitution is expressed through accepted condensation. If the condensation is removed, so is the joke. "What do you call a stick used by someone going for a walk?" "A walking stick, because I use it when I go out for a walk". This demonstrates a further attribute of the metonym, one that occurs when the grammatical use of a word is exchanged – the "walking" is changed from adjective to verb to create the joke. Another example would be "I walked the dog". Well, when the dog is literally taken for a walk, it is not walked by the person taking it out which would indicate manual manipulation of the dog's legs by the human accompanying it. There are other instances of this kind of substitution which are not acceptable, as in the sentence: "4 o'clock saw the room fill up". This is considered to be bad use of English as a clock does not have the capacity to see. But compare it with the proverb used above, "money talks".

In the search for modern (20$^{th}$ century) definitions of metonymy, Hugh Bredin, in his article on metonymy (1984a), reproduces a list which categorises the different kinds of metonym and suggests that there are relations between the two aspects of each category. There is an exchange in that either half of the metonym can be the deciding force providing the metonym. There are difficulties with Bredin's list, not least because there is an earlier version of it, quoted in Kenneth Burke's *A Grammar of Motives* (1969), where the list is subdivided (see Table 1 below). For Bredin, there are three types of metonym which Burke placed within the separate category of synecdoche. Neither Burke nor Bredin explain the source of the list and some of Bredin's examples are hard to understand. His list of references is, however, very useful. His table of the different types of metonym is also covered in the work of Michael Cameron in *Christ Meets Me Everywhere* (2012). Cameron cites the different classical writers who define each type. The sources of the different categories arise from Cicero, Quintillian and St Augustine. Unlike Burke and Bredin, he gives full references for each of his definitions. Bredin's table of metonymical relations is reproduced below:

**Table 1:** (Bredin 1984: 48).

| Metonymical Relations | | Examples |
|---|---|---|
| 1. Cause | Effect | (a) War is sad<br>(b) She is my pride and joy |
| 2. Inventor | Invented | (a) She was reading Virgil<br>(b) An enterprising scheme |
| 3. User | Instrument | (a) A walking stick<br>(b) A hired gun |
| 4. Doer | Thing done | (a) That car is a lovely driver<br>(b) Crime must be punished |
| 5. Passion | Object of passion | (a) She is my true love<br>(b) She is a slave to wealth |
| 6. Container | Contained | (a) A boiling kettle<br>(b) Milks, sugars (for milk-jugs and sugar-bowls) |
| 7. Place | Object in place | (a) Wall Street panicked<br>(b) I take my holidays at the seaside |
| 8. Time | Object in time | (a) A warlike century<br>(b) The age of science |
| 9. Possessor | Possessed | (a) The violinist broke a string<br>(b) The smart money is in computer software |
| 10. Sign | Signified | (a) Crown (for monarchy)<br>(b) Give me a Scotland (to a seller of rosettes at a football stadium) |
| 11. Concrete | Abstract | (a) The soldier is the enemy of mankind<br>(b) Youth is giddy and irresponsible |

It is worth taking the time here to explore his examples and add others. He lists 11 different categories of Metonymical Relations. The three categories which Burke also names as synecdoches are: 1. Cause and Effect; 6. Container and Contained; and 10. Sign and Signified. This places them within a separate trope. St Augustine, in his *De Dialectica* (1975: 10), examines how words can demonstrate "equivocal ambiguity". This is demonstrated in the above-mentioned example of the word "Nelson" which can refer to a statue, a historical admiral or an arm lock. The definition quoted from Cicero's *De Oratore* is: "a proper term is substituted for anther for the sake of ornament". What are more relevant here are the examples that he gave in *Rhetorica ad Herrenium*. It is worth quoting his examples in full as they are often referenced by others:

> Metonymy is the figure which draws from an object closely akin or associated an expression suggesting the object meant, but not called by its own name. This is accomplished by substituting the name of the greater thing for that of the lesser, as if one speaking of the Tarpeian Rock should term it "the Capitoline"; . . . ; or by substituting the name of the thing invented for that of the inventor, as if one should say "wine" for "Liber," "wheat" for "Ceres"; " . . . ;" or the instrument for the possessor, as if one should refer to the Macedonians as follows: "Not so quickly did the Lances get possession of Greece," and likewise, meaning the Gauls: "nor was the Transalpine Pike so easily driven from Italy"; the cause for the effect, as if a speaker, wishing to show that someone has done something in war, should say: "Mars forced you to do that"; or effect for cause, as when we call an art idle because it produces idleness in people, or speak of numb cold because cold produces numbness. Content will be designated by means of container as follows: "Italy cannot be vanquished in warfare nor Greece in studies"; for here instead of Greeks and Italians the lands that comprise them are designated. Container will be designated by means of content: as if one wishing to give a name to wealth should call it gold or silver or ivory. It is harder to distinguish all these metonymies in teaching the principle than to find them when searching for them, for the use of metonymies of this kind is abundant not only amongst the poets and orators but also in everyday speech. (1954: 335–337)

Quintillian, from "The Orator's Education", defines metonymy by stating "There is no great gap between Synecdoche and Metonymy which is the substitution of one word for another" (2001: 437). With these definitions of metonymy, slightly different, but allied in interpretation, it might be possible to think that metonymy is now well defined. There are two difficulties. The first is that Bredin's examples are possibly not altogether reliable, and the second is that the Russian Formalists, originating with the work of Andrei Belyj, define metonymy, with confidence, as something rather different, although the underlying principles are the same.

Working from Bredin's table, but referring also to Burke's classification of "The Four Master Tropes" (1969: 507–509), items 1,6 and 10 are synecdoches. They are in fact some of the easier types of metonym to understand: Item 1. Cause and Effect, the examples are "War is sad" and "She is my pride and joy". The aim is to find examples where the word substitution is based on using a word which denotes the cause of the thing rather than the thing itself. Another example is: "The final argument of kings" (attributed to Louis XIV who had *Ultima ratio regum* engraved on his cannons). The twist to this metonym is that it contains both cause and effect depending on which way you read it. Is war the final argument because it kills the king (i.e. the ruler of the enemy: cause then effect) or is war the final argument, because kings have the power to organise it (effect and cause)? Bredin's examples seem not to be clear. Item 6 is one of the more commonly used synecdoches: Container and Contained. Bredin's examples are "a boiling kettle" and "Milks, sugars" (for milk-jugs and sugar-bowls). Other examples might be "boil the kettle" (it's the water in the kettle that is boiled), "take a sachet" (when it's the contents which are eaten or drunk). And for the second metonymical relation – Contained and Container: "the mercury's up" (for thermometer measuring temperature). Another example might be: "time ran out" which is a reference to an egg timer which contains sand running through a pinch point. This denotes an abstract which is contained in a container and the contents (the sand) denote the action of time passing. Item 10, Sign and Signified, has commonly used examples, as in Bredin's "Crown (for monarchy)". To this can be added "sceptre" for power, "Washington" for U.S. Government. The second half – Signified and Sign – Bredin uses the example of "Give me a Scotland" (meaning a coloured badge to denote support of a particular team). What needs to be added here are the most commonly accepted forms of the synecdoche – those which denote a part of a whole to denote the whole. This would include the phrase "all hands on deck" (all people on deck, on board the boat), "many hands make light work", "vote with your feet", "an army marches on its stomach".

Of the other eight categories in Bredin's list, only some of the examples are easy to understand. Sometimes it is easier to think of alternative examples. Bredin himself accepts that a metonym "could be defined as any trope that is not a metaphor or a synecdoche". He comments on Jakobson's definition:

> He (Jakobson) describes metaphor as a trope based on similarity, a description at once traditional and clear. But to say, as he does, that metonymy is based upon "contiguity" is to cloud it in a convenient but unrevealing metaphor: contiguity seems in fact to refer to any type of relation whatsoever, other than similarity. In the realm of figurative language, it is made the common dumping ground. (1984a: 47)

The above description of the confusion surrounding metonymy provides some excuse for admitting that the examples Bredin uses in item 2 remains unclear. In item 3, the walking stick has already been referred to, the phrase "the jockey ran the race" (of course it was the horse not the jockey).

A radio broadcast (Heffernan: 2014) about the change of language use in a General Motors factory, highlights how metonymy is used as a useful tool in modern commerce. Bill McAleer noted that in the 1990's terms were changed. "Problem" was replaced by "issue"; "condition" by "matter"; and more seriously "defect" by "does not perform to design" or "discrepancy". As a result of his objections, McAleer's job was metonymically transformed to a "non-job" and he "went home" for eight years on full pay. Which of the Bredin classifications do these examples of metonymy represent? Perhaps this can be best established by expanding the words used in the above example into phrases: "there is/we have a problem" and "we have an issue (with someone/something else)" or "the issue is . . . ". This pushes the "doer" towards the "thing done" (Bredin no. 4) but how the metonymical relation is established is still unclear. What has been established is that the word has shifted to the opposite relation – from the active to the acted upon, which is largely what seems to happen with the other examples. There is no doubt that an Orwellian metonymic transformation has been adopted in the language usage in this example; but the classification used by Bredin does not appear to encompass this kind of metonymic usage.

Items 4, 5, 7, 8 and 9 are also not clear. Item 11: Concrete and Abstract, the examples are "The soldier is the enemy of mankind" the meaning of which is not clear, and "Youth is giddy and irresponsible". An example of Abstract to Concrete is: "with honour garlanded" and Concrete to Abstract: "keep you in the loop". This is certainly idiomatic language usage, but are the above suggestions correct? The difficulties with the various categories and the examples given indicate that the definitions and parameters of each category are not clear-cut. This is the kind of brain teaser that will either send you straight off to sleep at night or keep you wide-awake for hours struggling to think of examples.

However, there is another system of analysis which uses the structure of the metonym to explore its usage, rather than its actual combination of words. It is here that the work of Andrei Belyj and Roman Jakobson opens up the metonym for an understanding of how it is used in poetry. So far, the discussion has only involved examples from prose. Jakobson pursued his analysis of metonym through his interest in language disorders. In his essay "Two Aspects of Language" (1987 [1956]) he explores aphasia – where the person suffering from aphasia is either unable to understand the metaphor, or is unable to understand the metonym – positing that these two dysfunctions represent two poles of language usage. If a person suffers from the inability to understand metaphor they will recall events or recall words by using a sequence which approximates the metaphor; but they are associative words used in sequence. If a person suffers from the inability to understand metonymy then they will construct language usage through metaphoric form. Taking the first disorder: if there is the inability to remember things exactly then the person with the capacity for metonymy will use the word "knife" if they cannot remember the word for "fork"; "smoke" is substituted for "pipe", "glass" for "window", "heaven" for "God". Conversely the person who fails to understand metonymy, the connotation between words will use a replacement word which contains a metaphoric element. The word "telescope" becomes "microscope" and "gaslight" becomes "fire". In the same way "hut" may become "hovel" or "poverty".

In the work of Belyj, the analysis of the metonym and the metaphor is mathematically based. He understood metonyms to have the quality of contiguity – the word or words which were substituted for the originals were close in meaning to the original but sequential. In metaphoric language the words used in place of the literal ones had the quality of simultaneity, the substituted words overlaid the original ones in a simultaneous transference and not in a sequential manner, that is: metaphorically. Helle sums up Belyj's approach: "the metonymic juxtaposition becomes, in Belyj, an external juxtaposition by virtue of accidental relations of contiguity and not, as in metaphor, an organic connection by virtue of some motivated likeness between different elements" (1924: 42, 43).

In order to maintain clarity, it is necessary to make sure that both prose and poetry are considered, and that the definitions of metonymy and metaphor are clearly understood as existing within the different categories of semantics, syntax or semiotics. In the first part of the chapter the rhetorical origins of the classification were highlighted. It then became apparent that the metonymic can be either a single word, a phrase, or indeed, as will be demonstrated below, a whole style. The Russian Formalist definition of the metonym having the property of contiguity takes this trope outside the category of rhetoric and into the structural domain of the Formalist. The term becomes defined by its function in relation to the whole text, rather than by a definition of itself, in itself. Yes, it still has the qualities as Cicero stated: "A proper term is substituted for another for the sake of ornament"; but it also has a sequential structure – including the property of contiguity. The substituted words, construct the property of sequence, which in turn cntributes to the wider text. Once again it is demonstrated that a purely linguistic, as opposed to semiotic interpretation, of metonymy is not sufficient.

One further reference to lexical metonymy is the Anglo-Saxon use. Anglo-Saxon substitution of an attributive name for the actual person or item is distinctive in its poetry, including its riddles. It establishes a metonymical style. Riddle No. 40 is reproduced here (translated by Paul Baum (1963: online source: https://en.wikisource.org/wiki/Anglo-Saxon_Riddles_of_the_Exeter_Book/40 Accessed: 16/05/20: 12.06):

> I saw four things  in beautiful fashion  
> journeying together.  Dark were their tracks,  
> the path very black.  Swift was its moving,  
> faster than birds  it flew through the air,  
> dove under the wave.  Labored unresting  
> the fighting warrior  who showed them the way,  
> all of the four,  over plated gold.
>
> Ic seah wrætlice  wuhte feower  
> samed siþian  swearte · wæran lastas  
> swaþu swiþe blacu  swift wæs on fore  
> fulgum framra  fleotgan lyfte  
> deaf under yþe  dreag unstille  
> winnende wiga  se him wægas tæcneþ  
> ofer fæted gold  feower eallū

> [Answer:] Quill-pen. The four things are two fingers, thumb, and quill (or as in parallel riddles three fingers and pen). "Its" (l. 3) shows that the "four things" were a unit. The quill *qua* pen does not move faster than birds, but the expression is allowable hyperbole, or even an example of synthetic imagery, with possibly a humorous glance at the deliberation of some scribes. Similarly, the warrior is the guiding arm of the scribe. The "plated gold" has been explained as "the gold mount of the ink-horn."Other examples can be seen for example in *The Wanderer*; www.Anglo-Saxons.net – "The Wanderer" (no credited translator): "move by hand" (to row); "spirit-chest" (the mind); "treasure-chamber (thoughts); "gold-friend" (lord).

Jakobson provides a different angle in his analysis of metonymy. In his analysis of poetry he is interested, not only in the semantic and syntactic levels, but also the semiotic. This means that he understands that the metonym is expressed as a style of writing. This is a style which is formed by details which build a picture sequentially. Most of his examples are, however, from prose. He states that the author in pursuit of realism, inserts details which are not relevant to the plot – it is just that they may be of interest to the author and/or reader. Or the author pursues a style which, like cubism, builds a sequence of images and ideas which form a related whole but without necessarily being logically coherent. He notes that without sufficient control, metonymy can provide prose that becomes lost in its own detail. Jakobson provides an example in his essay "Two Aspects of Language". One such disintegrated portrait is cited in the monograph edition. It is by Kamegulov, *Stil' Gleba Uspenskogo* (Leningrad: 1930) . . . .

> From underneath an ancient straw cap, with a black spot on its visor, peeked two braids resembling the tusks of a wild boar; a chin, grown fat and pendulous, had spread definitively over the greasy collar of the calico dicky and lay in a thick layer on the coarse collar of the canvas coat, firmly buttoned at the neck. From underneath this coat to the eyes of the observer protruded massive hands with a ring which had eaten into the fat finger, a cane with a copper top, a significant bulge of the stomach, and the presence of very broad pants, almost of muslin quality, in the wide bottoms of which hid the toes of the boots.        (1987: 113, footnote 29)

Is this kind of metonymic discursiveness applicable to poetic form? This is a question which will be further explored in the praxis of the following chapter. Jakobson's work on the poles of language, the metaphoric pole and the metonymic pole, defines his definition of the difference between the two. However, clarity of the definition results in his statement that, metaphor is expressed in poetry and metonymy in prose:

> Similarity in meaning connects the symbols of a metalanguage with the symbols of the language referred to. Similarity connects a metaphorical term with the term for which it is substituted. Consequently, when constructing a metalanguage to interpret tropes, the researcher possesses more homogeneous means to handle metaphor, whereas metonymy based on a different principle, easily defies interpretation. Therefore nothing comparable to the rich literature on metaphor can be cited for the theory of metonymy. For the same reason, it is generally realized that Romanticism is closely linked with metaphor, whereas the equally intimate ties of Realism with metonymy usually remain unnoticed. Not only the tool of the observer but also the object of observation are responsible for the preponderance of metaphor over metonymy in scholarship. (1987: 113, 114)

Jakobson's own understanding of metonymy did not arise from a rhetorical foundation. But his interest in understanding how poetry functions and his theory of poetic function has given rise to a partially constructed theory of metonymic use in poetry. As stated above, the clearest underlying principle for Jakobson's position is his theory of the poles of language. In Chapter Two it was suggested that the metaphoric paradigm contains the attribute of simultaneity and the metonymic syntagm that of contiguity. This is because the syntagmatic metonymic pole contains sequence and therefore time, and is confirmed by Jakobson's use of the metonym's attribute of contiguity. The metaphor, constructed by two different ideas which are combined to ideate a different single thing or idea, realizes the simultaneity of the metaphoric pole.

A simple example of a metonymic sequence is: "food for thought". The phrase describes thinking, as a food, that to feed the brain is the same as feeding the body, and it has similar cravings and satisfactions. The phrase encompasses all of this as a sequence. The metonym places the words and ideas alongside each other. Perhaps it is helpful to use Jakobson's analogy with art:

> A salient example from the history of painting is the manifestly metonymical orientation of Cubism, where the object is transformed into a set of synecdoches; the Surrealist painters responded with a patently metaphorical attitude." (1987: 111). An example from Jakobson's understanding of the metonym is his analysis of a speech by Mark Anthony in Shakespeare's "Julius Caesar". He quotes the lines: "My heart is in the coffin there with Caesar/And I must pause till it come back to me." (Act III)

These lines describe how the stereotyped "I mourn for so-and-so" and the figurative but still stereotyped "so-and-so is in the coffin and my heart is with him" or "goes out to him" give place in Anthony's speech to a powerfully realized metonymy; the trope becomes a part of the poetic reality (1987: 90,91). The metonymy arises from the contiguity of the ideas. The ideas in the lines are not expressed through metaphor – two objects, ideas or persons united to construct a picture of one object or idea or person – but through a strong deictic placing which contains movement and therefore the passage of time: in this example, of one idea after another. Jakobson concludes his essay with his often-repeated statement that linguistics does not fully embrace the field of poetics. Poetry demands a semiotic analysis of its overall constructed form if it is to be fully understood.

Raymond J. Wilson III uses Jakobson's definitions of metonymy to explore a special use of this trope in the poetry of W B Yeats. His discussion of the scope of the metonym is detailed and his construction of the existence of an allegorical form of metonymy is a complex addition to the understanding of the trope (Wilson: 1994). His article: "Metaphor and Metonymic Allegory" is closely argued. Using the example of the phrase "Keels crossed the deep" (instead of "the ships sailed across the sea") he demonstrates how figurative metonymy is constructed by omitting the literal words to describe the action and replacing them with words which clearly indicate the same action (1994: 223). His analysis of Yeats' "Cuchulain's Fight With the Sea", shows how Cuchulain's rage and sorrow at killing his own son is metonymically portrayed in the poem as a fight with the sea. The sea becomes an allegory for the grief but by "retaining . . . the literal image of the tidal flow while attaining the *additional* meaning of grief demonstrates how metonymic allegory makes the literal level more meaningful rather than less." (1994: 225). Both of these examples retain characteristics of the Anglo-Saxon use of imagery referred to earlier.

It is clear from the above, that the metonymic trope has a complex theoretical history. It seems that the rhetorical origins of its naming have either not helped to define it sufficiently clearly or have been superseded. The tables used in Bredin and Cameron originated from the research of those who have tried to clarify its scope and type, going back to classical rhetoric. The origin of the meanings of the word, its classical and rhetorical sources, its fundamental attributes of substitution, condensation, euphemism, collocation, and idiom, have to be taken into account. The modern usage of the metonym in current affairs and advertising is a further development. The use of the metonym – of particular and pervasive use in Anglo-Saxon – poetry was used with the purpose of constructing the allegorical metonym in Yeats' poem. It is only through the analysis by Jakobson that the metonym reaches towards a semiotic structure. His classification defines it as a form which, through a sequence of sentences, establishes a metonymic style with a particular effect, an effect which Jakobson likens to cubism. The next suggestion of this chapter is that the metonym is ready for a re-categorisation of its different types, that the different levels of its structural use will make it easier to understand – semantic, syntactic and semiotic.

How is metonymy expressed in poetry and, in addition, does it have a special expression in city poetry? This form of verbal expression (both spoken and written) requires a complex analysis of phrases, sentences and, in some cases, an entire poem, before the full impact of metonymy and metaphor is revealed. The definitions of metonymy by linguists tend towards analysis of no greater than one sentence except within a particular definition, that of Discourse Metonymy. In recent years, linguistics has contributed a great deal by way of theoretical analysis of this particular trope. Grateful and appreciative acknowledgement is made to Jeannette Littlemore (2015) and Charles Denroche (2015), who have explored metonymy in poetry.

Littlemore's extensive review textbook *Metonymy* (2015) describes the cognitive (that is, the conceptual properties of the metonym) and the linguistic (the operational modes of the metonym) systems of the study of metonymy (2015: 9). The linguistic analysis incorporates the phrasal level of the use of the metonym (2015: 127), and how difficult it can be to define metonymic use and differentiate it from literal or metaphoric language (2015: 127/8). Littlemore quotes a passage from a novel which clearly reveals how the metonymy operates at textual and metaphorical levels of meaning arising from the text. It is difficult to reveal the full interpretation unless it is quoted almost in full. The passage is taken from *Goodnight, Mr Tom* by Michelle Magorian (1983):

> Mr Tom is remembering the birth of his child, who died of scarlatina soon after being born along with his mother, Rachel, Mr Tom's wife. Rachel had been fond of painting: 'Ent he beautiful' .... Yous'll have to git blue' .... for during her pregnancy he had bought her a new pot of paint for each month of her being with child. The ninth was to be blue if she had given birth to a boy, primrose yellow if it had been a girl.//After they had died he had bought the pot of blue paint and placed it in the black wooden box that he had made for her one Christmas ... as he closed the lid, so he had shut out not only the memory of her but also the company of anyone else that reminded him of her.//He glanced down at Will, who had become suddenly quiet. He gave a start and opened his eyes. His lips had turned blue (Magorian, 1983: 230)'. [Littlemore continues:] In this extract, the blue paint metonymically represents both the baby boy ... and Tom's wife Rachel (as it reminds him of her love of painting). The fact that the paint is now locked in a box is a metaphor for the fact that Tom's feelings are now "locked away" .... we can see that the source domain is still very much present (the pot of blue paint is still in the box), so this metaphor might be said to contain shade of metonymy. The literal references to the colours red and blue ... strengthen the dramatic effect of the metonymic and metaphorical references to red and blue.   (2015: 134,135)

As the illness scarlatina (reflected in its name) produces a red skin, the baby's lips in death are blue, and the blue paint interprets grief, the metaphorical level is also apparent. Littlemore makes clear in this passage how easy it is to slip between the two tropes – metonym and metaphor. She refers to various art forms – music, painting film – and at a linguistic level it is easy to understand that everything can become a representation of something else and be defined as metonymic – every camera angle, every musical phrase, for example (2015: 136,137).

On this basis, the interpretation of all that exists is a metonymic process. Poetry is included in this listing where it becomes clear that every word could be seen as metonymic – with reference to Saussure; the word stands for a meaning or a concept. It is acknowledged that "Metonymy can also serve as an important form of cohesion across a whole text or speech or even a whole book" (2015: 193).

Denroche posits a new methodology of metonymy in his book *Metonymy and Language* (2015). The book provides an exploration of a new model for understanding the use of the metonym. In his Introduction he writes: "The methodology used in this book can be broadly described as 'reflective' or 'speculative'; some would characterize it as 'armchair linguistics'". His thesis includes the early Aristotelian definition that "metonymy is located with metaphor". This is explored in more detail in his Chapter Four: "The Vital Role of Metonymy in Conceptualization and Communication" (2015: 56–80). He develops a model which differentiates between active skills and passive stores of language knowledge and use. His models are new and comprehensive. With reference to the theories of Jakobson, the models can be problematic because an expression of movement or dynamics is missing in them, although developments of, and movement in language are acknowledged, as expressed in the word "active". The category of the "novel metaphor", also mentioned by Littlemore in her overview of the different theoretical models of metonymy in her Chapter Three (2015: 55), will have some relevance to the analysis of one of the poems analysed in this book in Chapter Four.

For Denroche "simile", "metaphor" and "analogy" are all understood to be metaphoric comparisons (2015: 39). Jakobson provides a twentieth-century break with this definition and, from the perspective of the Jakobsonian axial model, Denroche's definitions raise problems. In the same chapter (2015: 53), the table which expresses Denroche's definition of the "Four domains of metaphor function", and which is shown as a grid, might well have been more clearly expressed as an axial model. His model provides a direct comparison with Jakobson's theory of Poetic Function. Denroche has made immense efforts to produce a new model of metonymic definition and use. These kind of models of thought processes can be very hard to visually delineate and express textually. Also, in his Chapter Four, Denroche's expression of domain theory (2015: 71–73) is so far removed from much of the Jakobsonian theory explored above that it is very difficult to relate the two theoretical approaches (this does not invalidate Denroche's approach which includes Lakoff's very important work). He writes: "Warren also makes a connection back to the traditional studies of figurative language recasting 'contiguity' as 'similarity in dissimilarity': "the approach presented here is a further development of the traditional view [is this an allusion to Jakobson, here?] that metonymy involves contiguity, whereas metaphor involves seeing similarity in dissimilarity." (from Warren, 2002:126; Denroche, 2015: 71). Denroche goes on to explore the possibility that metonymy (and presumably metaphor), can be expressed as a "strength" of how clearly the words used, express the metonymic.

Quoting Goossens' research, Denroche interprets another expression of the metonym within the context of the text: "Another of Goossens' metaphtonymy categories is 'metonymy within metaphor', where the metonymic element is embedded in a metaphoric expression, eg. 'to shoot your mouth off', in which mouth stands for speech (metonymy) and the expression as a whole means to reveal a secret (metaphor)." (2015: 76, 77). This approach enables Denroche's exploration of "Discourse Metonymy" in his Chapter Six "Metonymy and Metaphor in Discourse and Text" (2015: 106–132). Here, he provides a useful review of different definitions of Discourse Linguistics. Discourse Linguistics concentrates on the analysis of language within the context of larger texts which provide social meaning to interactions. These may be political, commercial, personal relationships, and so on. Semiotics is included in one definition by Blommaert to which he refers. But although the definition is referred to as "universal", poetry seems to be outside its frame of reference.

It is significant that many linguists (or perhaps "linguisticians" – please see Ian Hudson's thoughts at http://myweb.tiscali.co.uk/polymetis/writings/lang/linguisticians.html), usually refer to a range of only three of Jakobson's essays: "Linguistics and Poetics" (1987: 62–94[1960]), "Two Aspects of Language and Two Types of Aphasic Disturbances" (1987: 95–114[1956]), and: "On Linguistic Aspects of Translation" (1971: 260–266[1959]). Linguists' reference to analysis of metonymy in poetry has been left almost entirely to David Lodge's analysis of Philip Larkin (1979). Other examples of the study of the metonym in poetry and drama include the paper on Yeats by Raymond Wilson III (1994) (mentioned above) and a monograph on T. S. Eliot by Osterwalder (1978). It seems appropriate therefore to analyse some examples of the use of metonymy in specific poems in an effort to increase the number of poetic examples. This praxis forms the basis for the following chapter.

Jakobson, in his essay "Linguistics and Poetics", argues that poetics, linguistics and semiotics complement each other, and should not be exclusive. It is not enough, that the linguist studies language without its overall patterns of usage, or that the poetic theorist studies language without its formal structure. He wrote: "Poetics deals with problems of verbal structure, just as the analysis of painting is concerned with pictorial structure. Since linguistics is the global science of verbal structure, poetics may be regarded as an integral part of linguistics" (1987: 63). He goes on to explain the necessity of linguists to explore the poetic function of language as well as the referential: "The poetic function is not the sole function of verbal art but only its dominant, determining function, whereas in all other verbal activities it acts as a subsidiary, accessory constituent . . . . Hence when dealing with the poetic function, linguistics cannot limit itself to the field of poetry." (1987: 69, 70).

The study of metonymy, and the variety of disciplines which inform its definitions ensure that no one definition of the term will suffice. As has been mentioned above, The *NPEPP* states: "A figure in which one word is substituted for another on the basis of some material, causal, or conceptual relation" (1993: 783b). The entry then refers to the classical rhetorician, Quintilian's contribution (1993: 783b, 784a). The "Oxford Concise Dictionary of Linguistics" (Matthews, Oxford, OUP, 2005: 224) acknowledges the debt to Jakobson by referring also to the properties of metonymy as being contiguity and synecdoche. Charles Denroche and Jeannette Littlemore have been mentioned as providing two recent linguistics definitions which provide starting points for the complexity of metonymy: "Metonymy is a cognitive and linguistic process through which we use one thing to refer to another" (Littlemore, 2015: 1) and "as the highlighting of relatedness, usually part-whole, between closely-related concepts, things and signifiers" (Denroche, 2015: 56). It seems that there are two methods of defining metonymy – the rhetorical position based on the study of tropes and devices, and which is more commonly used in poetics, and the linguistic definition which is largely based on condensation and displacement.

A possible third argument is that by using the theoretical position of Jakobson, there is a crucial communication component in poetic language and poetic function provided by the movement of time inherent in the property of contiguity in metonymy, and that this is in contrast to a "simultaneity" communication component in metaphor. This acknowledgement of movement within the poetic trope of metonymy, can also be interpreted as a movement of the trope within the poem. The metonym can be defined firstly, as semantic (the actual words, the factual similarity), secondly, as syntactic, an expression of form and structure in a poem (the trope, the imputed similarity), and thirdly, as semiotic, through patterns of usage (artifice through parallels). It is further suggested, that within the Formalist structure, there is a similar acknowledgement of time expressed through metaphor – with the exception that it does not express time within its semantic or syntactic structure, only within its semiotic use. Having begun this research it emerged that Jakobson, crucially, has been very brief in his definition of the metaphor. This suggests a future area for research.

Metonymy was suggested by Jakobson as more the trope of prose than poetry. If it is found to be used in poetry as well as prose, then definitions of metonymy require some attempt to define poetry. Jakobson provides a definition of "poeticity" in his essay "What is Poetry?" (1987: 368–378[1933]):

> ... poeticity is present when the word is felt as a word and not a mere representation of the object being named or an outburst of emotion, when words and their composition, their meaning, their external and inner form, acquire a weight and value of their own instead of referring indifferently to reality.// .... Why is it necessary to make a special point of the

fact that sign does not fall together with object? Because, besides the direct awareness of the identity between sign and object (A is A1) there is a necessity for the direct awareness of the inadequacy of that identity (A is not A1). The reason this antinomy is essential is that without contradiction there is no mobility of concepts, no mobility of signs, and the relationship between concept and sign becomes automatized. Activity comes to a halt, and the awareness of reality dies out. (1987: 378[1933])

Jakobson's use of the words "mobility" and "activity" are indicators of the importance of the function of time in his poetic theory. This component is a development of his debt to, and understanding of, Saussure. Jakobson understands metonymy as a literary device which is of primary importance to realistic prose (see his essays: "Two Aspects of Language and Two Types of Aphasic Disturbances" (1987: 95–114), and "Marginal Notes on the Prose of the Poet Pasternak" (1987: 301–317). Jakobson adds insights into the use of metonymy in poetry through linguistic definitions which progress towards the semiotic. His definition of metonymy is further expressed in his essay "Linguistics and Poetics", as follows:

In poetry not only the phonological sequence but, in the same way, any sequence of semantic units strives to build an equation. Similarity superimposed on contiguity imparts to poetry its thoroughgoing symbolic, multiplex, polysemantic essence, which is beautifully suggested by Goethe's "Alles Vergängliche is nur ein Gleichnis" (Anything transient is but a likeness). Said more technically, anything sequent is a simile. In poetry, where similarity is superinduced upon contiguity, any metonymy is slightly metaphoric and any metaphor has a metonymic tint.//Ambiguity is an intrinsic, inalienable character of any self-focused message, briefly a corollary feature of poetry. (1987: 85)

The "self-focused message" refers back to his model of poetic function where poetry concentrates on the message for its own sake. The above definition is complex. There are problems here with the words used to describe the various qualities. Jakobson's use of the word "similarity" can give rise to some confusion. This difficulty has been analysed in Chapter Two. The current chapter is not concerned with metaphor as such but there are so many definitions of both metonymy and metaphor, that a brief mention of its characteristics is valuable. It is fundamental to refer to the axes, and Jakobson provides further analysis of the importance of time as a value.

For reference it has been noted that simile is understood to be a form of metaphor by Aristotle ("Rhetoric 3.4.140b" (2006: 367). Whereas the *NPEPP* defines the metonym of simile as: "A figure of speech most conservatively defined as an explicit comparison using 'like' or 'as' . . . . The function of the comparison is to reveal an unexpected likeness between two seemingly disparate things" (1993: 1149a). This definition also acknowledges, that the use of verbs such as "seem" "resemble" "echo", also defines simile (1993: 1149a). Simply put, metaphor can be understood to be revealed through the use of the verb "is". If an expression can be expressed logically and grammatically through the verb "to be" then this, very fundamentally, reveals a metaphor. Given the complexity of definitions of metaphor, this definition will, it is hoped, within the context of the chapter, suffice. The *NPEPP* definitions are comprehensive and it is interesting to note that many of them rely on stating that metaphor is not metonymy (1993: 760–766).

Using the analysis of the axes in Chapter Two, the present author accepts that the reference to metaphoric and metonymic poles is represented by two axes. However, any debate is rendered complex by the many attempts to understand its construction. For example, René Dirven, whilst being supportive of Jakobson's theories, agrees with the use of Saussure's earlier analysis, and he expressly develops his own axial model in his paper "Metonymy and Metaphor: Different Mental Strategies of Conceptualisation" (2002: 3 [1993]) (see Figure 4). The later edition is condensed. The debt to Jakobson and the definition of the two axes is quite clear. However, his listing of the attributes of metaphor and metonymy are not the same as Jakobson's:

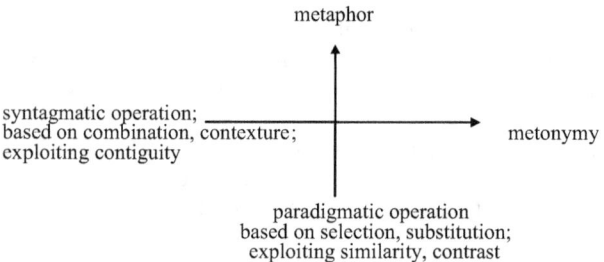

**Figure 4:** Dirven's Jakobsonian Axial Diagram.

Dirven's paper on "Metaphor and Metonymy" (1993) is almost entirely an exploration of metonymy. The terms he uses for the paradigmatic axis (in his words: paradigmatic operation) are similar to other models – including the axis explored above in Chapter Two. However, he also uses the terms "contrast" and, on the metaphoric pole, "contexture". He explains that metonymy has different levels of complexity, and can also contain the figurative. For Dirven this is interpreted with the concept that three levels exist within the axial diagram: "linear" (1993: 6/7); "conjunctive" (1993: 7/8) and "figurative" (193: 8/9).

> In metonymy two elements are brought together, keep their existence and are construed as forming a contiguous system . . . .//In metaphor, too, [as well as metonymy] two elements are brought together, but one of these i.e. the source domain is mapped onto the target domain . . . the source domain is wiped out, but in the process some or other aspects of its own structure are transferred to that of the target structure. The contrast between the two elements of domains is often so great that this disparity can only lead to full substitution of one domain by the other." (1993: 21)

Within metonymy, the "contrast" between the elements and their contiguous qualities does not result in the two terms used being transformed into a third expression which is metaphoric. It does, however, result in a condensation of terms which in its most complex form contains the "figurative". He uses the example: "I don't doubt but he's got a good head on him" – i.e. that this person is intelligent (1993: 8).

Jakobson's theory of poetic function is crucially informed by Saussure. However, he is critical of Saussure's understanding of time. He also criticised Saussure's definition of synchrony and diachrony in his diagrammatic representation of development of language. In his "Six Lectures on Sound and Meaning" (1978) Jakobson explains his objections to Saussure's definition. For Jakobson, time is, in itself, a value: "In postulating that the science of language has values as its object, the Saussurian doctrine failed to take cognisance of the fact that in a system of values the time factor itself becomes a value" (1978: 106). It has been noted that the axial model enables the inclusion of the quality of time in a definition of poetics. As has been shown, Jakobson indicates that metaphor occupies a position of simultaneity on the paradigmatic axis and that the metonym occupies a position of combination on the syntagmatic axis (requiring the passage of time).

Jakobson does not actually use the word "simultaneity", but his use of the axes provides this quality. Perhaps comparison with music and art is helpful. In music, simultaneity is represented by a chord – the simultaneous playing of several notes together which produces a sound which is not perceived as separate notes. In art simultaneity can be represented by colour where, for example, yellow and blue make green – they no longer have their own qualities of yellow and blue but make a third colour which exists in its own right. In language, the words selected and used in metaphor, provide a new ideation which does not entirely contain their original meaning. However, in the metonym the words combine, collocate and can be separated again. In the metaphor, the selection of the words provides ideation which, in its quality of simultaneity, is perceived as one not two ideas. Dirven provides this short definition of the two terms which demonstrates the inclusion of time within its construction:

> In metonymy two elements are brought together, keep their existence and are construed as forming a contiguous system . . . . /In metaphor, too, two elements are brought together, but one of these i.e. the source domain is mapped onto the target domain. Hence the existence of the source domain is wiped out, but in the process some or other aspects of its own structure are transferred to that of the target structure. The contrast between the two elements or domains is often so great that this disparity can only lead to full substitution of one domain by the other. (1993: 21)

It is important to note that in current thinking the use of the term "domain" has been largely superseded. Christine Brooke-Rose, with specific reference to poetry, analyses its shortcomings in coping with the complexities of metaphor in her definitive book *The Grammar of Metaphor* (1958: 6–13). Differing categorisations are currently much influenced by the conceptual categorisation of metaphor as in Lakoff (2003), Fauconnier (2002) and Gozzi (1999) (as, for example, in "anger is heat", "argument is war"). Here, metaphor is clearly understood to operate as a trope that does not include time within its construction. Jakobson's interest in metaphor constantly explores its function within the wider construction and use of language, he is not so concerned with the internal structure of metaphor as such.

In "The Development of Semiotics" (1987: 436–454), Jakobson, provides an overview of the importance of the American semiotician, Peirce, as well as other European semioticians, including Saussure. It is further evidence of Jakobson's interest in the semiotics of poetic language, that he combines Peirce's work with that of Gerard Manley Hopkins in his essay. The "similarities" enable the expression of artifice (see Chapter Seven below). These semiotic terms supplement the linguistic analysis. Jakobson found they were necessary in order to provide a methodology for the analysis of poetic structure. For example, a word can be used several times within the same poem and with differing meanings and connotations and this becomes a type of metonymy which can be used several times with a cumulative effect enabling imputed similarity and poetic artifice. It is a cumulative patterning. Further research is needed on whether the trope of metaphor can demonstrate the same characteristics.

Jakobson's understanding of time in poetics contributes not only to the construction of poetic function, as mentioned above, but also to the structure of metaphor and metonymy. In an interview with Krystyna Pomorska in 1980, he referred to his early essay "Futurism" [1919] where he stated that "Static perception is a fiction [untrue]" (1987: 30); and he alludes to analysis of all art forms when he refers to Saussure's synchrony and diachrony. While Saussure acknowledges movement/time, in his diagram of the development of language, for Jakobson it is an essential component of both of these axes. In a later interview with Pomorska (1985: 12) he said: "If synchrony is dynamic, then diachrony, which is the analysis and juxtaposition of different stages of a language over an extended period of time, cannot and must not be limited to the dynamics of the alterations of language alone." (1985: 12).

Here Jakobson is referring to film as well as language. For Jakobson, dynamics in language result in an expression of two aspects of time – simultaneity and succession. Both of these became aspects of his linguistic and semiotic poetic function. His Formalist analytical position understands, that time in literature, not only has internal developments which provide parallels and artifice within the specific text (1985: 25–27), but is also an essential factor in analysing the historical development of art, including literature and poetry. On a more specific level, Jakobson wrote: "Speech is transmitted at a rapid rate . . . In order for the utterance to be understood, attention to the flow of speech must be combined with moments of 'simultaneous synthesis'" (1985: 19). He compares the temporal qualities of the spoken and written word: "one of the essential differences between spoken and written language . . . The former has a purely temporal character, whereas the latter connects time and space. While the sounds that we hear disappear, when we read, we usually have immobile letters before us and the time of the written flow of words is reversible" ("Dialogue on Time in Language and Literature" 1985: 19/20).

Jakobson defined a special sense of "verbal time" which is expressed in poetry. We hear or read the text in its immediacy, we perceive its structure as it unfolds with the assistance of the semantics of the poetic text and, he stated: "in this way the verse becomes an integral part of the developing plot [or narrative]. It is difficult even to imagine a sensation of the temporal flow that would be simpler and at the same time more complex, more concrete and yet more abstract." (1985: 22). Within Formalism, linguistics and semiotics include the expression of an analysis of time held within their theoretical structure, and when analysis of time is expressed with reference to the theory of poetic function it establishes the poetic interpretation of both metaphor and metonymy. Jakobson's definition of poeticity, quoted earlier in the chapter, establishes the fundamental component of, to use his own word, "mobility" – that is, movement – as an aspect of function. This is within the defined term of Jakobsonian Formalist poetic function.

In the above analysis of the origins of metonymy and the changes which the term has undergone at different times and through differing definitions, it can be understood that the use of metonymy must not only be semantically and syntactically analysed but it must also be semiotically analysed through factual and imputed similarities, parallels and artifice, all of which are fundamental characteristics of poetry. In the next chapter, the theme of how a city poetic genre is constructed with respect to metonymy is analysed through both further theory and praxis.

# Chapter 4
# Formalist poetics – towards a praxis of a city poetic with special reference to the metonym

This chapter highlights the observation by Roman Jakobson in his "Two Aspects of Language" (1987: 95–114), that the metonym, with its quality of contiguity and association, is under-researched in poetry and poetics. He writes:

> The primacy of the metaphoric process in the literary schools of Romanticism and Symbolism has been repeatedly acknowledged, but it is still insufficiently realized that it is the predominance of metonymy which underlies and actually predetermines the so-called Realist trend . . . Following the path of contiguous relationships, the Realist author metonymically digresses from the plot to the atmosphere and from the characters to the setting in space and time. (1987: 111)

He adds to this, in the closing lines of the chapter that "Prose, on the contrary, is forwarded essentially by contiguity. Thus for poetry, metaphor – and for prose, metonymy – is the line of least resistance and consequently the study of poetical tropes is directed chiefly toward metaphor." (1987: 4). With reference to the developments in the theory of the metonym in the previous chapter, examples of city poetry are explored here to provide praxis for the theory. This includes the poems "Commuter's Pentameter" by Sarah Wardle (2014: 26); "Bedouin of the London Evening" by Rosemary Tonks (2014: 63); *Datashadow* – one sonnet – by Tony Lopez (2000: 17); and David Jones (1972:124–127), two pages taken from his book length poem *The Anathémata*. The reproductions of these poems are included with grateful thanks to both authors and publishers (see Acknowledgements).

For Jakobson, as previously demonstrated, the metonym has the properties of contiguity rather than simultaneity. With reference to poetry this can be expressed within a particular phrase or poetic figure or it can be understood as a structural expression of part of (a stanza) or of a whole poem. In the examples of poems now considered it is to be noted that there are at least two levels of metonymic use – those within the phrase and within the text, and those within the full text, in itself, within which there may well also be metaphors embedded. There may also be examples of metonyms which appear to slip in and out of metaphoric or literal interpretation as well. This means that metonymy operates on both an internal specific phrasal level, and also on a meta-level, as evidenced in a particular style of writing. Understanding this meta-level is essential if metonymy is to be understood as a poetic form of expression.

In Jakobson's analysis of Pasternak's poetry (1987: 301–317), he writes:

> the absolute commitment of the poet [Pasternak] to metonymy is known; what remains to be determined is the thematic structure of his poetry. The hero is as if concealed in a picture puzzle; he is broken down into a series of constituent and subsidiary parts; he is replaced by a chain of concretized situations and surrounding objects, both animate and inanimate . . . .//
> Show us your environment and I will tell you who you are. We learn what he lives on, this lyric hero outlined by metonymies, split up by synecdoches into individual attributes, reactions, and situations. (1987: 312,313)

Metonymy is therefore a method of construction of both the specific instances and meanings within the text and the text as a whole. It is understood as having linguistic and semiotic functions. These different functions enable different categorisations and definitions. This is further complicated by the different sources which provide the definitions in the first place (see Chapter Three) and the fact that, including going back to the classical rhetoricians, these are not altogether comprehensive or conclusive.

In the light of the complexity which Jakobson's model holds, two detractors of the poles of language are mentioned. Brian Vickers in his *Defence of Rhetoric* (1988) cogently explains how the study of rhetoric changed during the renaissance from the classical emphasis on the use of the various uses of rhetoric – including the art of persuasion and convincing legal argument – to an emphasis on the various tropes which formed the rhetoric, in itself. Jakobson's development, therefore which included the reduction of these various tropes into two over-arching categories, seems unnecessarily reductionist to Vickers:

> In Jakobson's work, as in Vico and White, rhetoric is fragmented and then subordinated to an alien enterprise. This is a pattern we have met before, in medieval rhetoric, with its disintegration of a unified tradition into components that were reused for different and usually more restricted ends. In Jakobson the guiding spirit is the binary opposition basic to structuralist phonology after Trubetzkoy, which here not only divides rhetoric into two terms, and two only, but then conceives of them in fundamental opposition. Vickers. (1988: 447)

Vickers has no interest in Russian influences on Jakobson and accepts Jakobson's importance but finds his reduction of all the tropes to those of metaphor and metonymy unnecessary and confused. But here it is important to remember some of the influences on Jakobson at the time. In his paper on Aphasia (1987:94–114[1956]), he cites the work of Hughlings Jackson, many of whose lectures and notes had been republished at the time that Jakobson's paper was written. Hughlings Jackson (1835–1911) established, through his clinical observations arising from many years experience at the London Hospital (now the National Hospital and Institute for Neurology in central London), that words in themselves convey very little meaning. Without meaningful arrangements of words (propositions), the patient conveys no meaning either to him/herself or to the listener. Neither can he/she absorb connected propositions and, for whatever reason (modern medicine has identified many), there is no capacity to interpret the speaker's proposition. Hughlings Jackson was extensive in his observations of the epileptic and the aphasic. The neurological principles of his research are still respected in the medical profession today. His work on aphasia is of great interest to those who study the formulation of early linguistics in the first twenty years of the twentieth century. Jakobson's quotes from Hughlings Jackson do not misrepresent him. He uses the following quotations: "It is not enough to say that speech consists of words. It consists of words referring to one another in a particular manner; and without a proper interrelation of its parts a verbal utterance would be a mere succession of names embodying no proposition" [Hughlings Jackson 1868: 66]; and: "Loss of speech is, therefore, the loss of power to propositionize" [Hughlings Jackson 1879: 114]. Jakobson needs only one other observation made by Hughlings Jackson to further explicate his analysis:

> Of course, we do not either speak or think in words or signs only, but in words or signs referring to one another in a particular manner, any more than we move single muscles, or muscles co-ordinated to a particular end. Indeed, words in sentences lose their individual meaning – if single words can be strictly said to have any meaning – and the whole sentence becomes a unit, not a word-heap. (1866: 56)

By the time that Jakobson wrote his aphasia essay (1956) linguistics was much more established as an area for academic study. Going back to Hughlings Jackson, it is interesting to note that there is a further relevant quote which directly informs linguistics:

> Words in themselves have no meaning; they are but symbols; it would matter nothing whether a certain small quadruped were called " cat" or " tac "; either would do as a symbol for the image we have when we think of a particular cat. Again, words only come to have speech value when they are in propositions; to speak is to propositionize, it is not merely to utter words. (Similarly, mutatis mutandis for pantomimic actions and pantomimic propositions.) Of course, a single word may be, in effect, a proposition, other words completing the proposition being understood, internally revived. Passing over the obvious cases of "yes" and "no," if a father calls to his son "Here," there is in effect the proposition "Come here.". Hence speaking is symbolizing a mental operation". (1893: 182)

For the development of linguistics in the early half of the twentieth century, abandoning the idea that people think in words (the prevalent wisdom in the late 19th century – see Head 1915: 13) – this system of differentiation of defining words and meaning enables the later linguistic and semiotic definitions of signs and the signified to be developed.

A second detractor, James Drake (1998), conducts an analysis of Jakobson's work which relies heavily on refuting Jakobson's understanding of aphasia. However, Drake's quotations (1998) from Jakobson are not referenced and in his longer essay (2002), he reveals that he has not understood the differing levels of perception which can be observed when people respond to situations which are challenged by their immediate condition. As Hughings Jackson observed, perception relies on previous information which the brain has already processed:

> In simple cases of delirium (partial imperception with inferior perception) as when a patient takes his nurse to be his wife, we find, I think, a going down to and a revelation of what would have been when he was sane, the lower and earlier step towards his true recognition or perception of the nurse.//The first step towards his recognition of her when he was sane would be the unconscious or subconscious, and automatic reproduction of his, or of one of his, well-organized symbol-images of woman; the one most or much organized in him would be his wife. To say what a thing is, is to say what it is like; he would not have known the nurse even as a woman, unless he had already an organized image of at least one woman. The popular notion is, that by a sort of faculty of perception, he would recognize her without a prior stage in which, he being passive, an organized image was roused in him by the mere presence of the nurse; the popular notion almost seems to imply the contradiction that he first sees her, in the sense of recognizing her, and then sees her as like his already acquired or organized image of some woman. We seem to ourselves to perceive, as also to will and to remember, without prior stages, because these prior stages are unconscious or subconscious. (1879: 125)

Jakobson (1987: 106,107) has correctly identified and referenced the parts of Hughlings Jackson's work which provide a definition of the trope as arising from linguistic thinking rather than that of the classical or renaissance rhetoric. Linguistics remains a central influence on Jakobson's thought processes and his definitions of metaphor and metonymy have to be understood as arising from this influence.

The work of critic Christian Metz (1982: 184/185) has defined Jakobson's theory of the metonym as "semantic" and "positional". This classification is originally postulated by Jakobson in his essay "Two Aspects of Language" (1987: 95–114 [1956]). Bertrand Augst's article "Metz's Move" (1981), refers to the classification as "Jakobson's 'move'" (1982: 37). It is examined in detail in Metz's work *Psychoanalysis and the Cinema: The Imaginary Signifier* (1982). The article "Metz's Move" by Bertrand Augst (1981) explains Jakobson's position as Metz interprets it: "this reshaping of the rhetorical tradition to a linguistic model was clearly Jakobson's doing and was fully recognized as such, although Jakobson himself did not fully develop his argument" (1981: 36). This is a clear acknowledgement of the shift away from centuries of classification of these tropes – metaphor and metonymy – from the rhetorical to the linguistic terrain and also demonstrates the influence of psychoanalysis. The reclassification may have shaped how modern linguists have understood metonymy as congruent with the categories of condensation and displacement rather than features of the rhetorical tradition, though not including an Aristotelian definition (Bredin 1984a: 89–103; and 1984b: 45–580). The reclassification leads to a possible over-inclusive definition of metonymy as condensation and opens an interesting area for discussion. Augst indicates that Metz: "shows very convincingly that Jakobson's realignment has been misconstrued to imply an identity between the two sets of opposing concepts: paradigm = metaphor, and syntagm = metonymy. Of course, Jakobson himself never made such a claim, as he has consistently maintained that these distinctions were parallel *but separate*" (1981: 37). Augst summarizes Metz's position:

> the paradigm/syntagm opposition is valid only if it is conceived in terms of another set of contrasting terms: semantic and positional, which were of course described in the 1956 article. This means that there are basically four types of relationships between linguistic units: a relation of similarity which can be either semantic or positional, and relation of contiguity which can also be semantic or positional. Thus Jakobson had really introduced not a two-term but a four-term homology. (1982: 37)

Metz's theoretical analysis indicates that similarity has two attributes – that of semantic or positional; and that contiguity, also has two attributes – that of semantic or positional. The reclassification of Jakobson's list, as published in his article on aphasia (1987: 95–114), which is based on the foundation word "hut" (1987: 110), can, it is suggested, in accordance with the four attributes as identified by Metz, be listed as follows:

> positional contiguity: hut~poor
> semantic contiguity: hut~den~burrow
> positional similarity: hut~cabin~hovel~palace (antonym)
> ~den~burrow
> semantic similarity: hut~little house~cabin~hovel
> ~palace (antonym)~den~burrow

Jakobson himself, in his "Two Aspects of Language" (1987[1956]), analysed the responses of individuals to particular words and suggested the following classifications:

> To the stimulus *hut* one response was *burnt out*; another, *is a poor little house*. Both reactions are predicative; but the first creates a purely narrative context, while in the second there is a double connection with the subject *hut*: on the one hand, a positional (namely syntactic) contiguity and, on the other, a semantic similarity.//The same stimulus produced the following substitutive reactions: the tautology *hut*; the synonyms *cabin* and *hovel*; the antonym *palace*; and the metaphors *den* and *burrow*. The capacity of two words to replace one another is an instance of positional similarity, and, in addition, all these responses are linked to the stimulus by semantic similarity (or contrast). Metonymical responses to the

same stimulus, such as *thatch, litter,* or *poverty* [to the word "hut"], combine and contrast the positional similarity with semantic contiguity.//In manipulating these two kinds of connection (similarity and contiguity) in both their aspects (positional and semantic) – selecting, combining, and ranking them – an individual exhibits his personal, style, his verbal predilections and preferences". (1987: 110)

The key to the interpretation of this information is in the paragraph of the Augst quotation above (1982: 37), in which Augst has summarized Metz's interpretation of Jakobson's work. The following is a full classification and tabulation of Jakobson's own examples, also with reference to the Augst paragraph above. The present author's classification of whether the word is, overall, metonymic or metaphoric has been added in square brackets. Briefly:

> HUT – the responses are substitutive, or predicative (i.e. complementary and narrative) to the original stimulus word: hut:
> burnt out; predicative, narrative, positional (syntactic) contiguity [metonymic]
> poor little house; predicative (double connection with word "hut"), semantic similarity [metonymic]
> cabin; substitutive homonym, metonym: positional similarity, semantic similarity [metaphoric]
> hovel; substitutive homonym, metonym: positional similarity, semantic similarity [metonymic]
> palace: substitutive antonym, narrative, semantic contrast [metonymic]
> den: metaphor: positional similarity, semantic similarity [metaphoric]
> burrow: metaphor: positional similarity, semantic similarity [metaphoric]
> thatch, litter, poverty: metonyms, positional similarity, semantic contiguity [metonymic]

The above system of classification implies that any word, which is similar to the foundation word (in this instance "hut"), in the sense that it can more or less replace it (as in "hovel"), expresses a positional similarity through its semantic similarity. Any word which is similar to the foundation word, in the sense that it adds to it, rather than replacing it (as in "burnt out"), expresses positional contiguity. Words can have both semantic *and* positional similarity. Narrative provides for predicative metonymic association. And there are gradations of whether the substitutive word depends more heavily on semantic similarity – simultaneous effect – metaphor – or more heavily on positional similarity which produces narrative – contiguous effect – metonym. Jakobson's examples are barely separable given the categories he provides. In any event, the metaphoric and metonymic axes are the basis for the analysis and this example provides gradations of the two attributes in his close analysis of the word "hut". However, there is room for confusion here: if a word substitutes another and is therefore substitutive, this is not metaphoric as such; it is metonymic in terms of displacement, especially within the terms of modern linguistic analysis. Linguists such as Denroche

(2018), and Goossens (1990), consider that there is always an element of admixture between the metaphor and metonym. The syntagm and the paradigm, as the classification quoted above indicates, provides the basis for understanding how, in this instance, the metonym, can occupy combinations of two positions – the semantic, the positional – and each of these positions are both contiguous and similar. But overall, metonymy remains syntagmatic. Within the context of the current chapter, these combinations of type must be reviewed with respect to poetry. For the use of the metonym in poetry, the Jakobsonian terms "factual similarity", "imputed similarity", "parallel" and "artifice" will be used.

Augst summarizes Metz by stating that the four independent axes, which interpret the different combinations of these semantic and positional metaphors and metonyms, are used with reference to filmic analysis (1982: 39). Dirven, in his paper "Metonymy and Metaphor" (1993), attempts a similar classification. Dirven's model, however, arrives at a classification based on three different syntagms. His model refers to Barthes' system of classification but does not refer to Metz's earlier paper. Dirven proposes analysis of the different levels of metonymy, suggesting that there is:

> a discussion of a third type of metonymy. Alongside the first type, which is based on a linear syntagm and does not involve semantic change, and the second type, which is based on a conjunctive syntagm and which is characterised by a systematic semantic change, we have a third type, which is based on an inclusive syntagm and always exhibits a figurative interpretation. (2003: 82/83)

Dirven defines the metonymic forms in increasing levels of complexity:

> Just as there are different degrees in metaphoricity, which has often been discussed in the literature, there are different degrees in metonymicity. The lowest degree of metonymicity is linear metonymy [*Different parts of the country* do not mean the same], since it is always non-figurative and non-polysemous. The next higher degree is conjunctive metonymy of the type *tea* for a 'large meal', which is non-figurative, but polysemous ... [*Tea* was a large meal for the Wicksteeds]. The third type is conjunctive metonymy as in *the Crown* for the (British) Monarch or Queen, which is both figurative and polysemous. This also holds for inclusive metonymy as in (*have a good head* for 'intelligence' ... [he has a *good head* on him]. Which just like metaphor in [Kreik-Lambik is *eating* and drinking together] can only be figurative. (2003: 93/94)

He uses the term "metonymic chain" (2003: 85), where he defines how the metonym holds different interpretations and forms within its structure. He uses the example of the process of thinking. Consider the example: "his brain worked slowly", where what is indicated is a number of different processes and perceptions taking place – the process of thinking in itself, assessment of intelligence, opinion and classification. Dirven states that these three kinds of metonymy involve the existence of three syntagms rather than their being three aspects of the same trope (2003: 85/86). He is, however, certain that the complexities of metonymy do not enable that shift from the syntagmatic or contiguous nature of the metonym into a metaphoric form. In his conclusion he uses the term "figurative metonymy" to describe the varying degrees of complexity of the metonym (2003:108/109).

However, classification of language usage is understood to contain its different semiotic levels – factual (with its emphasis on semantic/textual components), syntactic/imputed (with its analysis on meaning and form), semiotic/parallel (with its observation of verbal and rhyme patterns) and artifice (the sum of all these levels) and with particular reference to poetic function. – Using this classification, rather than depending on establishing a number of syntagms or axes, provides a model where the text (in this instance a poem) accumulates metonymic complexity as the text is considered through ever larger units – word, sentence, stanza, whole poem, or even whole poet's oeuvre, for example. Yeats, referring to his whole work as a "book" (part-for-whole metonym), is an example of this (Wilson III 1994: 223). Does it mean, therefore, that metonymy has a particular function within poetry? How is it expressed more particularly within the context of city poetry? These are questions that need answers.

The analysis of the metonym from the previous chapter uses the three categories of language – semantic, syntactic and semiotic to define the range of metonymic process. This same classification is transposed to assist in defining Jakobson's terms: factual similarity, imputed similarity, parallels and artifice. What follows is an introductory rather than definitive exploration. There is no attempt at a full Formalist analysis; the points discussed are with specific reference to the analysis of metonymy. What is of interest to note is the fact that the complex nature of the metonym emerges immediately once the metonymic analysis begins. The first example is the poem by Sarah Wardle "Commuters' Pentameter" from her collection *Beyond* (2014: 26). The lines have been numbered for easy reference.

Sarah Wardle: "Commuter's Pentameter"

| | |
|---|---|
| Where are you in this surging crowd? | 1 |
| Are you a separate body, or part | 2 |
| of the Leviathan, the lungs, the heart? | 3 |
| Can you hear yourself think out loud, | 4 |
| or are you suffocating in the throng | 5 |
| that marches down The Strand as one, | 6 |
| stringing along the soul of London? | 7 |
| Were you given a choice to belong? | 8 |
| Should there be an opt-out clause | 9 |
| for those who don't want to be confirmed | 10 |
| into the mysteries citizens learn | 11 |

| | |
|---|---|
| or are these more a blessing than a curse? | 12 |
| Is there solace in the rhythmic beat | 13 |
| that bears you on with iambic feet? | 14 |

The poem is a fourteen-line sonnet form, with a rhyme scheme. The iambic metric rhythm, which is explicitly referred to in the last line of the poem, has a slight irregularity to it which heightens the sense of the footsteps of the commuter crowd moving as one, but sometimes out of step (see lines 4, and 9 where it has the effect of a caesura). This is a clear example of the "inscape" which Hopkins sought to define with respect to city crowds (see Chapter Seven, below). The commuters in the title are metonymic for Londoners (part for whole) and workers (part for whole). The opening question in line 1 asks for the location of the one amongst the whole (part for whole) and sets a metonymic tone. Lines 2 and 3 are synecdoches: "Are you a separate body, or part/of the Leviathan, the lungs, the heart?" The use of the term "Leviathan" is also a metaphor within the synecdoche.

There is no communication from the commuters towards the narrator and this contributes to the remote rhetoric enabled by the viewpoint of the poet/narrator. However, the central lines (9 and 10) "Should there be an opt-out clause/for those who don't want to be confirmed" refers to contracts which have been entered into as commuters (in this instance) which provide a sense of entrapment. The viewpoint of the narrator, and the fact that the commuters do not speak, increases the power of the sequential questioning format of the poem. This also increases the sense of stasis. In line 7 the question: "stringing along the soul of London?" provides an example of a metaphor combined with a metonym. "To string someone along" is a dead metaphor. Its source is the idea of someone being controlled by string – as a puppet – and/or being tricked, sent along a wrong track. There is a double metaphor in effect – a pun/metaphor perhaps, but within the context of the poem the phrase is also a metonym – "stringing along the soul of London" features a literal sense of the crowd being pulled along in a line by the march (or shuffle) of the commuters' steps. "Soul" is, of course, a metonym (part for whole) for "human" (or perhaps whole for part), except that in the poem it refers to the "soul of London" and, since London is inanimate, this would seem to be a metaphor (the commuter *is* the soul of the city of London). The phrase has a double quality of both metaphor and metonym.

The viewpoint of the poem is significant. Viewpoint, is understood to mean the eyesight angle of the narrator of the poem – whether this is a persona or the poet herself. The *Deus ex machina*, God-like (a metonymic relationship of juxtaposition) viewpoint of the narrator of the poem is reinforced by the legal and religious imagery of lines 9–12. These specialist phrases: "opt-out clause", "confirmed" "mysteries" and "blessings" refer back to the use of the word "soul" (line 7) but

## Chapter 4 Formalist Poetics – towards a praxis of a city poetic – the metonym

the legal aspect of the phrase "opt-out clause" renders the religious phraseology imperfect. What might be an extended metaphor becomes broken. The "opt-out clause" is a synecdoche for a worldly life or Faustian contract and the religious terminology is therefore re-positioned. Perhaps the contract could therefore be described as whole-for-part metonymy within the metaphor.

The metonymy arising from the poetic language in the poem occurs not only as a result of the individual use of metonymy, but also from the repeated metonymy. In this instance, the distant poet/narrator/persona asks repeated questions and, from this, the poetic parallels are formed. The poem is a linked narrative with a constructed form and without random elements. Highlighting the metonymic within the poem has provided examples of the different usage – the factual (individual semantic use), the imputed (the combination of various uses in the text providing an overall meaning and form that is from semantic to syntactic), the parallel (patterns of usage, that is from semantic and syntactic, including rhyme) and, finally, the semiotic artifice (the poet's constructed whole). Jakobson stated that poetry "focus[es] on the message for its own sake, is the POETIC function of language" (1987: 69). The poetic function of the poem is partly constructed by these different levels of metonymic use. The poem demonstrates the metonymic relationship between the persona/narrator of the poem to the commuters and describes a relationship which reflects a metonymic positioning between the viewpoint of the poet, the power of the city itself and the inhabitants living in it. The metonymic positioning clearly delineates a city poetic genre.

The next poem to be analysed, "Bedouin of the London Evening" is the title poem of a collection by Rosemary Tonks (2014: 63). Again, the lines have been numbered for reference. The poem is quoted in numbered sections throughout the analysis.

Rosemary Tonks: "Bedouin of the London Evening"

| Ten years in your cafés and your bedrooms | 1 |
| Great city, filled with wind and dust! | 2 |
| | 3 |
| Bedouin of the London evening, | 4 |
| On the way to a restaurant my youth was lost. | 5 |

Both lines 3 and 6 are blank lines. The significant contribution of the poem is that it demonstrates metonymy of condensation of both content and form. The title uses the definite article "The". This makes the event time specific and yet what is wasted has a period of time expressed within it: "wasted youth". This is an example of a hitherto unexplored kind of metonymy – a temporal part-for-whole metonym.

| | |
|---|---|
| And like a medium who falls into a trance | 7 |
| So deep, she can be scratched to death | 8 |
| By her Familiar – at its leisure! | 9 |
| I have lain rotting in a dressing-gown | 10 |
| While being savaged (horribly) by wasted youth. | 11 |

Line 12 is also a blank line. The lines are uneven in length, there is no rhyme scheme and the text contains the quality of metonymic condensation, for example the opening line: "Ten years in your cafes and your bedrooms" can grammatically, though not so poetically, be expanded to: "I have lived for ten years in your cafes and in your bedrooms". The sonnet form is broken by the irregularity, and the insufficient number of the lines. However, if the spaces between the lines are added to the number of lines (i.e. the blank lines 3, 6 and 12) there are a sufficient number of lines to form a full sonnet (14). It can be argued that the blank spaces are a part-for-whole metonymy of the poem's form. The two gaps fragment the linked text. The sonnet is specifically indicated through a negative metonymic structure. The broken iambics, the broken sonnet form, both emphasise the representation of broken life expressed by the poem: "wasted youth" (line 11), for example. The poem therefore expresses condensation not only within its form (container for contained – or vice versa), it is also an example of cause-for-effect metonymy: spaces, broken lines represent the gaps in a broken life. This is more of a rhetorical than a linguistic categorisation. Tonks' poem contains a number of condensations, including the condensation of the sonnet form. The form of the poetic text, as a whole, is apparent on the page and provides visually apparent poetic interpretation as a sonnet. This provides an example of how Jakobson's imputed/syntactic similarity becomes a form of the poem as a whole – the parallel/semiotic.

It seems that the poem does not contain any easily defined metonyms. A simile is on the metonymic axis and the central part of the poem contains such a forceful simile "like a medium" (line 7) that the rest of the poem becomes influenced by it (possessor for possessed – literally!). This persona and the subsequent mention of the "familiar" appear to be random; but their full meaning is restored by the narrative which is completed in the last two lines of the poem. The Bedouin is evoked as a simile because his/her clothing is reflected in the narrator's dressing gown. This is referred to twice – lines 10 and 13. Line 10 is a metaphor – because "rotting" refers to her dissipation not actual rotting. The combined power of the similes in the poem influences its analysis. This is an example of imputed similarity. Line 2 contains a possible metaphor ("the city is filled with wind and dust") because a city is filled with buildings of concrete and tangible things, not ephemeral ones. But as these words stand in as a part-for-whole description of the city they are more strongly metonymic. It seems as if the linguistic terms undergo something of a transformation when subjected to the analysis of imputed/syntactic similarity of a poem.

The poem opens in a vocative mode. The "O" is omitted as is the implied "I have been" which, in ordinary prose, would be the opening words of the sentence. Anaphora is demonstrated by its later inclusion in the penultimate line of the poem. The factual similarity is rendered complicated by the quasi-anaphora. The Bedouin is not part of the invocation in lines one and two. But in line 3, it is possible to add a second vocative or to understand that the poet is referring to herself as a Bedouin. This is a metonymic complexity arising from the possible simile. The words "Bedouin of the London Evening" give rise to a number of levels of interpretation. It is the title of the poem, its third line and also the title of the book. The meanings become tripled because of the way the phrase is used. The fact that it is the book's title also provides inferred meaning to the whole collection of poems – the rootless traveller in a city. This is an example of poetic artifice.

The reference later in the poem: "I have lain rotting in a dressing-gown" (line 10), is surprising as this is one thing a Bedouin does not do, being by nature a nomad, or perhaps in the poem a "nemesis" (a metonymic connotation). The reference to wind and dust accrues to the Bedouin by virtue of what a Bedouin is. This makes "wind and dust" a metaphoric depiction as well as a metonymic one for the city itself. But there is also a metonymic quality in the use of "Bedouin". The poet's trip to a local shop in the evening in her dressing gown provides further tension between movement and the stasis of "wasted youth". In the final lines:

| | |
|---|---|
| I have been young too long, and in a dressing-gown | 13 |
| My private modern life has gone to waste. | 14 |

Another tension occurs through the juxtaposition of "My private modern life" with the public appearance of herself in a dressing-gown (a private form of attire). These suggestions point to a possible metonym of factual similarity – the factual form/similarity of the poem gives part for whole of the imputed form/similarity of the poet's life.

Line 5 "my youth was lost", is metaphoric but it can be interpreted as part for whole – "youth" for "life" or, perhaps, more generically, for "achievement". The condensation in the first line is metonymic. Line 5 has the same condensation. In prose it would read: "[When I was] On the way to a restaurant . . . ". The poem uses the very strong simile of the Familiar in the lines 7–11. A simile is, of course, metonymic; but it obtains its effect by having two parts for the whole – the medium and the person in the dressing-gown become inextricably linked by the simile. Lines 7–11 are an extended analogy of how the poet sees herself. "I have lain rotting . . . " also refers to her own "familiar" – which is "wasted youth". In line 13, the dressing-gown represents part for whole for the poet/narrator but it also has metaphoric qualities – it *is* the passage of time through the passing of youth. As such, it would seem to have both metaphoric and metonymic qualities, and is a condensation which is an imputed/syntactic similarity. The word "youth" can evince a negative attribute. Added to this is the phrase "life gone to waste" (line 4) and "young too long" (line13). And the narrative set up by this repetition provides a strong sequence of ideation – a contiguity.

The internal syntax of the poem provides both metaphors and metonyms. The imputed/syntactic similarity is metonymic because its overall message is that of mis-spent youth within the passage of life as a whole. The Bedouin, the dressing-gown, the Familiar – all provide metonymic part images of the whole "wasted youth". The word "youth" is used twice (lines: 5 and 11) and "young" in line 13. The parallels of the poem are based on condensation of form, including omission of lines and words, and this is metonymic. The poem's artifice, especially as it is also the title poem of the book, includes the condensation of time. The cross currents – "wind and dust" – are those of life's purpose and purposelessness: this is also a metonymic image which contains condensation. For the city dweller, the use of the metonymic condensation of the metonymic image provides a sense of how the city has power, albeit a moving, changing power, over the individual living within it. This is an example of how Jakobson's *function* in his "poetic function" is expressed as a semiotic function as well as a semantic and syntactic one. In the work of Dirven and Metz, discussed above, the metonymic word or phrase is also posited as possessing more than one property. The metonym can be expressed as a word which stands in for another, a word which interprets another and a word which has a figurative – but still metonymic – interpretation (Dirven: 1993). Jakobson's system describes four types of linguistic relationships: similarity and contiguity; positional and semantic (1987: 110 as quoted above).

The poem from *Data Shadow* by Tony Lopez is also in sonnet form (2000: 17). The entire sequence of poems is written in six titled sections. The sonnet comes from the second section in the sequence entitled "Imitation of Life". The poems printed in *Data Shadow* (2000) are a part of the sequence printed in *False Memory* (2012). The lines have been numbered for reference.

Imitation of Life: 6th Sonnet

| | |
|---|---|
| To the human eye, which cannot detect UV | 1 |
| That mental country is expected to decline | 2 |
| When compared with our thematic growth package. | 3 |
| War was unknown. Consumer groups approved | 4 |
| The packaged products and services of | 5 |
| Arethusa, who is the source of this sample. | 6 |
| The world is turning into information, | 7 |
| Store in an upright position. London ivy | 8 |

| | |
|---|---|
| The natural and delicious alternative | 9 |
| Sits awkwardly on screen. Asian tigers | 10 |
| Fail to bounce back for the demise of inflation. | 11 |
| Trainer and jockey in the best of form | 12 |
| Who wander into the Arcadian sunlight | 13 |
| Found in direct speech. One trillion bits per second. | 14 |

The entire sequence of poems is comprised of text which represents all the textual stimuli which we might encounter and then discard as not essential to our daily lives. The preface is written in the same style. Elucidation is not provided. This is not the usual definition of Data Shadow. It is as if the poem has eradicated the meaning even from itself – thus data shadow itself has been disrupted. The fragments have been fragmented. What does the term Data Shadow usually mean? One definition is: "A data shadow is a slang term that refers to the sum of all small traces of information that an individual leaves behind through everyday activities. It is a minute piece of data created when an individual sends an email, updates a social media profile, swipes a credit card, uses an ATM and so on" (www.techopedia.com).

The cover image of the book is a much-enlarged reproduction of the QR (quick response) code. The code was developed by Japanese car manufacturers in the 1990's to enable the data storage of greater quantities of information than, for example, a bar code. The enlarging of the code on the book cover effectively also eradicates its meaning. The text of the poem is condensed in the sense that it is comprised of phrases that, in fact, do not make clear sense when combined. The part-for-whole links are broken and, whilst the human brain makes constant efforts to make sense, the meaning is not readily available. These are not even novel metaphors or metonyms. The overall language is referential, but there are a number of metaphors and metonyms embedded in it. Line 2 has the metaphor "That mental country", line 3 "growth package". In line 6, the possible metaphor "source of this sample" is wiped out by the reference to Arethusa who is the Classical Greek goddess of water. Suddenly, the metaphor becomes a metonym. In line 7 "The world is turning into information" is both a metaphor and a pun. Line 9 is obviously part of an advertising slogan and, within its original context, is metonymic. However, as the slogan is linked with "London ivy", this becomes a less attractive combination, though still metonymic. The same sort of crash of trope takes place in lines 10 and 11 where the "bounce back" of the "Asian tigers" becomes metaphoric rather than literal when read in association with the information that this is the epithet given to Hong Kong stock exchange traders. The text plays with a kind of interchangeability between metaphor and metonym. Line 11 has a metaphor: "demise of inflation". Line 13 has a metaphor "Arcadian sunlight".

How does one read the poem, the sequence of poems? Is the poem as a whole to be read metaphorically or metonymically? A metaphoric reading, where the text of the poem becomes (is) our lives in the modern and urban world of today, is exhausting and frustrating, although not impossible. But these attributes fulfil the meaning of the title "Data Shadow". A metonymic reading, where the phrases are simply sequentially accumulated, is easier and more rewarding. The data-shadow accumulates (as it does in real life) and is used in a process of assimilation which has no conclusive use or function. But as the fragments are discarded it is best to leave them in their raw and unprocessed state and accept their unwanted, accumulative accretion. This is a metonymic process. The punctuation and grammar are not disrupted in any way but the random sources are placed in a "narrative" which is repeatedly fragmented. The artifice of the whole sequence of poems arises from this carefully constructed fragmentation of meaning.

The example also demonstrates what happens if you break associative threads. It is of interest because it demonstrates not only how interpretation of text takes place, but how it is also discarded. It can be very funny, as a breakage in sense linkage often is. If these chains become broken, is this a metaphoric or a metonymic break of text and language? Within this particular sonnet, it has been demonstrated that metaphors are embedded within metonymic phrases. But, in terms of Jakobson's analysis in his article on aphasia (see Chapter Three), the loss of associative conjunctions – in this example – between the phrases, results in an overall metaphoric communication. Analysis of other sonnets in the sequence may also reveal metonyms embedded with the phrases and that this characteristic happens to be in more than this particular stanza. Thus, there is evidence, again, that poetry has a number of levels of metonymic expression: the level of the textual form, factual similarity – semantic and syntactic – and the level of the whole poem as a patterned set of devices – the imputed similarity/semiotic.

The same operational levels can also be found in prose, albeit probably in a simpler form. It has been seen how poetic text can move between the qualities of metaphor and metonym as a result of context. This is not a negative quality, especially with reference to poetry, it enhances the imputed similarity of the text. Much of this kind of metonymic dysfunction reflects the plethora of stimuli in a city existence. The metonymic structure of the poem, with its embedded metaphors, can provide an interpretation of how city life accumulates stimuli to breaking point (a metonymic process); but the occasional linkage or image is absorbed, retained and processed as having a different quality or meaning (a metaphoric process).

Linguists have understood the presence of the metaphoric within the metonymic and vice versa. In what follows, the complexity of this structure is explored with reference again, to Denroche (2015) and Littlemore (2015). Denroche provides a review of some aspects of the phenomenon in his *Metonymy and Language*

(2015: 75/6) where Goossens' term, "metaphytonymy" is employed. Denroche understands that there may be degrees of complexity in the actual use of metaphor and metonymy and that under certain circumstances a word may be both (2015: 87–89).

Littlemore refers to the capacity of metonymy to operate at the level of the phrase (2015: 127/8). Also, in her Chapter Four, she provides many examples of how metonymy operates across various discourse types. These can cause "exophoric referencing" (2015: 83–5); that is, that the use of metonymy leads the reader/listener into a context outside that of the immediate text. Her section on "The interaction and overlap between metonymy and metaphor" (2015: 132–7), explores the complexity and difficulty of definition between the two tropes. It seems that, for Littlemore, these refer to examples which provide "factual similarity" within a text, rather than referring to the "imputed similarity" which arises from the form of the poetic text: the complexity of considering the full text structure, rather than just its components.

Discourse theory is examined in Denroche (2015: 106–132) with regards to specific registers; for example, text messaging or advertisements. Denroche also identifies and provides examples of three other groupings: "Textual Metonymy", "Textual Metaphor" and "Textual Metaphtonymy". Poetry is briefly mentioned in his chapter – he refers to David Lodge's analysis of Larkin. Lodge provides a definition that goes someway to describing poetic complexity of metonymic and metaphoric use. He wrote that in: "'The Whitsun Weddings', the metaphors are foregrounded against a predominantly metonymic background, which in turn is foregrounded against the background of the (metaphoric) poetic tradition" (Lodge 1979: 216). The definition gives an additional defining example of how the trope is both embedded in the word and phrase within the text and is also interpreted on meta-levels which are both intra- and extra-referential to the text – the imputed similarity which Jakobson described. Denroche concludes, in a later paper (2018), with reference to Lodge's analysis, that different types of Text Metaphtonomy occur: "We have seen that extended metaphor, metonymy clusters and metonymy chains have the capacity for setting up larger-scale structures within text and interactions at discourse level; but there is no reason in principle why the remaining three phenomena, 'metaphor clusters', metaphor chains' and 'extended metonymy', could not also form Text Metaphtonomies". (2018:30, 31).

Some of these definitions are useful in the consideration, which follows, of David Jones' poetry. In the Preface to his epic poem about London, *The Anathémata* (1972: 32 [1952]), Jones highlights the way that modern urban life contains so many stimuli that to attempt to describe it all in words would take far longer than the actual events. This much has been known since, at least, the publication of Sterne's *Tristram Shandy* (1759–1767). Unlike Lopez, Jones, as both poet and artist, uses his Preface in a more traditional way to inform the reader of some of the information, creative theories and techniques which elucidate his poem. David Jones (1895–1974) grew up in South-East London. *The Anathémata* was a personal autobiographical poem, much of which describes London from historical, archaeological, religious and cultural viewpoints. The resulting book-length poem is a highly complex and difficult work.

The current chapter looks at the opening pages of the fifth section of the poem "The Lady of the Pool" (for reproduction of the text without footnotes – 1972: 124–127 – please see below). Reading Jones' poetry can be said to be like being in a centrifuge. The reader is constantly pushed out of the text by the very large number of references and allusions within it. It is almost impossible to concentrate on the structure of the poem because the meaning has to be assembled, first, with reference to these multiple allusions, and secondly with reference to the reader's knowledge of the same allusions. The following short exposition of the opening 5 pages of this section will concentrate on the metonymic content to the exclusion of everything else. It is not asserted that the following represents anything like a full analysis of Jones' complex poem. For the text of the pages under discussion please see below. (For copyright reasons, the extensive footnotes in *The Anathémata* have had to be omitted here).

The Lady of the Pool:

(p124)
did he meet Lud at the Fleet Gate? did he count the top-
trees in the anchored forest of Llefelys
          under the White Mount?

Did ever he walk the twenty-six wards of the city, within
and extra, did he cast his nautic eye on her
                  clere and lusty under kell
in the troia'd lanes of the city?
And was it but a month and less from the septimal month,
and did he hear, seemly intuned in *East-Seaxna*-nasal
        (whose nestle-cock *polis* but theirs knows the sweet
gag and in what *urbs* would he hear it if not in Belin's
*oppidum*, the greatest *burh* in nordlands?)
(p125)
*Who'll try my sweet prime Lavendula*
*I cry my introit in a* Dirige-*time*
*Come buy for summer's weeds, threnodic stalks*
*For in Jane's ditch Jack soon shall white his earliest rime*
    Come, come buy
        good for a ditty-box, my fish-eye
        good to sweeten y'r poop-bower, cap'n.
    Come buy

                or else y'r duck'ill cry.
Come buy my sweet lavender
            that bodes the fall-gale westerlies
and ice on slow old Baldpate
when the Nore gulls fly this way that tell to Lear's
river a long winter's tale.
        Was already rawish crost the Lower Pool afore four o'
the clock this fine summer morning' – it might 've been
Lemon's Day. An' cuckoo seeming but bare flown and
Ember Ides not yet by a long way come, in pontiff Juliuses
'versal colander and them not yet sung their Crouchmasses
(p 127)
By tax-chandler's Black Exchecky Book nor yet thumbed
Archie's piscopal *Ordo* to figure out the moon of it.
            From the Two Sticks an' a' Apple to Bride o'
The Shandies' Well over the Fleet; from Hallows-on-Wall to
The keel-haws; from the ditch without the Vicinal Gate to
Lud's hill; within and extra the fending circuit, both banks
the wide and demarking middle-brook that waters, from the
midst of the street of it, our twin-hilled Urbs. At Martin
*miles* in the Pomarary (where the Roman pippins grow) at
winged Marmor *miles*, gilt-lorica'd on his wheat-hill, stick-
ing the Laidly Worm as threats to coil us all.
            At the Lady-at-Hill
above Romeland's wharf-lanes
at the Great Mother's newer *chapelle*
at New Heva's Old Crepel.
            (Chthonic *matres* under the croft:
springan a Maye's *Aves* to clerestories.
                Delphi in sub-crypt:
luce flowers to steeple.)
                    At Paul's
and faiths under Paul
where
        so Iuppiter me succour!
they do garland them with Roman roses and do have stitched
on their zoomorphic apparels and vest 'em gay for Artemis.
            When is brought in her stag to be pierced,
when is bowed his meek head between the porch and the
altar, when is blowed his sweet death at the great door, on the
day before the calends o' Quintilis.
            At the tunicled martyr's
from where prills the seeding under-stream.
            At Mary of the Birth
by her long bourn of sweet water.
            In where she mothers

Firstly, on pages 124, 125 – Jones sets up chains of metonymic associations in his references which lead the reader in and out of the text: away from, and back into, the text. But he does not provide the all-important context which makes the associations accessible. Then he breaks the metonymic threads by throwing in metaphoric material – in the footnotes even: see the story of Lud and the three plagues (line 1). And who is the "he" (see lines 1 and 3), who is being interrogated by the poet? Is the "he" himself? The form of the poem itself appears to be metonymic, but the intense cross-referencing of the text destroys the metonymic dimension. How do we "read" the poetic form of the extensive, necessary and intrusive yet vital, footnotes? Metonymy would seem to be the only way to describe this kind of structure. But, for example, (line 6) "in the troia'd lanes of the city?" – is this a reference to the multi-layered remains of Troy and if so, is this a metaphor?

The poem is also constantly interrupted by space (see the gap after lines 1 and 2); the blank page (opposite page 126 but un-numbered) between the notes and the inscription (drawn by Jones himself) also interrupts the text. In addition, the extra information in the footnotes renders the poetry diachronically interrupted whilst continuing on its associative course. Saussure used this model to describe how words change during the course of usage (2008: 240); but here the whole text is changed through the course of reading it. These interruptions constantly change the meanings expressed in the poem. Unfortunately, it is not possible to reproduce the notes here. They are extensive. It is possible that, on meta-metonymic and metaphoric levels, the poet expresses ideas that are within the text, through the methods by which the text is written: for example, by enabling a comparison of the textual form with the movement of water, the shifting sands of time.

Jones, who trained as an artist, would, more than likely, have considered the layout of the printed page important. The layout of the poem, with the positioning of the notes, must have been, at the very least, partly his choice. The gaps and interruptions are deliberate and have poetic purpose. The intense referencing provides a possible metaphoric interpretation because it is as if all of the people and things (though necessarily not everything that *could* be mentioned) become London. But the strong sense of the information in the notes, as associative to the text of the poem, provides a metonymic quality. Once again, Jones, as an artist, would probably have been fully aware of how different parts of a picture affect the relationship between other parts. The admixture of metonymy and metaphor seems complete. Another question to be asked is: who is speaking to whom? The lavender seller (125, line 1), it appears, is Jones' grandmother. This information is given in his own notes. But apart from this, who is the "he" referred to, on page 124? Given the multiplicity of voices and languages featured in the text, the matter has to be somewhat metaphoric because the "he" is a number of different people (is this also part-for-

## Chapter 4 Formalist Poetics – towards a praxis of a city poetic – the metonym — 109

whole metonymy?). The "he" is also metonymic because it is a pronoun standing in for a particular person, although the identity of the person is unknown. Another question ensues: are pronouns always metonyms? Analysis of pronouns as shifters is another component of Jakobson's theory (see Chapter Six) exemplified in his essay, "Shifters, Verbal Categories, and the Russian Verb" (1971[1956]).

So, is the poet talking to himself, the reader, his grandmother? Is he voicing the words of a sailor (nautical man) or does the vocaliser change when the italicised words begin at the head of page 125, so that we now have two voices plus the voices of the annotations which are by the poet? And, see note 1, page 125, for example: these are not objective notes. The poet is speaking twice or even three times simultaneously strongly indicating the metaphoric. Or is this to be understood metonymically when, through the complex referencing of the text, the reader is obliged to understand the speaking as one association occurring after another?

Added to this, there are a number of inscriptions, and, with the help of the footnotes, more voices emerge – Jones' image of a Latin inscription is itself, his own reproduction of an inscription: the history of those associated with it and its location are given in a footnote. The notes for page 127 are so extensive that a whole page is dedicated to them. The inscription engraved by Jones on the facing page: ROMA CAPUT ORBIS, SPLENDOR, SPES, AUREA ROMA translates as: "Rome head of the world, splendour, hope, golden Rome". This is a metonymic association for London, the subject of the poem. Jones acknowledges N.G. in the inscription (1972: 7) – but who is this? In the Preface, Neville George is mentioned, (1972: 37; with Bernard Smith). Neville George was a specialist in Welsh geology. Once again, the reader is taken away from the text on a different journey. The inscription illustrated on page 126 existed above the Porta San Pellegrino (meaning the pilgrim gate) in Rome, open until the fifteenth century (https://it.wikipedia.org/wiki/Porta_San_Pellegrino Accessed 12.8.22.12.05). The gate for pilgrims is one of several gates, constructed in the walls which fortified Rome. Jones' uses diachronic changing of meaning between cities and time to add layers of meaning to his text. This is contra to the Saussurean model, where the continuum of a word is occasionally intersected by a new meaning, this is a poetic text where the voices fire off ideas, viewpoints, words and meanings in very quick succession, both intersecting the text itself and changing readers' perception and understanding of the text line by line if not word by word. Is there a satisfactory analogy with music that is written with chords or several parts with the notes heard simultaneously in an act of musical condensation (see Chapter 3, above)? The reader hears the voice of the great city of Rome, the poet himself, St Peregrine, the geologist and more, all within the context of a single inscription.

Examples of metaphors within the specifically analysed text are "anchored forest" (124, line 2), "nautic eye" (124, line 5), "troia'd lanes" (124, line7), "threnodic stalks" (125, line3). On page 125, lines13/14: "long winter's tale./Was already rawish" is a metaphor which crosses two sentences, because "rawish" refers back to the "winter's tale" – without capital letters, so it is not the title of Shakespeare's play but a description of the weather/time of year/ and see book's original inscription: "IT WAS A DARK AND STORMY NIGHT, WE SAT BY THE CALCINED WALL; IT WAS SAID TO THE TALE-TELLER, TELL US A TALE, AND THE TALE RAN THUS: IT WAS A DARK AND STORMY NIGHT . . . .". On page 125, line17, "Lemon's Day" is both a reference to sharp weather as well as a reference to St Clement (see Jones' footnote). The condensation of references gives rise to a double metaphor. Page 127, line 2 – the phrase "figure out" is a metaphor but also a metonym because the two books referred to are historical manuscripts by which historians can compare the dates of events in history and thereby ascertain an accurate historical record.

The poet describes a history of London largely set within the context of London as a maritime trading city suffering attacks, invasions, defeats and victories, the events of centuries. But even the history referred to is dislocated. The text jumps through the various eras and locations of the Mediaeval, Celtic, Romano-British, Saxon, 19th century Cockney, Latin, the Saxon language, religious (Latin/French) folklore, slang, folklore (see for example: "Black Exchecky Book" (line 1, p127) – a kind of vernacular and, finally, "the moon of it", a folkloric form of dating or calendar.

The form of the poem would appear to be intensely metonymic, with association building on association. The fragmentation of poetic form is almost complete. In his Preface, Jones refers to "deposits" as a way of describing how the artist accrues, accumulates and embeds material. But the voices cut through the text and both break and inform its content and structure; links are broken through both place and time. The text is not, however, random, because Jones uses the layers, the "deposits", as a form through which he links all his references. The reader's brain is not informed as to every single one of these associations; is this the reason for inferring a metaphoric perception? The poet's (and the reader's) capacities are adjusted to full alert through these multiple allusions and the reading (and perhaps the writing too) of the text requires a bunching together of the allusions to such an extent that the only way that the reader can arrive at the meaning is by an absorbed simultaneity of stimulus that is metaphorical.

In Jakobson's essay on "The Metaphoric and Metonymic Poles" in *Fundamentals of Language* (1971[1956]), an accumulation of words is understood to be metonymic because of the lack of connecting words; but the overlaying of images, times and spaces can make the accumulation metaphoric in its sense of simultaneity. In Jakobson's 'Contiguity and Similarity Disorders' he concludes: "Metaphor is alien to the similarity disorder and metonymy to the contiguity disorder" (1971: 91). But it would not be useful to label Jones' poetry as an expression of a disorder. Jones' intense layering in his poem creates a metonymic structure for his city poetic which provides the reader with a historical diachrony, metaphoric in tone, which both shadows and guides his or her every step through the city.

In conclusion, as Metz pointed out, Jakobson's break with classical tradition through his definition of metonymy as residing on a syntagmatic axis provides a theoretical basis for this chapter. Various categories and definitions of the metonym which linguists have usefully differentiated and delineated have been discussed. In the praxis developed in this chapter, the modern classifications are used, many of which can be the same as the classic rhetorical ones: "part for whole", "whole for part", "part for part", "effect for cause" "cause for effect" (see also Bredin 1984). The examples of poetry, above, have demonstrated that the use of the metonym, in conjunction with the metaphor, in poetry can be frequent, complex and variable. The term "novel metonym" is not altogether useful because the reader tends to have no difficulty in interpreting new combinations of metonymic phrasing, thus rendering them immediately part of their syntactic and semiotic vocabulary. There are examples of the combined use of the metonym and metaphor within one phrase and the embedding of one trope within the other.

It is therefore argued, with reference to both semiotics and linguistics, that there are some extreme and complex uses of the metonym in poetry. The semiotic theories of Jakobson with respect to Poetic Function which include "factual similarity", "imputed similarity" and "parallels" and the axial representation of time within the use of language, provide the basis for a detailed examination of these various uses. These structures occur in text or speech, which may not be poetry; but they are more likely to occur and to be denser within the context of poetry. As Jakobson said in the 1921 publication "Contextual Glossary of Formalist Terminology", republished with additions in *Russian Poetics in Translation* (1977: "Poetry is language in its aesthetic function." (1977: 22).

With regard to metonymy – and the same is true of metaphor since the two tropes are almost always constantly linked and used in close proximity in any poetic text – there is a metonymy of factual similarity where the metonymic phrase might also be embedded within a metaphoric text and vice versa; a metonymy of imputed similarity, where the metonymy provides added meanings within the whole text (stanza or poem); a metonymy of parallels, where the levels of meanings within the poem are established through the use of patterns; and artifice, which is arrived at through analysis of all these levels and considers the whole meanings of the poem as more than the internal construction of it. There is also a meta-metonymic similarity which arises when the metonym is expressed by the associations which arise from the text but are not part of the text itself. Perhaps, with reference to Littlemore, these are exophoric-metonyms. Jones' poetry is just such an example of this phenomenon.

This chapter has been explorative rather than definitive. The application of Jakobson's theories of poetic function and his classification of the metonym and the metaphor has informed the discussion. It has been conclusively demonstrated in the examples of poetry analysed above, that the use of the metonym in poetry is not only frequent but also has some complex structures not employed in more prosaic texts. The chapter has also argued that linguistics is only one tool for the analysis of the metonym, that the complexity of the poetic metonym requires a semiotic analysis of structure as well. The use of rhetorical definitions can also contribute to the analysis. The Formalist understanding of poetic function with its incorporation of movement as a value within it, further enhances time, as well as place, as a particular expression of the metonym. This is a hitherto unresearched area of the metonym. There was evidence of just such a metonym of time in the Rosemary Tonks poem discussed above. Further contributions to the modern definitions and discussions of metonymy would be very rewarding.

Arising from the praxis of the poems in the above chapter, it has been indicated that there is an emergence of varieties of portrayal of the self. The portrayal of the poet, the self in each of these poems is different – Wardle suggests the presence of the greater force of the city over its inhabitants, and herself as one of them; Tonks' poem highlights how the persona of the poet is irretrievably altered by forces from her own past; Lopez presents an artfully created lack of persona; Jones presents multiple voices. As has also been demonstrated, in the poetic examples analysed above, the portrayal of the self in poetry is enriched through the use of metonymic juxtaposition. The next chapter considers how, with reference to the theory of shifters and deictics, the role of the self is expressed within a city poetic genre.

# Chapter 5
# Self and city poetry: Jakobson, deictics and shifters

Jakobson's analysis of deictics and shifters is significant because he does not, as the history of linguistics indicates, combine the two categories. Bühler's theory, as one of the earliest explorations of the combined categories is discussed below. Jakobson's theory of shifters: "Shifters, Verbal Categories and The Russian Verb" (Jakobson: 1984[1950/57]) which was published in his book *Russian and Slavic Grammar* (Mouton: 1984), includes interpretation of the spoken word and the first and second person pronouns. Critics of his theory have pointed out that he does not consider that his analysis of shifters applies to the written word. As a preliminary context for this significant point, Katie Wales (2001) does not mention shifters. Though she summarizes, with reference to Levinson, in her earlier book of 1996: "Jakobson calls the 1PPs and 2PPs [first person and second person pronouns] "shifters" (*embrayeurs*), since their referents are not fixed or stable, but shift according to the situation, as participants take turns to speak. Speakers become addressees, and vice versa: the use of 1PP or 2PP is therefore essentially context-dependent" (Levinson 1987: 57) (1996: 51).

For the purposes of this chapter, the type of message referred to is poetic. In the second part of the chapter there is praxis to accompany the theory of shifters, through one of Jakobson's own poems, written under the pseudonym "Jaljagrov" (1992 [circa 1914]). The term poetic indicates not only poetry but all word patterning – so the type could also include prose. The message is the words of the text itself – which of course, may also include the spoken word. But here is Jakobson's own defining quotation from his paper on shifters:

> A message sent by its addresser must be adequately perceived by its receiver. Any message is encoded by its sender and is to be decoded by its addressee. The more closely the addressee approximates the code used by the addresser, the higher is the amount of information obtained. Both the message (M) and the underlying code (C) are vehicles of linguistic communication, but both of them function in a duplex manner; they may at once be utilized and referred to (= pointed at). Thus a message may refer to the code or to another message, and on the other hand, the general meaning of a code unit may imply a reference *(renvoi)* to the code or to the message. Accordingly four DUPLEX types must be distinguished; 1) two kinds of CIRCULARITY – message referring to message (M/M) this is reported speech – speech within a speech; and code referring to code (C/C) [these are proper names – where someone's name does not do more than denote a particular person, there is no characteristic implied in a name – even 'Fido' the dog may not be faithful] 2) two kinds of OVERLAPPING – message referring to code (M/C) and code referring to message (C/M) these are the shifters proper which need the message in order to interpret the code. (1984: 41)

Here, with reference to shifters, it is Jakobson's category of Code/Message from his communication theory, which is of interest. He places his analysis within the context of speech which is something which has given rise to discussion (Fludernik: 1991). It is argued by the current author, that whether the Code/Message is spoken or written does not affect an understanding of shifters, especially within the poetic code.

Jakobson states that the term "shifters" originated with Jespersen (1923). He refers to Peirce's definition of the personal pronoun as an indexical symbol: "According to Peirce, a symbol (e.g. the English word *red*) is associated with the represented object by a conventional rule, while an index (e.g. the act of pointing) is in existential relation with the object it represents. Shifters combine both functions and belong therefore to the class of INDEXICAL SYMBOLS" (1984: 42/3). He also refers to Bühler's treatment of shifters as "mere indices", in other words the meaning of the personal pronoun is subsumed by its deictic function, its capacity as a pointing word. Jakobson wrote: "Every shifter, however, possesses its own general meaning. Thus *I* means the addresser (and *you*, the addressee) of the message to which it belongs." (1984: 43). Jakobson's breadth of reference to differing theoreticians also includes references to Husserl, and Bertrand Russell. Jakobson refers to children's acquisition of language in order to illustrate his points. He writes of: "[the] difficulties in defining the general meaning of the term *I* (or *you*), which signifies the same intermittent function of different subjects" (1984: 43).

A proper noun can also shift as is indicated by the following exchange: "'I met Florrie last week.'/'Who is Florrie?'(perplexed)/'Florrie is your mother' (also perplexed)/(Pause) 'Oh you mean Nana!'" In this example the personal naming crosses a generation by the last speaker as she refers to her own mother as 'Nana' – i.e. the name her children give their grandmother, Florrie. The spoken example, as reported and written here, indicates that the existence and function of the shifter is not affected by whether the words are heard or written. The particular use of the shifter had to be explained but was eventually both clear and acceptable as communication. Does the shifting have a special function in poetry as opposed to prose? As stated at the outset of the chapter, shifters are persistently included with deictics. It is interesting to note that Keith Green, in his PhD thesis: *A Study of Deixis in Relation to Lyric Poetry* (1992) has argued that there is no specific poetic deictic. His definition of deixis includes, as do almost all other analysts, shifters as part of a deictic category.

As shifters are usually considered to be a part of deixis, it is worthwhile to briefly examine the history of the development of the deictic category. Bühler (1982 [1934]) places the shifter firmly within a deictic category – the *origo-deixis* – that of the "I" within the "here" and "now" and he uses a diagram to interpret this (1982: 117) (see Figure 5):

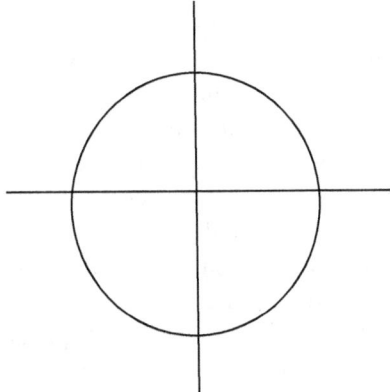

**Figure 5:** Bühler's diagram of deictic relationships.

He outlines a number of different categories of deixis, and for Bühler, the *origo-deixis* is the category which encompasses the shifter. He wrote:

> My claim is that if this arrangement is to represent the deictic field of human language, three deictic words must be placed where the O is, namely the deictic words *now, here, I*; ... the first demands, look at me, an acoustic phenomenon, and take me as a mark of moment; as a mark of place, says the second; and the third, as a mark of the sender (or characteristic of the sender). (2011: 117/8)

For Bühler, deixis is expressed through the words which denote position: "in front – behind, right – left, above – below" (2011: 145) and so on. Although these largely fall into the category of adverbs of time and place, other parts of speech also denote deixis. "The detective sits writing; the secretary stands waiting". The juxtaposition of the two phrases constructs deixis through the implied physical placing and timing of these two individuals. This is constructed through the use of the verbs. However, a much broader application of deixis can easily obscure the grammatical and linguistic basis for the term. A sense of place and time adheres to almost all human language exchange. Jakobson's understanding of shifters, written around twenty years later, describes the shifter "I", as has been shown, from the point of view of the context of the spoken word and reported speech. His emphasis is on the addresser, the code/message and the addressee rather than on the deictic place and time of the origo. This is, in fact, illustrated by Jakobson's vocative use in the opening and closing lines of a poem written by him, and analysed below, which further illustrates the special context of the shifter in poetic dialogue – the "For lovers" and "O you" readily become "we" for the addressee (or reader) and this specifically draws us into the chaos of the poem and its message.

In poetry the translation from the "I" to "you" or vice versa, is all the more readily made, as poetry contains an element of the spoken voice – through the heritage of recitation. Thus a poem, where even the personal pronoun is omitted, will contain the origins of thought whereby the reader (addressee) translates the author's (addresser's) experience, as either his or her own and/or the experience of the writer. The reader of poetry is more than willing – not to suspend disbelief as in drama – but to suspend differentiation in order to assimilate the full impact of the poem. The poem invites us to be there/here and to experience the same experience that the poet describes – this is seen as the valid purpose of the poet and the poem. Veronica Forrest-Thomson (1978), who refers to Jakobson's paper on shifters, understood the artifice of deictics and shifters in poetry very well. Her analysis of shifters in Eliot's "The Waste Land" interprets her theory of the "disconnected image" prevalent in modern and contemporary poetry. Her analysis also provides a connection to the second part of Jakobson's paper on shifters which is entitled: "Attempt to Classify Verbal Categories". She derives from Jakobson's work on participants, narrated events and verb tenses, an understanding that verbal tenses can shift in the use of verbs in poetry as well as pronouns. Of shifters she wrote:

> A contrast between 'now' and 'yesterday' of 'five years ago' in a poem does not lead us out into an empirical situation but tells us that a temporal contrast will be an important device for thematic organisation; and the same holds true for reference to 'I', 'we' and 'you': these oppositions, lifted away from external contexts, limit the invasion of the external world and provide scope for internal thematic expansion ... The fictionalized 'we', which refers not to an external class of persons but to a shifting function within the poem ['Homage to Sextus Propertius' by Pound], helps to distance the language from particular external contexts and to associate first-person pronouns with the self-reflexive process of reading and writing poetry. (1978: 35)

Analysis of shifters and deictics is only briefly referred to here, and it is now developed with reference to Formalist praxis. Jakobson, himself, wrote poetry as a young man. His entire poetic output is small. Praxis of one of his poems (see below), provides insight into how the shifter provides interpretation, not only of how it exists in its own right, rather than an aspect of deixis, but also as an example of city poetry. He adopted the pseudonym "Jaljagrov", a name which, in Russian, includes a coded reference to his own self (Vallier: 1987: 291–304). His poetry, which has been translated by Stephen Rudy, is available in *My Futurist Years* (1992: 249–261).

A focus of this chapter is city poetry. Mayakovsky, Jakobson's friend and contemporary, also wrote city poetry. His relationship with the city seems to be often negative. An early poetic image by Mayakovsky is that he "goes out through the city leaving his soul on the spears of houses, shred by shred" (Jakobson 1987: 289).

Although the early years of the twentieth century was a prolific and exciting artistic time in Russia, the Futurist relationship which poets had with the city is perhaps less sympathetic than artistic representations of the time, for example the work of Elena Guro and Olga Rozanova, with whom Jakobson printed a collection of verse. The title of this collection was *Gniga* (1916), which is a pun on book and gnat in Russian. Jakobson argues, quoting Khlebnikov, that "It is not new subject matter that defines genuine innovation." (taken from Jakobson's essay: "Modern Russian Poetry: Velimir Khlebnikov" (Brown 1973: 61). But he acknowledges the impact of the city, writing in the same essay, that: "The city offers material that fits neatly the structure of the verbal paradox and similar structures ... Urbanism offers opportunities for the application of a number of poetic devices: hence the urban verses of Mayakovsky and Khlebnikov." (1973: 66).

A poet himself, Khlebnikov, a contemporary and colleague of Jakobson, as quoted in the same essay, personified the city in the following way: "There's a certain fat gourmand who's fond of impaling human hearts on his spit, and who derives a mild enjoyment from the sound of hissing and breaking as he sees the bright red drops falling into the fire and flowing down – and the name of that fat man is – 'the city'." (Brown 1973: 66). This interpretation of the city can be compared with that of the Italian poet, Marinetti, who was also their contemporary. The following quote is from one of Marinetti's own manifestoes – also quoted in the same essay:

> We shall sing of the great crowds tossed about by work by pleasure, or revolt. the many-colored and polyphonic surf of revolutions in modern capitals; the nocturnal vibration of the arsenals and the yards under their violent electric moons; the gluttonous railway stations swallowing smoky serpents; the factories hung from the clouds by the ribbons of their smoke; the bridges leaping like athletes hurled over the diabolical cutlery of sunny rivers; the adventurous steamers that sniff the horizon; the broad-chested locomotives, prancing on the rails like great steel horses curbed by long pipes, and the gliding flight of airplanes whose propellers snap like a flag in the wind, like the applause of an enthusiastic crowd.
> (1973: 61)

If you combine the awareness of urbanism with futurism then the background dynamics of Futurist verse become clearer. Boris Gasparov (2014: 88, 89), reveals that Jakobson and his contemporaries – the futurniks – *budetliani* – regarded Marinetti with great suspicion. Livshits accused Marinetti of being superficial "without even trying to get beyond the surface of etymological categorization." (2014: 89). Marinetti's language is powerful and emotive, but Jakobson and his contemporaries were more interested in theoretical construction.

Jakobson's poem "How Many Fragments ... " is referred to, by Jakobson many years later, as an "oblique satire" on Mayakovsky's urban poetry (Rudy 1992: 343, note on Poem 7). Its overall mood is of both rapid movement and negative disassociation between the human and the power of the city. It is referred to here as it provides an example of how city poetry has an affinity to the use of deictics and shifters. The analysis which follows, is Formalist. Here is the full text of the poem, in English translation by Stephen Rudy:

How Many Fragments Have Scattered

For (O) lovers of coloured cardboard boxes and powdered elements
The city a lamppost the street's din and a car's horn the daughter of rooms etc.
Along their shattered nerves like words or crazy verses
Juggling the intersections the city's nights dance
What grief the street people are turning glued to a car's wheels
The sun Bunsen burner the sky over us coquettes a skirt spleen
The ill-fated one is run over by a truck and becomes a lump
The signboard thinks it's the city's friend
If it gets unstitched by passers-by (sic)
No city
It's just an absence of blue leit-lines
That's why that one invaded destroyed measure
as if it were a chimera
And don't seek
Why there's a superabundance of usual caresses. Again and again
Is that why all the colors have flown off the peacock's tail
And all that's left is the emptiness show your tickets
As of old the gazes of tongue-tied eternity shush
Four eyes the legs of a Viennese chair
It blows eveningly and windily
O you city ensured inhumanly'     (Jaljagrov: Jakobson:1992: 253)

The Formalist analysis of "How Many Fragments..." begins with examination of the shifters in the poem. The first line: "For lovers of colored cardboard boxes..." (line 1) is, arguably, a vocative line, containing a "hidden" shifter, which might be expressed as "O [you] lovers of cardboard boxes...". "Along their shattered nerves..." (line 3) is almost certainly a reference to "The lovers" in the first line, or perhaps a description of an attribute of the street. And the reference is combined with the deictic "Along" which describes both place and movement in one word. The fragmented grammar provides another dissociative technique – the association between the lovers, streets and nerves is indirect and blurred ensuring that the reader associates the nerves, not only with the lines (or streets) of the city, but also with human sensation.

Jakobson's "literariness" uses both linguistics and semiotics as a foundation for the interpretation of the text. In this poem – especially given that it is both a Futurist poem, and studied in translation – the parts of speech can be difficult to interpret. Any subsequent errors are the present author's. There is a shifter in line 6 – "us" and subsequent shifters occur towards the end of the poem: "your" (line 17) and "you" in the last line, which is also a vocative use of the pronoun. It is interesting to note that vocatives are defined by Jakobson, in his essay "Linguistics and Poetics", as decoder-oriented (1987: 67/68 [1960]. However, the hidden vocative in the first line seems to be addressed to the city inhabitants whilst the vocative in the last line is directed to the city itself. This was a point made by Professor Warwick Gould at a seminar where the poem was first analysed (19th March 2013).

It is important to remember that Jakobson was both linguist and semiotician. His semiotic analysis of Blake's poem "Infant Sorrow" in his essay "On The Verbal Art of William Blake and other Poet Painters" (1987 [1970]) is in contrast with his more linguistic analysis of Yeats' "Sorrow of Love" (1987 [1977]), although Jakobson agrees with Yeats in the introductory paragraph to his analysis of the poem, that patterning of words is more important than "mere story-telling". Analysis of "How Many Fragments . . . " is therefore partly one of choice, either to lean towards the linguistic, or to include the linguistic in a more semiotic analysis. The following analysis is hampered by the fact that the poem is translated from Russian and therefore only provides an indication of the kind of detailed analysis which Jakobson himself provides of any particular poem. Given that the title of the poem includes a disrupted meaning – the noun – 'fragments' – and the verb 'have scattered', then apart from noting the shifters in the poem, it would seem appropriate to also investigate how these shifters are affected by or influence the nouns and verbs in the poem.

Beginning with the title, the patterning of the words and grammar is, in itself, fragmented: fragments are, in the usual sense, the result of scattering rather than the cause of it: in a more usual prosaic sense the title would be "How Many Have Scattered Fragments . . . " There is an inversion of subject and object, of theme and rheme, not into a true passive verb because the inverted object is inanimate – fragments cannot be the actor (subject) controlling the verb – in this case "have scattered". If the verbs in the poem are categorised then a patterning can begin to emerge: the verb in the title is past perfect –and see line 16, where there is a past perfect question "have flown off". The meaning here, as in the title, is an inversion of actor and action: in a prosaic context, it is probably the peacock that has flown off not the colours. There are other simple past tense verbs: "invaded", "destroyed" are centrally placed in the text of the poem (line 12); "ensued" is in the last line (line 21); the past tenses are placed at the beginning, middle and end of the poem. The "glued" of line 5 appears to be almost an adjectival part of the present participle "are turning" which precedes it, although with a comma between the two words "turning, glued" would indicate two verbs placed together – one present participle and one simple past tense. The body of the poem is expressed in the present tense (lines 4–20). There is a present participle in line 4 "juggling" and "dance"- present tense; line 5 "are turning"; line 6 "coquettes" – which is really a noun made into a verb; passive present in line 7 "is run over" (this is not an inversion of actor and action as in the title and in line 16), followed by the present "becomes"; line 8 "thinks" – present, also "it's" for "it is"; line 9 "gets unstitched" – passive present; line 11 "It's" for "it is"; line 12 "measure" – is this a present tense or a noun?; line 14 "don't seek" present negative; line 15 "is" as in "there's"; line 16 "is"; line 17 "all that's left is" followed by present tense imperative: "show"; line 18 "shush"; line 20 "blows" – present tense. There is one verb tense which indicates a future, and this is the subjunctive in line 13 "were" – expressed future wish.

The title of the poem, the "is run over" in line 7 and the "gets unstitched" in line 9 are all a direct expression of fragmentation – this is picked up in line 16 "have flown off" – so the expressed fragmentation is in the passive tense. This increases a sense of dissociation – the question asked is: who is doing the fragmenting, the running over, the unstitching, the flying off? Respectively the answers are: the fragments, the truck, the passers-by and the colors. Within the structure the inanimate object as subject (except for "passers-by") renders the human attribute of the passers-by as less animate by association. The central section of the poem contains seven uses of the verb to be (lines 8–17), including the use of "becomes" and "were". The shifters are placed in the opening line (hidden) and in the last line, where the shifter is open to full view, as vocatives; in line 3, "their", the exact reference is unclear – does "their" refer to the lovers or the various features of the city itself in the proximal lines?; the "us" in line 6 is a pronoun which is overwhelmed by the structure and content of the line as a whole: "The sun Bunsen burner the sky over us coquettes a skirt spleen"; and in line 17 "your" where the placing within the imperative "show your tickets" can seem to include a deictic component but also serves to disassociate the human within the city environment – the command has no stated operator or subject.

Briefly – the nouns in the poem are numerous, forming almost one third of the total word number. Fragmentation governs the structure of the poem. Words which overtly interpret the fragmentation are: line 1 "powdered" (perhaps also with the sense of clouded or murky/misty); line 3 "shattered" and "crazy", "juggling"; line 9 "unstitched"; line 13 "chimera". But the chaos is made apparent largely through the interrupted and broken syntax. Sometimes it is difficult to ascertain the part of speech – as in "the city a lamppost the street's din" – are there implied commas in the line "the city, a lamppost, the street's din" or is there a hidden metaphor in the line: "the city: (is) a lamppost the street's din"; and in another line: "the sky over us coquettes a skirt spleen" – the word "coquettes" is a verb in this context but it is not normally used as a verb, there is a sense that the word "spleen" may also somehow have a double grammatical function – what is a "skirt spleen"? It would seem to be either two nouns, used one after the other, or one adjective and one noun. Or is the meaning more metaphorical in the sense of a skirt-sky is a spleen?

What is clear is that the central lines of the poem are full of things which are in a state of negation, absence and unreality – see Lines 8–15:

> "The signboard thinks it's the city's friend
> If it gets unstitched by passers-by (sic)
> No city
> It's just an absence of blue leit-lines
> That's why that one invaded destroyed measure
> as if it were a chimera
> And don't seek
> Why there's a superabundance of usual caresses. . ."

The "signboard" (line 1) would seem to be a reference to a billboard or advertisement hoarding. But the subsequent words indicate that what it shows is not the most important message. A speech made by Lenin to young people in 1920, a date almost contemporaneous with the writing of the poem, uses the word in just such a way: "We have no need of cramming, but we do need to develop and perfect the mind of every student with a knowledge of fundamental facts. Communism will become an empty word, a mere signboard, and a Communist a mere boaster, if all the knowledge he has acquired is not digested in his mind." (Lenin: 1920). The reference, contained in line 11, appears to refer to a painting by Burlyuk, exhibited in Moscow in 1912: "Leit-Line conceived according to The Assyrian Method and the Principle of Flowing Colouring" (Howard 1992: 146). The words: "absence of blue leit-lines", in line 11, connects with the line: "juggling the intersections of the city's dance" in line 4 –the lines and attributes of the city are visible and invisible – apparent and absent. The line "It's just an absence of blue-leit lines" is physically the central line of the poem. The analysis of both of these images – the signboard and the leit-lines – take the reader out of the Formalist critical process.

With reference to punctuation: full stops occur at the end of line 2, though this is likely to be because an abbreviation is used – 'etc.' and within line 15. There is no closing full stop. There is no question mark after the question posed from line 16 onwards. The meaning of the central lines of the poem imply that the passers-by unstitch the signboard and create "No city/It's just an absence of blue leit-lines". Significantly there is a word in brackets "(sic)". Within this context, the word is a deictic – as in the sense of here it all is, this is just as it is, thus. But the brackets take the reader out of the text and closer to the poet – there is an implied encoder comment here. The poet can be seen as placed between the poem and the reader at the central point. It can be argued that the central placing of this one word provides an axis or turning sensation to the images, and the line "No city" is a further jolt – is the city real or not? Or is it just the fragments which are real?

One last Formalist exploration of the poem uses the Jakobsonian interpretation of iconic shapes within the poem. The ensuing diagrammatic analysis (see Figure 6) is reproduced here and explained below:

How Many Fragments Have Scattered

For **(O)** lovers of coloured cardboard **boxes** and powdered elements
The city a lamppost the street's din and a car's horn the daughter of **rooms** etc.
Along **their** shattered nerves like words or crazy verses
Juggling the intersections the city's nights dance
What grief the street people are turning glued to a **car's wheels**
The sun Bunsen burner the sky *over us* coquettes a skirt spleen
The ill-fated one is run *over by a truck* and becomes a **lump**
The **signboard** thinks it's the city's friend
If it gets unstitched *by* passers-*by* (sic)
**No city**
It's just an absence of blue leit-lines
That's why that one invaded destroyed measure
as if it were a chimera
And don't seek
Why there's a superabundance of usual caresses. *Again* and *again*
Is that why all the colors have flown *off* the peacock's tail
And all that's left is the **emptiness** show **your** tickets
*As* of old the gazes of tongue-tied **eternity** shush
Four **eyes** the legs of a Viennese chair
It blows eveningly and windily
'**O you** city ensured inhumanly'

Jaljagrov

**Figure 6:** Poem with diagonals.

Here the words which denote squares are highlighted in **bold and underlined** (boxes, rooms, car, truck, signboard) and the words which denote circles, everything, nothing – are highlighted in **bold** (etc., wheels, sun, lump, No city, emptiness, eternity, eyes, O). Connectors have been drawn to guide the eye through the poem towards words which explore key ideas. Is it wide of the mark to see how the upturned chair legs (line 19) are loosely represented? A Viennese chair (line 19) is a bent wood chair invented by Thonet in Vienna in the mid 19th century and exported around the world. It is a chair that incorporates movement in both its physical manufacture and in its final form. The wood is steamed and glued into curved shapes. Is the reference in the poem one of something old-fashioned or something refashioned for the purposes of the poem? If there are four eyes then the chair is upturned showing the base of its four legs, regardless of whether it is a Viennese chair or not. The poem can be understood without this background information, but having it certainly enhances the meaning. Once again, the information takes the analysis outside the Formalist process.

Is this poem an integrated expression of chaotic movement, of things turned upside down, a truly Futurist expression in words? Antipov Pavel's painting: "Dance on the Viennese Chair" (2010) (https://forum.artinvestment.ru) is a recent Futurist style painting which includes a tumbling Viennese chair just to illustrate the point. Lastly, all shifters are underlined with a dotted line, all deictics shown in **bold italics**; there is a nexus of deictics of place ("over" and "by" used twice each) around lines 6–9; and in lines 15–18, the deictics are of time rather than place. But the vocative, implied at the beginning of the poem, and openly used in the last line, frames the poem.

For Jakobson a poem demonstrates a structure which can be analysed with reference to syntax, linguistics, and the semiotics of verbal patterning. Is it possible to apply principles which arise from Jakobson's later theories to the poem written by a young Jakobson, written originally in Russian and studied here in translation? Can the shattered nerves, crazy, juggling intersections, unstitched, blue leit-lines, be somehow understood to iconically construct the mechanics of a city: "O you city ensued inhumanly"? It can be argued that Jakobson's poem responds best to being read as bracketed by the vocatives of the beginning and end of the poem – encoder addresses decoder – and that within this there is the chaos of the city. For Jakobson, the human comprehension of the city, governs it. Or as Allen Fisher has asked, during his interviews with Scott Thurston (2001), and with reference to his own work (of which more below) why does the end of the poem have to be read last? The process of the text may be more clearly understood with the use of a different sequence.

Rather than go back to Jaljagrov's poem again, the idea of sequence can be developed with reference to a second example of city poetry: Allen Fisher's "African Boog", in *Gravity* (2004: 37–43). This poem has been chosen as it demonstrates Jakobsonian Formalist theory and the deictic of time as expressed in verb tenses. The poem is unfortunately too long to quote in full. Two short extracts are provided below. Fisher takes three quotations from Jakobson's article "Verbal Communications" (1972: 72–80). They are as follows: "Tomorrow we went to the forest"; "It happened I found myself tomorrow" and "It was tomorrow". The recurrent theme of the poem is in the repeated similar phrases which are quoted here: "moments when the go different two-beat series"; "Moments when series go different the two-beat"; "Moments when go different the two-beat series"; "Two moments when the two-beat series coincide"; "Moments when the two-beat series go different"; "Two moments when series coincide the two-beat"; "A mix of two-beat moments invigorates texture"; "Two moments two-beat series coincide when the"; "Two moments series coincide when the two-beat." (2004: 37–43).

The repeated phrase with its variations is interspersed with phrases that indicate a cross referencing of temporal and placing significance: "Juxtapose time a-cross-rhythm"; "Topological correspondences unfold similar linguistics together."; "Stratigraphical completeness sifted in differences"; "Juxtapose harmony-notes vertically chords"; "Older parallels and pseudo-parallels overlap"; "Juxtapose timbre vibrato to patterns vertically and horizontally"; "Speech patterned horizontally and vertically"; "'Temporal separation a tenacious illusion'" (2004: 37–43). These proximally juxtaposed combinations of phrases illumine the temporal shifting inherent in the quoted Jakobson phrases and demonstrate that there is an overtly explored temporal shifting or cross patterning examined as a thread throughout the poem.

The nature of time passing, inherent in both the verbal tense and the adverbs of time, indicate categories of deixis. The use of the terms, *anaphora* and *cataphora*, with respect to deixis, originate with Bühler (2011: 138). These derive from the actual construction of Greek texts which were written on scrolls: that what had come before was above the text – *anaphora* – and that which was to come, was below the text – *cataphora*. These terms are used by Bühler for the deictic defining of verbal tenses and adverbs of time – past, present and future, now and then, ahead. The phrases from Jakobson, which Fisher uses in the poem, contain a looking ahead (tomorrow) and a looking back (yesterday). When the overall fragmentary nature of the poem is also considered, then the Futurist sense of strong movement, here a strong chaotic movement of time, is a means whereby the city is expressed poetically. This is not a simple use of deictics, and Fisher's poetry is more than willing to express both borderline and impossible combinations of meanings.

The meaning of Fisher's poem is further fragmented, strongly highlighted by the apparently random use of the shifters "he" and "she" and the dislocational deictic phrase of place near the beginning of the poem "Watching myself burning from a distance". The action, both physical and intellectual is enclosed by opening and closing lines which refer to riding a bike in London. The different fonts used are as actually used in the poem:

> Went dicing on my bike
>     Disappearance
> Meaning given by timbre
> Relational invariants from a flux
> She lives in advance of her days
>     Speed..... (2004: 37)

and:

> 'Temporal separation a tenacious illusion'
> Every turn of the path seductions
>     Entrenching the desires of others

# Chapter 5 Self and city poetry: Jakobson, deictics and shifters — 125

> As best you can rapped from the brain bourne
> Jump on bike, figure of eight around rose beds, to the blackboard. (2004: 43)

The use of the pronoun "you" in the penultimate line of the poem suggests a further complication of shifter – that of an internal dialogue – an indication of levels of shifters within a text. This brief survey of temporal and placing deixis serves to indicate that further study both of shifters and adverbial and verb tense deixis would reveal many forms and levels. How is a nexus of placing, time and person relevant for the structure of city poetry? As an illustration of the nexus, the poem "Wrestle", taken from the fourth section entitled "Fame" of a long poem about London: *Shades of Light: A Triumph of City* (Coghill: 2006) by the current author, is discussed. This section of the poem was constructed with the use of Adobe Indesign software. Two versions of the poem are replicated here. The first is the published text, and the second version has the axial lines drawn across the text, as illustrated in the Jakobsonian analysis of the Jaljargrov poem above.

"Wrestle" is a poem which interprets specific points of the axis – syntagm and paradigm (see Figures 7 and 7 continued below). It is also a poem which is an experiment with themes, rhemes and the transition between the two. The city is the theme (see left of page), the transition (verbs) runs across the bottom and the rhemes – the humans – occupy the central space between the two. That space appears to rise into the distance, providing perspective. Using the computer software, lines were drawn where wanted and then text written along them. The perspective is an abstract street, with a foregrounded base. The themes and rhemes categorised in the poem are not expressed in the way they are usually defined with reference to the grammar of sentences. Some of the verbs appertain to the themes rather than the rhemes and this provides clustering, the meanings of which over-ride the usual clear-cut definitions of the terms.

This is an iconic poem, in that it expresses the paradigmatic and the syntagmatic axes of Jakobson's poles of language visually, and the human expression – that of the city-dwellers – is visually expressed in the space between the axes. The verbs on the paradigm are single action active present tense verbs. The verbs on the syntagm are present participles (indicating repeated actions) and there is a specific single defined person and action "my very eyes impulse participates". There are more verbs on the vertical than in the horizontal line across the bottom. Both paradigm and syntagm have 23 syllables.

The paradigm has many "s" sounds. The text in the space has a significant number of earthy references: "salt of the", "wastes", "not built up", "top dressing", "clean fresh", "fresh food". There is a counterpoint between "gang's leaders" and "exploding docks" which point to references to organised crime vs. references

**126** — Chapter 5  Self and city poetry: Jakobson, deictics and shifters

windows lance doors covet shadows leer streets shift dust gathers vision scars so far so stasis rules

writing graffiti salt of the

'the gang's leaders wanted televisions to watch....

hazard large enough

new conservatory assisted roof

in our jail 150 people killed

....'the world cup'

familiar slight

different place later wastes

the thames estuary

discomfort outragge runs on top dressing

all is well appropriate hub

not built up yet

keep tabs in a

clean fresh

accept stasis levels are low fearful of

general way

pulled down brought up to date new

exploding boat docks

want fresh food.

new kitchen new bathroom

happened moving faster taking place before my very eyes impulse participates rules

**Wrestle**
**105**

**Figure 7:** "Wrestle" without and with diagonals.

# Chapter 5 Self and city poetry: Jakobson, deictics and shifters

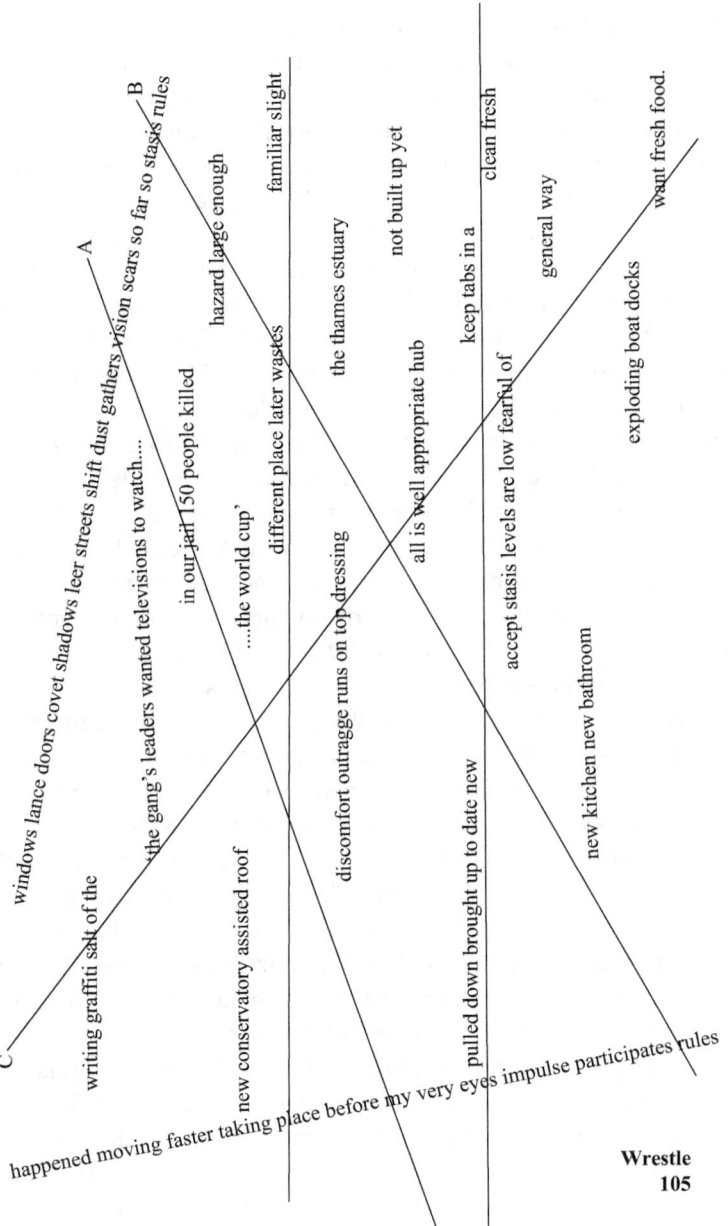

**Figure 7** (continued)

to organised efforts to be in touch with growing and fresh food. There is a "W" in the title and then also at the beginning of the poem and in last phrase.

Where is the pivot – the implied cross point between the vertical and horizontal? The only personal pronouns are "before my very eyes" and "our" – "in our jail". There are twenty human expressions in the space of the poem – is the pivot round the tenth – "the thames estuary"? Or is it to the physical centre of the text: "top dressing" – human existence as essentially "top dressing", if so, then should it be moved slightly further to the right or top of the page depending on which way up the page is? Or is it where the eye is led – to the top right corner: "want fresh food.", with the full stop indicating a final statement? There is no sense of a glorious future or positive horizon because the last phrase indicates the desire for an apparently unmet basic human requirement – fresh food.

Does the poem express the dynamic theme of the whole poem, Wrestle vs rules/stasis, the two words at the top of the paradigm? The poem demonstrates very fragmented thought, though there is some consecutive expression: "the gang leaders wanted television to watch . . . the world cup". Wrestle is echoed in "stasis", "wastes", "estuary". Sometimes it seems as if the themes are mentioned without additional reference – "hub", "tabs". Is there a combination of specifics and generic – "new conservatory assisted roof" and "stasis levels", "general way" and "thames estuary", "clean fresh" – specific vs. abstract? The axes in the poem seem to be visually acting as a pincer movement – as well as a construction of perspective – this is a metaphoric visual depiction, the visual perspective of words on the page constructs the human environment. Everything gets squeezed out of the people and the physical distance leaves room only for the basic cry "want fresh food."

The space in the poem is occupied by human activity, emotion and some references to physical environment – "conservatory", "estuary", "new kitchen, new bathroom". The first reaction is to deal with the poem as a sequence of metonyms with their attendant attributes: contiguous/random; linked/fragmented. There is also the metaphoric quality of torque, because the fragmentation over-rides the grammatical construction and any sense of overall meaning. There is little repetition and no apparent cohesion (for more information on these terms, see Chapter Two). There is some deixis: "down, "in" (twice), "later", on top", "yet". There is perhaps an emphatic deictic in the phrase: "before my **very** eyes". There is little sense of time as there is only one deictic of time, "later", and this perhaps shifts the controlling tenor of the poem towards the metaphoric paradigm. But there are no similes or metaphors in the language used, no use of synonyms or simultaneity. The over-riding emotional balance of the poem is between rules/stasis and the iconic sense of striving to escape the boundaries of these rules, by looking for a departure in the top right-hand corner. Then the eye travels back to the human flotsam on the way – it seems that the poem culminates on the water though it starts out with reference to buildings – the jail, the conservatory, "new kitchen new bathroom". The poem has movement in it in the sense that the buildings give way to various possible future and emotional options: "not built up yet", "thames estuary", "familiar slight", "clean fresh". The movement provides a time element and therefore the poem does inhabit the metonymic environment rather than the metaphoric.

Jakobson's Formalist analysis of Baudelaire's "Les Chats" (1987: 180–197), now provides the categories for a second analysis of "Wrestle" below. His list of selected categories is based on this particular poem – "Les Chats". A different poem will have different areas of analysis or a different emphasis of the important aspects for study. The following analysis provides the proof that any Formalist analysis of a poem must change with the requirements of the text (poem) analysed. However, what emerges from the use of Jakobson's own headings for analysis is that there is extensive common ground, despite the very great difference in the form and style of the poem. The intention here is to take each heading and develop it or leave it to one side:

**rhyme pattern** – there is no rhyme.

**feminine and masculine word endings** – this is not so important in English as French, but there is a predominance of masculine single syllable words at the end of each cluster, but see killed, dressing – also "of the, enough, up yet, in a, fearful of".

**how the beginnings and ends of lines are constructed** – on the theme vertical the words all begin with consonants; on the transition horizontal the only words which begin with vowels are in "eyes impulse". In the textual space the words beginning with vowels are: "our", "assisted", "outrage", "estuary", "appropriate", "is", "are", "accept", "exploding" – only "estuary" is a substantive, and the vowels "o" and "a" predominate.

**patterns of vowels/consonants; parts of speech/prefixes and suffixes** – there are several "s" and related sounds on the theme paradigm, but otherwise there is no over-riding prevalence of any particular vowel or consonant. The rheme part of the poem is of course comprised of the phrases which occur after the theme and verb (transition). However, in the poem, the theme vertical contains both substantives and present tense verbs and the phrases "so far so". The transition horizontal echoes the phrase with "before my very". But the transitional meaning is expressed not just through verbs, including participles, there are two adverbs – "faster" and "before" – and two substantives – "impulse", and "rules". But "faster" and "impulse" both have close connections to movement. "Rules" in both the vertical and horizontal is a verb not a substantive.

**stanza form** – the vertical and horizontal lines form one external stanza each and the internal and perhaps central stanza is comprised by the rheme phrases within this constructed space (but see the construction of the diagonals above).

**horizontal/vertical correspondences** – the page is governed by the horizontal transitional line as this is the right way up on the page (12 words). The eye then reads the vertical (17 words) as it appears to be a consecutive sentence at first glance. The rhemes in the space of the page are disconcertingly disparate, although some of them are connected through meaning on closer inspection (20 phrases). The software has enabled these phrases to be placed so that they are obviously not in a sequence. There are two apparently complete sentences in the rheme space: "the gang's leaders wanted television to watch the world cup" and "in our jail 150 people killed" – the second sentence would seem to be in answer to a question. The poem has two vertical lines drawn through it, in the Equivalence Diagram (Figure 7) above, in an attempt to designate how the poem occupies three "stanzas" or textual spaces. In the left hand "stanza" there are a number of transitions (15 verbs) amongst the rhemes: "writing" "wanted", "to watch", "killed", "assisted" (qualifier?), "wastes" (predominance of "w" and "a" letters); in the central "stanza" or section: "runs on", "built up", "pulled down", "brought up", "keep"; and in the third "stanza" or space, the verbs are: "accept", "are", "exploding", "want". These three "stanzas"– see above, each have 6,5,4 verbs in them respectively. The action decreases through the rheme text, with the reduced final verb of expressed need: "want". This takes the text back to the first group of "w" verbs in the first section of rhemes providing an echo of the participle "writing" – this is an active participle of political involvement.

**diagonals (which are constructed by grammar)** – In an effort to find the subject matter, the personal theme, the shifters, within the poem a diagonal (A) is drawn between the two pronouns in the poem: "my" in the syntagm and "our" in the third rheme within the spatial text, then the diagonal blocks off the lower left-hand corner from the rest of the poem. If a second diagonal (B) is drawn through the two final words on each axis – "rules", then a reverse structure of the pincer movement of the paradigmatic and syntagmatic axes is revealed. This means that the words which are placed after the diagonal A on the syntagm, provide a very personal viewpoint and which include the viewpoint of reportage and a desire for action: "my very eyes impulse participates rules"; and the words placed between the diagonals A and B on the paradigm provide a very negative outcome: "vision scars so far so stasis rules": this is plastic human political effort hitting immoveable inanimate objects (see Figure 7 above).

**grammatical contents and construction of each stanza** – or perhaps each phrase. The verbs, their modifiers and tenses – are mostly present, and include some present participles, verbs with prepositions "pulled down", "built up", some past tense "wanted televisions", "killed", "assisted" (or is this an adjective?), one negative, "not built up yet", and no passive tenses. The past tenses are clustered in the top section of the rheme stanza. The lower half (or right-hand half) contains expressions which introduce a possible future: "not built up yet", "all is well", "clean fresh", "new kitchen new bathroom" and the final "want fresh food". The phrase: "pulled down brought up to date new" combines these two characteristics and is situated juxtaposed to "eyes impulse" in the syntagm.

**construction of phrases/sentences – comparison of these, the nature of their clauses** – see all the comments on the theme paradigm, the transition syntagm and the rheme space between them.

**qualities of subject matters – descriptive/abstract adjectives** – when is an adjective a verb and vice versa? There is some ambiguity here: "assisted", "exploding". The adjectives used are not strongly associated with emphasis or emotion: "large", "new", "different", "appropriate", "fearful", "general", "new", "fresh".

**synecdochic tropes** (parts for whole) – many of the rhemes represent synecdoches – can they be paired up with themes and transitions or is any kind of meaning through combination ruled out? The themes portray the parts of the city as having its own characteristics: "windows lance, doors covet". The transition syntagm combines movement with place, with the suggestion of emotion: "impulse". The rhemes can be combined with the themes: "dust gathers . . . not built up yet" but this is not a comfortable method of combining the two parts of the poem.

**or other kinds of trope** – hyponymy (whole indicated by parts) perhaps this is more rewarding – the political and riotous elements of the poem – the prison riot, graffiti, are bounded by the stasis and rules of the paradigm and syntagm developing into a fragmented past and future struggle and effect in the populous city.

Jakobson's analysis also includes:

**point of view of the observer** – see "my", "our", and some reportage. But fragmentation of overall meaning results in disassociation rather than a coherent positional viewpoint.

**whether the subject emerges from within or is perceived from without, or moves from inside to outside** – see above – it moves from the lower left-hand corner outwards to the upper right-hand corner. Perhaps it is more strongly perceived from outside the text – the process of identification is not immediate or close – analysis of the fragments is important – this requires distance.

**content as subject or object** – the poem tends towards subject vs. object.

**theme/rheme** – see paradigm and syntagm and space for rhemes (which include some transitions).

**metaphor/metonym** – very metonymic, although the theme paradigm is slightly metaphoric – see below

**Does the poem contain equivalence?** – Jakobson writes in his analysis of Baudelaire's "Les Chats", with reference to the relationship between the stanzas in the poem, "the poem has appeared to consist of systems of equivalences which fit inside one another and which offer, in their totality, the appearance of a closed system. There is, however yet another way of looking at it, whereby the poem takes on the appearance of an open system in dynamic progression from beginning to end." (1987: 195). With reference to the definition of equivalence – this is a search for balances and parallels. The following is quoted from *NPEPP*: "equivalence in poetry serves to embed the atemporal within the temporal: as the lines proceed through their sequent schemes of meaning." (1993: 380b). That is, once selected, the lines proceed along the axis of combination – the temporal axis in effect. Metaphoric synonymy and antonymy, similarity and dissimilarity are called into play here as the metaphoric paradigm projects equivalence into the combination. It is a definition of how the parts combine and balance in order to construct the whole. The paradigm is metaphoric – doors do not covet or streets shift. The first rheme: "writing graffiti salt of the" is balanced by the final phrase: "want fresh food". These are both references to elemental human conditions – "salt of the" is a metaphor for human survival and worth, "want fresh food" is the expressed wish for human survival. The diagonal (C), runs through "top dressing"; but there is no passage of time here – "stasis rules". Any equivalence in the poem does not appear to express the passage of time, but the very combination of the phrases results in a temporality (imputed temporality). Any expressed combination is strongly resisted by the fragmentary nature of the rhemes. Any sense of the future or innate desire for hope or reconstruction which might be desired by the upward movement of the eye as it reads the rhemes towards "want fresh food" is thwarted. The movement of the poem pushes the reader back to the bottom left-hand corner where there is a lacuna between the axes. This has a strongly negative impact, it appears to be a "zero sign". The words and phrases: "scars", "stasis", "hazard", "wastes", "not built up yet", "levels are low fearful", "exploding", more than counterbalance the active present tense verbs in the paradigm themes – their negative metaphoric sense also adds to a sense of detraction rather than addition. The equivalence is therefore also between these metaphoric active verbs with their negative connotations, and the browbeaten rhemes, prompted and prodded by the more emotional movement of the transitions on the syntagm – "impulse participates".

**factual similarity/iconicity** – this can be seen in the Adobe Indesign constructed visual layout of the poem

**imputed similarity/iconicity** – for example the syllable count of the two axes (23 syllables each); the suggested three sections of the poem, each of which have largely different verb forms and see the section on **horizontal/vertical correspondences** above.

**equivalence/relational equivalence = parallels** – one final consideration – does this poem bear out the idea of reverse projection expressed within the axial model, as proposed by Turner (2012: 61)? Does the metonymical syntagm project into the metaphorical paradigm, rather than the poem being governed by the metaphorical projection? The proposed reverse axes suggest that it might. The poem has both factual and imputed axes. The imputed are more personal (involving the pronouns) than the factual.

There are two references which have a source: the "exploding boat" is a reference to SS Richard Montgomery – https://en.wikipedia.org/wiki/SS_Richard_Montgomery (Accessed 16.5.20) and many other references; and for the reference to the jail riots see: "some 150 people were killed, a quarter of them policemen..." and "The Mob Takes on the State" *Economist* 2006 Vol.379, No.8478: 39/40. This was after a criminal gang, based in the prison system, launched attacks on police stations, buses and bank branches in and around Sao Paulo, Brazil's largest city. The gang's leaders opposed their imminent transfer to a maximum-security jail, and wanted televisions to watch the soccer World Cup.

Both axes culminate in the word "rules" – the two axes govern human space, the rhemes. The paradigm and syntagm are single lines fixed by an invisible interstice. The human elements are plastic within the space that they occupy. The city lays down the rules (themes) and the rules of engagement (transition) and the humans (rhemes) take up the positions available to them. The axes in the poem construct perspective – this is a metaphoric visual depiction. The pivot of the axes can be in one of three places, as suggested above. One possibility, suggests the need for a change to the structure of the poem.

There is one deictic of place in the syntagm "before" and other deictics occur in the rheme space of the poem: "of" ("salt of the earth") "in" ("in our jail"); "on" ("on top dressing"); "up" and "yet" ("not built up yet"); "up" ("brought up to date"); "of" ("fearful of") There are only two deictics of time, "yet" and "up" which indicate that there is very little sense of time in the poem, and what there is, is centrally placed in the rheme space. Such a lack could propel the controlling mood of the poem towards the metaphoric paradigm. However, the content of the poem, as seen through the analysis above, results in the metonymic sense over-riding the metaphoric.

The Formalist examination of "Wrestle" is based on many of the headings suggested by Jakobson in his analysis with Claude Lévi-Strauss of Baudelaire's "Les Chats" (1987: 180–197). His full list includes other areas of analysis, many of which have already been explored in the above analysis of "Wrestle": organisation of the rhymes; sentence construction; stanza format; parallels of different visual parts of the poem; punctuation; themes or subjects and rhemes or objects; construction of diagonal lines linking syntactical structures and subject matter; syntactical similarities/dissimilarities; comparison of animate and inanimate subjects – their syntax and placing within the poem as a whole; the construction of verbs and their placing; patterns of vowels; coordinate phrases, similarity of phrases in content, syntax or tropic characteristic – alliteration, assonance etc.; structure of sentence clauses; use of metonymy, contiguity, synecdoche, metaphor; the use of the plural; use of masculine feminine nouns; construction of imputed similarity – poetic parallelisms.

Theory and poetry can often conflict in the sense that theorists prefer theory to poetry and poets prefer poetry to theory. The same problem can occur with linguists and semioticians – the two can seem mutually exclusive. Jakobson's theories bridge the gaps between these four categories. The chapter has attempted to provide analysis of how they might be combined. The use of semiotics with reference to linguistics gives rise to the study of patterns within poetry, leading to a study of artifice. The analysis originates from Formalist "literariness", or science of poetics. The combination of the analyses applies not only to different forms of poetry but also to different genres of poetry – here, it is suggested, that of city poetry. The chapter has included reference to shifters and deictics and how they need to be differentiated. The following chapter, with reference to women in the city, further investigates these two terms.

# Chapter 6
# Shifters, deictics and the woman narrator in city poetry: Theory and praxis

This chapter continues the investigation of Jakobson's particular contribution to the analysis of poetic language in his essay, "Shifters, Verbal Categories, and the Russian Verb", in "Fundamentals of Language" (1971[1956]). In his essay, Jakobson refers to the "shifter" as a part of spoken speech. His work has been criticised by Monika Fludernik in a number of articles, particularly, "Jespersen's Shifters: Reflections on Deixis and Subjectivity" (1989/90: 97–116) and "Shifters and Deixis: Some Reflections on Jakobson, Jespersen, and Reference" (1991:193–230). The analysis closely follows Jakobson's theory in relation to his own communication model. Jakobson's article (1971) does not fully explicate deictics and shifters. However, his separation of the two categories provides for future more detailed and distinctive analytical positions. As has been noted in the previous chapter, placing these two distinctive categories under the same term "deixis" results in continued difficulty. The deictic adverb is not at all similar to the shifting pronoun. If pronouns are persistently defined as having a deictic (adverbial placing) aspect, then the capacity of blending the personae is lost, which has particular relevance to poetic voice.

The term "deixis" has been defined in various ways and some definitions incorporate great complexity within their remit. Whole phrases or even sentences can be described as deictic. This can be such a wide definition that the term loses some of its precise meaning. An extensive definition is presented by Keith Green in his study of lyric poetry, where he incorporates shifters with deixis. Veronica Forrest-Thomson (1978), notes the importance of shifters in poetry in establishing the characteristics of the narrator. Roman Jakobson is the only poetic theorist to argue for a separation of the two when analysing poetry. The contemporary consensus, as illustrated by the definitions of Green and Jeffries, is that shifters and deictics should be considered as within the same category even when discussing poetry. The definition follows from the analysis of poetry by Keith Green and Leslie Jeffries which arises from Stylistics, of which more below.

Wales defines deictics as including: "the first and second person pronouns I, we, you; the demonstratives this and that; adverbs of place and time; and tense (present v. past)." (2001: 99). But it is argued here that shifters (personal pronouns) have a special function within poetry, and should be kept separate from deictics (prepositions of place, time and space), in order that the special function of the poet/narrator/self/ within poetry can be interpreted. The shifter, if defined separately from the deictic, is not a word which describes placing of a person, but a personal pronoun which describes human identification between poet and reader, and poet and text, as arising from the text. A poet may, as is often the case in Modernist poetry, refuse to use a pronoun at all. This can be interpreted as either the poet seeking to present themselves as absent from the text, or directly identifying with the reader. The poet may use various pronouns, "I", "we", "you", "they" and so on. The theorists who place these shifters within a deictic definition are emphasizing the deictic component of these words – as in the pointing meaning inherent in the use of the pronoun "you". But this denies the poet the complex range of interpretations and meanings of self within poetry and has a possibly deleterious effect on understanding the full complexity of the poetry. This is especially important when considering the poet as narrator, and also when considering how the reader identifies with the experience described by the poet in the poem.

Fludernik's close examination of Jakobson's theory reveals shortcomings in Jakobson's rather brief exploration (1971). She herself concludes that there are further problems to be overcome and posits that: "If *shifters*, as I have concluded, are empathy phenomena rather than functions of deixis (i.e. demonstrativity), they should be discussed as a sign of subjectivity, and so should be treated under the aegis of the emotive function – a *structural* relation of language." (1991: 223). There is also disagreement as to the shifter's availability as a written category. Fludernik suggests that the empathic aspect of the shifter is a dynamic process and this cannot be formalized within a "structuralist model of speech processes" (1991: 223). But if the "shifter" is specifically defined within the frame of a poetic text, then the expression (and it is noted here that poetry has access to special dramatic, empathic personae) of pronouns has a special range of definition: that is – differing species of shifters are dependent on the form of the text in which they are used.

Elena Semino in "Deixis and the dynamics of poetic voice" (1995: 145–160), provides further in-depth illustration of the uses of shifters in poetry. She includes, within deixis, verb tense, and adverbial placing, as well as personal pronouns. She notes that the: "Bakhtinian view that poetry, unlike fictional prose, is essentially monologic (Bakhtin, 1981) and the related assumption that poems, unlike novels, project single-layered discourse situations, i.e. tend to involve one level of communication between one addresser and one (set of) addressee(s)." (1995: 145). Semino analyses three contemporary poems, one each by Ted Hughes, Philip Larkin and Elizabeth Bartlett. Her conclusion highlights previously noted problem areas – the issue of how deictic shifting is expressed in poetry as opposed to fiction and speech:

> The shifts in deixis that I have discussed in relation to the three poems are in fact usually associated with the manipulation of viewpoint in fictional prose (e.g. Leech and Short, 1981: 340), and with the occurrence of deictic projection in ordinary conversation (e.g. Lyons, 1977: 578–579). This calls for a greater awareness of poetry's potential for the construction of complex discourse situation, and of the ways in which deixis can be used to achieve such complexity.
> (1995: 158)

The Bartlett poem referred to in the article, has such a complex shifting pronoun for all the voices – the poet's voice, the chronicler's voice and the voice of the subject – that it almost defies categorisation. If the use of shifters (Semino's "shifts in deixis") in poetry is recognised as complex, then a system of analysis specifically designated to understand them, would seem to be a useful theoretical way forward. The poem "Charlotte Her Book" is quoted in full in Semino's article. It is a poem of six stanzas of four lines each, imitating a ballad form. For copyright reasons, only extracts are reproduced here. The poem begins with what appears to be a simple poetic piece of autobiography:

> I am Charlotte. I don't say hello
> to people and sometimes I bite.
> Although I am dead I still jump
> out of bed and wake them up at night.

Charlotte (her voice, which is clearly and directly expressed), continues with a description of her mother and how she has drawn a picture of her, as a child would. Then, with what is more than a child's insight she says that she does not do what she is told and tells lies. The poem then states that she draws her father, and again there is slippage with the narrator, because the child's action of scribbling all over her drawing in order to destroy it, is then described, all with the use of the first-person singular pronoun but again with more than a child's insight. She continues, with overtones of a classical Greek tragedy, to describe how she would then eat her mother and make her "good and dead". She states that her mother is "sick in the head". Suddenly the mood darkens. The child states her age, again with the use of the first-person pronoun. But the poem then breaks into figurative, interpretive language:

> Although I am only four I went away
> so soon they hardly knew me,
> and stars sprang out of my eyes,
> and cold winds blew me.

As readers, we know that we are being given a text which describes Charlotte as others interpret her. External forces, such as metaphoric "stars" and "cold winds" are included. Then there is a further dislocation of time as she (apparently) records what her parents have told her, contradicting her own view of the family dynamic. Suddenly she writes her own epitaph and the shifter is entirely dislocated by the final narrated sequence of the poem:

> My mother always says she loves me.
> My father says he loves me too.
> I love Charlotte. A car ran
> over Charlotte. This is her book.

While the first part of the poem beguiles the reader into thinking they are simply listening to Charlotte's voice, the realisation then emerges that we are listening to the poet, or indeed Charlotte herself, recording Charlotte's voice. The sad fact that she is dead – and still writes her own epitaph – the poem – "This is her book", produces a deep complexity of voice which can hardly be interpreted. Semino assesses the "voices" as that of the adult recording the life of Charlotte but then provides a continuum for the interpretation with her note:

> The interpretation that I have offered is only one of the possible readings of the poem. A number of alternatives have been suggested to me in the course of seminars involving the poem. One in particular poses a valid objection to my own proposal. Some readers have argued that only Charlotte speaks in the poem, partly using the first person and partly referring to herself in the third person. This explains the simplicity and relative clumsiness of the syntax of the last two lines of the poem . . . .in the second sentence Charlotte's name is repeated rather than being replaced by a pronoun, [as in a child's syntax] and an active structure is used where a passive structure would have made more sense . . . The interpretation I have proposed does not account for these features of the text. On the other hand, the alternative reading fails to explain the presence of "adult" language in the poem and the prominent position reserved for Charlotte's book. (1995: 159,160)

None of the language usage in the poem detracts from it or is unacceptable to the reader. There seems, using the example above as an illustration, that there is a particular suspension of disbelief which the shifter enables, and which is only poetic. Would this kind of shifting be explicable in prose or even in drama? With reference to a city poetic, there is a strong dislocation and shift of identity produced by the last two lines of the poem, which, here argued by the present author, is a result of the factual brutal juxtaposition of city and the human.

It would seem clear that, whether the shifter is spoken, or used in written speech, it expresses its function as shifter. The present author suggests an example that could be written as well as spoken: "In my letter to you I wrote that he told me he was unable to meet her in my apartment at the same time as me" which is reliably translated, without thought by the addressee, listener or reader as: "In your letter to me you wrote that he told you he was unable to meet her in your apartment at the same time as you." Jakobson specifically examines how, in spoken communication, both addresser and addressee readily re-interpret the "I" and "you". Jakobson expressed this in his model of communication (see Chapter One).

In the current chapter, "shifters" and "deictics" are interpreted as stylistic terms in the exploration of the function of the personal narrator and its gender implications within the city poetic. An expansion of stylistic theory provides for a metaphoric and/or semiotic understanding of shifters if they are separated from deictics. The attribute of "shifters", which clarifies the position of the narrator and audience in poetry is lost, if they are classed as "deictics". The current understanding of deixis has left little room for interest in shifters.

In his thesis "A Study of Deixis in relation to lyric poetry" (1992) Keith Green defines deixis in relation to the narrator as: "The *I* is at the zero-point of the spatio-temporal coordinates of the deictic context. Language is a drama-event in which the first person takes the principal role." (1992: 44). In his investigation of the persona in modernist poetry, he concludes that: "the deictic devices serve to create a disjunction between text and reader or between addresser and addressee" (1992: 297). His subsequent analysis of specific lyric poems leads to his conclusion that "literary deixis" does not exist, and that "the difference between the deixis of a lyric poem and of, say, conversation is a difference in degree, not of kind" (1992: 347). In his analysis of the shifter, the personal pronoun, the narrator in poetry, is inseparable from the analysis of the deictic.

Lesley Jeffries interprets deixis as including shifters, even when she uses the example of children learning the precise function of pronouns (2000: 55, 56). This is the same argument made by Jespersen in his description and definition of shifters (1922: 123, 124). She specifically analyses poetry by Carol Ann Duffy as, for her, the poems seem to draw the reader towards the centre of the author's text (2000: 10, 11). Jeffries' definition of deixis, includes words that depict placing (here, there), time (now, then), and the narrator's position in terms of pronouns used. An authorial "I", makes the sense of the poem more intimate for the reader, and the other pronouns (you, they) make it more remote. Her 2008 article examines deictic theory where the narrator and reader blend to greater or lesser degrees. The definition of deictics is so broad that it becomes hard to define the meaning:

> the choice of a declared first-person viewpoint must be one of the main ones which will immediately involve the reader in a deictic shift into the relevant narrator's deictic center, whether that narrator is identified as a character in a tale or as the authorial voice. Other deictic elements of course contribute to this process of identification – present tense, proximal spatial and temporal adverbials and so on. (2008: 79)

In her book *Stylistics* (2010: 157–161), she describes deictic shift theory more fully and in a manner which, in relation to poetry, provides, for her, the best way of understanding how the text is absorbed and understood by the reader. As might be inferred from the above, deixis and poetry is a complex issue. Taking Jakobson's lead – the separation of the shifter from the deictic, makes the examination of the role of the narrator much easier within the poetic text. As Green conceded, deixis in poetry and prose are the same but in poetry it is a difference of degree (1992: 347). It is the current author's argument that the difference of degree is in fact so great that the ensuing complexity renders shifters a different species, and that it is vital to separate out the deictic and shifter functions in order to fully appreciate their complexity.

As has been suggested, one of the more significant aspects of investigation of the shifter, specifically in poetry, is that it opens out the complexity of the narrator within the poetic voice. Jeffries analyses this in relation to three poems in her paper (2008). Her "deictic shift theory", identifies: "the deictic triggers in a text which cause the reader to view the text world from a different angle. Thus, it is thought that the way that deictic expressions work in narrative is that they cause the reader to take up the deictic positioning of the character, place and time which are indicated by the textual triggers." (2008: 71). For Jeffries, the deictic shifting is identified in an analysis of all the aspects of deixis and shifting which she includes in deixis – verb tense, use of pronouns and adverbial placing. The purpose of the deictic shifting is to improve the range and accuracy of understanding by the reader of the authorial intentions in the text. It is obvious from the consideration of poetic (and often fictional) texts that a simple identification by the reader with the first person in a text is not a sufficiently wide parameter of analysis. There must also be: "a willingness to interpret the poem more broadly in a way that is relevant for the reader her/himself. This possibility that the reader retains some sense of self whilst also shifting into the persona of a character requires more investigation." (2008: 74).

Jakobson's work on the shifter arises from Otto Jespersen's earlier definition in 1923. Both Jespersen and Jakobson are brief. Jespersen's interest is explored through the examples of children learning that, both their names, as well as certain pronouns, identify them (1922: 123,124). Jakobson has developed this nascent theory and taken it into the linguistic sphere: "Any linguistic code contains a particular class of grammatical units which Jespersen labelled SHIFTERS: the general meaning of a shifter cannot be defined without a reference to the message" (1984: 42). Here, Jakobson is exploring in detail his diagrammatic representation of his theory of communication – addresser/addressee etc. For Jakobson the term "shifters" also applied to verbs. He wrote:

> The general meaning of the grammatical form called "shifter" is characterized by a reference to the given speech act in which the form appears. Thus the past tense is a shifter because it literally designates an event that precedes the given act of speech. The first-person form of a verb, or the first-person pronoun, is a shifter because the basic meaning of the first person involves a reference to the author of the given act of speech. Similarly, the

second-person pronoun contains a reference to the addressee to whom the speech act in question is directed. If the addressers and addressees change in the course of the conversation, then the material content of the form *I* and *you* also changes, they shift.      (1985: 23)

The "shifter" is not, however, confined to the spoken word. It can certainly be used in written reported speech, as well as in a fictional narrative. Jakobson's interest in poetry enables the term to be applied as having a more semiotic structure within poetry because of its relevance to the construction of the poetic voice. The analysis of Jakobson's point, that verbs are also "shifters", has, as yet, not been properly explored.

Katie Wales in *A Dictionary of Stylistics* (2001: 99,100) defines the deictic as a "showing" or "pointing" term – as in "this" and "that", "here" and "there". She also refers to how the deictic can define both time and space. It is interesting to note that the definite article in Early Middle English was used in a more deictic sense than it is today (2001: 100). As discussed in Chapter Five, the roots for a deictic centred definition, originate with Karl Bühler (1982 [1934]). He places the shifter firmly within a deictic category – as the origo-deixis. There are special considerations when poetry, as differentiated from prose, is discussed. Keith Green (1992) has defined the deictic with reference to lyric poetry. With regards to the personal pronoun, he defines this as the same as Bühler's "origo-deixis" and suggests that, within lyric poetry, "it mobilises the monologic "I" figure" (1992, p125). All of this contributes to the shifter being lost within the deictic category.

The complexity of the personal narrator in poetry is explored by Veronica Forrest-Thomson who, unlike everyone else, defined deictics as separate entities to shifters, although the definition is brief: "shifters are orientational features of language which refer to the situation of utterance: 'I' means the person speaking, 'now' the moment of utterance, etc" (1978: 34). Forrest-Thomson has gone where others have not. She proceeds to examine the shifter with reference to tenses of verbs in poetry. This is a direct use of the complex and under-developed work in the article by Roman Jakobson. With reference to a poem where the pronoun "we" is used she writes: "The fictionalized "we", which refers not to an external class of persons but to a shifting function within the poem, helps to distance the language from particular external contexts and to associate first-person pronouns with the self-reflexive process of reading and writing poetry." (1978: 35). For Forrest-Thomson, the shifting properties of the personal pronoun "I", "we" etc. provide a particular poetic "voice" which describes such a wide range of interpretation of the personal pronoun in poetry that it contributes to a "poetic artifice", and with this "A terrible beauty is born." (1978: 36) (see Yeats' poem "Easter 1916" in 2008: 193). This would indicate that in poetry (which bridges the written and the spoken) there is room for the shifter to expand and provide complexity of poetic language. It is within this analysis that the "poetic voice" is constructed. It is also the bridge between the linguistic or stylistic analysis of language and the semiotic.

Lesley Jeffries, in her "Introduction" in her paper (2000) writes that stylistics examines all texts, not necessarily literary or poetic texts. Her essay: "Point of View and the Reader in the Poetry of Carol Ann Duffy" (2000: 54–68) explores personal pronouns entirely within the definition of deixis. Her analysis provides evidence that, in Duffy's work there is a particular realized interpretation of the deixis, which expresses this woman's sense of place, time and identity. She explores the deixis within three categories: "Here and There", "Now and Then" and "Me, You and Them". All of these considerations are understood by means of the "distancing" aspect of deixis; that is, how separate or how closely identified the reader is from the author/poet or text. As with Jakobson, she identifies that children have difficulty in understanding that the pronoun, and the noun can be the same person. So, for the child the parent may say "Mummy's here" or "Daddy's here" rather than "You're here". And the child may well refer to themselves by their own name rather than "I" for a period of time whilst learning to talk (see also "Charlotte: Her Book" poem). In her section on personal pronouns, Jeffries, defines the characteristic of this part of speech as within a deictic parameter: "In deictic terms . . . "I" and "you" represent proximal and distal deixis respectively" (2000: 63).

In her analysis of Duffy's poetry, she therefore understands that a process of identification is established, or indeed blurred, through whether the poet is strongly identified as "I", rather than sometimes referring to "you" as a "generic narrative" form. This is a generalized form of "I", but not similar to the personal "I". "You" in this sense is understood as meaning "one", "someone", "anyone", or "everyone". This usage constructs different degrees of identification and understanding between the reader (addressee) with the poet (addresser). She concludes that the strong use of personal deixis in Duffy's poetry enables strong identification by the reader. She makes this analysis with reference not only to the personal pronoun, but also to the deixis of time and place. For Jeffries, the distancing effect of the pointing element of deixis affects not just the relationship between elements described within the text, or as here, the poem, but also the distance between the poem and the reader. It would seem that by its "pointing" deictic nature, it cannot promote a process of identification between the poet (addresser) and reader (addressee), it can only keep the two at a distance from each other. This is not a statement about women's poetry as such. But her understanding of the fluidity of personal deixis possibly enhances an analysis of women's poetry, where identity may, in itself, be blurred.

There is a further shifting category which can be identified with regard to gender. For the man or woman reader of a text, which is either written by a man or by a woman, there is a further shift which seems to take place. It is not just the "I" in the poem becoming "you" for the reader, it is the "I" becoming a "male you" or "female you" for the reader. Or this distinction may not in fact be made, either by the reader, or by the poet. The reader and/or poet can make a choice here. The shifting can be metonymic – one pronoun alongside another – or it can be metaphoric – the reader identifies with the poet as one and the same. This is a very complex type of shifting. The awareness that the male pronoun cannot enable identification of both men and women, is something which is currently more prominent in language usage. But, historically, the word "man" can be seen as generic, not specific. And, therefore, the pronoun "he" can also be seen in the same generic manner. This might well mean that a male reader only performs one shift – "I" to "you". The female reader makes not only this shift but another one, "you/he" to "you/she". If identification is taken from the generic sphere to the specific, then this results in a number of multiple shifts: "I" to "you/black man/woman/you" for example. This can, of course, have a distancing effect between the text and the reader – a loss of identification with the person speaking in the text. If the shifters are considered as a separate category from the deictics, does this enable the shifters to be more clearly defined? These considerations raise a number of questions and possible ideas for development of poetic theory. Perhaps these questions can be better answered in conjunction with the final consideration of the chapter, the possible special use of deixis and shifters as expressed within a city poetic genre.

It seems that poetry of the city derives characteristics from the concrete nature of the city. For those living in cities, there is no possibility that the city is anything other than an external concrete, steel, glass, brick and stone reality. The balance of human life within this actual reality is a particular concern for any city dweller. The city all too often appears to be hostile to survival. How to survive, and how to interpret that survival, provides special challenges of both form and content to the city poet. This is not obviously a poetry of relaxation, a contemplation of beauty, or of an aspect of the natural world. Because there is such a distinct difference between the human life and the concrete city, the use of deictics to interpret the city space is an essential means whereby this difference can be described and interpreted. The shifter also has a particular role to play. The nature of any shifting part of speech – and Jakobson has identified verbs as shifters as well as personal pronouns – means that it has characteristics which enable the interpretation of different personae, times and places simultaneously within the poetic form.

Within city poetry, a fluidity of personal function is required to interpret the exigencies of city existence. Within poetic form, fluidity can also interpret a sense of loss of identity. This is an aspect which may have special importance for the analysis of women's poetry of the city. If this is the case then a precise definition of the function of personal pronouns is a priority, in order to understand the person within the scope of the object (the actual city). Research into contemporary women's poetry from 1970 onwards, provides sources for women's poetic and theoretical input into a city poetic. It might be possible to discover a rationale for their contribution to a city poetic, or a rationale as to why this input appears to be lacking. The overall concern is to promote understanding of how a poet interprets human existence within the city.

It would seem to be, that in order for women to emerge as city narrators, as writers of city poetry, there needs to be a certainty of both self and *self within this environment* – something which may not be so strongly demanded within poetry which is not about city life. Women have indeed written city poetry and the detailed analysis of how the "I", and the sense of place is constructed in general, is work that still needs to be undertaken. The following list consists almost entirely of British women's city poetry. The list is not comprehensive. Some of the books mentioned here contain only some city poems amongst other subjects. Some American poets, who either originally lived in Britain (Loy and Levertov), or who have written a very significant amount of city poetry (Lorde, Bergman's anthology) have been included. Many women poets have written individual city poems. These poems, and more, could be collected into an anthology, and see below:

Bergman, D. (ed.) (1992) *City River of Voices* New Mexico: West End Press.
Coghill, M. (2006) *Designed to Fade* Exeter: Shearsman Books.
Coghill, M. (2012) *Shades of Light: A Triumph of City* www.cityofpoetry.co.uk.
Coghill, M. (2017) *Assay of Blood and Gold: London Poems* www.cityofpoetry.co.uk.
Crowther, C. (2007) *Stretch of Closures* Exeter: Shearsman Books.
Feinstein, E. (2010) *Cities* Manchester: Carcanet.
Levertov, D. (1979) *Collected Earlier Poems 1940–1969* New York: New Directions Books.
Lorde, A. (1997) *The Collected Poems of Audre Lorde*. New York: W W Norton & Co.
Loy, M. (1997) *The Lost Lunar Baedeker* Manchester: Carcanet.
Notley, A. (1992) *The Descent of Alette* Harmondsworth: Penguin Books.
Olsen, R. (2004) *secure portable space* Hastings: Reality Street Editions.
Pollard, C. (2005) *Look! Clare! Look!* Northumberland: Bloodaxe Books.
Rees-Jones, D. (2004) *Quiver* Bridgend: Seren.

Robinson, A. (2010) *The Finders of London* London: Enitharmon.
Rumens, C. (2004) *Poems 1968–2004* Northumberland: Bloodaxe Books.
Schneider, M. (2008) *Encircling the Core* London: Enitharmon.
Tonks, R. (2014) *Bedouin of a London Evening* Newcastle: Bloodaxe Books.
Wardle, S. (2005) *Score!* Northumberland: Bloodaxe Books.
Warner, V. (1998) *Tooting Idyll* Manchester: Carcanet.

The sense of self is complicated by women expressing a feeling of dislocation in their poetry, the woman writer who is not identified as to place, as in Carol Ann Duffy's essay, "A Stranger Here Myself" from O'Brien (1998: 160–170). For example, Carol Ann Duffy's poem "Originally" (from *New and Selected Poems*, 2004) describes how the impact of other children at her school, forces a sense of displacement from the environment which the speaker/girl belongs to, but over which she has little control. Everything is confusing and she describes, in a sequence of three stanzas, how everything depends on how she does not have the same voice (accent) as the others: they want to know where she came from "Originally" – the title of the poem. She has itemised moving home, being displaced into a city, going to a new school, and this destroys the validity of her own voice. For copyright reasons, it is only possible to quote one stanza from her poem. The poem is, however, freely available on the internet:

> All childhood is an emigration. Some are slow,
> leaving you standing, resigned, up an avenue
> where no one you know stays. Others are sudden.
> You accent wrong. Corners, which seem familiar,
> leading to unimagined, pebble-dashed estates, big boys
> eating worms and shouting words you don't understand.
> My parents' anxiety stirred like a loose tooth
> in my head. I want our own country, I said.

Here, in the final line, Duffy, makes a significant shift between personal self and identity of self as part of a group: "I want our own country, I said". The shifting pronouns are not difficult to interpret. Although Duffy is describing a personal loss of identity, she is also asserting that she has an identity, with the use of the pronoun "our". The reader of the poem also shifts the stated "our" to "my" when identifying with the poet's expressed sense of loss.

Within the scope of the discussion in the chapter, the "I" is positioned within the urban space. It might be useful to suggest that expressing diffidence about the exact nature of the "I" as myself, in itself, is not rewarding; there are several natures, several functions of the personal pronouns in poetry, and the city simply provides one environment for their expression and meaning. In order to function, the narrator needs to send a message out to someone who hears/receives. The narrator needs both a location, or a process of locating, and a process of explication. This can be done in a number of ways. Vicky Bertram suggests, in her book: *Gendering Poetry: Contemporary Women and Men Poets*:

> The pre-eminent position of the lyric "I", and the poem's movement from the private to a public sphere, are related to certain characteristics of the lyric mode, which is the most egotistical creative genre. In writing it, you describe the world through your own eyes, you cover everything with your words, your mark. Poets have to summon considerable authority in order to manage this feat. The reader has to yield far more radically to the poem's authority. (2005: 45)

This provides some explanation as to why women's sense of real existence within a city, and therefore a city poetic, might be problematic. But it must always be accepted that the reader may also have some preconditions and restricted vision, with regard to who the woman poet really is. It is with this in mind that the exploration of the shifter, the personal pronoun, has a special place of importance within the analysis of women's poetry of the city.

Within the humanist and geographical analyses, Gillian Rose, in her essay "No Place for Women?" (1993), explores the differences between humanist and feminist geographers and their differing relationship with time, space and place. An anthropocentric viewpoint of geography, by means of its masculinist approach, in fact, paradoxically, enables a validation of a feminist viewpoint within geographical theory. She writes:

> Feminist analyses of the power relations that humanistic geography neglects to address have understood homes and communities as sites of oppression – by the state, by capitalism and by patriarchy – and women have constructed their politics as theory through such socialist feminist discourses. Indeed, Ann Henley has recently remarked on a feminist literary "tradition of equating the loss of place with the acquisition of identity". The humanistic refusal to consider possible systematic [gender] differences in experiences of home erases consideration of feminist arguments, and suggests that only masculinist work could use the image of place as home so unproblematically. (1993: 56)

The quotation provides a useful background theory for a woman's gendered city poetic. Within a city poetic genre, "humanistic refusal", can be interpreted to understand that outdoor and work places, as well as the home, are important for an exploration of women's places. It certainly indicates that shifters must be gender identified.

And how is city space understood poetically? Deictics and shifters – words which describe placing in city space and the nature of the poetic persona respectively – are a crucial part of city poetic interpretation. Deictic placing is potentially fivefold (though others, as discussed above, have used different categories): placing in time: before, after, now, then; placing in location: before, behind, here,

Chapter 6 Shifters, deictics and the woman narrator in city poetry — 147

there; placing in space: inside, outside, inner, outer; placing of person, of self: I, you, he, she, we, you, (pl) them; and placing in relation to others: us, them, my, your, our. In the last two categories there is a crossover with the shifter. It is not just that these specific words are looked for (as in factual iconicity for example), or that these words are used as categories or headings for specific forms or genres of poetry, but that the poetry of the city itself can be interpreted through how these words are used (as in implied iconicity for example). As suggested earlier, this is not necessarily a poetry of beauty, emotion, lyric description, internal personal existence; but a poetry which interprets the person within the time, place and space of the concrete city. The subject matter requires analysis of both deixis and shifters.

This is one of the ideas behind the current author's book length poem *Shades of Light: A Triumph of City* (2012). It is an exploration of how humans and the city interact and co-exist, with special reference to London. There are a number of forces expressed in the poetry: equilibrium, constant movement, imbalance, construction, and destruction – sequences of events which are consecutive, concurrent or retroactive. Such considerations are not prescriptive of form or content; it is an exploration of poetics. In order to illustrate these points, some individual poems from the book are explored in detail. The analysis provides useful praxis and is Formalist in nature.

City poetry may not necessarily contain a large number of deictics, but interpreting a juxtaposition between the concrete and the human, may well demand them. As an example, it is noted that the last poem of *Shades of Light*: "Caravanserai" includes a high number of deictics (2012: 152–154). A section of the final part of the poem is reproduced here with the deictics highlighted (2012: 153,154):

> ***no*** light nothing personal pulling
> **past** the 5 star hotel the doorman
> stands **in** the window ***facing*** the street
> talking **by** mobile **to** the woman
> **right outside in** a waiting taxi
> derelict hospital
> ***the*** brand new hospital
> **this** is my ***last*** portal
> **into** the centre **now**

The highlighted deictics – both of place, time and space – include some words which are not specifically deictics – "last" for example (see italicised words) – which gives a strong sense of time/place/space. And this highlights the heart of the matter – a city poetic – the city with all its energy and activity – lines crossing, junctions – real and figurative – and the timing, placing and spacing, all demand deixis. The word "the" is also highlighted as a deictic, where appropriate (see

Wales, 2001: 100). It is still used in the poem in a deictic sense, as in: "the brand new hospital".

The deictics are interpreted through different forms in different poems, for example they are openly extracted from the text of the poem in "Shaking Out the Syntagm" (2012:127,128). In the poem the deictics of place and time – and perhaps even of space, as in time + place = space – are selected out to the right-hand margin. This highlights how the deictics construct an axis of their own. The text tends to be read on the left-hand side only and on a different level, the meaning is shifted by the format in order to enhance the sense of dislocation between factual life and the imagined. The poem is quoted in full.

Shaking out the Syntagm

Surely she has got used to death
                                                                                                          now
quicksilver sunny deep shadow
                                                                                                          after
eleven years and she twenty-six
                                                                                                          then
her going marked year
                                                                                                             by
year
I see her ghostly elegant stepping
                                                                            down towards
the quartet playing Janacek
she salutes their nationalist welcome sits
                                                                                amongst
them as they play they nod
                                                                                 across
their bows "welcome – enjoy the music"
I
                                                                                  nearly
jump
                                                                                 out of
my seat groan
                                                                               out loud
but choking keep my head
                                                                                    down
to cope of course
my heart threw arms
                                                                                 around
her crying at the same time
the embrace as close as lovers
movement harmony sympathy
                                                                                 when

I look up she has gone
leaving co-ordinates of more than one crossing
                  over

memory tingling peripheral senses
      sententious Time
      wearing great robes
     wielding mallet seconds
      pile driver minutes
      seismic tremor hours
      amniotic overbearing
    losing people vista parabola
                  now

    intimate working mechanisms
  curves start stretching reference to the years
    experience drifts any minute
                 now in

I do not notice the time is measured
                 out in

half-life unfocused eyes
blurring the plant and the filing cabinet
I think "what you would have said?"
                 what if
              what if that

if those arms truly embraced me
I would have known variable of recognition
                   that

too sharp moment
what I didn't and what you had
and what she lost and what you lost
                   then

my throat chokes
closes doors on malleable time
stop start stop start
                    up

[Author's note: with hindsight, the deictic "those" – eight lines from the end of the poem – is also a deictic.]

This is an explicit, iconic highlighting of deictics. Other poems within the book-length poem, highlight the deictics of balance and movement described in the poem through their titles, as in: "Substitution balance" (2012: 121) and "uneven motivations" (2012: 139). "Substitution balance" is the second of three parts of a poem: "Fulcrum at work" (2012: 120–122). (2102: 139–143). The understanding of balancing and placing is also portrayed iconically, in many of the poems of the section of *Shades of Light* entitled "Fame" (2012: 75–105): as in: "Random" and "Images Attached" (2012: no page numbers). This section of the poem was constructed through the use of Adobe Indesign software and produces poetic text which contains innovative structures. The full text, followed by analysis, of "Substitution balance" and "Uneven motivations" is reproduced below:

Substitution balance

| | |
|---|---:|
| another artic shudders by three cars | 1 |
| silencing the noise of my bus step up | |
| I am part of the lion's roar sitting | |
| in the belly of this wild animal | |
| carrying me home panther like it leaps | 5 |
| on through ranges of diesel adjustments | |
| gearing up and fine tuning its inbuilt | |
| balancing mechanisms veering to stop | |
| pressing itself close to the scratching post | |
| snapping doors open past the uvula | 10 |
| which hardly moves as the oysters file past | |
| do you go as far as the Elephant? | |
| the passenger error risks eviction | |
| sands flow nods crisis past not looking | |
| swipe the card he suddenly hey hey! hey! | 15 |
| someone turns the column of food stops dead | |
| as a small adjustment in the bite size | |
| takes place you didn't swipe your card beep | |
| beep the cry of oysters the lurching power | |
| driven begins and hassles and hastens | 20 |
| with the staring morsels counting down stops | |
| I read the paper but not much | |
| she reads a novel relentless | |
| he stares ahead into a file | |
| lying unopened in his brain | 25 |
| children laze about and mutter | |
| and squirm and snatch and pull | |
| the LED is a giveaway every | |
| bus arrives in seven minutes | |
| waiting REM sleep balances on the | 30 |
| cusp of waking Frozen Eye Glaze | |

("Shades of Light":121)

Uneven motivations

| | |
|---|---:|
| I have money in the bank | 1 |
| not a month goes by without | |
| more money going in and | |
| taken out I wish for more | |
| money in so does the bank | 5 |
| so much so that this month they | |
| charge me a lot more so they | |

can have much more that is mine
it's not a choice to stare so
long and hard magnifying                                      10
the sum column of figures
arabic numbers are so
curvaceous and enticing
the bank deeply responsive
to their allure sensual                                       15
sixes and sevens driving
forces behind the week's shop
I love irradiated fruit
figures attached delights
double choice half price buy three                            20
dear slips of receipts the cost
is heartbreaking seen clearly
only with glasses and by
2-D card listen the bank
laughs electronic counting                                    25
machines adjust totals bring
carry forward patterns bags
chattering happy clicking
uneven motivations
pour in and out at the base                                   30
of the calm smooth tower soft
movements iced with deaf glass
staff present papers figures
are set to advantage why
ask for the resident poet                                     35
at the Bank Tower humbler
life incompatible with
over-riding cell systems
this complete expression of
you have and have it from me                                  40
("Shades of Light":139)

It is interesting to compare the "I" in the first of the two poems, "Substitution balance", with the "I" used in the second poem, "Uneven motivations". It could be understood that the "I" in "Substitution balance" is more personal in the second half of the poem than at the beginning. In the first half the passengers on the bus are interpreted as a group through the use of animal imagery. In the second half it is indeed the poet as individual who reads the paper. The strong demonstration of the personal "I" in the poem's narrative, disturbs the reader/ text interface – the shifter with its distinctive individual meaning pushes the reader out of the text. The "I" in "Uneven motivations" seems to include both the personal and the generic. The poet and many others have money in the bank and many may also express sarcasm about the behaviour of banks. Here, the generic use of the shifter brings the reader closer to identification with the poet/text.

These two poems have been chosen because they highlight the relationship between the city as a concrete reality and how the humans, as living and malleable elements, negotiate their way around that which is largely immutable. The play of power and autonomy of existence is enhanced, in both poems, by the machines and buildings appearing to adopt attributes of the living. In "Substitution balance", the bus is likened to a creature with the attributes of a large and powerful animal – it is hungry and not altogether sympathetic with the humans which it carries/has eaten. The driver is the rider of this beast and is as powerful as the creature he drives. The impersonal deictic "it" (lines 5 and 7) sits uneasily with the personification of the bus as a beast "panther like" (line 5). There is a sense of dislocation, in that the intimate and complex range of meanings that shifters can have, has less of a range in the impersonal shifter "it". Wales (2001: 99) leaves this pronoun out of her list of pronouns as shifters. The humans in the poem are in a sense immobilized and cannot shift. This provides a dramatic tension. "I" is both a passenger (lines 3, 5, 22) and the poet/persona combined. However, line 2 refers to "my bus". This is a possessive pronoun which is discarded by the simile of the bus as animal and having a life of its own. As is indicated later in the poem, it does not even go where the passengers want to go. In line 15 "he" is the driver, although this is not immediately clear. This line is preceded by the words "not looking" (line 14) and this could be anybody shouting. In line 24, the "he" is depersonalized, depicting the generic. However, the children in line 26 are clearly particular passengers. The reader also makes adjustments through the shifters, in order to understand the metaphorisation of the bus as animal and recognize the passengers as de-humanised into fodder. Through the shifters, the reader adjusts between the particular and generic, between the poet's experience and the readers' individual or often repeated generic experience. We don't travel by bus once, we are often travelling by bus. Lines 11 and 19 refer to oysters (see Lewis Carroll: "The Walrus and the Carpenter") but of course this is also a reference to the Oyster Card London passenger travel passes. It is almost as if the bus (quasi animal) itself, takes offence at being asked if it goes to the "Elephant" as in "Elephant and Castle" (South London). The lack of punctuation enables several double readings in that the reader cannot tell if the lines move backwards to refer to something already mentioned or forwards to elaborate on something that is about to be mentioned. It all adds to the bumpy ride.

Further dislocation is provided by the fact that the personal pronouns, shifters in the poem, do not shift; but the use of similes, which indicate that the passengers are like mere fodder ("with the staring morsels" – line 21) for the bus, indicates that the shifting is also an attribute of similes – things are not as they

Chapter 6 Shifters, deictics and the woman narrator in city poetry —— 153

really are. This would be a different area for research. This form of shifting cannot apply to metaphor because by definition the two attributes are condensed by the metaphor and become a third, new, developed image. As indicated in the axial model (see Chapter Two, above) – similes are on the syntagm and have the property of time and therefore they can shift. How is the theorist to cope with the complexities of the use of language which occurs in poetry, the constant juggling of meaning, and arranging and disarranging of meanings? The word "shifter" seems to apply to so much more than the personal pronoun. There are levels of shifting. The shifter can also be applied to how the images and personification are constructed. So that, for example, the bus shifts from being a machine to an animal, the humans shift from being living and real to half digested ("frozen eye glaze") fodder.

In the poem, the use of deictics is closely aligned to verb usage. This enables a further question – is there a category of deictics which is very closely linked to action, as opposed to just being a "pointing" or "placing" element in language? The deictics which are linked to verbs in this way are: 'shudders by" (line 1), "step up" (line 2), "leaps/on" (lines 5, 6) and "close to" (line 9). However, in line 19, ("of") and line 30 ("of") indicate the possessive or establishment of the genitive case – the sense of belonging. It is only in lines 2 "step up", 26 "laze about" and 29 "balances on", that the deictic breaks through the verb, in order to establish an apparent deixis that is independent of its placing with the verb. There is one very clear deictic "this" (line 4) which establishes the simile of the bus as animal very clearly "this wild animal". But the deictics of time need to be considered as well as those of place. There is the phrase "every bus arrives in seven minutes" (lines 28, 29). Although the deictic "every" indicates the totality of buses – all buses – it also points us to the meaning that the arrival time is fixed or pinned in a certain position. This contains the pointing meaning which is always accepted as the main attribute of the deictic. But it indicates the timing rather than the physical positioning of the buses.

The shifters in both of these poems are more about the relationship of the city dweller with the inanimate aspects of city life than any expression of the female poet author's sense of identity within the city. However, it could be argued that the fluidity of the importance of the human within the environment reveals the power of the (inanimate) city to dislocate any sense of a human having control. It is the bus which has a life of its own, with the passengers (oysters) as food. In the second poem "Uneven motivations" the dislocation is caused by the power of money to control human life. In so doing it has human characteristics – the "bank/laughs" (lines 24, 25) and the supermarkets almost sing "happy clicking" (line 28). But the final line "you have it and have it from me", is slippage of meaning as in "you can take it from me". But the platitude is changed so that the double reading – you take my money and you can take this as true – emerges readily from the estranged use of the collocation. Rather than itemize each shifter and deictic, but bearing in mind the complex usages that have emerged from the previous poem discussed, it is noted that the poem also uses the technique of personification of the immutable bank. It is the human which gives way (gives the money) and the bank with mute staff who are behind sound proof glass ("deaf glass"), do all the taking. The "curvaceous and enticing" Arabic numerals hold out the promise of emotional reward while the bank does all the calculating and taking. The cluster of lines 5–8 has an enhanced use of shifters culminating in the one strongly deictic shifter "that is mine", which enhances the powerful placing of the ownership of the money about to be taken away.

The brief analysis above demonstrates that the shifter and the deictic both function in very different ways. These poems demonstrate the woman's life in the city, by referring to activities which are more usual for women: bus travel – which is cheaper than the tube – and the spending of money in the supermarket. But does the use of shifters and deictics change because of this emphasis? The controlling elements of the city itself, are highlighted as being more powerful than the humans within it, but this is not necessarily gender delineated. In these poems, the fluidity of the shifter does not necessarily indicate a loss of identity as a woman in the city, neither does it describe a specific dislocation of the woman within it. It describes a balance of power between the city itself and the humans living in it, jostling for survival.

The fluidity of interpretation of personal pronouns in poetry is a unique and a very important feature of poetics. The shifter therefore deserves to be analysed separately from the deictic. This chapter has argued that city poetry expresses a strong sense of movement, the placing of human persona within the often immutable and inanimate city structure, and that the two components of language, the deictic and the shifter, are very useful tools for the poetic interpretation of city space. From a contemporary viewpoint, writing poetry about crowded urban spaces, of necessity, requires focus on a poetic interpretative placing of people if we are not to be overwhelmed by topography, architecture, statistics, history, politics or sociology. Gender issues also need to be understood. Women must be noticed and recorded as users of city space. With reference to the city poem *Shades of Light*, travel (transition) and the streets (outside the home) dominate the poetic environment. Women are placed strongly within the city space.

The chapter has also argued that if the shifter is kept separate from the deictic, there is scope for a greater complexity of interpretation of the narrator in poetry. The differentiation also indicates how a semiotic analysis of the shifter can fully describe the nature of the poetic narrator, and perhaps, how the woman narrator particularly, is assisted by the shifter being defined as a separate category from the deictic. Jakobson's analysis of the shifter provides a basis for investigation. The complexities of this aspect of communication are apparent within poetics as soon as analysis is undertaken. Lastly the chapter has suggested how deictics and shifters, can be of special interest for the analysis of a city poetic genre. Iconic forms have been discussed. The following chapter explores the poetic theory of Gerard Manley Hopkins and his contribution to Jakobson's analysis of "parallels". The poetic use of repeated patterns and phrases in poetry, that is the implied forms in poetics, is a significant aspect of interpreting the city in poetry.

# Chapter 7
# Gerard Manley Hopkins: Parallels in poetry, parallels with Roman Jakobson

What is a parallel in poetry? How is the classical rhetorical work by Gerard Manley Hopkins relevant to the Formalist theories of poetic function offered by Roman Jakobson? Jakobson thought very highly of Hopkins' theoretical insights (for examples, see "Linguistics and Poetics": 62–94; and "Poetry of Grammar and Grammar of Poetry":121–144), both from (1987): and used them to develop some of his own theory of poetic artifice. If Hopkins' theories emerged from his classical undergraduate studies at Oxford University, then it would seem important to first establish what is implied by his rhetorical heritage and discover how it will also contribute to the details on metonymy and rhetoric to be found above in Chapter Three.

Classical rhetoric was, and still is, the art of persuasion and its degree of excellence was and is categorised by how effective the orator and his/her words are in influencing the audience. Rhetoric therefore has political and legal relevance as well as poetic. Poetry includes rhetorical eloquence – Coleridge, quoted by Hopkins, writes: "I wish our clever young poets would remember my homely definitions of prose and poetry; that is, prose = words in their best order; poetry = the best words in their best order" (Table Talk 12 July 1827) (footnote 84: 342). The various rhetorical figures, include such tropes as: chiasmus [repetition of words in reverse: ab:ba – it can be humorous or ponderous – "we fight to govern: we govern to fight"; apostrophe [as in soliloquy where speaker makes an aside – the is the vocative or exclamatory mode]; zeugma [one verb governs two nouns which use the verb differently – "Time and her aunt moved slowly" Austen, *Pride and Prejudice*, Chapter 43]. The American theory of New Criticism, much inspired by the work of John Crowe Ransom (1941), changed the nature of both literary and practical criticism in this respect. It changed the emphasis from that of studying the text within a rhetorical, historical or philosophical context, to that of using affective and psychological methods of analysis of the text. In the reference book of poetic theory, *NPEPP*, the entry on New Criticism states:

> The application of semantics to literary study, a development which owes much to critics like I.A.Richards and William Empson, was an important aspect of the New Criticism and has taken on even greater importance in subsequent decades. Yet the early Richard's affective bias and Empson's inveterate psychologising about both writer and reader run quite counter to the anti expressionistic tendencies of a T.S.Eliot, for example, or to the insistence on a *cognitive* criticism of other New Critics.                                              (*NPEPP*: 833b)

Understanding the rhetorical arts of speaking and persuading – especially in poetry – was abandoned to the pursuit of "close reading", to the study of the relationship between form and content which included the study of semantics. Crucially within literary art:

> knowledge is not essentially a matter of 'statement'; rather, the poem, drama, or fiction renders an experience, and in describing the nature of such an experience, many of the New Critics rejected the old dualism of form and content. (Here Ransom was a notable exception.) The way in which something is said often significantly affects the meaning of what is said. 'Form' becomes an integral part of 'content'. (*NPEPP*: 833b)

The *NPEPP* defines the three areas of the use of rhetoric as: "the author's relation to the text, the roles of the reader, and style." (*NPEPP*: 1047a). The definition of the author's relation to the text is of interest in establishing the role of the narrator in relation to the poet and is often referred to as the poet's "voice" (*NPEPP*: 1366b-1367b). The role of the reader in reader-response theory has risen to prominence in much literary theory and analysis in the past 50 years, as for example in the work of Jonathan Culler (*Structuralist Poetics*, 1975 [2007]). The third definition, the study of style, through the development and definition of poetic tropes, is the connection here between classical rhetoric and Jakobson's Formalism. The four major poetic tropes are here defined as: metaphor, metonymy, synecdoche (which is actually an aspect of metonymy "all hands on deck") and irony (including oxymoron [paradox – "Man is born free and everywhere is in chains" Rousseau Du *Contrat Social*]. Synecdoche includes hyperbole and litotes [praise of parts]). The study of the use of tropes is here used as a part of the Formalist analysis of poetry.

These tropes are understood through modern usage and Hopkins (1844–1889) may not have used or understood these terms in the same way. The study of rhetoric, and, for someone of Hopkins' era, the study of the practice of it, is something which is not considered to be so important today. For the purposes of this chapter, Hopkins wrote two very significant essays whilst an undergraduate at Oxford in 1865, "Poetic Diction" (1959) and "On The Origin of Beauty: A Platonic Dialogue" (1959). Hopkins' essay "On The Origin of Beauty" is written in the manner of a Socratic dialogue. It is not just the content which informs; he has used a particular literary and philosophical device as an exercise in persuasive rhetoric. The essay establishes that beauty is not dependent on symmetry; indeed, it is rather enhanced by a degree of asymmetry. It is during the development of the argument that Hopkins refers to "parallels". Parallels contribute to the complex interaction of words and form within a poem leading to artifice in poetry.

In Hopkins' short essay "Poetic Diction" (1959), he writes about the "structure of verse": "The artificial part of poetry, perhaps we shall be right to say all artifice, reduces itself to the principle of parallelism. The structure of poetry is that of continuous parallelism, ranging from the technical so-called Parallelisms of Hebrew poetry and the antiphons of Church music to the intricacy of Greek or Italian or English verse." (1959: 84). It can be seen from his definition that Hopkins is referring to some kind of repetition in poetic form. Hopkins elaborates further on the nature of parallelism in poetry:

> But parallelism is of two kinds necessarily – where the opposition is clearly marked, and where it is transitional rather or chromatic. Only the first kind, that of marked parallelism, is concerned with the structure of verse – in rhythm, the recurrence of a certain sequence of syllables, in metre, the recurrence of a certain sequence of rhythm, in alliteration, in assonance and in rhyme. To the chromatic parallelism belong gradation, intensity, climax, tone, expression (as the word is used in music), *chiaroscuro* [that is: the strong contrast between light and dark], perhaps emphasis: while the faculties of Fancy and Imagination might range widely over both kinds [of parallel]. (1959: 84, 85)

Hopkins' reference to parallels refers to patterns in poetry, patterns in poetic form which have not only a "marked" form, the use of poetic tropes, perhaps a factual structure but those patterns which give rise to "emphasis", a creation of mood. Hopkins describes these patterns as chromatic – having a range of sound and colour. This might also be defined as "implied" or "imputed" patterning – that is, it is not factual, arising from tropes and techniques – but arising from a contrived structure of the combined parts within the whole poem. The terms "factual" and "imputed" have relevance to Jakobson's own semiotic definitions of poetic structure, of which more below. But it is significant here that the meanings of the terms are similar enough to allow the later definitions to be an accurate interpretation of Hopkins' meaning.

It is interesting to note how the description by Hopkins of his terms includes references to painting and music. This must have increased Jakobson's sympathetic view of Hopkins. One of Jakobson's first published essays: "On Realism in Art" (1920) provides the early foundation for his communication theory. Like Hopkins, he did not restrict his analysis to verbal art. Jakobson's later essay, which included analysis of Blake: "On the Verbal Art of William Blake and Other Poet-Painters" (1970) includes analysis of the poetic text with reference to the paintings closely associated, by the poet, with the text of the poem. Hopkins' essay "On The Origin of Beauty" provides further discussion on the meaning of parallels. Hopkins wrote:

> All I want to shew [sic] is that there is a relation between the parts of the thing to each other and again of the parts to the whole, which must be duly kept. If from the volume of poems we take a dozen away, we [have] agreed there is no difference, the remainder are neither better nor worse. But if from one single work of art, one whole, we take anything appreciable away, a scene from a play, a stanza from a short piece, or whatever it is, there is a change, it must be better or worse without it. (1959: 97)

The repeated parts, the patterns or parallels within a work of art, is vital to its entirety, in order to create its artifice and, indeed, beauty. The patterns of lines, intersections, repetitions of forms and sounds, construct the poem as a whole. It has to be understood that Hopkins' definition of metaphor and simile indicates how his contribution, although very important, in fact differs from Jakobson's later developed model. He writes: "Then there are practically only these two kinds of comparison in poetry, comparison for likeness' sake, to which belong metaphor, simile, and things of that kind, and comparison for unlikeness' sake, to which belong antithesis, contrast, and so on. Now there is a convenient word which gives us the common principle for both these kinds of comparison – Parallelism." (1959: 106).

The placing of simile and metaphor together as a poetic trope used for "likeness' sake" rather clouds efforts to understand Jakobson's separation of the two tropes as belonging to different axes: the simile, as a contiguous or consecutive trope, along the syntagm and metaphor, as trope of similarity or simultaneity, along the paradigm. However, Hopkins' contribution is very important. Jakobson only discovered his work (see "Grammatical Parallelism and Its Russian Facet" 1987:145–179) later in his career. Jakobson refers to Hopkins in three essays: "Poetry of Grammar and Grammar of Poetry" [1960]; "Grammatical Parallelism and Its Russian Facet" [1966] and "A Glance at The Development of Semiotics" [1974], all in *Language in Literature* (1987). In "The Poetry of Grammar", Jakobson acknowledges Hopkins' paper, "On the Origins of Beauty", as one of the greatest contributions to poetics (1987: 127). He wrote that he agreed with Hopkins that "on every level of language the essence of poetic artifice consists in recurrent returns." (1987: 145).

However, there are other points to be raised from Hopkins' densely argued essay. He is concerned to define how prose and poetry are different. He writes:

> If therefore by poetry you understand all verse, we may define it as differing from prose by having a continuous and regular artificial structure . . . As for the nature of the artificial structure, from what we agreed before I think I may conclude you will say that rhythm, metre, rhyme, alliteration, assonance, and whatever other structural properties, may belong to verse, are cases of strictly regular parallelisms. (1959: 107,108)

Hopkins states that "verse is distinguished from prose as employing a continuous structural parallelism" (1959: 108). The parallelism may well also appear in poetic prose, but the added devices of rhythm, rhyme and metre are unlikely to be prioritised. It is the word "continuous" which is the giveaway. To his analysis Hopkins adds the term "continuous artificial structure" (1959: 108) as relevant to analysis of verse.

It is in the course of developing his argument that Hopkins defines a number of different parallelisms. These different categories refer to particular devices and the parallel use of them – assonance for example – but they also refer to the use of parallel structures which, in turn, also contain subordinate parallel structures. Hopkins refers to a poem by Shelley entitled: "Music, When Soft Voices Die", which Hopkins quotes as having the word "soft" replaced with the adjective "sweet":

> Music, when soft voices die,
> Vibrates in the memory;
> Odours, when sweet violets sicken,
> Live within the sense they quicken.
> Rose leaves, when the rose is dead,
> Are heap'd for the belovèd's bed;
> And so thy thoughts, when thou art gone,
> Love itself shall slumber on  (Shelley: *Posthumous Poems*: 1824)

Using this poem as an example, Hopkins identifies subordination of parallelism within the antithesis used in the poem. He writes (1959: 110):

> The idea of the piece then is thrown into the shape of an antithesis. Now this is illustrated in three metaphors, making with the couplet in which the idea is expressed a system of parallelisms in four members, the metaphors being taken from music, scented flowers, and rose-leaves. But now see further the subordination of parallelism to the parallelism. Each of three metaphors contains an antithesis within itself – "Music, when sweet voices die", "Odours, when sweet violets sicken", and "Rose-leaves, when the rose is shed" [sic] and answer to the antithesis in "thy thoughts, when thou art gone.

The parallels are therefore, with reference to the "subordinate parallels", identified as having different qualities, that is, different strengths or levels. Hopkins then identified a number of different types of parallel with reference to a poem by Richard Garnett called "The Nix" [a water fairy]:

> THE NIX
> The crafty Nix, more false than fair,
> Whose haunt in arrowy Iser lies,
> She envied me my golden hair,
> She envied me my azure eyes.
>
> The moon with silvery ciphers traced
> The leaves, and on the waters played;
> She rose, her arms my form embraced,
> She said: "Come down with me, fair maid."
>
> She led me to her crystal grot,
> She set me in her coral chair,
> She waved her wand, and I had not
> Or azure eyes or golden hair.

Her locks of jet, her eyes of flame
Were mine, and hers my semblance fair:
"O make me, Nix, again the same,
O give me back my golden hair! "

She smiles in scorn, she disappears,
And here I sit and see no sun,
My eyes of fire are quenched in tears,
And all my darksome locks undone.   (Garnett. 1893: 118)

To summarise Hopkins' theory of parallels, as well as the kinds of parallels mentioned above, he identifies the following, with reference to examples from the above poem:

> "individual" parallelism (1959: 112) – "more false than fair" [line 1] (heightened by the alliteration)
> "utilitarian" parallelism (1959: 113) – two clauses linked by "and" [last stanza, line 2]
> "independent parallelism" (1959: 113) – the use of "or/or" as a poetic device, which is not the grammar of prose (stanza 3, line 4). This can also be understood as a "parallelism of expression" (1959: 114), being poetic in style, rather than a structure which highlights sense over and above expression.
> "detached consecutive parallelisms" – where Hopkins indicates that the parallels are understood as separate constructions. However, he develops this into a further "higher" kind of parallelism:

> The two terms of a parallelism make a whole of beauty, but these wholes again may be the terms of a higher whole; as so many lines make up each speech in a scene, so many speeches each scene so many scenes each act, so many acts the play . . . I mean only that works of art are composite, having unity and subordination . . . each of the coordinates having a unity of its own towards its subordinates.   (1959: 114)

The analysis above indicates an understanding of what Jakobson was later to call "imputed similarity". The individual components of poetic structure are combined to construct a poetic composite whole, which is greater than its subordinate components. Before moving on to consider further similarities between Hopkins' and Jakobson's theory of parallels, it is important to remember that Hopkins' discipline was that of rhetoric and poetry. More modern systems of analysis use different categorisations – for example: semantics, linguistics, stylistics and semiotics. Before examining how Jakobson understood and used Hopkins' theories, a closer analysis of Hopkins' important terms "inscape" and "instress", will further inform an understanding of how Hopkins understood artifice in poetry, of which parallels formed a part. The following paragraphs are a brief overview and are not definitive.

*NPEPP* provides the following definition: "Inscape is Gerard Manley Hopkins' term for the pattern of attributes in a physical object that gives it at once both its individuality and its unity" (*NPEPP* 1993: 609a). Hopkins developed his own theory of "inscape" and "instress" with assistance from the 13th century philosopher and theologian Duns Scotus. Duns Scotus used the terms: "haecceity" ("thisness") and "quiddity" ("whatness") (Hopkins 2009: xxiii). For Hopkins, the important quality is the difference between the generic category and the individual qualities, properties or characteristics of a thing which make it a *particular* thing – the difference, for example, between man (people) and an individual. The person or object is at one and the same time its unity (inscape) and perceived individuality (instress):

> The individuality to which Scotus refers is more fundamental and abstract than that covered by inscape. He suggests that this uniqueness is part of God's concept of a person even before he has given him life and is far more radical than the incidental features by which we recognize individuals. Whereas Hopkins applies inscape [*quiddity*] to species, *haecceitas* [instress] is that which differentiates the individual from the species. (2009: xxiii)

However, John Llewelyn argues that the word "haecceitas" is not the same as instress (2021: 13,21 and 28). His argument, is based on close reading of Duns Scotus where he concludes that it is not possible to separate out Scotus' definition of the two qualities of being and individuality (1921:41). Are inscape and instress inseparable in the same way? Inscape is understood as the being, and instress as the individual nature of the people or things observed. However, in Llewelyn, this apparent echoing of Scotus is prevented by Hopkins' observation of movement in inscape. This can be seen from the examples provided by Hopkins below where he observes the movement of grasses and water. Llewelyn writes: "I take 'running' as a reference to a lapse of time in contrast to 'immediate' taken as a reference to an actual or imagined moment now". For Llewelyn, the inclusion of movement into the definition of instress is not a quality which can be included in the Duns Scotus "haeccitas" and "quiddity". It is therefore not possible to equate them.

Instress is also perceived by looking closely at something to see it anew. Hopkins wrote: "What you look hard at seems to look hard at you, hence the true and false instress of nature . . . Unless you refresh the mind from time to time you cannot always remember or believe how deep the inscape in things is" (2009: 204). Another example given by Hopkins is that he observes grasses nodding in the breeze and how they nod in the same manner but each individual movement is in fact different (2009: 214). He writes: "All the world is full of inscape and chance left free to act falls into an order as well as purpose" (2009: 215). Instress is both a state of existence and a dynamic, it is enabled through a perception of inscape. Instress is also inscape expressed as an impulse which recognizes the same in the other, person or object, but as individual to them. In 1872, Hopkins wrote about the water flowing in a brook: "I caught an inscape as flowing and well marked almost as the frosting on glass and slabs; but I could not reproduce it afterwards with the pencil" (1959: 227).

Another suggestion is, that as a classicist, is it possible that Hopkins derived his theories on inscape and instress from Plato's *Republic*? This might seem to be a digression but it provides a key to the transition between the semiosis in the ideas of both Plato and Hopkins, and is the reason why Jakobson finds Hopkins' analysis inspiring and useful to his own semiotic understanding of poetic function – in this case parallels in poetry as factual and imputed similarity.

As Plato makes clear in his Book X of *The Republic* (2000: 423–433). His model contains three forms of creation: the perfect object made by God, the real object made by the artisan (in Plato's example) the carpenter), and the image of the object constructed by the painter – which cannot be touched and is not real – but is a resemblance of the object which is understood to be an accurate representation. For Hopkins, his rhetorical understanding and categorization of parallels in poetry, is informed by these representations – the real or factual, and imagined. Using analogy: the table made by the carpenter comprises the category of "marked" (or factual) parallels (in poetry the actual poetic tropes – e.g. rhyme, alliteration). The image made by the painter comprises the sum total of the artistic devices which construct the image, (in poetry the sum total of all the devices within the poem which are not even understood by reading each individual line but only by reading the poem as a whole). The complex combination is higher level of the parallel and is therefore poetic artifice – imputed rather than factual similarity. Hopkins' sensitivity to parallels in poetry is also expressed by his appreciation of art, and he sees them as a vital part of poetic interpretation.

The overall argument for Hopkins is, that God created the world, and therefore all that exists within it. For Hopkins, the poet would be in the same category as Plato's painter – the poet imitates the perfect world but his/her poetry has no existence in itself – it contains the images of perfect creation – inscape – and the impulse of the poet who seeks inspiration to write about the created object is instress. The process of seeing and perceiving are directly linked to the divine created perfect model, though we, as imperfect humans, can only see imperfectly. A further quotation from Hopkins reveals that he understands that there is an element of chance, he wrote: "I saw the inscape though freshly, as if my eye were growing, though with a companion the eye and the ear are for the most part shut and instress cannot come" (1959: 214). Hopkins seems to be saying that the eye and the ear must be receptive to allowing the total of the individual and combined parts to be perceived and understood.

Hopkins applied his theories of "inscape" and "instress" to his observations of the city. This includes the depiction of crowds, an obvious aspect of city life.

William Thesing develops the idea in his chapter on Hopkins in Sulloway (1990): He suggests that Hopkins' poem "The Alchemist in the City" is almost the only poem which highlights a city environment. Here the Alchemist is seen as isolated, and is compared to the energy of the crowded streets below his window. The viewpoint of the city poet has been highlighted as important in city poetry – see the analysis of the poem "Commuter's Pentameter" (Wardle, in Chapter Four, above). Hopkins' entire poem has twelve stanzas of four lines each. It therefore has a ballad style form. Thesing quotes his first two stanzas:

> My window shows the travelling clouds,
> Leaves spent, new seasons, alter'd sky,
> The making and the melting crowds
> The whole world passes; I stand by
>
> They do not waste their meted hours,
> But men and master plan and build:
> I see the crowning of their towers,
> And happy promises fulfill'd.

Hopkins' poems on working men (for example: "Felix Randall", "Harry Ploughman") are studies of individual working men in themselves, not as part of a group of working men (people) in an industrial environment. His poem "Tom's Garland" incorporates a vision of how crowds are constructed and led to Hopkins perhaps recognising his inability to engage with city themes. Hopkins was never happy in the city. His knowledge of deep poverty, arising from his close proximity to it, especially as a parish priest, in Liverpool, distressed him. Thesing notes that Hopkins responded to crowds in two ways – how to "compose" a crowd scene, and how crowds, in reality, assemble on the streets. Hopkins described the crowd where honorary degrees are awarded in Oxford 1866. Here, the "inscape" is constructed by "all the heads looking one way thrown up by their black coats relieved only by white shirt-fronts etc: the short strokes of eyes, note, mouth, repeated hundreds of times . . . The short parallel strokes . . ." (Journals. 1959: 139, 140).

Hopkins witnessed many crowds, especially in Dublin where there were protests against British Rule. This included the rally in Phoenix Park in March 1885 and he wrote about it to his mother. The gathering appears to Hopkins to be random. He writes that he "cannot form a coherent composition of the crowd, cannot discover a single line of force or positive energy to capture an inscape because of the random competition inherent in the gathering" (Thesing: 144,145). Hopkins' brother composed an etching entitled, "Addressing the Free and Independent Electors" which was published in 1885, but Hopkins found it disappointing. He cannot find a unity of purpose in the constructed scene and considers that it lacks artistic construction:

As difficulties of perspective increase greatly with the scale so do those of composition. The composition will not come right of itself, it must be calculated. I see no signs of such calculation. I find it scattered and without unity, it does not look to me like a scene and one dramatic moment, the action of the person is independent and not mutual, the groups do not seem aware of one another.
(Thesing quoting Hopkins' letter to his brother: in Thesing (1990): 145)

In the final lines of Hopkins' poem "Tom's Garland", Thesing suggests that Hopkins "fails to find a line of unity to create an inscape of the dissolving image of 'packs' of the 'Undenizened' moving through the streets like an epidemic" (Thesing 1990: 151). Hopkins understands the crowd to be motivated by either hunger or rage but does not have a method of finding a poetic movement, or line of movement, which unifies and beautifies their movement. Hopkins' use of inscape informs his analysis of crowds, and provides a trope for such analysis, for both theorists and poets, even though he, himself, was unable to achieve cohesion in a poetic interpretation of city life. Hopkins' use of parallels in poetry further describes the repeated action of the crowded streets in the city. It enhances the power of how the city is expressed in poetry. It also provides an example of how both inscape and the parallel can be combined in the analysis of poetry and are found to be specifically useful in establishing a city poetic characteristic – the crowded environment.

How did Jakobson understand Hopkins' theory of parallels? It is clear that Jakobson understood parallels as semiotic. Jakobson's understanding of parallels in poetry, was first explored in his early essay "Realism in Art", ([1921] 1987, pp19–27), where he refers to "negative parallelism" (1987: 26). This is where a metaphor is replaced by the substitution of a descriptive designation. Jakobson's own example to demonstrate this trope is: "I am not a tree, I am a woman". The metaphor is constructed by the verb to be, "am", in this first instance, while the second use of "am" constructs a factual description. The sentences are repetitive in overall construction (i.e. parallels), but different in internal structure.

Jakobson, throughout his life, as a Formalist, was interested in the structure of poetry, and its form. He noted (1987: 94), with regret, that linguists rarely included the study of poetry in their systems of analysis. It was this separation which led him to construct his semiotic theory of poetic function. He explores the details of its construction in his essay "Linguistics and Poetics", written in 1960 (1987, *Language in Literature*: 62–94). Jakobson first studied parallels in poetry in his PhD thesis on mediaeval Czech religious poetry when he was living in Prague in the 1930's. He describes the contrapuntal effect of two rhythms – that of usual speech rhythm and that of the poetic stress running concurrently in the poem: "the *mounting* of the metrical form upon the usual speech form necessarily gives the experience of a double, ambiguous shape to anyone who is familiar with the given language and with verse." (1987: 80). He highlights Hopkins' analysis of parallels from his essay "Poetic Diction" as quoted above, summarizing his ideas as: "Briefly, equivalence in sound, projected into the sequence as its constitutive principle, inevitably involves semantic equivalence, and on any linguistic level any constituent of such a sequence prompts one of the two correlative experiences which Hopkins neatly defines as 'comparison for likeness' sake' and 'comparison for unlikeness' sake.'" (1987: 83).

Jakobson understands that the parallels provide a pattern for understanding "interaction between meter and meaning" and that therefore this "arrangement of tropes cease[s]" to be a free and unpredictable aspect of poetry (1987: 83). It is Hopkins' analysis of parallels which enables this understanding. Jakobson quotes from Hopkins at the beginning of his essay "Grammatical Parallelism and Its Russian Facet" (1987: 145–179[1966]). He uses a comparative study of Finnish, Russian and Chinese verse to demonstrate that all folk traditions use repetitions of words and phrases – including verses and choruses. The repetitive structure of some folk verse clearly demonstrates Hopkins' "figure of grammar" and "figure of sound" in his definition of parallels (1959: 289). For example, a poem may repeat a word at the beginning of each of several lines in a poem. In his chapter on "Grammatical Parallelism" Jakobson provides an overview of the study of biblical parallels. He mentions the work of Bishop Robert Lowth who, in 1799, published an analysis of parallels in Isaiah. Lowth's work is also referred to by Hopkins. Hopkins highlighted parallelism as a device in Hebrew poetry: "Hebrew poetry . . . is structurally only distinguished from prose by its being paired off in parallelisms, subdivided of course often into lower parallelisms" (1959: 106). Within Hebrew poetry the second parallel or colon is not a direct repetition of the first one, but a variant, for example, in the following quote from the *NPEPP*: "The poetic line is usually composed of two cola . . . [plural of colon] – sometimes three or four – which are parallel to each other either completely or partially in lexis or syntax. The words of the second colon repeat in different words the meaning of the first *(synonymous parallelism)*; reverse, negate, or contradict its meaning *(antithetical parallelism)*; or modify it *(synthetical parallelism)*" (*NPEPP* 1993: 501b).

Building on his strong sense of the semiotic in poetic form, it is a small step for Jakobson to understand the parallels as lines which can all be traced through the poem as diagonal lines. And, as is illustrated in Chapter Nine, below, even arcs or curved lines can be drawn through and/or across the whole poetic text. Jakobson writes of "vertical similarities", "horizontal similarities", a "falling diagonal", a "rising diagonal", higher and lower upright arcs, "inverted arcs" (1987: 134 [1960]). This is a dimension of geometric comprehension of poetic structure which Hopkins did not identify. It is possible, with the use of any analysis of parallels, to examine a poetic text and provide evidence of parallels through a repeated word, phrase, rhyme, alliteration, assonance and so on. A simple analysis may not be sufficient. An example, in conjunction with the use of Formalist analysis, has been demonstrated in a poem by Jaljagrov (Roman Jakobson's pseudonym) in Chapter Five, above. This has shown how the uses of certain poetic structures appear in clusters, which heighten the meaning of a poem.

The workings of such devices, are further demonstrated through praxis with reference to part of a poem by David Jones, "The Anathémata" (1972). Here an examination of personal pronouns, or "shifters" and "deictics", within the text reveals a complex process of how certain pages or passages of a poem draw the reader's eye towards clusters, parallel use and frequency within the text. These clusters form parallels within the text. The analysis demonstrates how parallels can be formed with the use of word patterns as well as with repeated phrases. This informs the understanding and meaning of the poem and the poet's intentions. As an example, page 157 (see reproduced text below) illustrates a patterned use of deictics of both time and place. David Jones' extensive annotations of his poem reveal a complex poetic exploration of London in historical, geographical, religious, ethnographical and personal terms. The praxis of establishing these patterns reveals the complexity with which theoretical and accepted usage of syntax is challenged by their use in poetry. It is also interesting and surprising to find that words which are not deictics in themselves, serve a strong deictic purpose. The quote is taken from the fifth section of the poem entitled "The Lady of the Pool". The section of the poem opens and closes with a reference to lavender sellers who peddled fresh lavender on the streets of London every August.

The deictics on page 157 (1972) are listed here. In sequence, within the poem, they occur: "when, upon, at, in, and in, before, within, and, at, on, against, between, when, and, such, new, in, on, that, about, that, such, when, then, by, that, that, what". Almost all of these deictics occur at the beginning of the lines and form a pattern. It is striking how, in usage, so many deictics of either time or place can be interchangeable as to function – for example, "before" is used as a deictic of place within the context of these quoted lines, but of course it also indicates a position of time as well as place. The deictics of place from the quote occur as a cluster largely at the beginning of the page, deictics of time are more concentrated in the second half of the page. Jakobson's Formalist analytical techniques are so detailed (and time consuming to implement) that he presents them with respect only to short poems. How his analysis can be made to work in a book length poem such as David Jones *Anathémata* would be a process governed by small units of the poem – in this poem even a section of it is daunting. With reference to this particular page, the patterning and the intensity of deictics provide a strong starting point for analysis. In the following extract the deictics are highlighted in bold and, additionally, for interest, the shifters are highlighted in bold italics.

>                     **When *he*** came to town
>
>                                                                        **upon** a'ass's pony:
>     **At** the lit board
>     **and in** the dark-hour garden
>                                         **before** the bishop's curia and
>                                           **within** the Justiciar's mote-hall
>                                         raised to the mock-purple
>                                    **and**
>     at the *column*,...cap-tin.
>                                                             **On** the ste'lyard on the Hill
>     weighed **against *our*** man-geld
>                                             **between** March and April
>     **when** bough begins to yield
>                                                 **and** West-wood springs new.
>     **Such** was ***his*** counting house
>                                         whose queen was **in *her*** silent parlour
>     **on that** same hill of dolour
>                                                   **about** the virid month of Averil
>     **that** the poet will call cruel.
>                                                 **Such** was ***her*** bread and honey
>     **when** with ***his*** darling Body (of ***her*** body)
>                         ***he*** won Tartary.
>     **Then** was the droughts of March moisted to the root **by that**
>     shower **that** does all fruit engender – and do constitute **what**
>
>     Excerpt from "Anathémata" by David Jones: from section:
>                                       "The Lady of the Pool". 1972: 157)

The shifters firmly place the text of the poetry as a perceived dialogue with the reader: "He, our, his, whose, her, her, his, her, he". The third person and first-person plural are balanced within the poem. The powerfully centrally placed "our" in the phrase "our man-geld" [meaning sacrifice/worship in AS and tax in Norman English] suddenly places the text as if it belonged to both the addresser and addressee (reader) "our". The complex rhyme systems recall and echo the poetic technique of Hopkins; "dark-hour/curia"; "counting-house/whose"; "hill/April"; "man-geld/yield"; and the "o", "ou" [ow] and "oo" sounds in the last lines of the page are coupled: "droughts" with "shower" and "root by /do constitute". Examination of the different verb tenses shows that the simple past tense is predominant with the central lines in the present tense: "begins" and "springs". There is one future tense: "the poet will call cruel". This again jolts the poem out of its own addresser time and towards the addressee or reader but at the same time it reminds the reader of the force of the addresser's or poet's perception and control of the artefact (It is also a reference to a mediaeval poem which T.S.Eliot also used in "The Waste Land").

The suggestion that words which are not usually associated with deixis are in fact deictics within the poem needs further examination. The categorisation of the words "such", and "and", as deictics is not an obvious choice, but it seems appropriate within the context of these lines. As Wales (2001: 100) defines "the" as a deictic word within its early Middle English usage, it might, within the context of these lines, be interesting to suggest that the word "and" also has a deictic meaning – as in the meaning that the poet is making sure that additional material is added, in the sense of pointing out this material. This might also be relevant as the passage has marked affiliation with older English usage. The word "such" as a suggested deictic is harder to define. It is an adverb of relative quantity. Within this context it seems to have such [sic] a strong qualitative meaning that it deictically points out the context of the drama which is unfolding within the short extract from the book-length poem.

Jones clearly understood the importance of deixis of both time and place as this example shows. His use of deictics reveals patterns within the text. The deictics are many layered, they interpret the subject matter. The deictic of place may refer to placing, both literally and, as an expression of poetics, as explored in the argument above. If the deictic of time is added to the deictic of place, then they reveal how the poem proceeds through various times, often in a dislocated manner – as is obvious in "The Anathémata" – through Roman and other time periods including contemporary periods. Understanding how parallels arise in a text provides analysis which is accessed through a variety of poetic tropes. The tropes – here shifters and deictics – can be the source for the semiotic analysis of parallels within a poem.

Jakobson further describes the qualities of parallels when, in his essay "Grammatical Parallelism", he makes a direct reference to Hopkins' theory of parallels: "on every level of language the essence of poetic artifice consists in recurrent returns" (1987: 145). These are "poetic patterns" and Jakobson further elaborates his description of how parallels in lines of poetry are constructed. He writes:

> Pervasive parallelism inevitably activates all the levels of language: distinctive features, inherent and prosodic, the morphologic and syntactic categories and forms, the lexical units and their semantic classes in both their convergences and divergences acquire an autonomous poetic value. This focusing upon phonological, grammatical, and semantic structures in their multiform interplay does not remain confined to the limits of parallel lines but expands throughout their distribution within the entire context; therefore the grammar of parallelistic pieces becomes particularly significant. The symmetries of the paired lines in turn vivify the question of congruences in the narrower margins of paired hemistichs [half lines] and in the broader frame of successive distichs [two line closed stanzas]. (1987: 173)

The discussion so far helps to shed light on a particular aspect of Jakobson's distinctive Formalist analysis of poetry. Jakobson's use of Hopkins' parallels relies heavily on Hopkins' work on artifice. He develops Hopkins' "artifice" in his essay "A Glance at the Development of Semiotics" (1987: 436–454). But Jakobson does not examine the different kinds of parallels which Hopkins identified in his essay on "The Origin of Beauty", as discussed earlier in the chapter: "individual", "utilitarian", "independent" and "detached consecutive" parallelisms. He has, however, suggested alternative types of parallel.

The different parallels which Hopkins identifies are largely patterns based on grammatical constructions, the use of conjunctive words to combine or separate the parallel expressions. Jakobson's exploration in the "grammar of poetry" provides more detail of how "lexical and grammatical aspects of language" construct parallels (1987: 122). His reference to the work of Edward Sapir in this paragraph indicates the linguistic source for the fundamental knowledge of patterns in language. He notes that in parallels there is either – or both – a material (lexical) concept of parallel or a relational (grammatical) concept. An example might be that a character is first of all described as "big" and then as "grand", this is a lexical parallel. Or a character might be described as doing one thing, then he is described as doing another. For example, he might "drive the cattle" then "ride a horse"; this is a relational parallel.

Hopkins' own categories of parallels (1959: 113,114) develop these more linguistic definitions so that the combination of the grammatical constructions reveals the parallels – not just a repetition of the lexical and grammatical components. The category of "individual" parallelism uses the trope of alliteration in his example. The link within the parallel is that one person is being described, but it is the alliteration that provides the trope, not the linkage between the terms of description. His example of "utilitarian" parallelism, is provided by the use of a conjunction word. This is the most purely linguistic parallel. He identifies that "independent" parallelism might seem to be lexical as it is defined by the use of the word "or" to link two phrases, but Hopkins himself, highlights how the use constructs a "parallelism of expression", the parallels are constructing a poetic form of parallel, not just a repetition of a single word. His "detached consecutive parallelisms" are described as separate constructions which follow each other. This is closer to Jakobson's definition mentioned above – the lexical and grammatical parallelism, but used to comprehend the structure of two phrases or sentences rather than two words or small combinations of words which are interior to a sentence.

Hopkins' "antithetical parallelism" contains a negation of some of the material presented in a sequence – it can be constructed by phrases, sentences, stanzas, two separate poems or even two separate books – as, for example, in Blake's *Songs of Innocence* and *Songs of Experience*. Hopkins in his analysis of the poem "The Nix" demonstrates how antithesis straddles the whole phrase, providing a parallel of opposite sensations – antithesis – within each idea expressed.

He further identifies it as having a "subordinate parallel", that it constructs a "higher whole" – that is that the construction of the stanza or poem as a whole comprises of groups of parallel expressions.

So far, the parallels discussed are ones of juxtaposition, though Hopkins' establishment of "subordinate" parallels constructs a more complex form. Time is established as an integral part of Formalist "Poetic Function". The negative parallel, is further identified, by implication, by the definition of time provided by St Augustine in his "Confessions", where he states that measurement of time is based on length, that something can be twice as long as another:

> I could not measure the movement of a body, its period of transit and how long it takes to go from A to B, unless I were measuring the time in which this movement occurs. How then do I measure time itself? Or do we use a shorter time to measure a longer time, as when, for example, we measure a transom by using a cubit length? So we can be seen to use the length of a short syllable as a measure when we say that a long syllable is twice its length. By this method we measure poems by the number of lines, lines by the number of feet, feet by the number of syllables, and long vowels by short, not by the number of pages (for that would give us a measure of space, not of time). The criterion is the time words occupy in recitation, so that we say "That is a long poem, for it consists of so many lines. The lines are long, for they consist of so many feet. The feet are long for they extend over so many syllables. The syllable is long, for it is double the length of a short one".  (1998: 239–240)

St. Augustine indicates that his definition is founded on the basis of the length of poetic lines and the number of syllables in the line. A line of poetry can be half as long as another or, as is suggested here, in a development of his definition, it can even be omitted entirely (see Tonks poem in Chapter Four above). The omission is then seen as a negative which can provide a negative parallel.

Jakobson's essay "A Glance at the Development of Semiotics" (1987: 436–454), provides material which draws his theories of poetics further away from Hopkins and into a different categorisation of poetic structure. It is Hopkins' development of the term "poetic artifice" which has so far formed the basis of the study of parallels as components of poetic structure. This chapter now refers to Jakobson's exploration of semiotic terms concerned with the definition of parallels, as influenced by Peirce, the American semiotician (1839–1914) and Saussure (1857–1913). Jakobson's understanding of Peirce is that Peirce's triad in respect of a sign's relation to its object – the index, the icon, the symbol (1987: 443) – should in fact be complemented with a fourth – the artifice of parallelism or imputed similarity.

In his essay "A Glance at the Development of Semiotics" (1987 [1975]) Jakobson refers to Saussure's ground breaking work on ancient poetry and then again to his own development of Peirce:

> "Parallelism" as a characteristic feature of all artifice is the referral of a semiotic fact to an equivalent fact inside the same context, including the case where the aim of the referral

> is only an elliptic implication. This infallible belonging of the two parallels to the same context allows us to complement the system of times which Peirce includes in his semiotic triad: "An icon has such being as belongs to past experience . . . An index has the being of present experience. The being of a symbol . . . is *esse in futuro*" (IV.447; II.148). The artifice remains the *atemporal* interconnection of the two parallels within their common context.
> 
> (1987: 452)

As discussed above in Chapter Two, the fourth mode to be added to Peirce's "icon-index-symbol" triad is therefore artifice. The example given is that of a horse: a picture of a horse is a factual index, the word "horse" designates a horse but is imputed, as the word "horse" does not at all look like a horse; how the horse is described in a poem for example, adds the parallels and, amongst other poetic devices, these combinations construct the imputed similarity, giving rise to the artifice. Whilst Jakobson's own analysis of a number of poems is often largely linguistic, his theories of poetics contain semiotic analysis. In the concluding paragraph of his essay "A Glance at the Development of Semiotics", originally written in 1975 (1987: 436–454), Jakobson demonstrates his commitment to semiotics:

> Semiotics . . . the science of signs . . . has the right and duty to study the structure of all of the types and systems of signs and to elucidate their various hierarchical relationships, the network of their functions, and the common or differing properties of *all* systems. The diversity of the relationships between the code and the message, or between the signans and the signatum, in no way justifies arbitrary and individual attempts to exclude certain classes of signs from semiotic study . . . Semiotics, by virtue of the fact that it is the science of signs, is called upon to encompass *all* the varieties of the signum.
> (1987: 454)

Jakobson's semiotics arose in part from Saussure's "Course in General Linguistics" (first published in French in 1915), and which was instrumental to the rise of interest in semiotics in the twentieth century. When defining linguistics and semiology Saussure wrote: "A science that studies the life of signs within society is conceivable; . . . I shall call it *semiology*. Semiology would show what constitutes signs, what laws govern them . . . Linguistics is only a part of the general science of semiology; the laws discovered by semiology will be applicable to linguistics." (1966: 16). Semiology was perceived by Saussure as a science of signs that were arbitrary in their relation between form and meaning. The more modern definition of semiotics has developed, so that it includes within its analysis, any system of signs which express human communication (as well as all communication in the known universe). Barthes' interest in semiology introduced non literary texts – music, menus, and advertisements (Barthes, (2000) [1957] *Mythologies*) – into the realm of the study of signs. John Deely, in his overview of the development of the various terms to denote semiotic categorisation of signs, suggests that "semiotics" has superseded other terms – semeiosis, sematology etc. (2006: 15/16) – and he defines it as "a renewal of intellectual culture around an increasing appreciation of the manner in which human experience depends upon signs for its life" (2006: 24). Semiotics, at the beginning of this century, had further widened its remit to include "animal semeiosis, plant semeiosis and even bacterial semeiosis" (Cobley 2001c: 8).

For Jakobson, linguistics is not sufficient in itself as a structure for an analysis of either poetry or poetics. His Russian Formalist interest in "literariness", the study of technique as a "structured system" within the text, makes the use of both linguistics and semiotics in the analysis of poetic texts important. His theories, which include a strong interest in poetic structure, require both linguistic and semiotic models to release the full meaning of these texts. As mentioned above, Jakobson argued that not only linguistics should be a part of semiotics but also that poetry, especially the study of poetic form, should be included within linguistics: "Since linguistics is the global science of verbal structure poetics may be regarded as an integral part of linguistics . . . . many poetic features belong not only to the science of language but to the whole theory of signs, that is, to general semiotics . . . since language shares many properties with certain other systems of signs or even with all of them (pansemiotic features)." ("Linguistics and Poetics" (1987: 63).

Jakobson also mentions how Peirce's terms are used with reference to poetry – a literary form which Peirce's semiotic analysis rarely covers: "The signs of a given art can carry the imprint of each of the three semiotic modes described by Peirce; thus, they can come near to the symbol, the icon, and to the index, but it is obviously above all in their artistic character that their significance (*semeisos*) is lodged. What does this character consist of?" (1987: 451). Jakobson wrote, that the clearest answer to the question is given by Hopkins – and the answer has already been referred to above: "The artificial part of poetry, perhaps we shall be right to say all artifice, reduces itself to the principle of parallelism" (1959: 84). And, as also illustrated above, these parallels can be expressed in patterns produced by single words, by groups and categories of words, as well as by the patterns constructed by whole lines or even whole texts in relation to each other. Jakobson understands that the whole poem, not only contains individual semiotic structures, its entirety is a separate semiotic sign in its own right. It is not just the contiguous nature of words on the page and their syntax, meanings and attributes, or even phrases which provide similarities in structure – a poetic structure – it is the poem as a whole which manifests these patterns or parallels of similarity. Jakobson gives Hopkins a further accolade, as having identified this fourth semiotic poetic structure: "Each and every sign is a referral . . . The parallelism alluded to by the master and theoretician of poetry, Gerard Manley Hopkins, is a referral from one sign to a similar one in its totality or at least in one of its two facets (the signans [code] or the signatum [message])." (1987: 452).

In conclusion the importance of semiotic analysis of poetry lies in understanding the overall construction of poetry, not just through understanding its components from the point of view of linguistics, semantics, stylistics or rhetoric. There can be the simple factual exploration of poetry where poetic tropes are examined as providing the meaning of a poem – for example the use of assonance, alliteration, rhyme. Or more complex patterns can be sought, where, for example, references to the shape of the verse, use of repeated phrases or ideas are analysed and reveal parallels and artifice.

Jakobson admired Hopkins' work, but he did not fully explore Hopkins' rhetorically-based analysis of different types of parallels in poetry. Jakobson used parallels extensively in his own Formalist analysis of poetry. He then developed the semiotic terms of Peirce to arrive at a definition of "poetic artifice", which defines a theory of the overall shape and structure of poetry. Jakobson's use and development of parallels provides a semiotic definition, where Hopkins' own definition of "poetic artifice" remains firmly within the rhetorical tradition. Poetic theory has moved away from rhetorical tradition, but in Jakobson's extension of Hopkins' theory of parallels into the field of semiotic theory, the rhetorical component becomes not only a historical but also a current aspect of the analysis, one which informed Jakobson's Formalist analysis. As noted above, Hopkins' theory of inscape, especially when combined with his theory of the different parallels, is important to a city poetic. Thesing's analysis of Hopkins' understanding of crowds, provides a component of a theoretical city poetic and praxis. The following chapter takes a closer look at another poet's theoretical praxis – not intended as a contradiction in terms – the work of Vladimir Mayakovsky. Here the "rules" of poetry as defined in Mayakovky's manifesto are very different to the rhetorical and semiotic theoretical positions of Hopkins and Jakobson. They are closely linked to his understanding of revolution in poetics, in post-revolutionary Russia.

# Chapter 8
# Vladimir Mayakovsky: Poetry: Rules and revolution

Mayakovsky's book *How Are Verses Made?*, was first published in 1926, and then in English translation by George Hyde in 1970, and 1990, both by Bristol Press. The book is a study in how poets search for, and find, their exact poetic form and expression. How does the poet balance such form, and a search for language which exactly interprets something? This chapter examines parts of this book in detail and places it within the context of more recent experimentation by poets influenced by modern technology. All references made to the poem "To Sergey Esenin", written in 1926, are from the same publication.

Mayakovsky's theoretical exploration on writing poetry contains many references which point towards Jakobson's theories. This is particularly true of the Russian Formalist commitment to communication through poetic function. Some of Mayakovsky's ideas are different in emphasis to Jakobson's. As has been shown in previous chapters, Jakobson's Formalist theory of poetic communication can be represented diagrammatically. This is not the subject of this chapter but the reader will find it useful to bear it in mind.

One of the important aspects of Formalist theory is the process of communication, which is, in effect, what is being referred to when using the term "function". With consideration given to the varied definitions of semiotic, linguistic and poetic communication, the chapter discusses the list of five propositions that Mayakovsky sets out in: "How Are Verses Made?" (*HAVM?*). These are studied, in part with references to his poem "To Sergey Esenin", which Mayakovsky regarded as one of his best poems. It gained great popularity with the public at the time (McLean. 1987: 34, 35). He begins: "What basic propositions are indispensable, when one begins poetical work? First thing. The presence of a problem in society, the solution of which is conceivable only in poetical terms. A social command. (An interesting theme for special study would be the disparity between the social command and actual commissions.)." (*HAVM?: 49*).

Mayakovsky writes in his conclusion, that in order to understand the social command accurately, "a poet must be in the middle of things and events" (*HAVM?: 88*). He goes on to describe how this requires being involved in what is going on and therefore not being objective about it. In *HAVM?* Mayakovsky describes how he wrote his famous poem on the death of Sergey Esenin. The description illustrates in detail, how he put into practice his own theories about writing poetry. Firstly, he tells us about his friendship with Esenin and he recalls an event in Esenin's life. In the early stages of his career, Esenin affected peasant dress even when he was already financially successful, but later switched to the more conventional suit and tie. Mayakovsky records that he shouted across to Esenin in public company: "'I win the bet, Esenin, you're wearing a jacket and a tie!'/ Esenin got very angry and went to take it out on someone else" (*HAVM?:* 59).

For three months Mayakovsky found that he could not write anything appropriate about Esenin's death. He explains: "When I got back to Moscow I realized that my difficulties and my slowness in writing were the result of too close a correspondence between my own circumstances and this I was writing about. / The same hotel rooms, the same water-pipes, the same enforced solitude . . . /Whence comes what is almost a rule: to do anything poetic you positively need a change of place or of time (*HAVM?:* 64)". Later in the text he adds: "That's why I got further with my poem about Esenin on the short journey from Lubyansky Passage to the Tea Marketing Board . . . after the silence of the provinces, there was the cheerful hubbub of buses, cars and trams; and all round, as though challenging the old lamplit villages, were the offices of electro-technical firms (*HAVM?:* 67)". Both observations highlight the importance of communication between addresser (as directed by the social command) and addressee, the receiver of the message, which is a central and vital component of Russian Formalist understanding of the poetic function of the poetic message. What he is also highlighting is that he responded creatively to a city environment.

The second suggestion demonstrates Mayakovsky's earnest search to be sincere and accurate in his poetry as an orientation towards communication: "second thing. An exact knowledge, or rather sense, of the desires of your class (or the group you represent) on a given question, i.e. an orientation towards an objective" (*HAVM?:* 50). This is a clear commitment to a message which reflects both the poet's intentions, and the interests of the addressee. With this in mind, he derides those who have used the Russian word *seryozhna* [серьёзно – seriously] when writing about Esenin. In Russian this is an epithet which is applied between close family members. He wants to talk about the poet himself – not other people's expressed notions of closeness. Esenin committed suicide and some wrote disparagingly about it as if his last action placed all of the poet's work in a certain light. Mayakovsky writes that he wants: "deliberately to neutralize the effect of Esenin's last lines, [this is a reference to Esenin's suicide poem] to make Esenin's death uninteresting, to replace the facile beauty of death by another beauty, since toiling mankind needs all its strength to sustain the Revolution it has begun." (*HAVM?:* 63).

The opening line of Mayakovsky's essay *HAVM?* states: "I have to write on this subject". The sense of compulsion which drives him to interpret the world poetically, also contains a sense of exasperation: "editors have no notion of the poetry of the past, or don't know what poetry is for" (*HAVM?*: 45). His strong commitment to the revolution encourages his urgent need not only for neologism – "Neologisms are obligatory in poetry" (*HAVM?*: 48), but also a new combination of words, presented in a language which his audience can understand. This affected not only the content, but his style. In a similar vein, Edwin Morgan makes the same point in his Scots' translation of one of Mayakovsky's poems: "Ay, But Can Ye?", and which appears in Morgan's "Collected Translations" (1996: 37). It is reproduced here in full, with the Scots glossary, by kind permission of Carcanet, the publishers:

Ay, But Can Ye?

Wi a jaup the darg-day map's
owre-pentit –
I jibbled colour frae a tea-gless;
Ashets o jellyteen presentit
To me the gret sea's camshach
cheek-bleds.
A tin fish, ilka scale a mou –
I've read the cries o a new warld through't.
But you
Wi denty thrapple
Can ye wheeple
Nocturnes frae a rone-pipe flute?

**Scots-English glossary**

jaup – splash, slap
darg-day – work-day
owre-pentit – painted over
jibbled – dribbled, splashed
gless – glass
ashets – dishes
jellyteen – gelatine
camshach – crooked
cheek-bleds – cheek-bones
ilka – each
mou – mouth
denty – dainty
thrapple – windpipe
wheeple – whistle feebly
rone-pipe – spout for rainwater

The vocabulary here is so very different from standard English that the glossary is essential. It represents an extreme adjustment of a language by the poet in consideration of his audience.

Mayakovsky's second proposition includes emphasis on theory which links with Jakobson's Formalist emphasis on "function" or communication. Jakobson's own definition of poetic function includes the statement that the "focus on the message for its own sake, is the POETIC function of language." (1987: 69). This might seem that emphasis by the poet on what is sincere communication, may obscure the clarity of the message. But both Mayakovsky and Morgan have a strong commitment to their own audiences, which can over-ride how the content of the message is presented with the need to communicate with a particular audience. Mayakovsky also read his poetry at huge gatherings where the audience often heckled and demanded that he read certain poems, and intense dialogue took place with regards to the content of his poems and the current state of political affairs (Jangfeldt. 2014: 519, 520).

Mayakovsky's third proposition is an exploration of how the poet produces the poetic message: "Third thing. Materials. Words. Fill your storehouse constantly, fill the granaries of your skull with all kinds of words, necessary, expressive, rare, invented, renovated and manufactured." (*HAVM?*: 50). In conjunction with this statement Mayakovsky suggests (*HAVM?*: 55/56) that for the experienced poet a notebook is vital and essential: "This notebook is one of the most important pre-conditions for the composition of the genuine article." (*HAVM?*: 55). But, for Mayakovsky, the printed word in a notebook is only one component of the final part of the process: "You can produce something good to order only when you've a large stock of preliminaries behind you." (*HAVM?*: 53). He speaks of words "hammering away" in his brain and some "fine rhymes', an American metre to be "adapted and Russified", some "tersely striking alliteration of a trivial poster". And eventually: "All these preliminaries are put together in one's head, and the most difficult ones are noted down." (*HAVM?*: 54). He speaks of his sense of "intensity" over his quest for poetic expression: "There was a time when I embarked on such work as if fearful even to utter words and expressions that seemed to me needful for future poems – I became gloomy, dull and untalkative." (*HAVM?*: 55/56).

In an article from a brochure produced to coincide with an exhibition of Mayakovsky's work in the UK in 1982, Edwin Morgan quotes from a letter written by Mayakovsky to an unknown recipient "The pre 1917 Cubo-Futurists have become the Communist Futurists" (1982: 11). In the following quotation, taken from Morgan (1982), Mayakovsky asserts that the process of writing poetry is:

> To affirm verbal art as mastery of the word not in terms of aesthetic stylization but in terms of ability to accomplish any task by means of the word:
> 1. To take up any task demanded by contemporary life, this involved the need
>    a) to work on the vocabulary (neologisms, orchestration of sound effects etc.)
>    b) to replace conventional iambic and trochaic meters with polyrhythms of language itself
>    c) to revolutionize syntax (simplification of the forms of word-combination, impact of un-conventional word-usages etc)
>    d) to revitalize the semantics of words and word-combinations
>    e) to create models for the construction of striking subjects
>    f) to bring out the poster quality of the words [this is a reference to *chastushka* – частушка – a traditional type of short Russian or Ukrainian humorous folk song with high beat frequency, that consists of one four-lined couplet, full of humour, satire or irony; a word which means a jingle or ditty].

Mayakovsky's commitment to communication demands the detailed constructed process of how to write poetry. In describing how his poem "To Sergey Esenin" was written he refers to the construction of the poem as using "building bricks": "When

I've produced almost all these bricks, I begin to size them up, putting them now in one place, now in another, attending carefully to their sounds, and trying to imagine what sort of effect they produce." (*HAVM?*: 77). His purpose is personal both for himself and for his subject:

> ... thinking it over, I decide: first of all I must get my listeners interested by my ambiguity, as a consequence of which they can't tell whose side I'm on, thereby taking Esenin away from those people who are using his death to their own ends... Winning over the audience, seizing the right to speak about Esenin's achievements... I unexpectedly shunt my listeners towards a conviction that Esenin's end was totally unremarkable, insignificant, and uninteresting: I have rephrased his last words, and given them a meaning opposite to the one he intended. (*HAVM?*: 77)

The lines Mayakovsky is referring to are the last lines of Esenin's suicide poem:

"In this life to die is nothing new,
But to live, of course, is nothing newer"

The last lines of Mayakovsky's poem on Esenin are:
"In this life
        to die
                has never been hard.
To make new life
            's more difficult
                    by far."

Once again this illustrates an aspect of Jakobson's Formalist theory of poetics. Here Mayakovsky emphasises the importance of the poet's interpretation of something in close conjunction with how the reader or hearer perceives it. This is the dynamic between the addresser and the addressee. Added to it is the understanding that the addresser – here Mayakovsky, the poet – is the encoder (originator/presenter) of the poetic message and the addressee – here the reading/listening public (receiver/individual respondent) – is the decoder of it. It is here that Mayakovsky's commitment to the "social command" is understood as part of his political commitment, not only in terms of politics but also in terms of poetics. Because of this commitment, he left behind his earlier adherence to Futurism, which included the prevalent use of words which were either neologisms or plays on words and grammatical structure. *Zaum* poetry expressed the Futurist ambition to write abstract poetry. In the notes to *HAVM?*, the definition continues: "taking the word as a musician takes a motif, or rhythm, or tonal cluster, or a painter a set of formal relations, a colour, and by means of what Marinetti called the 'wireless imagination' set off emotional associations of particular combinations of words" (*HAVM?* notes: 109.110).

It is interesting to note that the arts of music and painting (cf. Jakobson) are drawn into this definition. The example given to illustrate these ideas is Khlebnikov's laughter poem. Two versions of the poem are given in the notes of *HAVM?*:

> The poem ... is a set of variations on the morphological possibilities of the Russian word for "laughter", [cmekh – смех]. The first of these translations is "semantic" (or what Fyodorov calls "comparative-projective") in orientation, and to a certain extent interprets and explains the original; the second is closer to his notion of the "comparative-structural" processes of the Russian text while refusing to "explain" its meaning. (HAVM? notes: 111)

The reference to "Fyodorov" can be explored through a new translation of his book: Federov's *Introduction to Translation* (2021). Both Federov, and the above quotation, indicate that there is linguistic input by the poet into Futuristic verse. It also indicates that it is not just the meanings of the words which are broken apart, it is the grammatical structure as well. In the circumstances it is worth including both translations here. The first one is the "semantic" translation:

> O you laughniks, laugh it out!
> O you laughniks, laugh it forth!
> You who laugh it up and down, laugh along so laughingly;
> Laugh it off belaughingly!
> Laughters of the laughing laughniks, overlaugh the laughathon.
> Laughiness of the laughish laughers,
> counterlaugh the Laughdon's laughs!
> Laughio! Laughio!
> Dislaugh, relaugh, laughlets, laughlets,
> Laughulets, laughulets.
> O you laughniks, laugh it out!
> O you laughniks, laugh it forth!
> (*HAVM?* 1966: 110: note 13)

The second translation, the "comparative-structural" translation, reveals more of the literal verbal processes of the original:

> Hlahla! Uthlofan, laughlings!
> Hlahla! Uthlofan, laughlings!
> Who lawghen with lafe, who hlachen lewchly.
> Hlahla! Ufhlofan hlouly!
> Hlfhlf! Ufhljfan hlouly!
> Hlahla! Hloufish laughlings lafe uf beloght lauchflorum!
> Hlahla! Loufenish lauflings lafe, hlohan utlaufly!
> Lawfen lawfen,
> Hloh, hlouh, hlou! luifekin, luifekin,
> Hlofeningum, hlofeningum.
> Hlahla! Uthlofan, laughlings!
> Hlahla! Uthlofan, laughlings!
> (*HAVM?* note 13: 110 taken from Khlebnikov 1985)

For the English speaker, this poem holds extra difficulties as the word "laugh" is not pronounced as it is written, and this is something which the second translation addresses by changing the spelling. Mayakovsky, as recounted by Elsa Triolet in her *Memoir* (2002) of Mayakovsky, stated that he:

> thought the poems he wrote in 1912 were his most obscure and that it was these which most often caused the question of incomprehensibility to be raised: "Once it had been suggested to me that my poems weren't readily comprehensible. I committed myself to writing in such a way as to be understood by the largest possible number of listeners (from a Shorthand Record of a Speech 25th March 1930). (2002: 25)

Mayakovsky expresses the Formalist aspect of poetic function in his over-riding commitment to communication: the poet (encoder) considers both his audience (decoders) and the poetic message in his poetry. The Formalist "poetic function" enables Mayakovsky's commitment to communication to be formulated and expressed.

Mayakovsky loved poetry from his childhood. He became a socialist whilst still at school and was involved in the Russian Revolution from a very young age. He had been arrested four times already, by the time he was fourteen. Once he had to swallow the paper on which crucial information was written so that it did not fall into the hands of the police: "Caught in a raid in Gruzini. Our illegal printing press. Ate the notebook. A bound one with addresses. Presnenskaya Station. Secret Police" (Almereyda.2008: 43); and quoted from Vladimir Mayakovsky (2002). During and after the revolution, he designed posters, wrote plays, advertisements and morale boosting *chastushka* [jingles] for the government. Elsa Triolet (née Kagan), a well-known writer in her own right, was courted by Mayakovsky but he eventually formed a strong and lasting attachment to her older sister Lili, who was married to Osip Brik, the literary critic and writer. Mayakovsky won several prizes and became very famous, especially within Russia. Today, his flat, which forms part of a larger apartment building house, is open to the public. Seeing images of his rooms demonstrate the pragmatics expressed in Mayakovsky's fourth proposition:

> Fourth thing. Equipment for the plant and tools for the assembly line. A pen, a pencil, a typewriter, a telephone, an outfit for your visits to the doss-house, a bicycle for your trips to the publishers, a table in a good order, an umbrella for writing in the rain, a room measuring the exact number of paces you have to take when you're working, connection with a press agency to send you information on questions of concern to the provinces and so on and so forth, and even a pipe and cigarettes. (*HAVM?*: 50)

The use of city stimulus has already been mentioned above. As, too, has Mayakovsky's stipulation that in order to clarify what to write, one should seek the opposite kind of stimulus: "Whence comes what is almost a rule: to do anything poetic you positively need a change of place or of time" (*HAVM?*: 64). In the twelve numbered conclusions to *HAVM?*, Mayakovsky defines writing poetry as a manufacturing process. Using this description, he writes in paragraph six: "Don't set in motion a huge poetry factory just to make cigarette lighters. You must renounce the uneconomical production of poetical trifles. Reach for your pen only when there is no other way of saying something except in verse." (*HAVM?*: 88). And in paragraph nine he adds: "Only by approaching art as a manufacture can you eliminate chance, arbitrariness of taste and subjectivity of values." (*HAVM?*: 89). Mayakovsky expresses his belief that the poet's work is real productive work, and which is expressed in images which show the poet bowed down by books and work – a beast of burden. This describes his strong dedication to understanding the methods for the construction of poetry and the skill involved in producing it.

The emphasis highlights another Russian Formalist principle defined by Roman Jakobson, that of "literariness". The Formalists insist that any creative work – in this instance poetry – has its own inherent structure which can be defined in linguistic and semiotic terms. The poetry is not to be interpreted as a reflection of the poet's life, or as a reflection of ourselves or what the poem means to us, the readers, but what it is, inherently in itself. How it is constructed according to the rules of language, the science of poetics. For Jakobson, this means the use of linguistics and semiotics, the grammar and patterning of poetry. It is an emphasis which is essential both to the reader and analyst (the addressee), and to the poet, inventor of the artefact (addresser).

Mayakovsky's poem "Talking with the Taxman about Poetry" (1926) takes his analogy with manufacture one stage further. He wrote:

'sorry to bother you,
                    Citizen taxman!
        No thanks.. . ..
                Don't worry. . .
                    I'd rather stand.. ..
        My labour's
            no different
                    from any other labour.
Examine these figures
            of loss and gain,
    the production
            costs
                I have been facing,
    the raw material
            I had to obtain.. ..
    A rhyme is an IOU,
            as you'd put it.

> "Pay two lines later"
>                       is the regulation. . ..
> Upon my honour,
>                   Citizen taxman,
> words
>                   cost poets a pretty penny in cash. . ..
>                       (*Selected Poems Vol.* I. 1984: 173,174)

Mayakovsky writes further that he pays "fines in cash/and high interest on sorrow,/ the poet is/always/ the Universe's debtor" (1984: 177) and demands that the taxman "Calculate the impact of verse/ and distribute/ all that I earn/ over three hundred years!" (1984: 178). Within the context of his fourth proposition, Mayakovsky mentions the use of the telephone – new technology in his day – and it can be reasonably assumed that the use of computer software would have been on his list of equipment if he were alive today. This development will be discussed further below.

Mayakovsky's fifth proposition itemises the importance of poetics and includes an example to summarize the propositions he has already listed:

> Fifth thing. Skills and techniques of handling words, extremely personal things, which come only with years of daily work: rhymes, metres, alliteration, images, lowering of style, pathos, closure, finding a title, layout, and so on and so forth.
>
> For example: the social task may be to provide the words for a song for the Red Army men on their way to the Petersburg front. The objective is to defeat Yudenich. The material is words from the vocabulary of soldiers. The tools of production – a pencil stub. The device – the rhymed *chastushka* [jingle]. The result:
> My darling gave me a long felt cloak
> And a pair of woolly socks.
> Yudenich scurries from Petersburg
> Fast as a smoked-out fox. (HAVM?: 50)

The content of the jingle was both topical, and essential to Mayakovsky's fifth proposition. General Yudenich was in overall command of the Russian army from March 1917 but was unable to continue operations due to revolutionary developments, because of which he fled to Finland. After the defeat of his White Army at Petrograd in the autumn of 1919, he fled for the second time into exile in France.

Mayakovsky states, almost certainly disingenuously, "I know nothing of iambuses or trochees" (*HAVM?*: 49) and "I know nothing of metre. Only I am convinced, on my own account, that to communicate heroic or majestic sentiments, you must choose long measures with a large collection of syllables, and for cheerful sentiments, short ones." (*HAVM?*: 69/70). Later, in *HAVM*, he discusses the importance of alliteration and rhyme, using examples from how he wrote the poem "To Sergey Esenin". Robin Aizlewood observes in his *Two Essays* on *Maiakovskii's Verse* (2000) that Mayakovsky was almost certainly "self-masking" and possibly echoing Pushkin's similar disingenuity over his poem "Evgenii Onegin" (Endnote 5 to "Maiakovskii's Hexameter" 2000: 56). Aizlewood also concludes from his extensive study of metrics in Mayakovsky's verse that the poem "To Sergey Esenin" is written in free trochees (2000: 25).

Aizlewood identifies Mayakovsky's use of metre and interpretation of it "as a tension between the civic and the lyric in his poetry" (2000: 46), and that this is an important aspect of Mayakovsky's poetics. This arises from Mayakovsky's antipathy to *byt*. Jakobson gives a definition of this Russian word in his essay "On a Generation That Squandered Its Poets" (1987: 273–300) with specific reference to Mayakovsky: "Opposed to [his] creative urge toward a transformed future is the stabilizing force of an immutable present, overlaid, as this present is, by a stagnating slime, which stifles life in its tight, hard mold. The Russian name for this element is *byt*." (1987: 277). Aizlewood writes about the stasis of *byt* in connection with Mayakovsky's use of meter:

> also involved is the question of the epic strain in Maiakovskii, which for Jakobson is always the "heroic lyric on a huge scale". Moreover, thematically the hexameter is linked to one of Maiakovskii's most fundamental preoccupations, at the centre of his mythology for Jakobson: this is liberation from confinement and the extension beyond set limits, which links in turn to the problematics of movement and stasis, "I" and "not-I", life and death.
>
> (2000: 46/47)

Aizlewood examines Mayakovsky's knowledge of hexameters and iambics in his poetry, specifically with reference to two poems "1500000000" [Fifteen billion] and "Chelovek" [Man]. Aizlewood notes how Mayakovsky also often freely interpreted these metrics. The poem "1500000000" is a political polemic on how the huge Russian peasant, Ivan, repulses Woodrow Wilson's American involvement in Russia's civil war (1917–1923) and "Man" is a personal love poem. Aizlewood notes that they both use two of these poetic constructions: the hexameter to demonstrate the heroic associations of the poem and the iamb to describe constraint: "the hero's actual fate as imprisonment, in society, religion and ultimately in millennia of unrequited love." (2000: 47).

*Byt* [быт] as a central theme of Mayakovsky's work needs some further explanation. Its meaning is by no means easy to translate. Any consideration of *byt* must also include a reference to the Formalist understanding of movement. *Byt* contributes to an understanding of how movement within communication exists between the text and the poet/reader (addresser/addressee). It is an important concept which influences the vocabulary of the Formalist poets. Conceptions of movement, time, plus aspects of how it is measured, in the context of the city, provide a framework for the construction of a poetic space.

Mayakovsky developed an esoteric definition of the function of time which is discussed by Pomorska (1985). Unfortunately, much of her article is in Russian and not translated. The quest for the relationship between the word and the thing, between art and life, for Majakovsky and the Russian Avant-garde, was a quest for the two to be one and the same thing. Pomorska quotes from Mayakovsky: "'Why should literature occupy its own little special corner? Either it should appear in every newspaper every day, on every page, or else its totally useless.' ... Consequently, the task of poets is *to make* new language. The radical side of this task was the theory of *zaum*, or the 'supraconscious language'" (1985: 50).

In a poem written in 1920: "Extraordinary Adventure", Mayakovsky "explicitly accuses the sun of generating time – that vicious circle, the senseless succession of days and nights." (1985, p54). Was this by implication an accusation that the sun generates *byt*? For Mayakovsky time was a trap. How was he to resolve the antinomy or contradiction between the poet and life? Pomorska identifies his struggle as an expression of *byt*. Mayakovsky transforms *byt* through "poetization" (1985: 67). Mayakovsky was a passionate and dedicated poet of the revolution. In his definition of the revolutionary requirements made of the poet, the need for "anti-*byt*", he wrote:

> The poet's revolutionary call is directed at all of those "for whom life is cramped and unbearable," "who cry out because the nooses of noon are too tight." The ego of the poet is a battering ram, thudding into a forbidden Future; it is a mighty will "hurled over the last limit" toward the incarnation of the Future, toward an absolute fullness of being.
> 
> (Jakobson 1987: 277)

The complexity of *byt* can lead to misunderstanding. *Byt* [быт] is not the same as the word as *byt'*, [быть, the verb to be], spelt slightly differently. *Быт* [быт], denotes a noun – meaning "way of life" or "life itself". This latter meaning of the word, *byt* [быт], is that of a stasis which is felt as an obstructive, immobilizing force. It is almost impossible to denote the difference in meaning through use of the Western European alphabet, however see Carrick below. Jakobson quotes Mayakovsky more fully:

> Inertia continues to reign. It is the poet's primordial enemy, and he [Mayakovsky] never tires of returning to this theme. "Motionless *byt*." "Everything stands as it has been for ages. *Byt* is like a horse that can't be spurred and stands still. . . . In fall,/winter,/spring,/summer/ During the day/during sleep/I don't accept/I hate this/all./ All/that in us/is hammered in by past slavishness/all/that like the swarm of trifles/was covering/and covered with *byt*/ even our red-flagged ranks." Only in the poem "About That" [*Pro Eto*] is the poet's desperate struggle with *byt* fully laid bare.
> 
> (Jakobson 1987: 278)

A second quote adds more imagery: "The poet is oppressed by the specter of an unchangeable world order, a universal apartment-house *byt*" (Jakobson.

1987: 279). An early image of Mayakovsky is that he "goes out through the city leaving his soul on the spears of houses, shred by shred'" (Jakobson. 1987: 289). And he eventually feels that *byt* has defeated the poet (1987: 280). He came to interpret the word as meaning not just "'rubbish with its own proper face,' but 'petty, small, vulgar rubbish' . . . 'swarm of trivia'" (Jakobson 1987: 294).

There are also issues which arise because of language differences and the Russian Cyrillic alphabet. This is addressed in detail, with regard to *byt*, in Rosy Carrick's PhD thesis (2016) which provides analysis of how possible inaccuracies of both the translator – Edward Brown and even Jakobson – have arisen. Carrick addresses the issues which arise from misunderstandings caused by mistranslating the Russian word *byt*: "when I note the difference between the Russian words Быт [daily life] and Быть [to be], the only lexical difference between which is the soft sign [ь], I distinguish between them in transliteration thus: byt and byt' [the apostrophe here indicates the Russian "ь", a letter that has no sound of its own]" (2016: 4). She carefully explains the different kinds of *byt* Mayakovsky is referring to, using examples of how translators have not taken the time and trouble to differentiate between the terms, thereby missing the complexities of meaning. The confusion has been misleading with regards to understanding Mayakovsky's work and sometimes creates a negative effect in people's attitude to the poet and his work. In her PhD thesis, Carrick writes about the development in the meaning of *byt*:

> At its most basic level, *byt* does indeed translate as 'everyday life', but in early Soviet Russia the term was far more complex. It ceased altogether to represent one single concept, and became instead split into two opposing concepts: old *byt* and new *byt*. Old *byt* referred to the stagnant daily life before the revolution, the practical conditions of the culturally and industrially backward, largely illiterate and impoverished population and, alongside that, the parasitic greed and extravagance associated with the bourgeoisie. New *byt* represented the ideal communist way for the "new soviet man" to live: a life of classless equality which embraced technology, education and good physical health. When Mayakovsky writes, as he often does, about his hatred for *byt*, it is always made explicit that it is the old *byt* to which he refers – and not to domesticity in general. Likewise, there are many poems in which he vigorously extols the virtues of the new *byt* as a central element of the revolutionary goal.
> (2016: 8, 9)

Carrick uses examples of Mayakovsky's poetry to illustrate her arguments and analysis. Some of these are translated, for the first time, in her thesis. Her first concern is to provide details of how the term contains the two concepts which emerge from Russian history. Quoting Svetlana Boym she writes:

> . . . dating back to the period of Russian Orthodox Christianity, the notion of *byt* has existed in binary opposition to another word *bytie*, the latter of which represents the human ideal: a higher spiritual existence, in which context mere *byt* has been considered inferior and fleeting in its concerns with earthly existence . . . Muscovite culture may have 'developed out of

the experience of East Slavic peasants in the nearly impossible conditions of life in the northern forest and in response to external aggression' [Boym] – a level of hardship which developed a particular "conservationist mentality [which] did not seek to preserve a traditional or idealised Slavic 'way of life' but [only] to preserve life itself" [Boym]. Such a mentality is inherently opposed to the notion of *byt*, on the grounds that *byt* is an element of life – or rather a way of experiencing life – that only those who have not endured such hardship may pursue or value. (2016: 99,100)

With the Soviet revolution, came an intolerance of the past, and thus a new, old *byt* and new *byt* emerge (see first quote from Carrick above: 2016: 8.9). Carrick explains later (2016:134) that the word *bytie* is a neologism and is accompanied by a second neologism *bytik*. These terms are used in Mayakovsky's poem "Love" (1926). The interpretation may best be translated in English as "old man byt": "We *adore* the rallies/such *elegant* anthems!/Leaving the meetings,/we speak with such beauty,/but often/beneath it,/covered with mould,/is little-old-grotty-old bytik." (2016:180).

Problems for translators have arisen because these differences of interpretation are not observed or understood. It is not that Mayakovsky hates domestic life or the little things of life, he has an intense revolutionary commitment to living life in a new way – including within the domestic sphere. Carrick writes: "The *byt* of Mayakovsky's time, like Janus, has two faces. It looks both to the past and the future – and maps out the transitional space between." (2016: 115). The mistranslation of Jakobson's essay "On a Generation that Squandered its Poets" has particular relevance, as Carrick states that not only did Jakobson need to provide more context for his quotations from Mayakovsky in his essay (see Carrick, 2016: 122,123), but that the essay has also been mistranslated leading to misinterpretation of Mayakovsky's poetry. She explains:

Jakobson's article was first published in the book The Death of Vladimir Mayakovsky [Смерть Владимира Маяковского] in 1931, which makes his description of Mayakovsky's relationship to *byt* the first in existence following the poet's death, although it was not translated into English until 1967 . . . . Particularly influential, as we will see, are his [Jakobson's] unsubstantiated accounts of Mayakovsky's alleged battle against time ('Majakovskij's conception of the poet's role is clearly bound up with his belief in the possibility of conquering time and breaking its steady, slow step'), suicide as a weapon against byt-as-stagnant-time ('[t]he motif of suicide [. . .] continually recurs in the work of Majakovskij, from his earliest writings, where 'madmen hang themselves in an unequal struggle with byt [. . .] in the Tragedy'), and his hatred of children ('[t]his constant infatuation with a wonderful future is linked in Majakovskij with a pronounced dislike of children, [. . .] and with undying hostility to that "brood-hen" love that serves only to reproduce the present way of life . . . . . . .

Jakobson does in fact, as we can see above, quote from a number of other poems which really do have the early Soviet concept of byt as their main subject, but he gives no context to these lines, and as, prior to the translations made by me for the purpose of this thesis, none of them have ever been translated into English before, it is impossible for the reader to know

> that in each one of the poems from which these lines are taken Mayakovsky's revulsion is levelled quite explicitly at the seemingly immoveable characteristics of *old byt*, a natural connection instead being suggested between Mayakovsky's views on *byt* and domestic life in general. (Carrick 2000: 122, 123)

Carrick also questions the translation of Mayakovsky's suicide note: "The inaccurate simplification by Brown [the translator of this essay by Jakobson], quoting from Mayakovsky's suicide letter, in translating *byt* as 'the daily grind' further cements the misrepresentation [of Mayakovsky], inextricably linking the concept of *byt* to 'everyday life' in the minds of almost every subsequent writer on Mayakovsky" (2016: 123). This has special importance with respect to discussion about the meaning of *byt*, in his poem *Pro Eto*, which addresses Mayakovsky's revolutionary commitment to *byt*. It is also important that the poem is understood as a political expression, not merely a personal one, which has hitherto been the case (Carrick: 128–130). Mayakovsky also understood *byt* as something which he disliked about certain forms of poetic expression. Carrick's close analysis of Mayakovsky's use of the word *byt*, includes mention of a further complication:

> The distinction in Russian between 'life' ('zhizn') and 'way of life' ('byt') means that it is possible in that language to speak of 'zhizn bez byta' – whereas 'life without daily life' sounds absurd in English. Nevertheless, even in Russian that phrase refers specifically to a primitive way of living, with an emphasis on the preservation of life over any kind of traditional or idealised 'way' of life – being 'alive' over being part of a 'culture'. (2016: 138.139)

Carrick summarises Mayakovsky's approach to *byt* and poetics: "Mayakovsky both attacked and supported *byt's* contradictory manifestations in a broad, detailed and politically rigorous manner which covered the following areas . . . [including] The criticism of poetry which, in Mayakovsky's opinion, is overly concerned with the trivial matters associated with the pre-revolutionary bourgeoisie – the 'new trash' – and which, in being so, stagnates and undermines communist progress." (2016: 205/206).

Jakobson's essay "On a Generation That Squandered Its Poets" (1987: 273–300) highlights, with deep regret, the suicide of several Russian poets in the 1920's – of which Mayakovsky, who committed suicide in 1930, was one. The others were: Nikolai Gumilev (1886–1921), first husband of Anna Akhmatova; Alexander Blok (1880–1921); Velimir Xlebnikov [Khlebnikov] (1885–1922) and Sergei Esenin (1895–1925). But is Jakobson ultimately ambivalent about Mayakovsky's skills? He describes the public's response to Mayakovsky's performances:

> "About That" [the title of a poem] is a long and hopeless cry to the ages, but Moscow doesn't believe in tears [a reference to one of the lines in the poem]. They [the audience] stamped and whistled at this routine Majakovskian [sic] artistic stunt, the latest of his "magnifi-

cent absurdities', but when the theatrical cranberry juice of the puppet show became real, genuine, thick blood, they were taken aback: Incredible! Inconsistent! (1987: 292)

For Jakobson, who left Russia in 1920, the suicide of so many poets from his peer group, must have produced ambivalent feelings, including anger, that his native country did not protect those with whom he had formed his ideas and with whom he was still in touch. The loss of poets leads him to state that: "As for the future, it doesn't belong to us either . . . . When singers have been killed and their song has been dragged into a museum and pinned to the wall of the past, the generation they represent is even more desolate, orphaned, and lost." (1987: 300).

Jakobson makes a reference to the power of *byt*, in his words "pinned to the wall of the past". His essay seems to ratify the dark tone of *byt*, rather than interpret the life of the poet in the way that Mayakovsky was determined to do in his poem "To Sergey Esenin". Mayakovsky really wanted Sergey Esenin to live on in his poetry and did not want Esenin to be understood through the veneer of his death. With reference to his fifth proposal in *HAVM?*, Mayakovsky writes about how he establishes a living rhythm for writing poetry, and with specific reference "To Sergey Esenin" he writes: "I walk along, waving my arms and mumbling almost wordlessly, now shortening my steps so as not to interrupt my mumbling, now mumbling more rapidly in time with my steps.//So the rhythm is established and takes shape." (*HAVM?*: 68). He goes on to liken this rhythmic "dull roar" to the sound of the sea, a door slamming, even the rotation of the earth and the whistle of a high wind.

Mayakovsky's interest in technology was demonstrated in an illustration by Rodchenko. There is a photomontage designed for the back cover of Mayakovsky's early poem: *"A Conversation with a Tax-collector about Poetry"* (published first, separately, in 1926 and then in later collections). Here, a picture of Mayakovsky is shown with the top of his head covered by a globe of the world with aeroplanes flying round it. It demonstrates how his poetry was dynamically interpreted though different and contemporaneous technology and media. Mayakovsky continues:

> I get my metre by covering this rhythmical roar with words, words, suggested by the objective (all the time you ask yourself: is this the word I want? Who must I read it to? Will it be understood in the right ways? and so on.) – and with words that are regulated by a highly developed sense of appropriateness, by one's abilities, and one's talent. (*HAVM?*: 70)

He begins with ra ra ra and fills in as he develops the lines:

> You went off ra ra ra ra ra to a world above
> It may be you flew ra ra ra ra ra ra.
> No loans for you, no girls and no pub.
> Ra ra ra/ra ra ra ra/sobriety. (*HAVM ?*: 70)

He rejects lines which include words which just fill in a metric form, for example the words "for ever" as too impersonal or too formal; lines which break the rhythm or do not hold enough meaning; lastly he demands rhyme: "without rhyme (understanding the word in a wide sense) poetry falls to pieces.//Rhyme sends you back to the previous line, reminds you of it, and helps all the lines that compose one thought to hold together." (*HAVM?*: 74). He considers that rhyme can occur at the beginning of lines or you can rhyme the end of one line and the beginning of the next, but that it must not be too "rich, too transparent" as in "sobriety" and "impropriety'". Mayakovsky breaks down the components of words in his search for rhyme – remembering that his choice of words as the example – is all in translation from Russian:

> Taking the most characteristic sound of the rhyme word [in this instance he is referring to the word 'sobriety" – in Russian: трезвость (trezvost)], "briet" [part of the word sobriety], I repeat it to myself over and over again, attentive to all its associations: "riot", "iota", "right", "righter", "brighter". And a good rhyme has been found. An adjective, not a noun: and ceremonious to boot! (*HAVM?*: 76)

Other important techniques are the development of images, similes, metaphors, the use of metres which have new twists to them so that they have fresh power. He also suggests the usefulness of exaggerated images as in the example: "so that Kogan scattered that way and this/Impaling passers-by on his moustache's bayonets"; and imagery based on an opposite principle to the preceding subject matter: "In the rotting wagon were forty men-/and four legs" (both *HAVM?*: 80). This is an antithesis of interpretation which in its effect, nearly destroys the meaning of the poem itself. He itemises how a single line will go through as many as twelve stages from the outset to the finished result. He wants the "magic of words", "to be a result of 'technical work'". He takes his audience into account. If the poem is to be performed then the tone must fit the occasion – "persuasive or pleading, commanding or questioning" (*HAVM?*: 84). If the poem is to be read aloud he writes that: "Metre and rhyme are more significant than punctuation, and they bend punctuation to their will when it follows established patterns." (*HAVM?*: 85). To illustrate the point he quotes a line from Alexei Tolstoy where the interpretation of the meaning is unfortunately, and humorously, governed by the punctuation: "Shibanov stopped talking. From his pierced leg/Blood streamed in a red jet . . . ", which he states everyone reads as: "Shibanov stopped talking from his pierced leg . . . " (*HAVM?*: 85). He quotes another example from Pushkin where he suggests that if you divide a line into two, into hemistichs, this removes confusion as to both sense and rhythm. A hemistich is a half-line of verse; the two halves are divided by a caesura.

As the modern technology of his day was important to Mayakovsky, there follows an analysis of a poem, which uses computer software in its construction, by way of an illustration of his point. As technology has moved on from the 1920's, the poem

"Shout!", by the current author, is used as an example of poetic form which reflects technological developments in software. It is from the sequence of city poetry *Shades of Light: A Triumph of City* (2012), a section of which, "Fame", was written with the computer software Adobe Indesign. This poem contains interpreted methods from the work of the Russian poet and painter Elena Guro and Jaljagrov (Jakobson's pseudonym as a poet). The title of the poem is derived from a lithograph by Lul'bin, circa 1913 (Rowell and Wye, 2002: 73). There are six drawings and the last one depicts someone with an open mouth and words projecting from it. This is a sequence of drawings which are illustrations from a booklet with the neologism title of "Explodicity" by Kruchenykh (1913) (as quoted in Rowell and Wye: 2002). The title of the poem "Shout!" plays with the construction of the word "Shout" and related words and meanings. As such it therefore reflects the more futurist aspect of early Russian Formalist ideas. The concluding text of the poem has been reversed, and amongst the words written in reverse are "poesie" transcribed into numbers (903513). The idea comes from a poem written by a Brazilian poet, Philadelpho Menezes (1993). He wrote the poem originally as "poesia" using the numbers displayed on a small digital calculator as in the numbers shown above. The calculator thus has a voice. "Poesie", in the poem below, emerges again in its clear and usual format suggesting that whatever the city throws up, poetry will survive in some shape or form.

At the end of the poem there are words which are broken, truncated as well as reversed, and which directly signify how the human communication is broken by the impact of – in this instance – legal trauma. The parts of words have no meaning in themselves, but they signify a mood. They are not new words as such, but dislocated speech. New words, which as yet have no meaning are labeled as "zero signs" or "zero signified" (Rudy, 1987: 281).

With respect to the term "zero", it is worth briefly referring back to the axial model based on Jakobsonian theories and ideas. The linguistic concept of "zero" indicates that absence indicates meaning (see Wales: 411). Jakobson, very early in his career (1921) wrote an essay on Futurism where he explains the term. It is analysed by Stephen Rudy (1987: 277–290). The English translation of the title of Jakobson's article is: "The Newest Russian Poetry". The article itself has not been translated into English. The development of sounds into words, and words into meanings is traced as a process whereby meanings of the original word become lost through habit. Only in poetry, with its capacity for dense re-interpretation of words, can the habitual meaning be broken. Rudy quotes from Jakobson's article "The Newest Russian Poetry" (1921) in his paragraph:

> "The mechanical association between sound and meaning by contiguity is realized all the more rapidly as it is made from habit. Hence the conservatism of practical speech. The form of the word quickly dies out" (1921:330). In poetic language, on the contrary, 'the connec-

tion between the sound aspect and meaning is tighter, more intimate, and consequently, language becomes more revolutionary, inasmuch as habitual associations by contiguity recede into the background' (1921: 304). The type of revolutionary estrangement that occurs in "Distraction" [poem by Aljagrov] is so severe that familiar words are wrenched from their habitual meanings and aligned on the basis of similarity and parallelism with nonexistent words that actually begin to function as autonomous beings . . . . On this level, the poem's global meaning lies in its disruptive gesture. (Rudy, 1987: 280)

Deriving from this, in conjunction with the Russian Formalists' interest in Futurist sound poetry, the idea of the "empty word" becomes established. Jakobson understands that habitual use constructs the meanings of a word. Rudy provides an overview of Jakobson's view: "Thus one has an opinion 'as to what it should not signify' without knowing 'what it should signify'. Jakobson uses the technical linguistic concept of the 'zero sign', . . . 'or any word one knows to exist in a given language without remembering its meaning', as not a signifier without a signified but a signifier with a 'zero signified'." (Rudy. 1987: 281).

The term "zero signified" can therefore represent the use of a word that can be placed on the negative space of the axial model – on the left of the paradigm and either above or below the syntagm (see Chapter Two, above). Insofar as the city poetic requires the interpretation of densely crowded space – crowded with both humans and structures – there is significant scope for unmarked words which are inspired by the sounds and sights of the city. An interesting example is from the work of Uruguayan poet, Alfredo Mario Ferreiro. As highlighted in Tim Conley's article:

> In "Moving Train," a poem, from his 1927 book El Hombre que se comió un autobus (The Man Who Ate a Bus), may be mimicking the sound of the engine he admires or, more tantalizingly, learning the language of the object of his affection . . . For all its absurdity, the poem has a rhythm that is gradually compelling, even erotic. Anyone can read it, for trainspeak knows no borders. As the title of Ferreiro's book reveals, the experience of mass transit can be consumed, absorbed, internalized.
>
> Toco-tócoto
> trán trán.
> Toco-tócoto
> trán trán.
> Racatrácata, paf-paf.
> Chucuchúcuchu
> Chas-chás,
> chucuchúuchu
> cháschás.
> Tacatrácata, chuchú
> tacatrácata, chuchú.
> Chucuchúcuchu
> chás-chás,

racatrácata, paf-paf.
Búúúúúúúúúúúúúúúúúúúúúúúúúú
Chiquichíquichiquichi
chiquichíqu chiquichi
chiquichíquichiquichi
chiquichíquichiquichi . . . .         (2014: 350–51)

These non-words do not confuse the reader/listener. They quite obviously represent and interpret the sounds that trains make. Here, Mayakovsky's concern about not being understood is overridden by the non-words which are perfectly clear in their intention. The inspiration for the poem "Shout" was the forced attendance at court where the processes of the legal system resulted in a defeat which had personal implications. The poet here expresses the "social command" enforced by altering the word "poesie". The poem is written in the shape of claws. Perhaps in a darker, modern twist, the *byt* expressed here is not the stupefying stasis described by one of the Russian uses of the term, but of the movement backwards to a past situation which contains destruction (see quote from Svetlana Boym above). Even stasis has advantages when faced with this kind of destructive movement. Please see text of the poem below:

## SHOUT! SHOO! OUT! SHUT! SHOUT!!

                                            hirsute and
                                     nipping claws
                                heaving eating
                       termagent termagent
                 scything tossed
            arrant mites
        fulminous over
    rough dregs
nice
    stropp ergonomics
        in numbers
            bearing down
              born borne
                  to smithereens
                    comng at us
                        caissonous teeth
                              nice

              midden happy
                  crawing claws
                      music in their ears
                          terror pinches
                              how they drone
                              how they fly
                                  how they come
                                          nice
                              for the crumbs
                            hoping hopping
                            landing eating
                       strike once
                          and once past
                          not enough
                                  not enough
                            noise ose ise  noise ose ise
                            nice one nice  nice one nice
                                      903513
                                    313509
                                  POESIE
                                POESIE
                       POESIE

Jakobson's Formalist theory provides a theoretical background for the pragmatics of Mayakovsky's *HAVM?*. Earlier in the chapter, it was mentioned that Mayakovsky moved away from Futurist ideas in his commitment to communication – in itself a Formalist structure. Mayakovsky was energetic in his assertion that any word, however insignificant in itself was significant within the poem – even the simple adjective "big" (Jakobson, 1987: 93). Jakobson in his essay "The Poetry of Grammar and Grammar of Poetry" (1987: 121–144) uses another example of Mayakovsky's poetry to illustrate how the careful use of Russian grammar – using a particular linguistic example of an unstated dative object – adds spatial dimension to a particular poetic phrase.

This reference is rewarding if examined closely. It not only reveals Jakobson's intense attention to detail it also demonstrates how the intricacies of foreign language translation can illustrate the complexities of a native language, and, arising from this, further knowledge of how our own language operates. It is important to quote the full paragraph before attempting to unpick the contribution to poetic theory that this small example provides:

> When in the finale of Majakovskij's poem *Xorošo* – "i žizn / xorošá // i žít´/xorošó //" [и жизнь / хороша, // и жить / хорошо //: taken from section 19 of the poem *"Хорошо"*: https://ru.wikisource.org/wiki/хорошо (accessed 11.am 14.3.19)] (literally, both life is good and it is good to live) – one will hardly look for a cognitive difference between these two coordinate clauses, but in poetic mythology the linguistic fiction of the substantivised and hence hypostatized process grows into a metonymic image of life as such, taken by itself and substituted for living people, *abstractum pro concreto*, as Galfredus de Vino Salvo, the cunning English scholar of the early thirteenth century, explains in his *Poetria nova*. [See E. Faral, *Les Arts Poétiques du XIIe et XIIIe siècle* (Paris, 1958), pp.195, 227.] In contradistinction to the first clause with its predicative adjective of the same personifiable, feminine gender as the subject, the second clause with its imperfective infinitive and with a neuter, subjectless form of the predicate, represents a pure process without any limitation of transposition and with an open place for the dative of agent. (1987: p124)

The example of Mayakovsky's poetry referred to here is from a long poem which has been translated as "Fine!" (1986: 207–277). Unfortunately, the rather free translation does not help with the analysis here cited. Jakobson's paragraph needs extra analysis. In Russian "žizn" or "жизнь" means "life" and has a feminine gender. The "predicative adjective" referred to is how "i žizn / xorošá [и жизнь / хороша,] is constructed. The subject is "life" and it is qualified by a corresponding adjective, "good". The adjective takes the feminine construction in agreement with "life". The subsequent imperfective infinitive in Russian "žít´" (жить – to live) is the present infinitive with its Russian innate imperfective meaning of something that is not complete or repeated – "imperfect". This is qualified by a variation of the adjective "xorošó" [хорошо – it is good] which, as Jakobson points out, removes the gendered predicate (object). The form also propels the word towards being an adverb "well". *And* then Mayakovsky adds to the complexity of his meaning by removing the dative agent. In this instance, in English, it would be "and it is good [to me] to live". This is meaning revealed by a negative – the meaning arises because something has been left out. It means that, in reading the poem, the personal element (to me) has been removed and the poet's voice expresses the wider general meaning of: "it is good (for all) to live". This is an example of *abstractum pro concreto* (see below). Added to it is the meaning (in Russian) that "to live" inherently contains the imperfective meaning "to continue to live", or "to be alive", providing a positive colour to the words.

There is a wider implication here: that poetics – and, in this instance, metonymic poetics – adds meaning not only by how it is constructed grammatically but also by leaving words out. A negative, an omission, *adds* meaning and levels of meaning. This painstaking analysis reveals evidence that the axes of language have a negative space which *really* exists and can be interpreted. The negative space (see Axial Diagram in Chapter Two) is represented by the space to the left of the paradigm, both above and below the syntagm. Here also, a metonymically constructed meaning – *abstractum pro concreto* – has been revealed. For Jakobson, in his chapter "Poetry of Grammar" (1987: 121–144) it is referred to as a "figure of grammar". Of course, in this instance he means a figure of poetic grammar.

The Galfredus de Vino Salvo to whom Jakobson refers is usually given the name of Geoffrey de Vinsauf (early 13th century). The term "*abstractum pro concreto*" derives from his Latin poem "Poetria Nova" or "The New Poetics' (c1210–2012). It is a term which contributes to metonymic understanding of the use of language. An English translation of Vinsauf's original Latin text has lines with differing numbers in different texts. The edition used for this particular quotation provides different numbering to that of the edition used by Jakobson in his reference; but, after careful research, they have been established as the correct lines:

> Bring forth such a statement as this: The feeble man desires the doctor; the sorrowful man desires solace; the destitute man wants support. Words flower better in this scheme: Feebleness needs the doctor; sorrow needs solace; destitution wants support. In expressions there is a natural delight in thus placing the abstract for the concrete. Hence change *the feeble man* into *feebleness, the sorrowful man* into *sorrow, the destitute man* into *destitution.*
> 
> (lines 971–977. Gallo: 1971)

Vinsauf's further definitions of metonymy are of additional interest with respect to metonymy as defined by substitution of effect for cause and instrument for use. His examples are not used by Hugh Bredin (see Chapter Three). The reason for Jakobson's referring to Vinsauf as "cunning" are unclear, except that Vinsauf seems to have survived various very serious quarrels and difficulties to continue his rhetorical teaching career in different cities in the UK and Europe throughout his life.

Jakobson's Formalist theory examines poetic grammar; Mayakovsky's intense commitment to poetics provides a rationale for producing highly crafted poetry from raw material. These are commitments, not only to the techniques of writing poetry, but also a commitment to linguistics and semiotics. Mayakovsky, in his intense awareness of his revolutionary audience, is careful to write poetry which linguistically interprets the particular requirements of his audience. His commitment to semiotics is demonstrated through his deliberate and informed choice of poetic metric structure. Rhyme, for example, which Mayakovsky also found very important, produces parallel and referential structures within poetry – it is not a simple metric tool. As can be seen from "*HAVM?*", the Revolution in Russia inspired Mayakovsky's poetic revolution. The breaking of old rules in both poetic revolution and political revolution constructed new rules for Mayakovsky. His opposition to *byt* as stasis, gives rise to a city poetics that fights for survival when up against the pressures of revolutionary city life. This goes so far as to demand the use of negative space in poetics, and is further expressed by the omission of the reference to the human, replacing it with a quality of emotion which is identified in Vinsauf's metonymic trope: *abstractum pro concreto*.

There is a statue of Mayakovsky in Moscow, the size of which reflects his stature as a poet. It is six metres high, designed by A.P. Kibalnikov. Mayakovsky's personal giant stature (he was over six foot) was delineated in the statue in such a way that the observer at ground level forms the impression that he is about to step down from the pedestal and join the crowd again. His left hand holds a notebook, a core symbol of Mayakovsky's commitment to poetics. His work continues to inform both emotionally and in terms of poetic skill. The following chapter explores two poems about city bridges, both analysed using Jakobson's Formalist analysis. Mayakovsky's poem on Brooklyn Bridge highlights the use of deixis and shifters. Hart Crane's contemporaneous poem, "The Bridge" is similarly analysed and compared with Mayakovsky's poem. The Formalist praxis used in analysing these poems contributes to a city poetic genre.

## Chapter 9
## Poetry of the city, Mayakovsky and Hart Crane – the construction of form and landscape: Theory and praxis

Is contemporary poetry of the city inspired by particular forms? By "form" is meant not only the type of poem, a sonnet or ballad for example, but also the linguistic and semiotic construction of the text with which the ideas are expressed. For Roman Jakobson, writing as a theorist rather than a poet, this is the "grammar of poetry" (1987: 121–144). It is within his construction that the linguistic and semiotic Formalist analysis takes place. The specific poems referred to in the chapter are "Brooklyn Bridge" by Vladimir Mayakovsky (1893–1930), written after his visit to America in 1925, and "To Brooklyn Bridge" written by Hart Crane (1889–1932), the American poet. The poem was published in a collection entitled *The Bridge* 1930 (in 2001). An apology is required here as, regretfully, Mayakovsky's poem is analysed in an English translation, taken from Mayakovsky (1985). The Russian title of his poem is: Бруклинский Мост. A "scientific" study of the literary text is used in order to discover its "literariness" (for a definition of the term see Chapter One, above), with special reference to Boris Èixenbaum's definition. It is Formalist theory which is used here for the basis for analysis. The city poetic genre provides the literary category.

Both the poems discussed here are entitled "Brooklyn Bridge". The bridge was built in 1883 and links two large suburbs of New York – Brooklyn and Manhattan. Its construction was a giant engineering task and involved the use of caissons. These are large underground chambers which, in the 1880's, were excavated by hand and then filled with concrete, providing the foundations for the supporting structures of the bridge. The construction took over fourteen years and there were an estimated twenty to forty deaths, and many casualties (McCullough: 505,506). The caissons were often so deprived of air and under such high pressure from the depth at which they were excavated, that the workmen could only work underground for a very short time. The engineer, Washington Roebling, himself suffered a devastating attack of "the bends" and was unable to supervise the completion of the project (McCullough: 2009: 318,319). These details demonstrate how the celebrated engineering feat was only completed with a cost to human life.

How does the poet construct an image of Brooklyn Bridge? Analysis of the poems suggests that an answer may lie in the "point of view" constructed in the poem. This demonstrates the relationship between the poet's physical position to the city space described; for example, it can be at eye level, looking upwards or looking downwards on the subject matter, close up or distant. A deictic understanding of the position is an important influence on form. This, combined with a structuralist analysis, demonstrates the poet's relationship with the city. It is with this in mind, therefore, that the analysis of Mayakovsky's poem, "Brooklyn Bridge", begins with a Formalist study of the shifters (pronouns) and deictics. As noted above, the discussion is based on the English translation of the original Russian text (1985: 161–163) reproduced here in full. The lines have been numbered for reference.

```
        BROOKLYN BRIDGE
Coolidge, old boy,                                    1
give a whoop of joy!
What's good is good –
            no need for debates.
Blush read with my praise,
       swell with pride
              till you're spherical,
though you be ten times
             United Sates
of America.                                          10
As to Sunday church
            the pious believer
walks,
      devout,
            by his faith bewitched,
so I,
     in the grisly mirage
            of evening
step, with humble heart,
       on to Brooklyn Bridge.                        20
As a conqueror rides
       through the town he crushes
on a cannon
       by which himself's a midge,
so –
     drunk with glory –
            all life be as luscious –
I clamber,
     proud,
            on to Brooklyn Bridge.                   30
As a silly painter
       into a museum Virgin,
infatuated,
      plunges
             his optics' fork.
so I
```

                    from a height on heaven verging
look
          through Brooklyn Bridge at New York.
New York,                                                                40
          till evening stifling and bewildering,
forgets
          both its sultriness
                    and its height,
and only
          the naked soul
                    of a building
will show
          in a window's translucent light.
From here                                                                50
          the elevators
                    hardly rustle,
which sound aloud,
                    by the distance rubbered,
betrays the trains
                    as off they bustle,
like crockery
          being put by
                    in a cupboard.
Beneath,                                                                 60
          from the river's far-off mouth,
sugar
          seems carted from mills by peddlers,
it's the windows of boats
                    bound north and south –
tinier
          than the tiniest pebbles.
I pride
          in the stride
                    of this steel-wrought mile.                          70
Embodied in it
          my visions come real-
in the striving
          for structure
                    instead of style,
in the stern, shrewd balance
                    of rivets and steel.
If ever
          the end of the world
                    should arrive,                                       80
and chaos
          sweep off
                    the planet's last ridge,

with the only lonely
            thing to survive
towering over debris
            this bridge,
then,
        as out of a needle-thin bone
museums                                                         90
        rebuild dinosaurs,
so future's geologist
        from this bridge alone
will remodel
        these days
            of ours.
He'll say:
        this mile-long iron arch
welded
        oceans and prairies together.                           100
From here old Europe
        in westward march
swished
        to the winds
            the last Indian feather.
This rib will remind
        of machines by its pattern.
Consider –
        could anyone with bare hands
planting                                                        110
    one steel foot
        on Manhatten
pull Brooklyn
    up
        by the lip
            where he stands?
By the wires –
    those tangled electric braidings –
he'll tell:
    it came after stream, their era.                            120
Here people
    already
        hollered by radio,
here folks
    had already soared up by aero.
Here life
    for some
        was a scream of enjoyment,
for others –
    one drawn-out,                                              130

                hungry howl.
From here the victims of unemployment
dashed headlong
                into the Hudson's scowl.
And further –
                my picture unfurls without a hitch –
by the harp-string ropes,
                as the stars' own feet,
here stood Mayakovsky,
                on this same bridge,              140
and hammered his verses
                beat by beat.
I stare like a savage
                at an electric switch,
eyes fixed,
      like a tick on a cat.
Yeah,
            Brooklyn Bridge…
It's something, that!
            (1925)

The original Russian version of the poem can be found on the world-wide web (accessed 12/04/19: 12.10) https://ru.wikisource.org/wiki/Бруклинский_мост_(Маяковский). There is a literal translation of the poem available through "Google translate" on this page, but it has not been referred to here, as it does not make enough sense for it to be a reliable research document. However, it is important to know that the 1985 Raduga translation is also not necessarily accurate. For example, in the original Russian, Mayakovsky refers to a giraffe (жираф – line 27). This is not found in the Raduga translation. Again, the lines are numbered for reference.

        БРУКЛИНСКИЙ МОСТ
Издай, Кулидж,
радостный клич!
На хорошее
        и мне не жалко слов.
От похвал
    краснеj,
        как флага нашего материйка,
хоть вы
    и разъюнайтед стетс
        оф              10
Америка.
Как в церковь
    идет
        помешавшийся верующий,

```
как в скит
        удаляется,
                строг и прост, -
так я
        в вечерней
                сереющей мерещи                    20
вхожу,
        смиренный, на Бруклинский мост.
Как в город
        в сломанный
                прет победитель
на пушках – жерлом
                жирафу под рост -
так, пьяный славой,
                так жить в аппетите,
влезаю,                                            30
        гордый,
                на Бруклинский мост.
Как глупый художник
        в мадонну музея
вонзает глаз свой,
                влюблен и остр,
так я,
        с поднебесья,
                в звезды усеян,
смотрю                                             40
        на Нью-Йорк
                сквозь Бруклинский мост
Нью-Йорк
        до вечера тяжек
                и душен,
забыл,
        что тяжко ему
                и высоко,
и только одни
        домовьи души                               50
встают
        в прозрачном свечении окон.
Здесь
        еле зудит
                элевейтеров зуд.
И только
        по этому
                тихому зуду
поймешь -
        поезда                                     60
                с дребезжаньем ползут,
```

как будто
           в буфет убирают посуду.
Когда ж,
           казалось, с под речки начатой
развозит
           с фабрики
                    сахар лавочник, -
то
                    под мостом проходящие мачты        70
размером
           не больше размеров булавочных.
Я горд
           вот этой
                    стальною милей,
живьем в ней
           мои видения встали -
борьба
           за конструкции
                    вместо стилей,        80
расчет суровый
           гаек
                  и стали.
Если
           придет
                    окончание света -
планету
           хаос
                  разделает влоск,
и только                                   90
           один останется
                  этот
над пылью гибели вздыбленный мост,
          то,
                  как из косточек,
                           тоньше иголок,
тучнеют
           в музеях стоящие
                  ящеры,
так                                              100
           с этим мостом
                  столетий геолог
сумел
           воссоздать бы
                  дни настоящие.
Он скажет:
           - Вот эта
                  стальная лапа

соединяла
  моря и прерии,        110
отсюда
  Европа
    рвалась на Запад,
пустив
  по ветру
    индейские перья.
Напомнит
  машину
    ребро вот это -
сообразите,           120
  хватит рук ли,
чтоб, став
  стальной ногой
    на Мангетен,
к себе
  за губу
    притягивать Бруклин?
По проводам
  электрической пряди -
я знаю -           130
  эпоха
    после пара -
здесь
  люди
    уже
      орали по радио,
здесь
  люди
    уже
      взлетали по аэро.  140
Здесь
  жизнь
    была
      одним – беззаботная,
другим -
  голодный
    протяжный вой.
Отсюда
  безработные
в Гудзон           150
  кидались
    вниз головой.
И дальше
  картина моя
    без загвоздки

```
            по струнам-канатам,
                           аж звездам к ногам.
       Я вижу -
                   здесь
                           стоял Маяковский,                            160
       стоял
                           и стихи слагал по слогам. -
       Смотрю,
                   как в поезд глядит эскимос,
       впиваюсь,
                   как в ухо впивается клещ.
       Бруклинский мост -
       да...
                   Это вещь!
         [1925]
```

There is another website which includes notes to the poem (accessed: 13.06.21, 10.12): http://mayakovskiy.lit-info.ru/mayakovskiy/stihi/stih-238.htm. These notes indicate that the reference to the unemployed throwing themselves from the bridge – the lines which occur in both Mayakovsky's poem and Crane's (see below) – were added later at the suggestion of someone in the audience when Mayakovsky read the poem in New York.

Jakobson's system of Formalist analysis carefully abstracts and analyses the linguistic, semantic, syntactic and semiotic components of a written poetic text. With reference to "Brooklyn Bridge", the analysis begins with locating and categorising the pronouns in the poem (see Table 2). It should be noted that a shifter is here defined as separate from a deictic (see Chapters Five and Six, above). The tables below are not a strictly Formal linguistic analysis, and words other than pure shifters have been included in the shifter list – for example: possessive pronouns or pronominal adjectives. With regards to the selection of deictic words, again, these are not purely pointing words or prepositions. A word can have a "deictic tone" without being strictly speaking, in a linguistic, syntactical sense, a deictic. Not only have words of placing been selected and included, but also words which indicate a deixis of time. Deictics of time is an under-researched categorisation. In the table below, pronominal shifter words are listed:

**Table 2:** Shifters.

| – my | 5, 72, 136 | – his | 15, 35, 141 |
|---|---|---|---|
| – you're | 7 | – he | 22, 97, 116, 119 |
| – you | 8 | – himself | 24 |
| – his | 15, 35, 141 | – they | 57 |

**Table 2** (continued)

| – I | 16, 28, 36, 68, 143 | – it | 64, 149 |
|---|---|---|---|
| – he | 22, 97, 116, 119 | – its | 43, 45, 107 |
| – himself | 24 | – my | 5, 72, 136 |
| – they | 57 | – I | 16, 28, 36, 68, 143 |
| – it | 64, 149 | – ours | 96 |
| – its | 43, 45, 107 | – you're | 7 |
| – ours | 96 | – you | 8 |

The first column lists the different pronouns and the numbers of the lines in the English translation of the poem (see above) in which they occur. The second column lists the pronouns by category – third, second and first persons, again with the line numbers listed alongside. The dominant pronoun in Mayakovsky's poem is the third person (see second column – first four lines), as in "his", "he", "himself", the plural "they" and the impersonal "it", "its", and is closely followed by use of the first-person pronoun "I", or the possessive form "my", and he uses the possessive plural once: "ours"; the second person is the least used pronoun – as in "you're", "you". The categories in the first column reveal that, numerically, the third person is dominant in the poem. But if the pronouns are analysed specifically through each precise grammatical form, then the pronoun "I" is actually the most frequently used pronoun.

The analysis of deictics in the poem begins with Table 3 below:

**Table 3:** Deictics.

| – on to | 20, 30 | – out of | 89 |
|---|---|---|---|
| – through | 22, 39 | – together | 100 |
| – with | 26, 84 | – from here | 101, 132 |
| – into | 32, 134 | – to | 104 |
| – from | 37, 50, 64 | – on | 112, 146 |
| – only | 46 | – up | 114 |
| – by | 15, 54, 58, 64, 107, 115, 117, 137 | – where | 116 |
| | | – those | 118 |
| – off | 56, 82 | – after | 120 |
| – beneath | 60 | – here | 121, 124, 126, 139 |
| – in | 17, 69, 71, 73, 76, 102 | – already | 122, 125 |
| | | – further | 135 |

**Table 3** (continued)

| – of | 18, 70, 75, 77, 79, 107 | – without | 136 |
|---|---|---|---|
|  |  | – at | 144 |
| – over | 86 | – that | 149 |
| – this | 87, 93, 106, 140 |  |  |
| – then | 88 |  |  |

Deictics provide positioning of the subject material in place and time. A second table of deictics (see Table 4), see below, lists two categories:

**Table 4:** Deictic analysis.

| Category 1 | |
|---|---|
| – by | 15, 54, 58, 64, 107, 115, 117, 137 |
| – in | 69, 71, 73, 76, 102 |
| – of | 70, 75, 77, 79, 107 |
| **Category 2** | |
| – this | 87, 93, 106, 140 |
| – then | 88 |
| – here | 121, 124, 126, 139 |
| – from here | 101, 132 |
| – that | 149 |

It should be emphasised that the original Russian text would not indicate the same deictic use. In English, the use of certain prepositions – "by", "in" and "of", occur naturally very frequently, these have been listed in the first category. They often modify verbs, the Russian language is not constructed in the same way. The second category lists the deictics which prioritise placing. For the purposes of the chapter, any analysis of poetic meaning arising from the study of language use in the poem will concentrate on the demonstrative deictics (second category), such as "here", "then", "this" and "that"; and those deictics which indicate placing through time: "after", "already", "till". In English, some deictics can be used with either significance – that of either place or time – such as the deictic "further" (line 135). This can be used to indicate further away – as is this use here – or further ahead in time: "And further-/my picture unfurls without hitch". The scope of the chapter does not allow a full Formalist analysis of the complicated structure of deixis, as well as shifters in the poem. It is also hindered by analysing the poem in translation.

It has been noted that the shifters express the third person more than Mayakovsky, the poet, as first-person narrator, in the poem "Brooklyn Bridge". The question is then asked if the deictics reinforce this poetic position. The use of the first person provides a close identification with the subject, the poet's response. The use of the third person provides the perspective of the more distanced poet/narrator writing about what he sees. The most frequently used deictic is "this", as opposed to "that" and "here". The deictic "there" is not used at all, although there are two instances of "from here". It is noted that these deictics all occur in the second half of the poem. Please see table 5 below:

**Table 5:** Deictic analysis.

| – by | 15, 54, 58, 64, 107, 115, 117, 137 |
|---|---|
| – in | 69, 71, 73, 76, 102 |
| – of | 70, 75, 77, 79, 107 |
| – this | 87, 93, 106, 140 |
| – then | 88 |
| – here | 121, 124, 126, 139 |
| – from here | 101, 132 |
| – that | 149 |

Bringing together the study of the shifters and deictics, the reader notes that Mayakovsky uses a rhetorical form of the first person "I", in the first one third of the poem. He uses it as an exclamation which is monologic and self-referential. He uses the form three times (lines 16, 28, and 36). This provides a sense of distance between Mayakovsky, the person, and his response to the bridge. The next passage (lines 40–77) describes the city as viewed from a great distance. The following section (lines 78–134) is a description of how the future will look back in time at the structure and meaning of Brooklyn Bridge – a deictic of distant time. It is within this section of the poem that deictics of time are used three times – "after" (see line 120) and "already" (see lines 122 and 125), please see table 6 below:

**Table 6:** Deixis and time.

| – after | 120 |
|---|---|
| – already | 122, 125 |
| – till | 7, 41 |

The poet has now distanced the city by both place and time. Mayakovsky crowns this with the use of celestial imagery – "the harp-string ropes,/as the stars own feet" (lines 137, 138). Then he is back to earth (both in place and time) when he describes himself as a "savage" (line 143). Finally, in the last line of the poem, he uses the deictic "that!" (line 149). This places both the poet/narrator and the reader at a distance from the bridge. Mayakovsky is using a number of devices to distance himself from the bridge.

Mayakovsky's use of verb tenses is also very revealing of the poet's "point of view" towards his subject – "Brooklyn Bridge". The table below is collated with reference to the Raduga translation quoted above. The verb tenses in the Russian original are not always comparable. The categorisation below, in Table 7, is therefore only a guide:

**Table 7:** Verbs – analysis.

| verbs: numerical usage | |
| --- | --- |
| imperative | 2 |
| present | 27 |
| past | 13 |
| past perfect passive | 1 |
| infinitive | 1 |
| future conditional | 2 |
| future | 5 |
| passive | 1 |
| future passive | 1 |
| rhetorical | 2 |

There are two rhetorical uses of verbs in lines 2 and 27. The grand effect at the beginning of the poem becomes a distant effect as the poem progresses. There is some use of the future tense when he uses the device of a narrator within the poem – "He'll say" (see line 97) and "he'll tell" (line 119) and he refers to "the end of the world" (line 79). There is one other future tense "will remodel" (line 94). Although evening is described (lines 40–49) there is no sense of a passage of time as there is only a description of particular events and aspects of the bridge's structure, and the present tense is used throughout (lines 50–70). The poem contains similes and analogies, but these are not presented as a sequence of time but as aspects of the bridge, even though there is reference to historical events. Overall, the majority of verbs used in the poem are in the present tense. There are two future conditionals: "should arrive" (line 80), and "could . . . pull"; (between lines 109–113). The use of the future tense (line 106) "will remind" has a strong backward movement through time inherent in its meaning. Significantly, the end of the poem is a mix of present and past tense, with the use of the past tense producing a rhetorical effect (lines 135–149).

In the final lines of the poem, Mayakovsky compares his poetic work to that of the people who built the bridge: "here stood Mayakovsky,/on this same bridge,/ and hammered his verses/beat by beat." (lines 138–142). His reference to himself in the third person, where earlier in the poem he uses the pronoun "I", distances himself from a personal response to the Bridge and yet the simile constructed by the "beat by beat" which echoes the "I pride/in the stride/of this steel-wrought mile" (line 70) and "shrewd balance/of rivets and steel" (lines 76,77) indicates that he first expresses his identification with the vast structure and effort of its construction, and then distances himself from the sense of twisted and warped human suffering which accompanies it – "the victims of unemployment/dashed headlong" (lines 131,132). This is confirmed by his phrase "I stare like a savage/ at an electric switch" (lines 143, 144). The bridge mesmerises and appals – both in the sense of identification with personal suffering within the vast scope of the city's activities, and also in the sense of how human lives are perceived through the passage of time "He'll say" (line 97) and "He'll tell" (line 119). In this short examination of shifters, deictics, and verb tenses, it becomes clear that Mayakovsky's poetic skills have not only provided a complex relationship between the poet himself and the city bridge which he sees, but he has also drawn lines which are ties to the past, present and future, to the simultaneous immediate personal experience of the city and its panorama of experience. It is suggested that the web of complex links echoes the network of the suspension cables of the bridge itself.

Hart Crane (1889–1932) wrote his book of poetry *The Bridge* to which the poem "To Brooklyn Bridge" was the proem, in the years 1923–1927. It was first published in 1930. The poem "To Brooklyn Bridge" was written in 1926. It is therefore contemporaneous with Mayakovsky's poem. It is interesting to note that there are similarities in some of the subject matter. The full text of the poem is reproduced below, with kind permission of the publishers, W.W.Norton and Co. The lines are numbered for reference:

To Brooklyn Bridge

How many dawns, chill from his rippling rest     1
The seagull's wings shall dip and pivot him,
Shedding white rings of tumult, building high
Over the chained bay waters Liberty--

Then, with inviolate curve, forsake our eyes     5
As apparitional as sails that cross
Some page of figures to be filed away;
–Till elevators drop us from our day . . .

I think of cinemas, panoramic sleights     9
With multitudes bent toward some flashing scene

Never disclosed, but hastened to again,
Foretold to other eyes on the same screen;

And Thee, across the harbor, silver-paced 13
As though the sun took step of thee, yet left
Some motion ever unspent in thy stride,--
Implicitly thy freedom staying thee!

Out of some subway scuttle, cell or loft 17
A bedlamite speeds to thy parapets,
Tilting there momently, shrill shirt ballooning,
A jest falls from the speechless caravan.

Down Wall, from girder into street noon leaks, 21
A rip-tooth of the sky's acetylene;
All afternoon the cloud-flown derricks turn . . .
Thy cables breathe the North Atlantic still.

And obscure as that heaven of the Jews, 25
Thy guerdon . . . Accolade thou dost bestow
Of anonymity time cannot raise:
Vibrant reprieve and pardon thou dost show.

O harp and altar, of the fury fused, 29
(How could mere toil align thy choiring strings!)
Terrific threshold of the prophet's pledge,
Prayer of pariah, and the lover's cry,--

Again the traffic lights that skim thy swift 33
Unfractioned idiom, immaculate sigh of stars,
Beading thy path--condense eternity:
And we have seen night lifted in thine arms.

Under thy shadow by the piers I waited; 37
Only in darkness is thy shadow clear.
The City's fiery parcels all undone,
Already snow submerges an iron year . . .

O Sleepless as the river under thee, 41
Vaulting the sea, the prairies' dreaming sod,
Unto us lowliest sometime sweep, descend
And of the curveship lend a myth to God.

The poem is now analysed using aspects of a Formalist analysis. For the sake of being able to compare it directly with Mayakovsky's poem the same format of analysis will be attempted – categorisation and analysis of pronouns (shifters), deictics and verbs. This is not to exclude the proper consideration of other techniques used in the poem which may well be more revealing of the poet and poem's intention and meaning. The poem was chosen because it was written about the same subject, at around the same time and contains some similar responses. In "To Brooklyn Bridge" by Hart Crane, the shifters/pronouns occur as follows:

| | |
|---|---|
| his | line 1 reference to the seagull |
| him | line 2 reference to the seagull |
| our | lines 5,8 |
| us | lines 8,43[stanza 2, lines 5–8 very close identification with the reader] |
| I | lines 9, 37 |
| Thee | line 13; this is the only capital 'T'. The rest of the stanza has two instances of "thee" and two instances of "thy" – none with capital letter. Is this a fractioned idiom – the split between the god-like magnificence of the whole and the mythological rhetoric of it (see analysis below)? |
| thee | lines 14,16,26,41 |
| thy | lines 15,16,18,24,30,33, 35,37, 38 |
| thou | lines 26,28 |
| we | line 36; there is a sudden concatenation of the remote other worldly of "thee" and "thy" to the purely grounded human inclusive "we". The words: "condense eternity" (line 35) actually describe what the first-person pronouns in these two subsequent lines actually do – bring everything to the purely personal individual human level. And this is followed by "I" in the next line (37). |
| "us | line 43 completes the nexus of first-person pronouns which occur almost entirely in stanzas at the beginning and the end of the poem. |

There is a stunning avoidance (line 44) of 'thy' in the final line where he uses "the" and "a". If he had written: "And of thy curveship lend thy myth to God", the biblical sense would be greatly heightened and the link to the human world greatly diminished. Also, God is spelt with a capital 'G' – and suddenly the bridge is a myth and this reminds us of stanza three where the cinema uses "panoramic sleights". Crane succumbs to a divine pre-eminence in his last line but by not using 'thy' in this same line, he distances the links that the bridge has with divinity. The imagery and use of shifters throughout the poem demonstrate that distance.

The use of the biblical pronouns mentioned above, with reference to Bühler, can be called "origo-deictics" in the precise sense. This is where the pronoun has less of the property of a shifter (personal pronoun) and more of a demonstrative or pointing (deictic) property. (Bühler. 2011: 117 and 145). There is a strong placing of the self in the environment, both space and time, with these shifters. Given their archaic form, which refers back to English usage where the definite article, has a stronger quality of the deictic (as in "the man", meaning "that man", for example), they should be considered as a separate category. Where Mayakovsky, perhaps, gains his effect through juxtaposition of human with the object, the bridge; Crane is placing himself and the reader by using biblical pronouns which enforce a pointing aspect – the divine is distant in relation to the human. These particular origo-deictics occur in the greatest number in the last three stanzas. The use of capital letters is selective:

| | |
|---|---|
| Thee | line13 This must be a reference back to the Statue of Liberty, where, in line 4 "Liberty" is spelt with a capital letter. |
| thee | lines 14,16,41 |
| Thy | line 25 (beginning of the line) |
| thy | lines 15,18,33,35,37,38 |
| thou | lines 26,28 |
| thine | line 36 |
| Unto us | line 43 (beginning of the line) |

Other deictics have a variety of qualities, some are positional in terms of place, some in terms of time and some in terms of quantity. There is only one deictic of movement, line18 "to" which is a reference to the suicide. Suggested deictics of place: "high" (line 3), "over" (line 4), "on" (line 12), "across" (line 13), "out" (line 17), "to" (line 18), "momently" (line 19), "from" (line 20), "Down", "from", "into" (all line 21), "that" (line 25) and "under" (line 41). Suggested deictics of time are: "then" (line 5), "Till" (line 8), "ever" (line 15) and "again" (line 33). Suggested deictics of quantity are: "some" (lines 7 and 10), "other" and "same" (both line 12), "some" (line 17) and "all" line 23). The use of the word "how" (lines 1 and 30) seems to be a special category of deictic which imposes a rhetorical quantity on the subject matter of the poem. This is in the sense that if everything were quantifiable the word used would be "all". Deictics are here emerging as having a range of qualities which could be usefully further explored.

In the poem, however, the shifters and deictics are governed by the poetic image of the catenary. Shifters reveal the relationship between poet, subject and reader very clearly. It is interesting to note that the Formalist approach to analysis gives rise to difficulties when two poems are compared strictly according to the same aspects of the formalistic process. It can be a masking of what the poem in itself has to offer. The process of the use of pronouns in the Mayakovsky is not useful in fully understanding the Crane poem. Crane uses the declamatory and religious pronoun 'thee' very prominently throughout the poem. He refers directly to himself only twice: "I" in the third stanza (line 9) and penultimate stanza (line 37). Another very significant moment in the poem is the opening of sixth stanza – midway through the poem – here, the viewpoint, for the first of only two times in the poem, is from the bottom up – giving the reader the personal perspective of the human underneath the magnificent catenary of the bridge. This aspect of Crane's perspective is the overall compelling attribute of his poem. His catenaries are sweeping parabolas and curves. And this central form is discussed in the Formalist analysis that follows. A catenary is a curve which hangs in a parabola of its own making, depending on the span of its two anchor points and its own weight. It is not strictly a parabola as such, because it is dependent on these two factors. But because of these factors it has an equilibrium which gives rise to a pleasing innate aesthetic. A catenary is a term which is used in both mathematics and art. However, in one sense, the curve of the cables of Brooklyn Bridge is not a catenary because the cables are anchored in more than one position along their length. It is also, in artistic terms, a catenary which is observed from an angle, rather than end-on for example, and which introduces an asymmetrical quality to the curve.

The poem propels the reader to an overarching (literally) view of the bridge as it sweeps across the bay (panoramic curve). Each stanza is analysed with reference to curves, panoramas, parabolas and catenaries below:

1. the seagull 'dips and pivots' – first catenary – and 'shedding white rings of tumult . . . . over the chained bay' – another catenary. He states the bridge's location and its fundamental nature quite clearly in his first verse. "Liberty" (obviously the statue) in line 4 is only visible while standing on the centre of the bridge. The reference cannot be to the island as it was called Bedloe Island until 1956. The poem provides another level of catenary in that it indicates not only a sweeping curve of vision from the bridge to "Liberty" but also through its sweeping description of the bay and what it contains – birds, bridge and statue of "Liberty". The ground rules between the real and the metaphysical are laid out as the language glides easily between a description of the actual bay to a metaphorical "other world" interpretation of the visual cues. There is a neo-concatenation "Liberty" with the words "statue of" left out so that the iconic statue and all it stands for is fractioned here. What is something which is fractioned? To use the word as a verb rather than a noun is archaic – please see *OED online* (2022): "fraction *v.* to break into fractions or pieces. 1841 T. CARLYLE *On Heroes* ii. 81: The Nation, fractioned and cut asunder by deserts." Crane himself uses the word as an adjective in line 35. In terms of the poem it counterbalances the word "inviolate" (line 5). There is more on this aspect of the poem later in the chapter.

2. here is a catenary in the first line: "inviolate curve". This stanza provides vertical lines, as in: "sails that cross,/Some page of figures", "elevators drop", but these images which involve lines crossing or falling are surrounded so strongly by the curves that they are submerged. These vertical lines conjure up the image of the cables which tie the single upper curved cable to the bridge itself.

3. "panoramic sleights" establishes a mythological arena and contrasts to the cinematic where the screens can also be curved. He establishes the parameter of the myth, that cinematic image is reality and here the images are seen over and over again. He has deleted the passage of time here – the cinematic myths are foretold to other eyes on the same cinema screen but "Never disclosed". There is no revelation of knowledge – this is a false panoramic of time.

4. "And Thee" – here the bridge is given a capital letter, it is God-like but then it slips back to the small "t" – "thee" in the next line. He uses a simile here: "As though the sun took step of thee", in other words the sun could encompass and measure the bridge. And there is "Some motion ever unspent in thy stride, –" The bridge is boundless in its impact and motion but the chains are there: "implicitly thy freedom staying thee!". The vision of the bridge is contained by its curves.

5. in this stanza even images that might designate lines are adorned with curves – 'speeds to thy parapets' as if not walking but ascending so quickly as if to fly – another curve or trajectory. And then "tilting there momently", there is a concertina of perspective as the sight of the human falling is interpreted as a "jest falls from the speechless caravan". The noise of the crowds is silenced by distance, the tragedy is a jest, and with a transferred epithet, the shirt is "shrill". The suicide tries to convey a message but the catenary of despair is silenced by the distances of the other humans – double interpretation of distance – literal human distance and poetic visual distance.

6. "Down Wall" – his crashing image slices through the poem exactly half way through. There are no neologisms in the poem but there is a neo-unification of meaning in the irreconcilable and dominant double noun: "Down Wall" (line 21). Crane has spelt these two words with capital letters. "Down" is explicable as the first word of this line, but the capital in "Wall" enforces a consideration of the poet's intention here. It becomes a proper noun, an embodied thing, perhaps a channel of communication between the sky and earth, God and man. This profoundly strong vertical line breaks the poem in half and the following image emphasises this with "Rip-tooth" in the next line. It is a reference to saw teeth which do not have an angled edge, they work more like little chisels. The image recollects the blinding flash of sunlight through some slicing mechanism, the visual effect of looking skyward through the cables. To say that the derricks turn is a transferred movement, as it is the sun that turns, the human viewer who stands and looks at the cables and pillars of the bridge through the shifting light, another curve. In spite of the vertical "Down Wall" the catenary has emerged once again. And then suddenly the bridge is stationary again – "Thy cables breathe the North Atlantic still".

7. "guerdon" means reward; there is movement here as the reader thinks upwards towards heaven and downwards again to receive the "accolade". The bridge in its location over the river, sea and within the free sky above, gives its own reward. The most overt metaphysical reference is denied the true metaphysical expres-

sion of metaphor – simultaneity – and is given a poetic form which expresses ideas consecutively – the simile.

8. here the deity is "fused" with the human construction – not the human soul, 'thy' consistently spelt with a small "t" and is therefore not a reference to God but the God-like hugeness of the bridge and its meaning. The words: "mere toil align thy choiring strings!" – describe that even the harp strings are unfettered. The harp, and later fusion of both God and the celestial followed by the reference to the unwanted of human society – the pariah and the forbidden lover's cry. This is a filmic panoramic sleight or sweep of vision.

9. "traffic lights that skim thy swift unfractioned idiom" here the power of 'thy', with a small "t", is not God, but the bridge, and the catenary is unfractioned, absolutely entire and unbroken with the power to construct its own idiom and not reliant on another's interpretation. It is not prosaic but having an inherent meaning of its own. But in grammatical or poetic and semiotic terms, what is an "unfractioned idiom"?

An idiom, with reference to one of many definitions, is "a group of words established by usage as having a meaning not deducible from the meanings of the individual words" (*OED online* 2019). Hart Crane, who read (and disliked) T.S.Eliot, wrote in a letter dated 9th February 1923: "Tate has a whole lot to offer when he finds his way out of the Eliot idiom." (Weber: 121). This is an example which defines the meaning of idiom as: "A distinctive style or convention in music, art, architecture, writing, etc.; the characteristic mode of expression of a composer, artist, author, etc." (*OED* online: 2022). There is a more literary interpretation of the word idiom: "A specific form, manifestation, nature, or property of something, now chiefly as *figurative*". The *OED* online (2022) quotes an example of this meaning from G. M. Hopkins:

> I noticed it [snow] before me *squalentem* (rough, dirty from neglect), coat below coat, sketched in intersecting edges bearing 'idiom', all down the slope:- I have no other word yet for that which takes the eye or mind in a bold hand or effective sketching or in marked features or again in graphic writing, which not being beauty nor true inscape yet gives interest and makes ugliness even better than meaninglessness. (1959: 195)

John Unterecker in his biography of Crane, mentions (quoting from a letter by Crane) that Crane read Hopkins in 1928 (1969: 526). Crane first wrote "To Brooklyn Bridge" in 1926 with revisions mainly to the typeface as noted by the Liveright "Complete Poems of Hart Crane: The Centennial Edition" (2001 [1933]). However, the book "The Bridge", to which "To Brooklyn Bridge" formed the opening poem, was not published until 1930. Crane was deeply impressed by Hopkins' poetic achievements but was not able to purchase a copy of his poetry until 1931(Mariani. 1999: 292). There is no evidence that any changes to the poem were made as a result of his reading Hopkins. In the light of discussion about the nature of the idiom, Crane gives a description of Brooklyn Bridge in a letter to Waldo Frank written in 1924 (Weber: 1965: 181), where he indicates the power the bridge has for him, resulting as it does, in his famous poem to it. It has become an idiom for him: "And I have been able to give freedom and life which was acknowledged in the ecstasy of walking hand in hand across the most beautiful bridge of the world, the cables enclosing us and pulling us upward in such a dance as I have never walked and never can walk with another." (1965: 181). In a letter to his mother a few weeks later he wrote:

> Everytime [sic] one looks at the harbor and the NY skyline across the river it is quite different, and the range of atmospheric effects is endless . . . Look far to your left toward Staten Island and there is the Statue of Liberty, with that remarkable lamp of hers that makes her seen for miles. And up at the right Brooklyn Bridge, the most superb piece of construction in the modern world, I'm sure, with strings of light crossing it like glowing worms as the L's and surface cars pass each other going and coming. (1965: 183)

And in a later letter to Waldo Frank in June 1926 he wrote:

> These "materials" were valid to me to the extent that I presumed them to be articulate or not at least organic and active factors in the experience and perceptions of our common race, time and belief. The very idea of a bridge, of course, is a form peculiarly dependent on such spiritual convictions. It is an act of faith besides being a communication. The symbols of reality necessary to articulate the span – may not exist where you expected them, however. By which I mean that however great their subjective significance to me is concerned – these forms, materials, dynamics are simply non-existent in the world. (Weber, 1965: 261)

The term "idiom" has already been discussed as being connected to condensation and euphemism (Chapter Three above), both metonymic forms. However, "idiom" although closely linked to these two forms, is ultimately metaphoric. The words, as they are, do not add up to a meaning that is clearly represented by these words. Eliot, himself uses the word in his 1918 essay "A Dialogue on Dramatic Poetry" (1948: 48), and in his essay on Jonson (1948:149 – both in *Selected Essays*). He wrote that Jonson, in his play "Catiline", fails because he "was not alert to his own idiom" (1948: 149). "Idiom" is clearly a word which describes how a specific writer uses and interprets words to produce his own particular personal language. As such, this is therefore a metaphoric form – the idiom of the language, *is* the writer. Here in the poem "To Brooklyn Bridge" Crane has, by inference, thought about a "fractioned idiom" because he has written "unfractioned idiom" (line 34), and he himself has used a "fractioned idiom" (line 4) by omitting the word "Statue of" from the word "Liberty".

Is it possible to define an idiom, as discussed above, as a metaphor, and a fractioned idiom therefore a metonym? As it is a form of wording which by its nature provides a definition or image of something unrelated to the words which are used, it must therefore be metaphoric in quality (e.g. "the goal posts have moved" meaning changing times and allegiances). But if the idiom is fractioned then does each part retain its overall metaphoric whole image/meaning? In Crane's poem it certainly does. "Liberty" is used without the words "Statue of" but it is quite clear from the subject matter of the poem that this is partly what he is referring to. He presents the fractioned image as a condensed whole and it therefore loses none of its metaphoric quality. Although it might be seen as a synecdoche – that "Liberty" is a part of all that the "Statue of Liberty" stands for. In his poem it literally refers to the Statue of Liberty because we know that this statue can be seen from Brooklyn Bridge if you stand in the middle of the bridge. The same line contains the word "chained": "Over the chained bay waters Liberty – ". The word "Liberty" therefore holds connotations which refer not only to the statue itself but rather to that freedom which can be reached beyond the bridge-bound waters of the bay. Therefore, using the implication of the viewpoint, the imprisoned human looks far outwards to liberty or freedom. It is at this moment that the word "Liberty" seems to be both metonymic, and metaphoric. It is metonymic (referring to the name of the "Statue of" literally). It also has a meaning which has burst beyond the bounds of the idiom (The Statue of Liberty), even though it is fractioned. The idiom is a metonym as well as a metaphor, and the open view beyond the statue doubles the strength of the metaphor of Liberty (also an allegory on account of the capitalisation of the word, without the full name of: "Statue of Liberty").

In line 34, "Unfractioned idiom", refers to the entire structure of the bridge. In the context, it is the bridge which has its own language. He is not only referring here to the unbroken catenary of the bridge cables but also, by inference, to how it cannot be split up (fractioned) into separate parts, the bridge cannot exist unless it is comprehended as the full sum of its parts. Within the context of the particular stanza of the poem, the bridge reaches up to the stars, is celestial in its attributes and lifts night in its (catenary) arms. The bridge is unfractioned and all the attributes become the idiom of the bridge – this is a metaphor.

Using the example of "the goal posts have moved", as an example of an idiom, if this is fractioned and only the words "the goal posts" are used, then they mean little more than the actual items – though it might be understood as a concatenation of the idiom by inference – because the receiver of the message "the goal posts", knows within the language and context that the words "have moved" are implied. "Have moved" means very little on its own, its scope of reference is so broad. Crane is therefore doubly interesting because it would seem that he understands the difference between an idiom which loses all its metaphoric meaning when fractioned and he is careful to emphasise the idiom by using the word "unfractioned". But in his use of the word "Liberty" he presents a fractioned idiom which loses none of its metaphoric power. Using a broad definition of the idiom, it is possible to refer to it as a metonymic form, as in "the goal posts have moved", which is a displacement of the more literal meaning "things have changed". But inherent in the idiom "the goal posts have moved", is the image of the misfired goal (because the goal posts have been moved) and therefore the failure of something. On balance it would seem to be a metaphoric structure. Crane's fractioned idiom, "Liberty", is one where the word "Liberty" takes on not only an allegorical meaning (because of the capital letter) but also (because of its known position), one which interprets the open sea, the sea is liberty. If the image were unfractioned then "Statue of Liberty" does not hold the same layering (see Hopkins' example) of meaning. The rules do not seem to be hard and fast here. The fractioned idiom, in this instance can be seen as a synecdoche – that "Liberty" alone represents the whole "Statue of Liberty" and constructs the whole from the part. But it would seem to be only one aspect of the full meaning of the idiom. "Liberty" as used in the poem's context here in Crane's poem means so much more than the "Statue of Liberty". To label the word "Liberty" as only a synecdoche of the Statue of Liberty, is to lose sight of the full metaphoric meaning of the image.

Here, in the penultimate catenary of the poem, the bridge is seen again from a low viewpoint looking upwards. It is fixed and unchanging and provides the same power as the sweeping curve of the actual bridge, and the sweeping curve of its magnificent meanings for the poet, viewer, reader, is constructed by the words: "night lifted in thine arms". The parabola means that the lights on the bridge have lifted the darkness upwards. It is the city's fiery parcels that are all undone but the bridge is unfractioned – snow, iron year – even the weather is measured (controlled) by the iron's response to it (see the following stanza).

10. in line 42 there is the final parabola – "vaulting" and then "lowliest", "sweep" (another curve) and when this descends (penultimate line), it "gives a myth to God". God is given the capital letter and suddenly all the splendid glory of the bridge's construction is seen as within that which is even greater – but the power of the previous detailed description overpowers the word God. Within the dense concentration of curves in the poem, the nouns and pronouns hardly seem to have the power that one would expect. The single use of the first-person pronoun in stanza 10, which places him at ground level looking up, enhances the sense of how the bridge belongs to the metaphysical other, leaving the poet firmly grounded in the shadows.

11. and then the bridge is referred to as a myth. The other time the word "myth" is used in the poem, is with reference to the cinema, to a human constructed

artefact – films. This suddenly places the bridge back into its human constructed reality rather than something from which meanings soar over and above the iron reality. With "Unto us lowliest", the biblical language grounds the human firmly into the lowly human condition.

In order to conclude the short Formalist analysis of the two poems, the verb usage in Crane's poem is listed below in Table 8:

**Table 8:** Verb usage.

| present | 17 (inc.1 negative) |
|---|---|
| past | 10 |
| past perfect | 1 |
| past conditional | 1 |
| present participle | 7 |
| archaic present | 2 |
| present passive infinitive | 1 |
| indeterminate | 1 (line 35) |

There is a predominance of past verb tenses in the first half of the poem (especially stanzas 3 and 4). But apart from this, the verb tenses are intermingled throughout the poem which leads to a sense of indeterminate time in the poem as a whole. It provides the metaphysical atmosphere of the poem. Overall Mayakovsky uses more verbs than Crane. There is an indeterminate verb "condense" in line 35. Here the language itself is condensed and it is unclear if this is an infinitive or an abbreviated adjective. A similarly complex poetic meaning occurs in line 24 where the cables "breathe" the ocean's "still" – where "still" can have the triple meaning of: a brewing still, a reference to eternal existence, or how the distinct ocean appears to be still though the perspective of distance though of course it is in perpetual motion.

In conclusion, although the difficulties which arise from studying a poem which has been translated from its original language have been taken into account, it is still clear that Mayakovsky's varied use of shifters and deictics in his poem sets up a complex web of time and place. Particularly, the wide range of use of different pronouns provides differing positions in relation to his subject matter: Brooklyn Bridge and New York City, and his presence there which results in a variable point of view. The device of the reported speech, the reference to the person of the future introduced with the words: "He'll say", and "he'll tell" (lines 97 and119) all contribute to the varied relationship. The detailed Formalist analysis has indicated that differing "points of view" have emerged through the use of shifters, deictics and verb tenses.

Hart Crane's poem provides "points of view" that are governed by his imagery, specifically his use of the curve – parabola and catenary. These are all-pervading throughout the poem. His position, although shifting in relation to the bridge, does not have the variability of Mayakovsky's response. Crane's predominantly biblical use of the archaic pronoun "thee", and "thy", provide a rhetorical effect, almost like the anchor points of the true catenary and on which the curve depends. His refusal to use this biblical pronoun in the last line of the poem, even though, if he did use it, there would be no rhythmic disruption, provides an outward-curving sweep for the reader which propels him/her away from the imagery of the bridge itself into wider considerations of the relationship between the human and the metaphysical.

The use of the Formalist approach to the analysis of text – the text in itself – provides some interesting insights into the poems which have been considered in detail above. But Jakobson's own Formalist praxis has not yet been sufficiently well used to provide a reasonable corpus of text analysis. Analysis of these two poems from different cultures and in different languages, but on the same subject, provides some interesting comparisons. But it is hard not to think outside the "Formalist box". Any reader of these two poems, so close to each other in time of composition, cannot fail to be struck by the similarity of content – the references to a sense of history, to indigenous American populations; to the sugar factory on the docks below (Crane's father was a sugar manufacturer); the description of the suicide falling, including the description of the shirt billowing out; the reference to the unemployed. Crane had an antipathy to air travel, which he does not mention in the poem itself. Mayakovsky refers to aeroplanes as a force where the machine controls the human. But such observations as these, lie outside the remit of the Formalist analysis, when the text in itself is analysed as a priority, the fruits of the analysis will always help to inform the understanding of the poem and poet all the more.

Jakobson's Formalist analysis includes how poetic images and structures arise from the text and how the poetic text provides patterns of lines and balances which link the poem and its stanzas across the more classic perception of the poetic stanzas or line as separate units. This, as a semiotic expression of his Formalist analysis, is explored in more detail in the following chapter. The above analysis of Crane and Mayakovsky has concentrated on particular parts of speech – the shifter, the deictic, and verbs. Crane's strongly defined pattern of curves in his poem is revealed through the use of Jakobson's Formalist method of analysis. It gives an implied/iconic poetic and factual/iconic dimension to the Jakobsonian "equivalence" (there is more on iconicity in Chapter Eleven). A balancing and communicating poetic structure has been constructed within the poem. The Mayakovsky poem is more elusive. This is partly because of the difficulties of dealing with a poem in translation. Mayakovsky appears to express ambivalence to his material – Brooklyn Bridge, New York City and America – as expressed by his changing shifter position and his use of deictic time. But as discussed above, the connective lines drawn between the pronouns, deictics and verbs provide a network which echoes the structure of the bridge itself.

And in addition to this, especially with reference to the Crane poem, a city poetic genre is enabled through understanding the structure of the term "idiom". The landscape of a city poetic has been established through three characteristics revealed in the above analysis: variable position of self in time, curved movement, and idiom. In the following chapter, metaphor, metonym and analogy are explored with the purpose of further establishing the forms and tropes of a city poetic genre.

# Chapter 10
# "Courage conquers the city" ("Смелость города берёт", a Russian proverb): Metaphor, metonym and analogy in poetry of the city

The proverb in the title of this chapter may not be the best literal translation of the Russian, but it can be used to interpret a poetic of the city. Three poems on London are studied here (authors: Blake, Wordsworth and Wardle) and the work of the Russian poet Elena Guro is discussed. The title of the chapter suggests that it takes some courage to interpret the city and, therefore, perhaps some courage to analyse the text. It is within the context of Russian Formalism that the tropes of metaphor, metonym, and analogy, in the three poems will also be discussed.

A combination of linguistics and semiotics in the analysis of poetry is very clearly demonstrated in Jakobson's essay "On the Verbal Art of William Blake and Other Poet-Painters" (1987: 479–489 [1970]). In the first part of his essay, Jakobson specifically analyses one of Blake's "Songs of Experience" entitled "Infant Sorrow". The text of the poem is reproduced here:

> My mother groand! my father wept.
> Into the dangerous world I leapt:
> Helpless, naked, piping loud;
> Like a fiend hid in a cloud.
>
> Struggling in my fathers hands:
> Striving against my swaddling bands:
> Bound and weary I thought best
> To sulk upon my mothers breast.
>
> William Blake (from *Songs of Experience.* 1794)

Jakobson's analysis demonstrates how the linguistic structure of the poem is reflected in the artistic structure of the poem. As a detailed examination of this artwork is included in Jakobson's analysis, the relevant picture is reproduced here (see Figure 8), as is Jakobson's diagram (see Figure 9). The Blake illustration is downloaded from: https://www.bl.uk/collection-items/william-blakes-songs-of-innocence-and-experience /page 44 in the digital reproduction:

Chapter 10 "Courage conquers the city": metaphor, metonym and analogy — 225

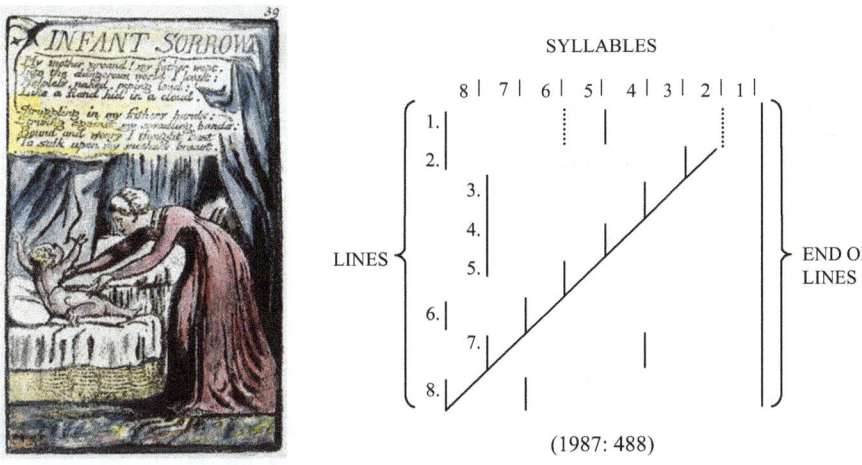

**Figures 8 and 9:** Blake's illustration of "Infant Sorrow" and Jakobson's semiotic diagrammatic interpretation.

The diagonal created within the drawing is reflected in the structure of the poem. With pure Formalist technique, Jakobson reveals how the linguistic workings of the poem, through its verbs and rhymes construct a pattern. His summary is quoted in part:

> The distribution of pauses in Blake's octastich illustrates its stunning symmetry. In the diagram below, numerals followed by a dot show the order of the eight lines; the subsequent vertical indicates the beginning, and the oblong vertical at the right of the table, the end of the line. The syllables of the line from its end toward its beginning are designated by the upper horizontal row of numerals. The vertical between the two limits of each line renders its inner pause, while the secondary, optional inner pause is represented by a dotted vertical. A slant marks the increasingly regressive tendency displayed by the disposition of the interlinear and then, in the last couplet, prelinear pauses. (1987: 487)

Jakobson notes, with reference to Hopkins, that the poem is rich in semiotic "figures of grammar" and "figures of sound" (1987: 489). For Jakobson, the linguistic parts construct the semiotic poetic whole. The poem by Blake, entitled "London", is now analysed, with reference to Jakobson's Formalist techniques, as used in the poem "Infant Sorrow". Blake's original illustration (see Figure 10), depicts an elderly bearded figure, apparently being guided by a child. Strong diagonals are apparent in the illustration of his city poem, as also are the shadows and angles of the cityscape behind the figures:

**226** —— Chapter 10 "Courage conquers the city": metaphor, metonym and analogy

"London"

I wandered through each chartered street,
Near where the chartered Thames does flow,
A mark in every face I meet,
Marks of weakness, marks of woe.

In every cry of every man,
In every infant's cry of fear,
In every voice, in every ban,
The mind-forged manacles I hear:

How the chimney-sweeper's cry
Every blackening church appals,
And the hapless soldier's sigh
Runs in blood down palace-walls.

But most, through midnight streets I hear
How the youthful harlot's curse
Blasts the new-born infant's tear,
And blights with plagues the marriage-hearse

    Blake (from *Songs of Experience*. 1794)

**Figure 10:** Blake's poem "London" https://www.bl.uk/collection-items/william-blakes-songs-of-innocence-and-experience /page 43 in the digital reproduction.

# Chapter 10 "Courage conquers the city": metaphor, metonym and analogy — 227

Movement is readily understood as an important characteristic of a city poetic genre and therefore, the verbs are the first linguistic structure to be analysed. The first line of the poem opens with the simple past tense "I wandered". All other verbs are in the present tense. All the verbs are verbs of movement. The one verb describing emotion "appals" (line 10), contains both strong emotional movement and stasis in terms of impact on the recipient. There is evidence in the poem of elision, the opening two lines have too many syllables if the words "wandered" and "chartered" are not elided. It perhaps indicates that the verb "appals" in line 10 could also be already elided and be doubly interpreted as both "appals" and "apparels" (or "clothes").

Blake's poem has a strong narrative content. Within the narrative, the "I", can be understood as largely metonymic. The poet is placing himself clearly as a direct narrator of the events in the poem. The metaphors are perhaps in lines 3 and 4 "mark" and "marks"; "mind-forged" in line 8; "appals" in line 10; "Runs" in line 12; and "Blasts" in line 15. But some of these examples may well be metonyms rather than metaphors. The use of the word "mark/s" in lines 3 and 4 may refer literally to the pox marks associated with venereal disease or indeed the marks of poverty as in thinness, this would render the use of the word a metonym. However, there is a specific use of the word "mark" which was conversant at the time of Blake. It designated the marks used to measure the depth of water on a plumb line. In this case, referring back to the description of the River Thames in lines 1 and 2, this would represent a metaphor where there was an image of drowning in the faces of the people on the streets of London. The "mind-forged manacles" are an image constructed by the word "cry" in lines 5 and 6, the "voice" in line 7, and then the recursive sensory verb in line 8 "hear". The cries are voiced and heard by sensory perception and therefore relate to the mind. This requires the "mind" part of "mind-forged" to be metonymic and only the "forged" part of the expression to be metaphoric – it is an image from the foundry or the blacksmith.

"Appals" in line 10 is metonymic if it is simply how the church responds to the physical cries of the chimney sweeper. If it is an elision, "appals" in the sense of "apparels", then this is metaphoric because it is a metaphoric "clothing" in soot of the blackened steeples and walls of London's churches as representing the church as an institution. Even if this elision is not accepted the verb contains the emotional movement – the cry of the chimney sweep, by metonymic contiguity, clothes the church spires in a sooty pall. Or it can be argued that the churches are clothed in guilt and/or blame by the cries of the child chimney sweep, and this indicates more of a metaphoric interpretation of the image. There is a similar transposition from the metonymic physical to the metaphorical in the use of the verb "Runs" in line 12 ("Runs in blood down palace-walls") and "Blasts" ("Blasts the new-born infant's tear") in line 15. There are therefore three possible metaphoric verbs in the poem "appals", "Runs" and "Blasts", one possible metaphoric noun, used twice "mark/marks", and one metaphoric adjective "mind-forged".

In summary, the verbs carry the metaphoric meaning within the poem, in each stanza this is expressed in the last line except for the final verse which carries the metaphor in the third line. In the poem, the metaphors are contained within a metonymic sequential narrative. In the first stanza, the repetition of "chartered" reveals a sense of control, the "marks" are symptoms of disease which controls the fate of the inhabitants; the cries itemised in stanza two result in the further control of the minds, in stanza three the images of soot and blood give evidence of the results of these controls – disease and death; and in the final stanza the description of venereal disease paints a ghastly picture of the sins extending down the generations. The final image of the poem "the marriage-hearse" requires special mention. This is a metonym. There is a hyphenated combination of two images – that of marriage and that of the funeral hearse – the beginning of procreative life and the last journey of life in death. If the words are understood as a synecdoche within the metonym, then extra power is released – the marriage is part of the hearse (the adjective to the noun). Perhaps this is a cogent example of Jakobson's definition of the poetic language: "In poetry, where similarity is superinduced upon contiguity, any metonymy is slightly metaphoric and any metaphor has a metonymic tint" (1987: 85). Poetic language use is extraordinarily complex, and perhaps it is an example which proves Jakobson's observation, arising from his analysis of "*Les Chats*" by Baudelaire, that poetry contains "transitory grammar" (see Chapter 11, below). The present chapter has only provided an initial exploration of the textual complexities of Blake's poem.

The Wordsworth poem, "Upon Westminster Bridge" was written in 1802 (first published 1807). It is a poem which differs from Blake's "London" because the viewpoint is different. The text is reproduced below:

Upon Westminster Bridge, September 3rd 1802

Earth has not anything to show more fair:
Dull would he be of soul who could pass by
A sight so touching in its majesty:
This City now doth, like a garment, wear
The beauty of the morning: silent, bare,
Ships, towers, domes, theatres, and temples lie
Open unto the fields, and to the sky;
All bright and glittering in the smokeless air.
Never did sun more beautifully steep
In his first splendour, valley, rock, or hill;
Ne'er saw I, never felt, a calm so deep!
The river glideth at his own sweet will:

> Dear God! the very houses seem asleep;
> And all that mighty heart is lying still!
> (Wordsworth:1969: 214)

Blake's poem describes London from the street upwards – he wanders through the streets, he sees the churches and the palace-walls from the street level, there is the sense that the marriage-hearse is seen close up. The last stanza of "London" is prophetic in its observations – here the poet has the courage to observe and proclaim, in spite of the dreadful vision that arises. Wordsworth's poem sees London as a distant whole – he describes its different buildings glittering in the sun and the river flowing through the landscape. The viewpoint results in a distance from city life which enables the rose-tinted view of its characteristics. The poem contains little metaphoric expression, even the "mighty heart" in the final line, which is a metaphor, is portrayed as not functioning, as in "lying still". In line 4, what could be a metaphor "This city now doth, like a garment, wear" is expressed as a simile. Or perhaps it is possible to interpret line 11 as metaphoric – "Never saw I, never felt a calm so deep!". But once again the metaphoric possibility is counteracted by the antithesis expressed in the word "never". In the penultimate line, once again, the image of the houses asleep is pushed towards the simile rather than the metaphor, as they "seem asleep". The poem uses words in its opening lines to depict that which is incomparable. Line 4 refers to "This City" with a capital letter, it is a demonstrative gesture, line 7 describes the city as "Open unto the fields", the emotions are extreme: "never felt a calm so deep". Can it be argued that the poem does not contain any metaphors? However, the poem as a whole is in a metaphoric mood, although the linguistic text of the poem is strongly metonymic. This supports Jakobson's ideas on the "grammar of poetry", how poetic language is structured through both linguistics and semiotics, as the poem in its whole is constructed by the poetic grammar of its parts.

An analysis of metaphor and metonym in Sarah Wardle's poem "At White Hart Lane" reveals a viewpoint which combines the street level view of Blake's "London" poem and the distant bird's eye view of Wordsworth's poem. The poem is reproduced here with kind permission of the author:

At White Hart Lane

> Waiting for a train this winter evening,
> as a distant siren calls and fallen rain
> reflects still swings, a red bus makes
> progress into the future, and something
> like a comet or prophecy from *Macbeth*,
> or the cockerel on a weather vane,
> moves for North London, pointing
> in the direction of the wind, speaking
> words of Dylan, telling of a ruler's fall,

> when Stamford Bridge next comes to
> White Hart Lane. The tournament at
> Old Trafford revealed ill-gotten gain is
> no substitute for the true score crossing
> the line. Some things can't be bought
> but go deeper, like a father and son now,
> walking along Love Lane. Tonight's tempest
> brings voices and stands singing, 'The Club
> for England, Hotspur and their King'.
> 
> Wardle (2005: 26)

Whilst the action takes place at street level, the greater skyline is also denoted: "a distant siren calls"; "the red bus/makes progress into the future", "pointing/in the direction of the wind"; "Tonight's tempest/brings voices and stands singing". "Stands singing" is a strong metonymic image. It is a reference to the stands at the football stadium, but there is no visible reference only a reference to the noise which comes from their location. This is an example of the more distant viewpoint. Anyone who has stood outside a football stadium recognises that it seems as if the whole stadium is singing, rather than the human beings within it. The metonym arises from the juxtaposition, the contiguity of the stands and the singing. We know that the stands are not singing, this would be metaphoric, as in "the stands are singing" – we understand that there are two connections placed alongside – the stands and the sound of the singing. The title of the poem refers to "White Hart Lane". This, at one and the same time, reflects mediaeval hunting imagery – the hunting of the white hart (deer), heightens the sense of Shakespearean epic and refers to the location of a football team and Tottenham Hotspur Football Club. If the hunting imagery is prioritised, then the phrase may contain the metaphoric – the football team is the team of huntsmen hunting the white hart. Or again it may be accepted that it is a reference to a modern location in London without the imagery from centuries ago, simply reflecting the powerful football team located there. This would be a dead metaphor becoming a metonym.

This system of symbols refers back to Jakobson's semiotic interpretation of Blake's poem "Infant Sorrow". The symbols in Wardle's poem interpret the sense of movement in it and therefore, by association, the structure of the city – the lines crossing – people standing, the "fallen" rain – not "falling", "true score crossing the line", "father and son now/walking along Love Lane" (the road which actually runs from the stadium towards the nearby train station). The "Shakespearean" sense of epic comes from the dislocation of sequence of place and time – "the bus makes progress into the future... like a comet or prophecy" (lines 3/4). The use of symbols to interpret the sense of movement through place and time in the text is something which, in the poem does not appear to have a strongly ordered pattern The overall sense of the poem is a heroic chaos of epic effort.

The present chapter set out with the intention of establishing that the emotional quality of courage is required in order to conquer the city. Such a hierarchical system of analysis – that the city needs to be controlled or that the city controls, even defeats us, the inhabitants, is not necessarily the best relationship to have. However, the quality of courage is certainly required. In Blake's poem "Infant Sorrow", there is a prescience which directly arises from the poem as one of the sequence – a "Song of Experience". The odds are stacked against the innocent child who must bear his accident of birth like the marks referred to in the poem "London". Also, in the poem: "London", it took the courage of the poet to perceive and understand the enduring victimisation of the city dwellers. The courage of the city-dwellers themselves, in the face of great adversity, is not in doubt. In Wordsworth's poem the sense of courage is also seen within the poet's viewpoint – the city seems too great to understand as a whole, too magnificent in its "majesty". But Wordsworth, in effect, retreats from the city he feels unable to control. He attempts to control it by perceiving it as a distant, even inert object but the expressed antithesis in the poem belies his intention. In Sarah Wardle's poem, the sense of courage is part of the subject matter – the grand scale of an important football match. There are direct references to epic Shakespeare plays – Macbeth (in line five) and Henry V (final lines). For Wardle the city *is* courageous. Her displacement of movement between place and time contributes to the epic atmosphere. The poem contains strong metonyms which appear to contain the metaphoric. These are three poems about a metropolis and three interpretations of the relationship between the city and courage.

Each poem demonstrates a preponderance of the metonym above the metaphor. Although a Formalism is the basis for the above discussion, it is not a complete Formalist analysis. It is suggested that the strong narrative content of these particular poems – albeit the narrative is dislocated in the Wardle poem – provides the context required for the trope of metonym which, as Jakobson himself pointed out is more readily used in prose. Does the use of the metonym in poetry affect city poetry especially? What other aspects of these poems make them specific to city poetry? The nature of the city, its physical space, the enforced physical co-existence, over a period of time, of concrete, glass and stone, with the plastic human frame, requires a particular poetics in order to adequately describe it. This chapter suggests that a poetics of courage, both by the inhabitants, the poet and even the researcher, is required – not necessarily in order to conquer the city but in order to confront it, understand its effects, and then to enjoy its poetics. It is for this reason that the poetry of Elena Guro is now discussed.

The Russian Formalist and revolutionary writer and artist: Elena Guro (1877–1913) wrote both poetry and prose associated with the city. Her themes follow a number of threads, all of which are significant studies in their own right: Futurism and Formalism; revolution in language, including supraconscious poetry; women's contribution to both Futurism and Formalism; the Holy Fool. All of these ideas can contribute to a contemporary city poetic. The contribution of Elena Guro's ideas, enables the exploration of some of the intersections between both the theory and praxis of Elena Guro, and Roman Jakobson. It is suggested that contemporary poetic theory and practice, with special reference to city poetry, can be explored more fully as an expression of innovative – perhaps even revolutionary – poetics through a discussion of the revolutionary thought of the Formalists and Futurists of a century ago.

The early Russian Formalist literary revolution was a powerful movement in revolutionary Russia. Early in his career as a semiotician and linguist, Roman Jakobson wrote two early essays entitled "Futurism" (1987:28–33 [1919]) and "Realism in Art" (1987: 19–27 [1921]). His earliest semiotic expression was firmly grounded in an interest in art. The ideas proposed in his essays formed the basis for his later theory of poetic function. This, and his lifelong emphasis on the "literariness" of the text under consideration, rather than its background and the biography of the writer, has a scientific aspect from which his later semiotic theory developed. Jakobson was himself also a poet and both he, and one of his contemporaries, Elena Guro, made strong and unique contributions to the Formalist literary revolution through the Futurist movement. This was expressed in a number of ways. Elena Guro was an artist, poet and fiction writer. Her art is not, unfortunately, central to this chapter. Her paintings use bold colours and often express a strong interest in the well-being of animals.

Some of Guro's work is available in English. Here, only her poetry is considered. Her diaries and letters are also available – partly translated (see Lunggren and Nilsson 1988 and 1995). Guro experiments with juxtapositions of unconnected words in her work as well as the construction of new words. Jakobson, who only wrote around fifteen poems in total, all of them very early in his career, also experimented with different innovations in word patterns and the construction of new words. The experimentation is part of *supraconscious* or transrational poetry and the poets called themselves *zaumniks*. Further information on this can be found in Rudy's essay (1987) "Jakobson-Jaljagrov and Futurism" in Pomorska (1984: 277–290); and Lass on "Poetry and Reality: Roman O. Jakobson and Claude Lévi-Strauss" in Benfey and Remmler (2008: 179–184).

Elena Guro's contribution to poetry has a strong visual expression. It was part of Futurist/Formalist revolutionary thought, that choice of printing materials, was an expression of the break with the conventional. One book was printed on pieces of wallpaper. It included the cover of a book containing artwork by Guro, entitled: *Sadok Sudei II* [Садокъ Судей II] and in translation, *A Trap for Judges II*. Another example shows the front cover of a book entitled: *Tainye poroki akademikov* [Тайные Пороки Академиков] and in translation, *The Secret Vices of Academicians*, published in Moscow (1915). The cover contains a black line drawing which appears to show a stone wall being peeled back to reveal something underneath. It is a small limited-edition booklet with covers made of brown paper. It includes short essays by various authors, Ivan Kliun, Aleksei Kruchenykh, and Kazimir Malevich, who highlight the key differences between Futurism and Symbolism. The futurist cover and three lithographs were by Kliun. The booklet contains an essay by Kruchenykh attacking Russian symbolism and its romantic, escapist tendencies, and in which he praises Futurist Russian poet Elena Guro for her use of transrational language.

Part of the Formalist literary revolution expresses the rejection of *"byt"*, the Russian word expressing the antithesis of movement (for more analysis, please also refer back to Chapter Eight). Jakobson mentions the possible influence of Pyotr Chadayev (1794–1856) on Mayakovsky (1987: 277), and the life and work of this philosopher reveal that his influence is one that could be seen to be of significance for the development of Russian thought as a whole, not just Mayakovsky's own path though ideas and energies.

If *"byt"* [быт] (and see Chapter Eight for detailed explanation of the word) is the mass of everyday mundane things which submerge everyone to the point of stasis, then this is a negative cultural movement which represents all that Russia succumbs to, including transference of ideas both from, and to, Western Europe. There is a Russian history of discussion of this transference which Chadayev did much to instigate. He was certified insane during his life and placed under house arrest by the Tsar. But his is a very thought-provoking insanity. The antithesis of *"byt"* is movement, rather than stasis, of ideas and energy which alter the course of life and constantly improve it. "Anti-byt", represents a desire to transfer ideas from Western Europe to Russia. This was opposed by many Russians. A history of Russia's ideologies – historical, geographical, religious, political etc. – is not appropriate here, but if the word *"byt"* is to be fully understood, then what the word countermands has also to be understood. *"Byt"* appears to denote a compelled stasis, its antithesis must therefore be a release to freely access all that is new, different and changing. It is to be regretted that the quote from Chadayev which Jakobson reproduces is unreferenced:

> We recall that in the early nineteenth century, during the time of Čaadaev, there was the sense of a 'dead and stagnant life,' but at the same time a feeling of instability and uncertainty: 'Everything is slipping away, everything is passing,' wrote Čaadaev. 'In our own homes we are as it were in temporary quarters. In our family life we seem foreigners. In our cities we look like nomads.' (1987: 277)

What is considered here is the energising which results from the rejection of *"byt"* – the embrace of movement as a principle for poetic expression. The emphasis on movement derives from the principles which are central to Futurism – and is discussed further below. Creativity is engendered where the moveable hits the immovable – thus interpreting functionalist communication. The Formalists sought to reduce the distance between life and art. Rejection of *"byt"* would seem ideologically central to their ambition. It was perceived as a stasis and impediment to both change in life and art at one and the same time. It has implications for a city poetic as explored by Dalgård in his paper "The City as Symbol and Metaphor" (1987). Dalgård analyses selected city poems by Brjusov, Blok and Majakovskij. He contributes detailed observations on the nature of city poetry based on the poems he discusses. He observes how poets' use of colours, viewpoint, fragmentation, and folklore, all create confusion or complexity, dissolution of time of day – light and dark, and the blurring of the edges. All this contributes to an urban poetic.

For Jakobson, Futurism is "The overcoming of *statics* . . . ", he understands that art may express simultaneity and, writing in his essay on "Futurism" (1919), he goes on to quote Carrà's *Manifesto*: "If Cubism, following Cézanne"s behests, constructed a picture by starting from the simplest volumes – the cube, cone, sphere – . . . then the Futurists in search of kinetic forms introduced into the picture the curved cone, the curved cylinder, collisions of cones, with sharp curved ellipsoids . . . ." (1987: 30). This is a process not only of movement but of fragmentation. Jakobson's poem entitled: "How Many Fragments Have Scattered" is quoted and discussed in full in Chapter Five. In the final two lines of the poem he wrote: "It blows eveningly and windily/O you city ensured inhumanly" (1992: 253). The poem experiments not only with fragmented experience but suggests neologisms which, in this instance, in translation, are adverbs. Jakobson also wrote three "Futuristic Verses". The last of these fragments, translated by Stephen Rudy, experiments with elision and with sound and word association. Reading the poem results in laughter, but this is not necessarily the effect it is supposed to have. Rudy's translation of the first two "stanzas" are quoted:

> chr. greet fg evl if clear don't see. ressur words sent bottom ressurwooods yr mnd. wt save skn splyd mowgli shush
>
> spit not t eat shchi so'd year shu = year pop weave bipl. O futpud. I be glss this thrughted forgt. nakd bipl (for through carrying away wmns remns beep only taking wrds) . . . . (1992: 251)

In Mayakovsky's poem "Adišče Goroda" ("Адище Города") ("Invocation of the City" or more literally: "Huge Hell City") *byt* is used to describe: "the poet's attitude to the humdrum of everyday life (*byt*) in the urban hell" (Dalgård. 1987: 8). The problem for Mayakovsky, and perhaps for the city poet today, is that he has a dislike of the city. His poetic skill in representing it, does indeed give rise to "urbanism" but a romantic antipathy to the city – the city as an anathema to the soul, may still be present.

# Chapter 10 "Courage conquers the city": metaphor, metonym and analogy

Elena Guro was, as has been noted, a significant contributor to the Futurist and Formalist movements (Winner 1977: 503–514). She wrote a poem which, according to her husband, the revolutionary musician, M.V. Matushin, was a description of her contemporaneous Futurist colleagues:

> Scatterbrain, madman, soarer,
> maker of spring storms,
> sculptor of restless thoughts,
> driving the azure!
> Listen you mad seeker,
> rush, dash,
> shoot past, unshackled
> intoxicator of storms
>     (Banjanin 1986: 242)

Guro, in her representation and interpretation of city life, was both more open-ended and more personally identified with the suffering existing in cities, than Mayakovsky. Women's contribution to movements can be neglected and it may be hard to uncover the records of women's contributions to this period of Russian cultural and political history (see Banjanin and Guro: 1986: 230–246). Her interests lay in form and technique rather than in beauty and romantic language. Her work highlights the connections between the Futurist and Formalist movements.

Guro began with a more positive interpretation of city space but found that she was "simultaneously attracted to and horrified by the city" (Banjanin and Guro: 1986: 236). Her later inspiration was a communion with the natural world and a spirituality which was expressed through the innocence of children, nature and animals. Her earlier poetic and prose work, inspired by the city, expressed, what Jakobson called, with reference to Pasternak, an "appropriation of reality". In her collection *Hurdy-Gurdy* (1909) she wrote a poem entitled "The City" ("Gorod" ["Город"]) which has been translated by Jamie Bennett in her Dissertation (2008), of which more below. Her work contains imagery of a city that often adversely affects people's behaviour and which has a darker side. She wrote in her unpublished diary: "Free rhythms. Prose into verse, verse into prose. Prose that is almost verse . . . Sections of stories taken as color and leitmotifs . . . !" (Banjanin and Guro: 1986: 243). Her city prose reflects her theoretical position: "Streets curve around the city without beginning or end. Windows. Droplets. Window-sills. Cats, pigeons. Ahead it unfolds, shuts itself up, opens up. Turn after turn. Reflections, resonant voices. Secrets, unknown desultory thoughts, scraps of flowers, scraps of conversation" (quotation from *Šarmanka 10*, [Шарманка: 10] (Banjanin and Guro: 243: 1986). Such language is on the edge of a definition as prose. Comparing this with American poets more than a century later, Bronwen Tate, in her article on Bernadette Mayer and Lyn Hejinian (2016), highlights how listings of city events and attributes can be interpreted as simply a prose listing and without poetic form or tropes. And she argues that "metonymy is a device easily taken for granted . . . [and can] hover without resolution" (2016:49). But in her analysis, it is a way in which women particularly experience and then identify with the city and the outside world.

The perspective contained in Guro's description is very interesting – she interprets the view as from a camera lens – "Streets curve around the city . . . ". The following is a quotation from Juliette Stapanian-Apkarian's introduction to Guro's work in *Russian Women* Writers, where she describes how Guro's language in a short story in this same collection portrays "the dynamics of Futurist breakup and manipulation of fragmented form . . . a Futurist elasticity of imagery in its convergence of interiors and exteriors, struggle against confines (it had become the room "too white and bright and narrow") and use of fragment and periphery ("the dusty edge of the table")." (Tomei 1999: 395). The painterly use of perspective and movement are characteristics which also emerge in her city poetry as explored by Banjanin:

> Although windows act most often as barriers, we should note that the window in Guro's works is not understood as a barrier between physical reality and inner mood. In this, she differs from Baudelaire and Blok, for example, because they use the device of a window in their poetry to express feelings of alienation and solitude . . . She, however, needs the interaction and transition between these two worlds to help her define her existence. In Guro's work there is a constant interchange and juxtaposition of the outside world and the inner mood through the frame of a window. Thus she uses numerous verbs of perceptions: "saw", "looked", "discerned", "perceived", "painted", "hummed", "smelled". The frequently used verb . . . . "to seem" indicates the subjective quality of the perceived reality that "appears" rather than "is".   (Banjanin, "The City as Framed Spectacle in Elena Guro".2000: 42–57)

The understanding that the window is not a barrier but something which can add richness to her perception, is something which is a significant tool for a city poet. For Guro, the window provides a theatrical perspective – it seems to be a proscenium arch through which life unfolds before her. Guro's poetic prose and its close affiliations to the theatre are highlighted by Banjanin in his discussion of her prose poem "The Street" ("Ulitsa" ["Улица"]), written in 1905/6. Banjanin only quotes extracts from the poem, which like other examples of Guro's city poems and prose, contains a description of a city with a dark interpretation. Guro uses perspective, descriptions of movement, focuses on specific people and events in the street like shafts of light on a stage: "The street seethes with black and fiery patches. From secluded corners of houses, small dark insects are thrown on to the street. Immediately the crowd, and the crush of noises and shapes, rush deafeningly at them . . . Stunned, they look for a harbour within the roaring river of the street" (Banjanin. 2000: 46)

Windows, especially high up windows, are a thematic perspective used in city poetry. They can be used to create a distance between the perceiver and the outside world, but they also have to be understood as a perspective of the poet who lives more indoors than out. This can be particularly relevant to the woman city poet. Guro has demonstrated a significantly altered "take" on this which indicates a particular tool of perception for contemporary city poetry. As an additional example, the following poem from the city poem *Shades of Light* by the current author is discussed. "Uninvited" (Fame section: 2013) uses a number of techniques which, by referring to the experimental processes of Futurism and Formalism, can be helpful in constructing tropes for contemporary city poetry. The poem is set out in frames which denote windows in a building. The viewpoint indicates that the windows are seen as a sequence which reveals how the building was constructed, both technically and in terms of how large buildings can be interpreted as structures – an expression of eidometropolis. The poem observes the construction of the building – with windows – from the outside, but moves into the building in the final stanza, on completion of the building. The strike weight of the text box borders has been left visible so that there is a sense of a building structure. Numbers have been added so that there is an indication that the text should be read upwards from the ground floor to the top:

## Uninvited

**31.** hosed down the site
        ordered multiple cradles
for nearby blocks to have their windows
        cleaned
(not paid for in the original contract)
    laid the floors (which are underheated)
after months of preparation
        we clad and clothe
shelve and iconise think of a name
        employ a concierge
sanitise the bathrooms
        I have no complaint
the lack of noise is fine

**32.** the lack of fresh air is death
        it is a sickly puling
crablike thing
        throw out the baby
with sights on the profits
    I find that I am working here
for the next 8 years
        if only once going upstairs
to the director's suite
        great view of 'Keep Out!'
sights on the bedroll stored
        above parking lot architrave
with the pigeons stumbling

**21.** basement is sealed
        first floor over ramped for cars
and in the heat and cold without shelter
        only the massive crochet of
scaffolding
  picked at by the harness of the dandling
crane
        the swarms of workers rise with
layers
        health and safety calls
weighs and measures
    gives instructions as to feed amounts
purification

**22.** the lights go on
        in the framework
the wires spread-eagle
        over the dust laden floors
the glass fixed panels
        are suctioned into place
the hermetical sealing begins
        over the genetic fault
they have turned off the arc lights
        lowered the stirrups
of the scaffolding
cleaned up the hoarding
        with disposable towels

**11.** the architect draws up terms
        with the midwife
they strike bargains over space
        here and so big
there are many that are similar
        who knows
will this one be born perfect
        in business the midwife togs up
puts on gloves shouts orders
pile drivers generators gather round as
    the archaeologist cleans the site for the
new timekeeper – time and motion study
  swings his digital watch for the protegée
the workers cry

**12.** we have built foundations
        like this before
knocking and reverberating
the drivers and cranes and pumps
        and scaffolding
and the endless succession of
        dawns
nightfalls bring out
        a rash of arc lamps
hoarding is rasped by padlocks
    the graffiti stains like cradlecap
dust on surrounding
        buildings forms eczma
first echo triumphant as the

**glass glint steel strength beneath granite thock pluck chemical change ridged & stressed resiliance cracks flexibility against the riven dirt and pigeon droppings**

## Chapter 10 "Courage conquers the city": metaphor, metonym and analogy

Reading poetry from the page, not necessarily from top to bottom was, in this instance, inspired by the poetic work of Allen Fisher. In his city poems in *Gravity* (2004), he does not use numbered sequence to assist the reader. He has left it to the reader to decide in what order they would like to read and understand the text. There are four sections to the poem "Ballin' the Jack", but it is only Fisher's discussion of the text which explains it. Here is a quotation from Thurston's interview with Fisher in 2000:

> Some of the poems read up and downwards, backwards on each other, like "Ballin" the Jack" does, In "Brixton Fractals" (*Gravity*: 2004: 20-23). There's four stanzas I think, so you read from top to bottom on the first one and then, if you then read from bottom to top on the second one, you'll see a relationship quicker than you will by reading in the normal direction, and the same happens to three and four. One of the things that's going on there is transformation". (Thurston 2001: 150/1)

The "transformation" that Fisher refers to here is an aspect of his theory of writing poetry. Fisher's own definition of his term includes the idea that: "the words have very different connotations when pulled into relation by the transformations going on . . . Again, 'the smoke above the town' might also find its rhyme in the notion of 'heavy water'" (Thurston: 2001:187). And Thurston quotes Fisher as saying: "At the level of words in the text [. . .] transformations may be used which deliver word links through the use of sound (rhyming), comparable meaning (rhetoric), disruption of meaning (poetic), and damaged pasting [. . .] together of different parts" (Thurston, 2001:187–8).

There is more on Fisher's work in the next chapter. While Fisher explores transformation, amongst other techniques, Guro uses a technique which modifies the simplicity of the narrator. Jensen in his analysis of Guro's work (1977) has highlighted some very interesting forms of construction in her poetry. He noted that her use of the narrator in *Songs of the City* is fluid. He observed that while there is often no consistent plot line in the poems, time is more sequential and stable. Jensen quotes frequently from Guro's poems in his analysis but only uses the Russian poetic text. Here is Jensen's summary of one of Guro's poems, *Songs of the City*. This is a city poem where the apparent narrator, who addresses the city, interacts with the city itself:

> It seems as if the appeal is given by a person, "I" to "a man with long dishevelled locks." We logically assume that the "I" stands for the narrator, but in light of following complications . . . we will come to realize that the "I" might be the city, personified. For the man is said to have spent his day walking around the city in a state of half madness, thinking about his dreams . . . The time indications show that the day has passed between the beginning and the end of this address. Thus the address could have been made to him by the city while he walked around. He walked around dreaming about the real life of the city, but he walked around in the daytime. (Jensen 1977: 92)

The role of the narrator, when considered with the benefit of its specific "shifter" category (see Chapter Six above), is not only open to distinctive interpretation but also has recognizable characteristics within the context of women's poetry. Guro uses a male persona in her poem but it is the poet herself who is expressing the complexity of interpretation.

Guro's use of how courage and strength are required to live in the city, takes the form of both an exploration of violence against women, children, animals and poets, and the spiritual strength required to understand and rise above the violence. Her work has been interpreted by Jamie Bennett through the perspective of the Russian Holy Fool. She is the author of the unpublished dissertation on Elena Guro: "Elena Guro and the Holy Fool as Prophet, Performer, and Poet" (2008). Her analysis understands Guro as more than a Futurist poet: "In an attempt to unlock the seemingly impenetrable oeuvre of the poet and artist Elena Guro (1877–1913), this dissertation identifies a recurrent element that offers an interpretive pathway: a hero figure who, though he appears in several guises, is always fundamentally a holy fool. Guro represents her holy fool/hero as a prophet, a performer, and most importantly for Guro, as a poet." (2008: 4).

Guro's poetry was written with the intention of informing her readers and encouraging greater insight and wisdom. As such she introduces audiences into her work and these spectators become a medium for ourselves, the readers. This is similar to the way in which windows are used in her work. The audiences she depicts are interpreters of the quasi-mythical action. Her heroes, heroines, children and mythical creatures are central characters. The city is often the backdrop for the performance of the central character in the poem in front of the inhabitants of the city. And this is an audience which exists within the poetry/prose, and which is depicted as mocking or ignorant. Guro's relationship with children, animals and innocence in her poetry and prose, is also crucial to its understanding. The imagery of light and the perspective of a viewpoint from a window are other recurring themes, as mentioned above.

In her *Songs of the City*, written in prose/poetry, the poem "So goes life", tells the violent and distressing story of "Nel'ka". The poem has been translated by Bennett. Here the innocent child becomes a violently degraded prostitute. The city is the backdrop to the cruelty and loss of innocence:

> [Men] walked right ahead so as not to lose their self satisfaction.
> She was small among them, with shy, quick
> legs. They controlled her, looked at her with self satisfaction,
> pushed her, ordered her, ordered their own
> women, whistled to their dogs, whistled to her, forced her
> to walk behind them. They beat her, leaving on her body
> the pain of embarrassment. And through all this, graceful

and elegant men walked by without even noticing her, and
in passing, thought – "woman" – and they felt like Lord and
Master. And electricity obediently illuminated her for them.
(Bennett: 2011: 105)

In this prose poem the child Nel'ka is unable to leave her situation and subsequently ceases to have insight into it. In her depiction, the city, and its ways, is triumphant over this child. Guro's use of audiences within her work provides two levels of interpretation of the situation she describes – the reader, him or herself, and the people whose responses are described within the text. This has the opposite of a cushioning effect. It is as if we, the reader, see the action with double the intensity – from both inside and outside the text. Her use of different perspectives provided by the double audience requires a semiotic interpretation of the text. The use of the stage in various forms within her work provides the setting for this requirement. Her poem "The City" explores the brutality expressed by the crowd of city inhabitants. Guro has the courage to speak and she conquers the city through her understanding of the importance of human integrity and desire for good. The sacrifices she describes are, however, very great. In Ljunggren and Gourianova (1995: 14, 15) the method used by Guro to develop her construction of this poem is described. She uses a sequence of sketches and études. It is important to remember that Guro was an artist as well as a writer: "The etude as a genre borders on the sketch but is not entirely identical with it. This "etude" vein, which is a key to understanding Guro's poetics, clearly reveals the intertwining of the verbal and visual "languages" in her art. The brevity of the etudes lends them considerable semantic tension, as selected salient painterly details are supplemented by a metaphorical interpretation focused on conveying a mood." (Ljunggren and Gourianova 1995: 14).

The painterly details which make up the different "études" – here rendered as separate stanzas – provide separate images which then construct the whole: "The first phase [of the writing process] consisted of études which often registered some visual effect. The semantic space between these points was then filled with text, followed by the somewhat revised complete version." (Llunggren and Gourianova 1995: 15) Here is the full text of Guro's poem, translated by Bennett:

    The City
It smells of blood and shame from the slaughter house.
A tailless dog pushed its ridiculed backside against a post.
The prisons are orderly and calm.
[There are] women's hats with flowers in a lacy haze.

Glances with scabs, hopeless glances
They beseech the stones, they beseech the
    executioner. . .

> Hubbub, trams, automobiles
> Prevent one from looking into the weeping eyes.
>
> They walk by, walk by, gray and incidental
> Without ever altering their cardboard gaze.
> And the terrible one and the secret one uttered:
> "Someone's time has come and shame!"
>
> Beauty, beauty in eternal trepidation,
> Is created by love and creates from a dream,
> The image from the profaned heavens
> Is conveyed in every breath.
>
> — So welcome every poet with mockery!
> Strike him with your whip!
> So that he receives his song like a sacrificial offering,
> And walks in the kingdom of your power with blood on
>     his face.
>
> So that at that time, when before the howling crowd on the
>     streets,
> And there is blood streaming from his cheek,
> He understands that in the world of butchers and machines
> He has come to profess – love!
>
> So that his love, eternal love,
> Is sold like a whore, facing mockery and spit, —
> And around him they laugh, laugh with ecstasy,
> Invested with the right to kill the good-hearted one!
>
> So that when it is all over, [and he is] already exhausted,
> He falls before all who are laughing, onto the stones
>     half-inebriated, –
> And all that is reflected in the laughing, unblinking eyes,
> under the fashionable hat
> Is that same cardboard emptiness. (*Sochineniia*: 363)
>     (trans. Jamie Bennett 2008: 166–168)

In keeping with her religious ideation, the literary device in the poem is neither metaphor nor metonym, it is the use of analogy. This is a device which sits outside either the categories of metaphor, or perhaps even the accepted understanding of metonym. Guro adopts a number of different narrators throughout her work. The work of Boris Uspensky in "A Poetics of Composition" (1973) provides a theoretical analysis of how to understand different points of view of the role of the narrator, of which more below. In her poetry Guro adopts both male and female personae. The addition of the audience within her text, as in the poem above, provides a new level of interpretation for the reader. We see: what the poet sees;

## Chapter 10 "Courage conquers the city": metaphor, metonym and analogy

what we see; what the audience sees; and we also see what the poet wishes us to see. There is both description of events and also a description of responses. The narrator has more than one role and this affects the nature of the text and its subsequent interpretation. These are analogous roles as they do not construct a single complex identity. Analogy is understood as the literary device which interprets the position of the narrator in Guro's poetry. How is analogy defined as a literary device? The *NPEPP* defines analogy within the entry on "symbol". If the imagery:

> is presented as if it were literal, but as it develops we see that it is rather, a dream, a vision, a fantasy or an imaginary action and hence, [or] there is literal action and situation, but certain metaphors and similes are also presented in relation to one another and to the literal action so as to produce an additional level of meaning . . . Thus, symbolism resembles figures of speech in having a basic doubleness of meaning between what is meant and what is said (tenor and vehicle) but it differs in that what is said is *also* what is meant.
> (1993: 1252b, 1253a)

The word "analogy" comes from the Greek, and means; "a comparison between one thing and another" (*OED Online 2022*), in effect a placing beside. Archbishop Richard Trench provided definitions useful to understanding analogy in literature when he wrote about the nature of the Christian parable:

> the parable differs from the fable, moving as it does in a spiritual world, and never transgressing the actual order of things natural – from the mythus, there being an unconscious blending of the deeper meaning with the outward symbol, the two remaining separate and separable in the parable – from the proverb, inasmuch as it is longer carried out, and not merely accidentally and occasionally, but necessarily figurative – from the allegory, comparing as it does one thing *with* another, but, at the same time, preserving them apart as an inner and an outer, and not transferring, as does the allegory, the properties and qualities and relations of one *to* the other.
> (Trench: *The Parables of Our Lord* 1850: 12)

The essential description of analogy is therefore suggested, as that which is described as not an overlaying of one image with another in such a way as to displace one element with another but: "the two remain[ing] separate and separable in the parable". John Deely, in his article "The Absence of Analogy" (2002: 521–550) does not specifically mention the parable as a form. His essay, taking inspiration from St Thomas Aquinas, is an explication of two different forms of analogy. First, he defines analogy: "The doctrine of analogy at its highest point undertakes to explain the proper nature of the unity of the concept by which being as such is presented objectively as an object distinctive of human understanding." (2002: 523). This exposes the heart of analogy as an ideation – we are two things because we know that we exist. He considers that Aquinas described the tools for analogy but did not name it as such (2002: 524). For example, the earthy example of the quality of urine is used to indicate health in a living being and this is analogy: "'Health,' thus, is said directly of the state of the organism, but, on the basis of, or from that usage, 'health' may be applied secondarily – analogously – to such related other things as medicine and urine." (2002: 532).

Deely suggests that if the quality of proportionality is added, then Aquinas can be said to have:

> added a distinction between an analogy of proportion and an analogy of proportionality. The former occurs when we speak by analogy of two different things which yet belong to the same order, as "health' said of an animal, of medicine, and of urine. The latter, an analogy of proportionality, occurs when we speak by analogy of two things belonging to entirely different order, for example, one to the order of *ens reale* [a being that exists independently of any finite mind – OED online 2019] and the other to the order of *ens rationis* [an entity of reason, a being that has no existence outside the mind – OED online 2019], or one to the order of created being and the other to the order of uncreated being, where there is an absence of proportion between the two things talked about. (2002: 533,534)

The above explicates the metaphysical connotation of the word "analogy". Aquinas himself goes back to Aristotle and Deely provides a summary definition: "The bottom line, then, is that analogy as Aquinas treats it is a doctrine about how we use words to express what we know, and transfer words from one meaning to another in order to illumine related things and to develop their connections in discourse. Aristotle calls it 'equivocation by design'; Aquinas calls it 'analogy'" (2001: 535). An example is that the bark of a dog and the bark of a tree are denoted by the same word and contain some of the same meaning – bark indicates a tree and a dog's bark protects the house. This is equivocal analogy because of the reference to protection as a function of "bark". The definition of "analogy" differs between Aristotle and Aquinas. Deely, quoting McInerny, writes: "we would have to say that where Thomas [Aquinas] is talking of analogous names, names analogously common to many, Aristotle speaks of things said in many ways, with reference to one and the same nature, and not equivocally" (2002: 540).

Here it must be remembered that the modern meaning of the verb "to equivocate" can make this argument obscure. The modern meaning is to quibble. But here, it is simply that several words can be used to describe the same thing, not merely that there is simply another word to mean the same specific thing. Analogy is further developed by the philosopher Cajetan. Deely (please refer back to the word "bark") summarizes Cajetan's work: "When words have related senses as a result of a property which is intrinsic and essential to the objects designated by each, the result is what he calls 'analogy of proper proportionality.' This alone is what Cajetan titles the analogy of being. Two things quite different, a frog, say and a meteorite, yet both exercise existence." (2002: 541). Without succumbing to too much detail here, Deely usefully suggests that "The problem lies in the idea that 'being', because it turns out that it must be said in many ways, is an intrinsically or irreducibly analogous term, when no term is intrinsically or necessarily (outside of the manner in which it is here and now deployed) anything according to signification." (2002: 543).

How is meaning to be communicated? Very easily, it seems, because analogy does the work. One word can be used by one person, and another by someone else, but the meaning is communicated between both speakers because the process of analogy facilitates it. It constructs the link with which the meaning of analogy is used linguistically. Although Deely, (2002: 548), quotes an example of how analogy can be made which leads to erroneous conclusions (that "niggardly" is not to be permitted because it is deemed to have the same root as the word "nigger", which it does not). Fowler, in *Modern English Usage*, defines analogy in a similar way. Analogy is the term which describes how specific words are added to, changed and also misused (2004: 51).

The overview of the definitions of analogy provided above, indicates that analogy, as a poetic trope, is metonymic. The definitions mentioned by Deely with reference to Aquinas and Aristotle show this clearly. Analogy is constructed through the use of consecutive words/phrases and provides a substitutive element which aligns it to synecdochic metonymy. As a trope, analogy, not only definitely exists, it can be shown to be used within poetry, as analysis of the poetry by Guro demonstrates.

Jakobson, responding to the work of Saussure, uses the category of the "code" in his theory of communication to express the analogical use of language. He wrote that all communication needs: "a CODE fully, or at least partially, common to the addresser and addressee (or in other words, to the encoder and decoder of the message)" (1987:66). Saussure understood analogy as strongly affected by time. Saussure investigated the mutability of language within his theoretical linguistic framework. He demonstrated that continuity of meaning is established through the passage of time. Saussure used the term "continuity" to define how language legitimately changed over time, that language, over time, throws up different words to describe things. For him this is a legitimate history of language: "Language differs with time, and at the same time differs or diversifies in space. A language observed at two different dates is not identical. Neither is it identical if observed at two points more or less distant from its territory." (2008: 99).

In Saussure's definition of the difference between language and *Langue*, he uses analogy to provide the definition for his "Characteristics of Language":

> But the analogy with 'customs' is itself highly relative ... 1. Language, belonging to the community, like 'tradition', corresponds in the individual to a special organ primed by nature. This fact, in itself, bears no analogy.//2.*Langue* is above all a means, an instrument, which has to fulfil *its aim, purpose and effect constantly and immediately:* which is to make oneself understood. A people's traditions are often an aim in themselves – feast days – or else a

> very indirect means. And since the aim of language, which is to make oneself understood, is absolutely necessary in any human society as we know it, it follows that every society, is characterized by the existence of language//An excellent analogy for related languages is to be found in divergent glaciers, giving insight into a common origin, new elements, different time periods, without the idea of a living organism (2008: 120,121)

Language is a system of analogy for Saussure. Words represent things and ideas. Different words, for the same things and ideas, are different in both the same, and other languages but the meaning is the same. But analogy lies at the heart of his exploration of language.

In the *Oxford Dictionary of Literary Terms* (2001) analogy, "is another story or plot which is parallel or similar in some way to the story under discussion" (2011:11). Mark Schorer's paper "The Matrix of Analogy" (1949) used the term "analogy" to develop a trope. He identified the "matrix" from a sentence spoken by Heathcliff in Emily Bronte's *Wuthering Heights*:

> The application of this landscape [the moors] to the characters is made explicit in the second half of the novel, when Heathcliff says, "Now, my bonny lad, you are mine! And we'll see if one tree won't grow as crooked as another, with the same wind to twist it!" This analogy provides at least half of the metaphorical base of the novel. (1949: 545)

He goes on to demonstrate how terms referring to the weather and weather events overwhelmingly shape the descriptions of the characters and their actions in the novel. This is analogy which is used as a trope for how the novel expresses a powerful message.

The parable, based on the use of analogy, includes that which has a religious content. But for poetry where does the true meaning and expression of analogy lie? The existence of analogy in poetry affects the structure of the poem – that is, how the idea is developed through the text. It is usefully expressed by Schorer's idea of the "matrix of analogy". A poem can be entirely analogical and can be perceived by the reader as such. Guro's "Poor Knight" is a Holy Fool and is an analogous interpretation of a perceived and recognisable religious expression for her audience. But in her poem "The City" she constructs a sequence of images that eventually crescendo into how the poet is welcomed with every mockery, his/her love is sold like a whore and he/she eventually falls and the audience who caused the downfall is a "cardboard emptiness". It is possible to use knowledge of Christianity here to understand the meaning of the described event, using Saussure's idea of "continuity", not only within the meaning of single words, but also within the meaning of the culture, including religious, ideation. The poem is further interpreted through Guro's use of stage effects. Here she is using the device of enactment – that of life as a play on the stage – to heighten the impact on the reader through an analogous device.

Uspensky, in his book *The Poetics of Composition* (1973), explains how the artistic form of the literary work is constructed so that the reader (and/or the character) is sometimes outside the text and sometimes within it. He demonstrates this with reference to pictorial perspective. His chapter "The Structural Isomorphism of Verbal and Visual Art" (1973: 130–172) provides several examples of how the perspective of the reader or viewer is altered as a result of how the subject matter is depicted. Visual examples include how, depending on the importance of the person or object, they can be larger or smaller in relation to each other – based on their importance, not on actual perspective; repeated images (for example several mountains) can be reduced to a depiction of 2 or 3 symbolic mountain peaks, the position may be peripheral and viewed from a different perspective (not pictorially accurate); and the furniture, or the placing and size of hands can be altered depending on whether the artist him/herself perceives these from within the painting itself or from in front of it:

> The function of the second person, representing the audience or viewer, may be compared in some cases to that of the chorus in ancient drama, which represented the spectator for whom the action was performed. The author often finds it necessary to establish the position of a perceiver – to create an abstract subject from whose point of view the described events acquire a specific meaning (and become significative and, correspondingly, semiotic)". (1973: 147)

Uspensky wrote that "The frame of the work is created by a shift between the internal and external authorial positions" (1973: 151). He goes on to explore the different viewpoints used by the author to provide these multiple narratorial positions. In Russian, because of the construction of verb tenses, the shift (as noted by Jakobson: 1984) can be manifested through verbs as well as names and pronouns. Uspensky gives examples from Tolstoy's "War and Peace" (1973: 153,154). Where in English the repeated event is described by the conditional tense, in Russian the imperfective tense as opposed to the perfective tense is used. The actions are never completed, and they therefore lose some of their power. There is also a role for puppet-like characters in his theory, those characters who are not fully named and provide only a peripheral function, often non-speaking, within the literary work (in Uspensky, 1973: 160.161). An author may well step completely outside the work of fiction in order to end it, by using some kind of statement of summary. (Jane Austen, in the last sentence of *Northanger Abbey*, writes "I leave it to be settled by whomsoever it may concern, whether the tendency of this work be altogether to recommend parental tyranny, or reward filial disobedience (2006: 261).")). Examples from literature are understood as operating within the reader's understanding of a framing of the personae and events. There are comparisons with the stage proscenium arch and the boundaries for the actions which preclude (more often than not) the players addressing the audience or coming out of the drama to assert themselves as existing independently from the events. Analogy is a literary form which assists in providing the opportunity to break the suspension of disbelief. The effect of this can be to draw the reader or listener into the text, as well as into identification with the author/poet.

This armoury of devices gives the author strong control of the text. Guro exercises control in her poem "The City". Her use of the audience within her work is a similar technique. This is not metaphor – the subject matter "is" not the audience – and it is not metonymy – the subject matter is not "as" the audience. The audience sees what we, the reader sees, but their response informs our own response, rather than becoming our own. This is an analogical device. The audience in "The City" is depicted within the poem, the cruel outcomes described are caused by their response and become an analogy for the reader – does the reader respond in the same way as the audience within the poem? Guro is brutally forcing the question: how much identification with, and responsibility for, the action, does the reader feel for the audience's actions within the poem?

Guro's use of analogy in her poem "The City" demonstrates how courage in a city poetic is required, both in order to experiment with tropic form, and also to experiment with responses which provide full understanding of what the city requires of its inhabitants, how the inhabitants respond to the city and how this is to be expressed as a culture. "Courage conquers a city poetic" is an adaptation of the title of the chapter. This extends investigation, into understanding that a city poetic may require increased knowledge beyond the usual range of poetic tropes.

In conclusion, the questions which the Futurists and the Formalists asked about how to use words to register complexity of movement are very relevant with regard to city poetry today. The consideration of city poetic genre is new. Does city poetry inevitably contain the Futurist and Formalist understanding of "function" and movement? Is analogy a literary form with special importance to a city poetic? It may seem that the selection of material in the chapter is too broad a mixture of techniques – fragmentation, neologisms, different perspectives, focus, tropes and styles. All of these components will readily reflect and interpret city life. Guro's early work about the city contains bold and innovative techniques. But there are tensions in her work. She does not naturally or harmoniously identify with the pace and experience of the city. Her recounting of manipulations by the city of people's lives, women's lives, is disquieting. Her story of the abused daughter Nel'ka, from "Hurdy-Gurdy" reminds any reader that city life, not only in the events themselves, but also the interpretation of events, is always problematic, that disturbing incidents may not contain positive resolution or clarity. Is catharsis a trope for a city poetic? The answer is no, when considering Guro's poetry. The contributions of Guro and Jakobson provide sources of how revolutionary use of language, analysis of movement and viewpoint, adoption of new techniques and tropes, all contribute to experimentation that can enable the expression of contemporary innovative poetry of the city. As suggested earlier in the chapter, discussion of Jakobson's Formalist analysis of poetry with reference to the existence of lines which link subject matter and text is significant for city poetry. The following chapter provides further analysis for the city poetic genre with reference to the London poetry of Allen Fisher and iconicity.

# Chapter 11
# City as source: City as destination – formalist praxis, iconicity, and the city poetic genre

Within the context of the present chapter, it is suggested that the projection within poetic function contains not only a metaphoric function but a metonymic one. The city as source can be a sequential juxtaposition of ideas. These denote an accumulation which represents the busy life of a city. The chapter therefore argues that how the city provides source material is crucial to understanding a city poetic genre. The immediate sense of the city as a place is the easiest understanding as source for poetic text. Jakobson's model for poetic function can be further structurally developed to produce an axial model as seen in Chapter Two, above. Jakobson's definition of a grammar of poetry is expressed through factual and imputed similarity. His definitions of these terms were outlined in Chapter Two, where it was suggested that with the help of these terms, a city poetic genre can be constructed. Gerard Manley Hopkins' contribution to the definition of these terms, a discussion of parallels and poetic artifice, was reviewed in Chapter Seven, above. Veronica Forrest-Thomson's contribution to understanding poetic artifice is referred to in Chapter Five. There are two further terms that need to be added – those of factual iconicity and imputed iconicity. These terms are considered as necessary to fully interpret the city in poetry. They introduce a theoretical discussion which is based not only on Jakobson's ideas but also on a specific part of Peircian theory, that concerned with the icon.

Jakobson, writing in his essay "The Development of Semiotics" (1987: 436–454), understood Peirce's icon as acting "chiefly by a factual similarity between its signans and signatum, between the picture of an animal and the animal itself; the former stands for the latter 'merely because it resembles it'" (1987: 415). Going back to Peirce's "icon", briefly – a picture of the object is the icon but the words which describe it are not – they are the "index". This definition is Jakobson's: "The *index* acts chiefly by a factual, existential contiguity between its signans and signatum" (1987: 415). He continues with a quotation from Peirce: "'psychologically, the action of the indices depends on association by contiguity'" (1987: 415) Jakobson continues: "Smoke is an index of fire . . . any interpreter of smoke [can] infer the existence of fire . . . Robinson Crusoe found an index: its signans was a footprint in the sand, and its inferred signatum, the presence of some human creature on his island" (1987: 415). Jakobson later states: "(1) the *index* is a referral from the signans to the signatum by virtue of an effective contiguity; (2) the *icon* is a referral from the signans to the signatum by virtue of an effective similarity; (3) the *symbol* is a referral from the signans to the signatum by virtue of an 'imputed' conventional, habitual contiguity" (1987: 443). Jakobson develops his theory of parallelism and artifice in poetry as deriving from the Peircean analysis, with the assistance of Gerard Manley Hopkins (and see Chapter Seven above). He continues:

> The 'artifice' is to be added to the triad of semiotic modes established by Peirce. This triad is based on two binary oppositions: contiguous/similar and factual/imputed. The contiguity of the two components of the sign is factual in the *index* but imputed in the *symbol*. Now, the factual similarity which typifies *icon* finds its logically foreseeable correlative in the imputed similarity which specifies the *artifice*, and it is precisely for this reason that the latter fit into the whole which is now forever a four-part entity of semiotic modes.
> (1987: 451,452)

It is from the above paragraph that the iconicity – both factual and imputed – derive. Jakobson, has already used the terms factual and imputed similarities. It is suggested here that these are added to, so that the factual, empiric reality of the city can be seen, represented and understood as iconically interpreted in poetry. That there is factual iconicity and imputed iconicity in the same way that factual and imputed similarity has been explored (see Chapter Seven). It is not suggested that this is only relevant to city poetry. The point is illustrated with reference to a poem by e e cummings analysed below.

There are further summary definitions of the icon which indicate that this is not necessarily the conclusion that other semioticians and experts in Peirce would accept. Merrell provides a succinct definition of the icon in referring to it as part of:

> The trichotomy of signs, including INDICES and SYMBOLS. An icon is a sign that in one way or another resembles its semiotic object. A caricature of a famous person is an icon. The relationship established between a few sketchy lines on a flat plane and a well-known celebrity is in part constructed, since everything is like everything else in some form or another, and it is in part a natural relationship, since the caricature bears some similarity to the familiar face with which virtually anybody can identify.
> (2000: 232/233)

Petrilli develops what is implied in the Jakobson and Merrell quotations above, that habit forms an essential part of the recognition of the icon: "For iconic signs to obtain the effect of convention or **habit,** social practices or special functions must be added to similarity. Iconic similarity is a special kind of similarity: it is an abstraction on the basis of a convention, for it privileges given traits of similarity and not others" (in Cobley, 2010: 242). There is further discussion of one of Peirce's systems of signs, known as his "decalogue" in the next chapter.

As a development of the definition of "habit", it can readily be understood, that city poetry deals with habitual life in the city. The city itself has to interpreted, and lived in, with reference to its factual reality. Within the definitions used above, which include the term "iconic similarity", a similar definition of the link between the icon (the factual city itself) and the habit of living in it, the terms "factual similarity" and "factual iconicity" arise. "Factual iconicity" is poetry which can include factual representations of the city through actual lines drawn in the poem. Fisher's use of actual diagrams within the text of his poetry is a clear example of factual iconicity. Fisher's poetry is discussed further below. However, it is further argued, that within the context of a semiotic analysis of poetry, the factual iconicity must, inevitably, as the poem progresses, contribute to a patterning, an artifice, and therefore an imputed iconicity.

Jakobson's definition of poetic function provides an important background for a theory of a city poetic genre. His Formalist method of poetic analysis provides a methodology. The following discussion of the theory and methodology will be illustrated by poetic examples. Formalism studies the text itself, not the author, or its context. It can be a difficult theoretical position to maintain in practice but is the basis for the structural analysis which Formalists developed. The function of the text is therefore inherent and is expressed, through the message (the text), as the movement between the addresser (in this instance the poet) and the addressee (the reader or listener). Any projection within this poetic function contains the movement which is essential to both express – and interpret – the poetic structure. The Formalist approach therefore understands that there is placing and movement, not only within the text at the centre of the analysis. There is also movement which arises from the text itself through communication to the addressee.

Arising from the core acceptance of movement within the model of poetic function, Jakobson adds his suggestion that there is a further role, that of the "recoder". This arises from his discussion (1980d) of both Saussure and Peirce. He argues, with reference to Saussure, that: "The relation between a *signans* and a *signatum*, which Saussure described as arbitrary, is, in reality a habitual, learned contiguity, which is obligatory for all members of a given language community. But along with this contiguity the principle of similarity, *la resemblance*, asserts itself" (1980d: 33). He goes on to state that the basic linguistic difference between the *signans* and the *signatum* "is that the *signans must necessarily be perceptible whereas the signatum is translatable*" (1980d: 35). Here is Jakobson's use of the "habitual" and the "learned" in action. He uses the examples of the physicist and the linguist: "He [the physicist/scientist] transforms these indices given in nature into his own system of scientific symbols. In the science of language [to include linguistics] ... The symbols exist immediately in language ... here an exchange of symbols occurs between the participants of a communication. Here the roles of addresser and addressee are interchangeable" (1980d: 36). Jakobson's argument is developed with the intention of clarifying the process of translation between languages. But he develops his description of communication further. He states, in italics: *"One must distinguish sharply between two positions, of the encoder and the decoder, in other words: between the role of the addresser and that of the addressee"* (1980d: 37). When interpreting any sign, there are three vital forms of communication. To this he adds a final aspect of the communication process which is required in order to communicate effectively between the speaker/author and the hearer/reader – that of the "recoder", and which interprets the use of the habitual. He writes that when a text is constructed, the encoder uses probabilities in language usage to establish an accurately encoded text. The decoder uses the same processes but in reverse: "when he pronounces in English/SAN/ he knows precisely whether he meant a son or a sun; whereas the hearer must use a different method of probability in order to solve the question" (1980d: 37). It is not enough for the decoder to use only the "grammatical analysis of immediate constituents . . . he cannot exclude meaning. Meaning can be excluded only when one works from the position of the decoder, since for him meaning emerges only as a conclusion, whereas for the speaker meaning is primary" (1980: 37). He continues with his definition of his fourth term:

> Many things will become clearer . . . when a clear demarcation is undertaken and the proper attention paid to the different modes of observation of the encoder and decoder. The modes of observation, however, are not exhausted by those of two kinds. One should also take into account the considerable process of "recoding": in this case one language is interpreted in the light of another language, or one style of speech in the light of another one.
>
> (1980d: 37, 38)

Cobley (2019) states that Jakobson's contributions to the work of Peirce have greatly influenced subsequent Peircean analysis (more of Peirce's work was published in America from the 1950s onwards, following the initial volumes of *The Collected Papers* which appeared in the 1930s). Cobley suggests that Jakobson's theories do not recognise the importance of the "interpretant" in Peircean semiotics (Cobley: 2019: 38, 39). It is here suggested, however, with reference to the above essay by Jakobson (1980d) that Jakobson's terminology of the "addresser". "addressee", "decoder" and "recoder" all fall into the remit of the term "interpretant". And, according to Jakobson, that all of these functions establish final meaning of the text.

Jakobson's analysis of Peirce clearly establishes how the meaning of all signs are enabled through the habitual:

> One of the most important features of Peirce's semiotic classification is his shrewd recognition that the difference among the three basic classes of signs is merely a difference in relative hierarchy It is not the presence or absence of similarity or contiguity between signans and signatum, not the purely factual or purely imputed, habitual connection between the

> two constituents which underlies the division of signs into icons, indices, and symbols, but merely the predominance of one of these factors over the others. Thus the scholar refers to 'icons in which the likeness is aided by conventional rules.' (1987: 417[1965])

He develops his argument with reference to the different indexical meanings of the pointing finger in various cultures (1987: 418). Arising from this, it is impossible to escape the sense that the "icon" has a deictic component, which immediately highlights the importance of the addresser/addressee and decoder/recoder structure. As has been argued above (see Chapters Five and Six), deixis illustrates both place and time. Peircean theory is further explored in the next chapter, with reference to the poem "Arches".

A sense of time provides a more complex interpretation of source. If place as source, is the basis of the city as text, then Allen Fisher's poems about London with its title "Place" (2005) is a clear exposition of the connection. The first theoretical form discussed, is the use of deictics in city poetry. Deictics are words which provide a sense of both place and time in verbal and written language. The use of deictics in language is complex and intriguing. How deictics are defined is also complex, as has been seen from previous chapters. How placing occurs in the poetic text, is readily comprehended by the use of prepositions such as here and there, now and then, and these indicate how the person is placed within the context – and in this instance, the city. A sense of movement is therefore implied between the person and the location. For example, I can say that I am here in the city and the city is there, i.e. exists in itself, with myself in it. There is connection and interaction. The sense of movement inherent in the Formalist definition of poetic function is therefore very useful here.

The placing of a poem can be simply made explicit in the title, although it does not necessarily mean that the city is really the theme of the poem. William Wordsworth's sonnet "Composed Upon Westminster Bridge" (1802) describes the city, but in reality, he brings the pastoral to the heart of the poem (see Chapter Ten, above for discussion of the poem). The theme of place or location in the city is explored by Peter Barry (2000). His discussion of Roy Fisher, Allen Fisher, and various Liverpool poets, amongst others, is based on finding both a theoretical means by which to counteract the pastoral romantic and also reasons why the contemporary poet engages so little with the urban environment in which most of us live. Location is therefore very important in the construction of a city poetic genre. It seems that the poet must at least give some verbal indication that a city location is the subject of a poem. One section of Barry's book (2000) describes how women have not so clearly placed themselves within the city, and that this is the reason why they have not strongly expressed a city poetic genre. His short analysis of women's poetry uses examples from work by Denise Riley and Deryn Rees-Jones.

Poets may place their subject matter within the city by describing events and actions taking place within it. An example is Roy Fisher's sequence of poems "City" (in 1996), which is about his home city of Birmingham. It is interesting to note that a number of the poems are about a city which is disappearing, being literally demolished, by the developers' bulldozers. Developing from these poetic positions there can be poetic devices – for example, tropes – used within a poem which may reflect an attribute of the city. Wordsworth reflects one such device with his description of London's "raree show" (1969: 540a) in the seventh book of his *The Prelude or, Growth of a Poet's Mind* (1969 [1850]) which describes his residence in London. Here, he describes, in a long list, all the people and events encountered whilst walking in London, resulting in a sense of madness which overpowers the author. The device of the metonym is the poetic trope which interprets such a listing. The city is the associative sum of its parts. In the example, the poet presents these parts as the poem. The impact and comprehension of the city is as a result of the accumulation of these parts. Mark Bruhn (2006), in his article on Wordsworth's *Prelude* uses the deictic to analyse Wordsworth's position, or viewpoint, in relation to what he sees, and the impact the positioning by the poet has on the forcefulness of this part of the poem. He notes that Wordsworth relates his list of stimuli using eye-level deictic placing which provides a very immediate sensation of being overwhelmed. The metonym can, therefore, be used to describe the impact of the city – its people and events – and when employed as a poetic device it reflects the divisive and fragmenting pressures of densely packed city activity. If the metonym is used as Wordsworth uses it, the movement through the densely packed city crowd of experiences can have a powerful effect.

The suggestion is that Jakobson's definition of poetic function is useful in understanding that certain tropes and devices may be particularly relevant to city poetry and that the inherent movement in the Formalist function is of special interest here. Also, the Formalists' understanding of the term *"byt"* as stasis, or an immoveable "petty, small, vulgar rubbish . . . . swarm of trivia" (Jakobson 1987: 294), provides an antithesis to the sense of movement which Jakobson's theory of function demanded. A theory which demands movement as one of its central components is very useful in defining a possible city poetic genre. As has already been indicated in the previous chapter, in Russian, the word "жизнь" [zhizn] means life as being active, being alive. This is the word which describes life with vital energy and movement. It may be translated with the same word in English "life", but the force and movement of *"zhizn"* is antithetical to *"byt"*. In Chapter Eight, above, the subtleties of the term are discussed with reference to Carrick (2017).

With reference to Allen Fisher's work *Place* (2000 [1976]), and "Brixton Fractals" in *Gravity* (2004), the metonymic devices are used in a fragmented, or apparently incoherent, way so that the text appears to be variously disordered or unintelligible. This use of the metonym interprets a frequent city experience for dwellers in cities. Robert Sheppard, in his essay on Fisher (in 2011: 31–54), writes: "*Place* was itself a conceptual response to *readings* about place, rather than of improvised field-notes or site-specific spontaneous jottings, but some of the most effective passages are where the past and present are juxtaposed." (2011: 35). Part of "Place IV", Fisher (2005) demonstrates this. With apologies for the placing of the text which is not a strictly accurate representation of the published text but is as close as possible:

>  the Effra is a torrent
>     carrying the waste of a dozen villages
>
> 'six miles south of London"        /1890
>     the unbridled YFRID
>   bricked over
>       "for convenience of Mr Boffin, chemist"
>
>   Effra Road/Effra Parade
> divider of Kennington & Vauxhall
>
> wide enough, a Lawn Lane gardener says,
>     to bear a large barge
>
>       Lord Loughborough obtaining a private Act of
>       Parliament to make this navigable
>         from Brixton to Thames" (2005: 43)

A second quote from Fisher (2005) reveals the use of location as a very visual deictic trope within the sequence of poems:

> elevated & well-drained north bank
>
>         raised Taplow terrace
>
>             city of London
>
> River Thames
>
> low-lying marshy south bank
>
>         low natural sand bank
>         raised one meter above
>         the marsh

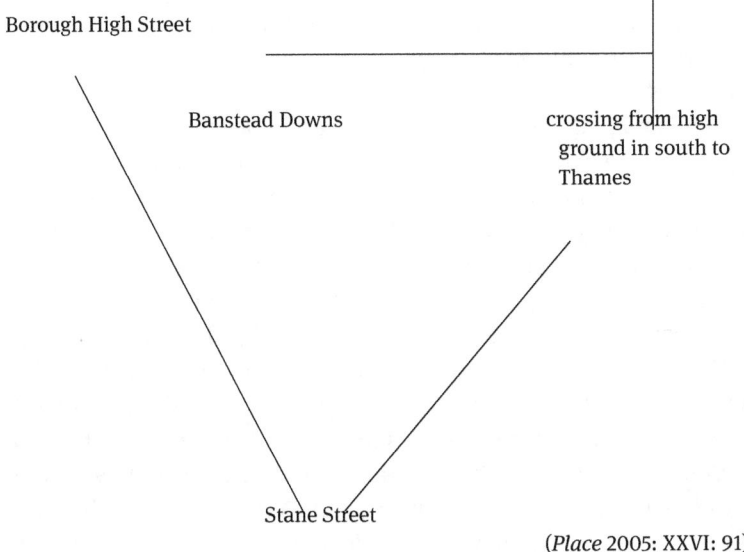

(*Place* 2005: XXVI: 91)

It is immediately apparent from these extracts that the deictics of both place and time are strongly manifest. The history sources are mentioned in proximity to present knowledge – "Effra Road" in Brixton is named after the local history of it as a river: "the Effra is a torrent/carrying the waste of a dozen villages", and see also the reference to Lord Loughborough. In the second extract the actual textual existence of the diagrammatic lines linking the text on the page delineates the travelling between the locations. The lines are used as a factual iconicity within the poem and which enhance the imputed iconity of the city poetic genre. This is explored further, below, in the current chapter.

In "Brixton Fractals" the same deictics are in use with additional complexity. With reference to "Bel Air" in *Gravity* (2004: 44–52), Allen Fisher introduces several characters – or personae – who interact, and provide a strong sense of movement through the text. Not only is there a fragmented metonymic succession of actions, places, responses, there are also the interactions between the personae – the Engineer, Photographer, Painter, Mathematician, Burglar. The same use of personae occurs in "Black Bottom" (2004: 66–73). Here the poem zig-zags between locations (Brixton, Streatham), actual events (a bicycle puncture), dialogue between personae and their actions, and a manifestation of William Blake. The poem also uses a number of forms and carefully wrought poetic designs. Allen Fisher has defined his poetic constructive devices as "Procedural" and "Processual". Scott Thurston (2001) discusses these devices in his interview with Allen Fisher. These devices are the amassing of material without constructive alteration (Procedural), and the use of device to significantly construct the poetic text – often in unorthodox ways (Processual). The brief definition does not do justice to Fisher's complex use of devices which process his procedural text. This is his own summary in the Introduction to "Brixton Fractals" in *Gravity*: "Brixton Fractals" provides a technique of memory and perception analysis. It can be used to sharpen out-of-focus photographs; to make maps of the radio sky; to generate images from human energy; to calculate spectra; to reconstruct densities; to provide probability factors from local depression climates." (2004: xi).

Allen Fisher is also an artist and his work illustrates his poetic techniques. Whether his painting – "scattered X" (2000) (http://allenfisher.co.uk/gallery accessed: 11.21) – is of the city or not, the shapes, explosions of shape and colour in the painting are readily assimilated as a representation of Fisher's multi-layered juxtaposition of ideas which he uses to represent and interpret the city. The triptych, "Views of the City: Barbarian, Savage and Civilian; 1991–93") seems to evoke an apocalyptic after-life of the city. Here the city has become desert inhabited by animals – which adds a prophetic ideation – which have taken over and are using human methods of destruction.

The factual iconic representation of the city is demonstrated in the diagrammatic example above, taken from Fisher's poem in *Place*, entitled: XXVI (2005: 91). It is here that the present chapter recapitulates the ideas suggested by the theories of the Russian Formalists already mentioned. There is a poetic function which, through projection, includes movement. The movement can be interpreted not just as words progressing from top to bottom of a page, or ideas progressing steadily with poetic tropes through a sequence of ideas, decoded and recoded by the reader. Allen Fisher's ideas of procedure and process indicate that other movements may be indicated. Where poetry of the city is concerned, the present chapter argues that the complexity of city life demands both a fragmented and also a synthesised structure and interpretation.

In Fisher's poetry, the subject matter is accumulated from many sources. These are then overlaid and broken up into fragments. The senses, sights, sounds, locations, emotions, conversations are all dislocated, interjected and interwoven. Fisher has indicated that there is a similarity between the assorted structures of the city – streets, distances, different times (see the examples used above) and he has interpreted these not only in a factual way (as can be seen from the diagrammatic lines in the second example above) but also as part of a more complex poetic structure. He fragments the information and also uses voices and devices of personae to interpret the city in his poetry. He uses both the structure of the city, which in the example above is diagrammatically represented, to represent and interpret the city, as well as a patterning of words and ideas to construct a city poem. The individual components of his poetic construction combine to provide parallels or imputed iconicity.

"Black Bottom" from "Brixton Fractals" (in *Gravity* 2004) is placed in the city by its content: "Laned on my bike/black High Road/iced from repetitions./Apocalypse/came down the hill spitting/Never saw him/Simply fragments/Frozen refuse, A/dry throated discourse,/A metal gas/to stifle analysis,/She smashed milk bottle/as bus moved sat/and cried/on a back seat, her head contracted by a rear-view glass/on the window . . ." (2004: 66). Interwoven with the city imagery of road lanes, a bus, rear-view mirrors, are ice and glass imagery, positioning – the use of deictics are both factual and imputed. In the following quotation from "Bel Air" in *Gravity* (2004), the factual iconicity of the city is introduced into the poem, not only by stating "we are in a city", but also by describing factual components of a front door, surrounding sounds and the sense of "alarm" which is a familiar response to unexpected city events. All of these give rise to an imputed iconicity. The accumulated details provide a nexus of city attributes. We know that this is a city poem:

> There is talk suddenly of mortice locks,
> with another, hasp and staple,
> inside an alarm sounds
> from a car in the road
> we know, beforehand, we are in a city
> We call this knowledge but
> are also in out of place
> no room to move without limits
> The Burglar rings a bell for help
> It is a mistake
> We are alarmed and our
> vibration changes colour
> randomly our rhythm chocks
> and my breath catches hers.
>                     (2004: 47)

If "we know, beforehand, we are in a city" then this foreknowledge is predicated on what we understand the city to be. The deictic of time – "beforehand" – places the content of the poem as a previous perception of the location – the city is therefore understood as imputed rather than just factual. The city is interpreted. The poem contains many references to a "star map", several personae, political satire: "A Burglar near the end of the century/looks out over his balcony/and reinterprets the State" (2004: 44). The Burglar is mentioned several times in the poem and appears to have a variety of functions and roles. The poem as a whole is conversational, there is a great deal of human interaction recorded. The last section again explicitly mentions the city environment: "'Anyone else want to ring the bell?'/ the conductor asks./I cross the city road to the walkway . . . /Children are roller skating with/a ball on new paving" (2004: 52). This section then moves into what could be described as a summary of how the city must be felt and interpreted – how its forces and energies must be recorded and synthesised:

> I lift a tract from the shelf
> and weigh it. No physical
> entity escapes this surveillance.
> It frees all concern about issues
> of internal consciousness – violent
> motions, unknown forces, tortuously
> curved, even multiply-connected
> geometry. Dealing with a point
> simply makes contradiction. This
> swarming, the mathematician
> calls multiplicity. "it's a
> matter of intensities," the Painter adds,
> "And velocities and temperatures and
> decomposable distances,
> You have to use your
> intelligent body
> to *feel* it." So much need to be done
> to know the consequence of shape.
> (2004: 52)

Fisher, in these lines, is indicating how the city is to be understood and interpreted. His statement, that he weighs the information that he has access to, provides a factual iconicity which is then added to a metonymic succession of ideations which construct a city existence, which is imputed iconicity. The context of these lines seems to indicate that he really does weigh it. His action of lifting the book from the shelf is metonymic, the metaphoric phrase "to weigh information", is converted to the metonymic, and here, it is suggested, it is therefore interpreted as factually iconic. His mention of forms and forces and how they are a "consequence of shape", is a paraphrase for how the imputed iconicity is constructed from the factual iconicity of city stimuli.

Iconicity in poetry is therefore a way of understanding both content and form. Within the context of a city poetic genre, these can be expressed through factual reference (names of streets or diagrammatic lines which interpret movement direction). Space, sequence and succession are all components of poetry which Fisher does his best to dislodge and disrupt, but in the process, it is apparent that the unprocessed material is his starting point. Fisher adapts his city material from procedure (the amassing of material) into a processed space, sequence, layers of perception. Fisher's techniques are primarily metonymic. He is using the axis of combination referred to in Jakobson's definition: his city as both source and as text. Does this in itself give rise to a construction of a city poetic genre? Deixis provides one aspect of how the text is ordered, disordered, laid and overlaid; the use of the metonymic trope provides another source for city poetic structure; another input is from the Formalist ideas of function which provide movement in understanding the construction of both factual and imputed iconicity.

Iconicity in poetry is a complex structuring of poetic tropes. Max Nänny, in his chapter "Iconic Dimensions in Poetry" (in Waswo, 1985) uses the overall term of "poetic signification" to explore iconicity. His definition includes the categories of: spatial configuration, sequential motion and successive change to describe different iconicities. His analysis of e e cummings' poem about the grasshopper is an effort to understand the structure of contemporary poetry which may well be also useful in an analysis of city poetry. The text of the poem is reproduced in Figure 11 below. This is not a city poem, but the factual iconicity used by e e cummings, clearly illustrates a methodology of iconicity.

Nänny suggests that if the reader follows a sequence which is the most similar to the usual method of reading text – line by line, from top to bottom of the page and from left to right – then the reading pattern represents a similar motion to that of a grasshopper's movement. The reading process follows: "words, syllables or letters that hop down one or two lines, vault typographic voids, skip up to capitals and down to small letters; we are interrupted by stops and reversals as well as puzzled by a saltatory [abrupt, dancing movement; movement of nerve impulses] punctuation" (1985: 134). Nänny goes on to describe how the words are used to construct the activity of the grasshopper by means of their spacing and placing, and that the sonnet form of the poem is dislocated:

> Furthermore, the word "grasshopper" itself, whose eleven letters behave like grasshoppers in a bait box, wildly hops around in the poem, leaping lines, landing in the middle of a word (line 5) or a sentence (line 12). Even the title of the poem, I suggest, has hopped from its proper place to line 7 ("The") and line 15 ("grasshopper") thus disguising the fact that the poem has the fourteen lines of a sonnet.           (Nänny 1985: 134)

Nänny notes the use of onomatopoeia, so that the movement of the grasshopper is reflected in the sounds of the words as well as their placing. He also interprets the mood of the poem:

> the sequential unscrambling on the part of the reader is an iconic imitation of a gradual change in the perceiving subject, of a gradually firmer perceptual grasp of the nature and identity ("The," l.7) of the evasive object called grasshopper. Hence, the initially slow and laborious act of rearranging the letters can be seen as an iconic reenactment of the subjective process of perception that bundles disparate sensory impressions into the whole of a meaningful 'gestalt'. The progressive recognition of the poem's genre as a titled sonnet matches this process in terms of poetic form.           (Nänny 1985: 134)

Nänny calls the poem a "poempicture" and a "virtuoso poem". His final interpretation of the iconicity of the poem is revealed with a diagram in which he has delineated the grasshopper:

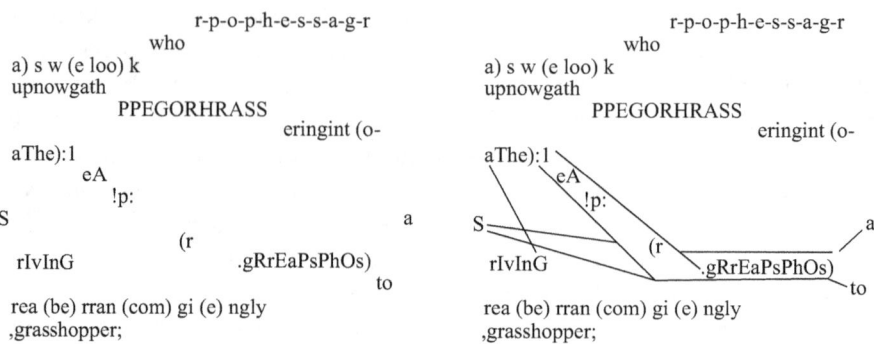

**Figure 11:** e e cummings: Grasshopper poem complete with drawing (Nänny 1985: 134, 135).

Poetry can not only construct and be constructed by factual iconicity, as indicated by the examples used above, but it can also construct and be constructed by imputed iconicity. Imputed iconicity in poetry takes the form of a range of devices. At the least intricate, this is demonstrated by the simplest patterning such as, for example, the drawing of a line, alliteration, or the use of a chorus. At the most intricate, this is constructed by a nexus of iconicity which ranges from the factual through to the imputed, by the structure and tropic use in the poem as a whole. Even further, by complex forms which can defy analysis or even lead to doubt as to whether the poet intended (or succeeded) in achieving the results observed. Within this range, linguistics and semiotics provide forms of analysis which reveal the patterns. The Formalist focus on the text is the only method which can reveal such complexity. The factual similarity/iconicity and imputed similarity/iconicity are terms which define these areas of analysis. This is a theory of iconicity in poetry which has been partly enabled by Jakobson's lifelong interest in the techniques of modern art. This area of study assists in analysing Jakobson's own Formalist analysis of poetry. His analysis of "Les Chats" by Baudelaire is a pivotal example. The Formalist analysis of the poetic text, as can be demonstrated below, puts no limit on its complexity. And finally, forms such as the use of anagrams, which seem to be almost beyond the Formalist remit are discussed.

It is notable that Jonathan Culler, in *Structuralist Poetics* (2002) negatively criticised Jakobson's Formalist analysis of Shakespeare's sonnet "Th'Expence of Spirit" and Baudelaire's "Spleen" poem "Quand le ciel bas et lourd…". Jakobson's Formalist analysis of the poem has been published in a number of languages, but not in English. Culler uses the original French version of Jakobson's article which was published in 1967 (*Tel Quel*, No: 29) and then, later, in the book *Questions de Poétique* (Jakobson with Tzvetan Todorov: 1973). Culler uses his own translation of the poem and his translation is central to his discussion. Culler also wrote the Introduction to McGowan's translation of Baudelaire's poems (1993). On close examination, it is revealed that while asserting that Jakobson made some grammatical errors in his analysis, Culler too, is not entirely accurate (1975: 64–86). In Jakobson's article written with Susan Kitron: "On Poetic Intentions and Linguistic Devices in Poetry: A Discussion with Professors and Students at the University of Cologne" (1980b), Jakobson states that the "author [Culler] made the experiment of taking a few lines out of one of my essays in order to interpret them from the point of view of poetics. The result was really extremely negative" (1980: 88). Later, Jakobson refers to this criticism in his interview with Krystyna Pomorska in *Dialogues* (1983: 119–122). His critique of Culler's analysis of his own work indicates that, without doubt, Culler failed to understand either the method or the results of the Formalist techniques. Culler, who has championed the role of the reader throughout his career, had little interest in Formalist technique which highlights the poet's skill in constructing a poem and how the poet, therefore, exerts a significant degree of control of a text.

Jakobson notes that Culler failed to observe the pattern of odd and even stanzas in the poem, with their differing use of personal and reflexive pronouns. He also notes that Culler failed to notice the patterning of the use of pronouns throughout the poem and he further states:

> Finally, Culler should not pass in silence over the semantic difference that diametrically opposes the movement 'from the bottom to the top' of the even stanzas to the progression 'from the top to the bottom' of the odd stanzas, especially since the entire metaphorical system of the "Spleen" [this is the overall title of poem sequence of which "Les Chats" was included] is in fact based on this antithetical motion. (1983: 121)

Jakobson's comments on the role of the poet in creating poetry are also of importance here. He writes:

> It is hard to understand why critics do their best to neglect grammatical figures in Baudelaire when the poet himself constantly referred to the 'vocative magic' of grammatical structure, the expressive force of grammatical categories, and the poetic pertinence of such evident factors as 'regularity and symmetry'. That great expert on the work of Baudelaire, Théophile Gautier (1811–1872), devoted particular attention to the 'trade secrets' hidden in this work and 'invisible to outsiders'. (1983: 122)

However, Culler does not refer to Gautier in the bibliography of his *Structuralist Poetics*. His translation removes the use of allegory by spelling "hope" with a small "h" when it is capitalized in the French (see stanza two), and this leads to a subsequent different use of pronoun – "it" instead of "she" – in the next stanza. In the fifth and final stanza, 'Hope' is, however, spelt with a capital letter. The observation of fine detail is not to question all of Culler's analysis; but it highlights the importance of being precise, especially as he criticised Jakobson's close Formalist analysis, which is based on exact interpretation of the poet's words, especially the pronouns, as imprecise. Jakobson went on to discuss the rhyme patterns and metrics of the poem. Jakobson's analytical vocabulary is precise, and he refers to the work of Lucien Tesnière (2015 [1965]) when analysing the use of adverbs and sentence construction.

It is possible to compare the two analyses by Jakobson and Culler and discover difficulties with both of them. But it is not advisable to dismiss the points raised by Jakobson. Close reading of both Jakobson's original analysis and Culler's critique reveals that some of Culler's frustration with Jakobson arises from his own realization – after he has already done much analytical work – that dense poetry contains "transitory grammatical forms" (1975: 71). This interesting term is not defined or explored by Culler and it is, in fact, a term which Jakobson used previously (1973: 428, 429). Jakobson only uses it within the context of the precise terminology of language used in his analysis. In itself, however, it is a term which provides an interesting theory for the use of language in poetry. It is a possible indication that the term "shifters" applies to grammar as well as pronouns. For Culler this is perhaps a "let-out" phrase for his eventual realization that Jakobson's work is remarkably detailed, even accurate – and that he cannot dismiss it, although his own dedication to "reader theory" compels him to dismiss the Formalist theoretical position. Jakobson referred to "épithètes ou complements adnominaux" [adnominal nouns or complementary adjectives] (1967: 428), this is where an adjective can be used as a substantive. He later analysed the grammar of the poem by referring to "asyndète" [asyndeton] where a conjunction is omitted. The detail of his analysis includes his knowledge, that parts of speech, perhaps especially in poetry, often occupy more than one grammatical function. It is appropriate here to provide a translation of part of the essay that Jakobson wrote:

> The 4 first person pronouns, of which one is a substantive (I/4 'nous') and 3 are adjectives (III/4 'nos'; V/2 and 4, 'mon') appear in the odd stanzas whereas the 2 even stanzas are entirely lacking [in first person pronouns, though II has a 3$^{rd}$ person pronoun: 'ses']. Of these first person pronouns, 2 plural and 2 singular, the uneven stanzas bring together equally, the 4 pronouns in the third person, of which 2 in their turn are plural and 2 are singular and of which, one of the new ones, is a substantive (I/4 'il') as opposed to 3 adjectives (III/1 + 4 'ses', 'ses', 'son'). The 2 'ses' in III, in the same way, as the 2 'mon' in V, the first connects to the feminine substantives ('traînées', 'âme') and the second to a masculine one ('filets', 'crâne'). The passage with the double plural 'nos' (more correctly understood as plural adjectival pos-

sessive pronouns in the first person plural) to the double singular 'mon' (or more precisely, the singular adjectival possessive pronoun of the first person singular) create the gradual process towards a focus.'     (1967: 421) [translated by the present author Coghill]

Jakobson then moves on to discuss the use of adjectives in the poem. Culler takes issue with Jakobson's analysis of "gémissant" (1975: 70). But on balance he is not correct. He argues that it describes the subsequent phrase more than the "l'esprit", but as there is no comma after "l'esprit", it must refer back to this word and not forward to "en proie aux longs ennuis". He states (1975: 76) that Jakobson's prose can be equally analysed to discover symmetries and asymmetries, which invalidates this kind of analysis of poetry. But in stating it, Culler only proves to himself that prose can be just as rich in poetics as poetry. This, in itself, does not invalidate the analysis; it merely extends it. Culler's analysis of Jakobson is detailed. Unfortunately, it is undertaken with a destructive remit. His irritation and sense of frustration with Jakobson's techniques leads him to disparage the man without necessarily invalidating the analysis.

There are further details in the history to the argument between Jakobson and Culler. Jakobson's original essay was entitled: "Une Microscopie du dernier 'Spleen' dans les Fleurs du mal": (*Tel Quel* 1967, 29: 12–24, also 1973: 428–435). Culler's article was published in *Language and Style*; (5:1 1971) with the title: "Jakobson and the Linguistic Analysis of Literary Texts". Jakobson himself rebutted Culler's criticism in a "Postscriptum" to *Questions de Poétique* written in 1973 (485–504). Culler's book *Structuralist Poetics* (1975), contained much of the material from his original article on Jakobson. Jakobson's "Postscriptum" does not mention Culler by name but contains a focussed critique of Culler's argument (1975: 496–497), which centres around the exact nature of adjectives and their grammatical designation. On reading Culler's original article in *Tel Quel* ([1967] 1971) it is clear that Culler is incensed with Jakobson on a false premiss. He understands Jakobson to be a Formalist who depends entirely on linguistics for the analysis. It becomes frustrating for Culler when Jakobson analyses the balancing of the strophes in the "Spleen" poem because it exposes the limitations of his own analytical brief. Jakobson's is not just a linguistic analysis of the poem, it is a semiotic one. Culler himself states, quite correctly, "linguistics does not give the critic a finite set of categories whose distribution in a text can be determined automatically and exhaustively" (1971: 55). Jakobson would be the first to state that linguistics was not his only tool for Formalist analysis. The debate refers to detailed linguistic analysis. Jakobson refers to Culler as a critic who is a "nebulous" and "bizarre" (1973: 497). It is interesting to note that Jakobson refers to the work of Tesnière as a final explicatory source for his grammatical and linguistic analysis. Culler refers to Tesnière's *Eléments de Syntaxe Structural* (1965) in his bibliography (1975) but there is no evidence that he has actually used any of his theory. The English translation of Tesnière's book was published in 2015 as *Elements of Structural Syntax*. The extremely dense material of his book is challenging even when reading it in one's native language. Jakobson's quotation from it does not, unfortunately, provide a page reference. This is a debate which is hampered by the fact that Jakobson's original article "Une Microscopie . . ." (1967) is still only available in French. A publication of the material in English is needed and now overdue. The exact grammatical nature of verb participles in poetry is something which challenges the reader, as is also demonstrated in the following chapter which includes Formalist praxis of a poem by the present author, Coghill.

Culler would be glad to have the last word on the antipathy that he has towards Jakobson's theories. As a possible conclusion to the confrontation, he refers especially to Jakobson's theory of poetic function in his Outgoing Presidential Address to the American Comparative Literature Association (2001). The value of reader theory is that it enables the critical reader to interpret Culler with more, or perhaps less, kindness than he intended: "Among the six elementary functions of language [of Jakobson] was the poetic function, which involves, in a famously rebarbative phrase that all students of theory once knew by heart, 'the projection of the principle of equivalence from the axis of selection into the axis of combination'". As has been demonstrated in Chapter One, above, close analysis of Jakobson's poetic function reveals a dynamic heart to Formalist poetic theory, which is both sophisticated and impossible to ignore.

Anagrams have been mentioned as a part of this discussion. It is an area of Jakobson's poetic function which has caused some uneasiness. In his essay, "Une Microscopie . . ." (1967: 434, 435), Jakobson analyses the patterns of consonant and vowel sounds, not as an exercise in alliteration and assonance but as a sound pattern which reflects the overall title of the four "Spleen" poems. There is no suggestion that the words are spelt out and replicated within the text of the poem as a reproduction of the word of the title, but that it produces a poetic "fureur du jeu phonique" (literally, a passion for gambling), something which was understood by Saussure, in a letter from him to Meillet (1967: 434). Jakobson adds further quotations:

> et l'entrelacement insolite des significations formelles, grammaticales, donc abstraites, ne peuvent pas ne pas jouer un rôle primordial dans l'œuvre du poète qui prit la langue et l'écriture « comme opérations magiques, sorcellerie évocatoire (Fusées, VI, XVII). ["and the unusual networks of formal and grammatical usage, even though they are abstract, cannot but play a primeval role in the work of the poet who took the spoken and written words "as magical processes, evocative sorceries" (Fusées, VI, XVII) [translated by the present author, Coghill]. (1967: 435)

Saussure's interest in anagrams is explored in *Words upon Words: The Anagrams of Ferdinand de Saussure* by Jean Starobinski (1979). This is research which Saussure undertook early in his lifelong work on linguistics and semiology. The theory is at one and the same time fascinating and unrewarding. Starobinski, in analysing Saussure on this subject, discerns that Saussure found his anagrams sometimes by chance and then built on the nature of the occurrence. He then postulates that even more might emerge –including the incidence of the hypogram. The hypogram is defined as: "These [sound] structures [which] range from paired repetitions of sounds, either individually or in groups, to the looser reproduction in the phonic material of the work of elements of a *key-word* (*mot-thème*, later, *hypogram*) central to the plot of the text." (*NPEPP*: 1993. 69b). Whether it was chance or the conscious design of the poet, Starobinski suggests that "Perhaps Saussure's only mistake was to have posed the alternatives so sharply between "chance" and "conscious deliberation". Why should one not see in the anagram an aspect of human speech . . . . neither haphazard nor fully conscious." (1979: 122).

Anagrams are present in the patterns of letters, syllables and sounds within poetry. Saussure's study revolved around examples taken from classic poetry. But ultimately, the work is frustrating because the researcher cannot distinguish between what is a purposeful addition to the poetics of a text and what is merely haphazard. Starobinski again: "He (the critic) resigns himself badly to remaining alone with his discovery. He wishes to share it with the poet. But the poet, having said all he has to say, remains strangely silent. One can produce any hypothesis about him: he neither accepts nor rejects it." (1979: 123). The composer, J.S. Bach, was also interested in these forms in music. The anagram is something which interests any Formalist researcher. However, Starobinski sums up the unease which this study evokes:

> Ferdinand de Saussure interprets classical poetry as an art of *combination*, whose developed structures are tributaries of simple elements, fundamentals which are required by the rules of the game to be both conserved and transformed. Only it happens that all language is combination, even without the intervention of an explicit intention to practice combination as art. Decipherers, whether they be cabalists or phoneticists, have a free range: a reading which is symbolic or numeric or systematically attentive to a partial aspect can always bring to light a latent depth, a hidden secret, a language within the language.     (1979: 129)

It is not the critic's or the researcher's desire to be chasing formulas of language that might be based on chance and co-incidence. Logic, it is felt, must prevail. However, in an echo of Sidney's earlier definition: "Now for the poet, he nothing affirmeth, and therefore never lieth" (1959: 38), Brooke-Rose wrote in her conclusion to her analysis of Pound's "Usura Canto": "I think the essential function of literary discourse is to perform what it says rather than to prove it" (1976: 67). But the poet's remit is wider than this. When faced by the complex discourse of a poetic text it might seem a mistake to limit oneself only to logical processes in its analysis. In this light, given Jakobson's interest in art, is it possible to suggest that Jakobson in fact analysed the "Spleen" poem as a form of painting, specifically a cubist painting? Cubism can be defined as: "the artists aimed to show different viewpoints at the same time and within the same space and so suggest their three-dimensional form. In doing so they also emphasized the two-dimensional flatness of the canvas instead of creating the illusion of depth." (Tate Gallery: https://www.tate.org.uk/art/art-terms/c/cubism Accessed: 12.00 13.8.19).

It is relatively easy to generate ideation of form from Jakobson's analysis of the "Spleen" poem. He discussed in detail the balancing of the stanzas – anterior, posterior, outer, inner, alternate – odd and even. Then he analysed the pronouns and their functions in the text – this would be equivalent to the cubist understanding that a painting can be seen from different viewpoints – that the perspective may not be interpreted as entirely coming from a single vantage point of the creative artist. It seems therefore that the fragmentation can lead to a loss of sense. The image is re-interpreted through its movement as well as its actual shape, and then the words of the poem are to be interpreted not just by their placing on the page but in their relationship to each other and which includes the different vantage points of the artist. This is how the poet uses the words to create an imagined image that includes movement which is seen from different vantage points. It is suggested that Fisher's poetry, discussed above, has the same characteristic.

Perhaps this can only be understood as happening – or not – if the poem is re-interpreted as blocks or shapes with lines and connections which emerge to provide linkage between the images (both in terms of word language and art language). This is an exciting semiotic possibility. The complexity renders the analogy almost impossible to construct. It's difficult enough just trying to follow Jakobson's verbal analysis. He divides the five quatrains (5 stanzas of 4 lines) stating a preference for the uneven number. The odd (*impaires*) stanzas are 1,3,5, and even (*paires*) stanzas are 2,4 with a central stanza (3). He then argues that the placing and designation (singular or plural) of the pronouns selected in 1,3,5 are influenced by the anterior (1,2), and the posterior (4,5) and these two linkages are characterised by convergent and divergent impulses. The grammar which supports his analysis is complex. Jakobson quotes from Baudelaire: "cette une chose douloureuse de voir un poète . . . supprimer . . . les adjectives possessives ["it is a distressing thing to see (read) a poet who removes possessive adjectives" translation by Coghill]" (Jakobson, *Questions de Poétique* 1973: 422), and he uses the phrase "d'une mise au point" – which refers to the camera lens or a visual artistic focus. In the final paragraph of the essay Jakobson again quotes Baudelaire, and the spatial arrangement as well as the syntax of the words, which Jakobson had analysed in a very detailed manner, assumes importance:

> Baudelaire tout en reconnaissant la qualité dramatique du sujet dans l'art, confesse que la ligne, avec ses inflexions, est à même de le pénétrer 'd'un plaisir tout à fait étranger au sujet' et qu'une figure bien dessinée 'ne doit son charme qu'a l'arabesque qu'elle découpe dans l'espace'. Il exalte la noblesse de l'abstraction contenue dans la ligne et la couleur de l'artiste (1967 : 435). [Baudelaire, while recognizing the dramatic quality of the subject in art, acknowledges that the line, with its inflexions, is the same as entering into 'a pleasure which is completely separate from the subject matter' and that a well constructed device 'owes its appeal to its arabesque shape, as well as to the shape which it creates in space'. It excites the nobility of the abstract contained in the line and the paint of the artist [translated by the present author, Coghill].

According to Jakobson, the poem, so far, resembles a cubist painting which, it is suggested in Figure 12, could look something like this:

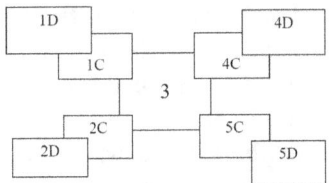

**Figure 12:** Baudelaire: poem as a cubist painting.

Here the stanzas are numbered 1–5 and the 'C' represents the impulse to converge and the letter 'D' to diverge (1967: 421) in relation to the poem's grammar and vocabulary as a whole. As already mentioned, with reference to another poem, "Infant Sorrow", by Blake, Jakobson demonstrates how his theory of "poetic function" could be illustrated with reference to art forms. In his essay: "Poetry of Grammar and Grammar of Poetry" (1987: 121–144[1960]) he writes: "In this connection it seems to me suitable to restate the 'remarkable analogy between the role of grammar in poetry and the painter's composition based on a latent or patent geometrical order or on a revulsion against geometrical arrangements'" (1987: 132/3). And: "In particular, the headwords, the principal clauses, and the prominent motifs which fill the diverging outer couplets stand out against accessory and subordinate contents of the contiguous inner couplets, quite similar to the converging lines of the background in a pictorial perspective" (1987: 486).

Jakobson undertook several other Formalist analyses, some of them are published in *Questions de Poétique* (1973). These essays include a number of different poets but do not comprise the full scope of his Formalist analysis of poetry.

His analysis of an Italian sonnet by Martin Codax, analyses the balancing power of strophes by the poet and the poet's use of sound patterns [1970]. The essay is republished in English in *Selected Writings III*: (1981: 169–175). He analysed a sonnet [1966] by Dante which includes discussion of metre, rhyme, grammar, semantic levels, and tertiary organization of poem. His analysis is also republished in English in *Selected Writings III* (1981: 176–192). A sonnet by Du Bellay is analysed with reference to subject matter, strophes, grammar, phraseology, verbs, pronouns, adjectives, nouns, adjectives, genres of grammar, verse structure, rhyme structure, phonetics, and the overall structure [1973]. This is also republished in *Selected Writings III* in French (1981: 239–274). Jakobson again analyses the balancing of verse structure in a poem by the Romanian poet Eminescu, which is in the form of a dialogue. He examines metre, the balance between the verses, the use of pronouns [1962]. This is republished in French in *Selected Writings III* (1981: 536–545). He also analyses a poem by Brecht 'Wir sind sie' [we are], which contains a large number of pronouns. The analysis highlights the occurrence of parallels, punctuation, the structure of the verses and their relationship, as well as alliteration and assonance. His overall view of the poem is defined as Brecht's "Le jeu dialectique des antonyms" [a game of opposites] (1973: 461 [1965]). This essay was originally written in German and is also in *Selected Writings III* (1981: 660–676). And lastly, poetry by Fernando Pessoa, where the analysis of "Os Castellos" is based on the balancing of strophes, metre and the strict symmetry belied by the oxymoronic subject matter [1968]). This is republished in French in *Selected Writings III*: (1981: 639–659). The study of Jakobson's Formalist processes is incomplete without studying these, and other, essays.

Christine Brooke-Rose, in her Formalist analysis of the "Usura Canto" (Canto 45) by Pound (1976) set out to interpret Jakobson's Formalist technique and extend the body of work which has been subjected to this form of analysis. She observes that iconicity arises from the text – a patterning which is more than an imputed similarity – as can be understood from the quotation below. As with all detailed analysis of this kind it is not only very lengthy to compile by the analyst, but also to decipher by the reader. Brooke-Rose set out her theoretical considerations:

> I shall now try to analyse Pound's Usura Canto as both a spatial object and an event in the reader's (my) mind, using the Jakobson levels but fusing them in my own way and order, that is, adapting them to the text in question and organising them around basic semantic polarities. To do this I shall start with a superficial look at the text as a spatial structure, including the first impact of grammatical parallelisms. This will be followed by a consideration of one specific point brought out by this first glance, in relation to Jakobson's shifters, as analysed by Benveniste. (1976: 9,10)

For many critics, analysis is complicated by the discovery that some of the levels of the poetic text under consideration are only discoverable once very detailed investigations have taken place. But is it a statement of the obvious that a poetic text contains exo-textual or subliminal elements which both entice and reward the reading of a poem? The desire to explain the text, as a theoretician and reader, leads to a refusal to accept that this is a valid result of critical analysis. In her reading of Riffaterre, she disagrees with his findings. She quotes from Riffaterre: "many of the patterns Jakobson finds are based on components that absolutely cannot be perceived by the reader and therefore must remain outside the poetic structure, whose function is to emphasize the form of the message, to make it more 'visible, more pregnant'" (Riffaterre, 1971: 316 and quoted in Brooke-Rose, 1976: 4).

These unperceived components in poetry can surprise the semiotician, linguist and reader alike, but as is summarised by Starobinski (1979), the poet presents his/her text and is then "strangely silent" (1979: 123). Problems of how to categorise and analyse the poetic text are constantly evolving. Is it a sure foundation for analysis, to accept that the poet has presented a pattern of words, which for the analyst or critic, can only reveal the full drama of its structure by being prepared to accept the illogical and/or unexpected? Jakobson, in his model for verbal communication, stated that poetry alone concentrates on the message simply for the sake of the message. In her development and analysis of his theoretical position, Brooke-Rose carefully processes the arguments which support this approach. She considers whether they are complemented by an understanding that the message (poem) is not only a thing in itself but also an event in the reader's mind. However, this produces the usual difficulties in how to define the reader. The qualification of "superreader" (see below) is a hard one to acquire, one that even the poet may not necessarily have. She comments that "the error . . . in many would-be scientific critics lies in considering a text solely as an object, rather than also an event in the reader's mind". And also, crucially, in the poet's mind. She quotes from Stanley Fish (1970: 140–141), but without entirely agreeing with him: "A criticism that regards 'the poem itself as an object of specifically critical judgment' extends this forgetting [of the text's movement with our mental movement] into a spatial one; it steps back and in a single glance takes in a whole (sentence, page, work) which the reader knows (if at all) only bit by bit, moment by moment." (1976: 7).

The qualification of "superreader" is defined by Riffaterre who says that the quality of "retroaction" by the reader must also be included (Brooke-Rose: 197: 7). Riffaterre himself states: "This tool of analysis, this 'superreader' in no way distorts the special act of communication under study: It simply explores that act more thoroughly by performing it over and over again." and:

> My 'superreader' for "Les Chats" is composed of: to a limited extent, Baudelaire (correction of line 8, placing the sonnet in the ensemble of the collection); Gautier (his long paraphrasis of the sonnet, in his preface to the third edition of the Fleurs), and Laforgue (some echoes in Sanglot de la Terre, "La Premiere Nuit"); the translations of W. Fowlie, F. L. Freedman and F. Duke; as many critics as I could find. (both from 1966: 215)

Barthes' reader in his work on "Sarrasine" assumes that his analysis is not based on a "first reading" (1976: 7). Brooke-Rose sums up: "Literary competence is incompatible with total virginity" (1976: 7). Brooke-Rose recognises the unexpected in analysis and here we, the reader, should perhaps recognise the effect of unexpected sarcasm on the part of the critic. It is possible therefore to conclude here, that for Brooke-Rose, the message of the text has to be the over-riding consideration in Formalist analysis.

However, it seems that the analysis of the impact of poetry lies beyond that of linguistics – grammar, semantics and syntax – and even semiotics. The poem may suggest that which was not hitherto known – the "surprising". As Brooke-Rose herself demonstrates, the only path to the discovery of the skills of the poet is through a structured and Formalist analysis. This is not to say that it is something that every reader or analyst wishes to undertake. She is well aware of the pitfalls: "I have said that we cannot *a priori* know whether our method will confirm our intuitive grasp of the text as a poem. I should like to add that neither can we know whether a particular method will prove to be a super-system applicable to all poetic texts (a naïve though unfortunately attractive notion), let alone whether it will elaborate a grammar that will generate all possible poetic sentences" (1976: 8). She goes on to shift the argument into one which clearly reveals how there is a supertext, never mind a superreader: "I think it is too often forgotten, even today, that all rules, whether of harmony in music, or of meter in poetry, or of grammar, are in the first instance elaborated as a description of what people do (composers, poets, speakers) and only tend to become prescriptive (and so automatically entail deviance) in a secondary instance, imitative, pedagogic, pedantic." (1976: 9).

Her analysis of Pound's Canto 45 is based on the poetic levels of understanding defined by Jakobson, but adapted "to the text in question" and organised "around basic semantic polarities" (both 1976: 9). More fully, her analysis investigates spatial structure with special attention paid to shifters, as defined by Jakobson, semic polarities, consideration of various parallelisms and finally attention to sound patterns. She has adapted a model produced by Jean-Claude Coquet (1972) which is based on various parallelisms in the text and their possible rupture. These parallelisms are: grammatical, conventional, phonic, prosodic and semantic (Brooke-Rose: 1976: 6). Her model is specifically adapted to the analysis of this particular poem.

She uses a number of diagrams to describe and explore the Formalist analysis of the text. These delineate complex relationships in the poem. As an example of the nature of what she does and how she presents the material, there are two diagrams reproduced here (see Figures 13 and 14 below). They are semiotic both in terms of their own structure and in what they reveal about the poem. It illustrates how the word "usura" is used, in terms of its placing throughout the poem. It demonstrates the shape of the usage of the word within the poem. Brooke-Rose wrote: "there is an initial/end pattern over the poem on the single word *usura*" (1976: 65). The second diagram shows the pattern of usage of *usura* within part II of the poem (1976: 65). These diagrams have been selected because they highlight the use of the key word of the poem, the title word. Apart from the sound patterns which the reader hears (or speaker produces) when reading the poem, the diagrams demonstrate how the network of usage produces links which tie the poem together as a whole in a very obvious way. The imputed iconicity is revealed through the patterning of word usage, which the diagram itself factually depicts. The model is more than imputed similarity as the patterning is revealed through the Peircean iconic use of lines arising from the patterns in the text.

Close examination of the patterns within the text of the poem demonstrates how the effects of the poem are achieved. The question of "so what" is the chorus of the irritated critic of Formalist analysis. "So everything" is the answer. The dense analysis of the techniques (or indeed, either lack of them, or surprising ones) communicates the skill of the poet in constructing a message which the reader responds to all the more intensely, intimately, with pleasure or displeasure. There is no need to criticise the detail of the analysis, only to understand that there is an echo in the reader (decoder and recoder) of the techniques that are so complex that it can remain elusive as to how the full poetic effects are created. These two diagrams have been highlighted here as they refer to how the rhyme scheme of the poem has been constructed throughout the poem as a whole, an aspect of poetry which compels attention from any reader of poetry.

Brooke-Rose includes the word "azure" (line 41) within the rhyme scheme and it is of interest to note that in the preceding line "usura" is referred to as "her" which has the effect of producing a silent rhyme which the reader may insert, as an exophoric connotation, "uxora" (also derived from the Latin): from which the word "uxorious" is derived. This interpolates a further meaning of "usura" into the poetic text. If anagrams are of interest to the Formalist analyst, then word associations can also form a part of their structure. The exophoric connotation certainly enhances the ideation of slavery which the poem addresses in the relationship between usury and humans.

Rhyme schemes are always perceived when reading or reciting poetry. The stresses of the poetic lines, and how these accumulate to provide the atmosphere

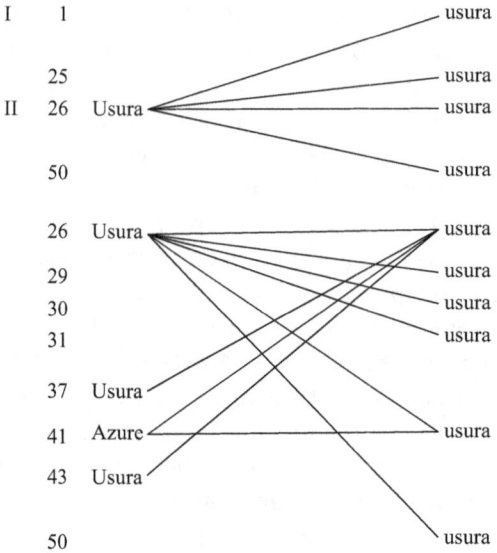

**Figure 13:** Patterns of word usage: "usura" from Brooke-Rose (1976: 65).

of the poem are also of central importance. The second semiotic graph diagrams reproduced below demonstrate the Formalist conclusions of this in Jakobson and Rudy's analysis of Yeats' earlier and later versions of "The Sorrows of Love". In the analysis, Jakobson, with Stephen Rudy, compares two versions of the same poem, written 23 years apart. Where the diagram above by Brooke-Rose demonstrates the pattern of rhyme, the diagrams below demonstrate the pattern of mood. Jakobson and Rudy divided the poem into three quatrains. Jakobson is always concerned with establishing how the parts (stanzas or verses) of a poem, balance with each other and here he uses both the stress patterns of the lines, and also where these stresses fall within the words, as a method for understanding which parts of each line have a primary or "heavy" downbeat. He notes that there are significant differences between the versions.

The reaction to the analysis is to look for an assessment of which version is more powerful or whether there is a flattening of emotion. But this is not what Jakobson and Rudy provide. Their Formalist analysis investigates the structure in great detail. The variations, which occur when the two versions of the poem are compared, remain a technical comparison. It is tempting to perceive a flattening of emotional depth in the second version because the graph lines show fewer depths and heights. The Formalist analysis goes no further than the analysis of the structure. Once again, the graphs are a factual iconicity of the imputed iconicity of the text. In this instance the analysis is very detailed and technical. Please see reproduction below:

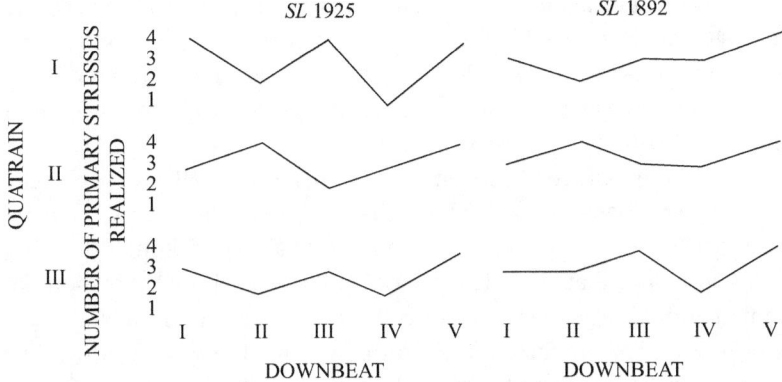

*Frequency of primary stresses on the downbeats in the two versions*

**Figure 14:** Diagram of mood: "Frequency of primary stresses on the downbeats of the two versions" (1987: 238).

As with the Brooke-Rose analysis, the Formalist stopping point leads to a sense of irrelevance of the analysis. Everyone wants to know what the poem *means* and *how* are the effects in terms of surface structure achieved? But the Formalist critic, analyses more than the surface structure as a consideration of rhyme, assonance, onomatopoeia etc. He/she also provides the tools which dissect the text right down to its semantic, syntactic, and semiotic heart, and including its artifice. These tools also reveal much about how a language is constructed and used, when placed in complicated patterns. Sometimes verbal meaning and grammar are placed under stress – that is, not used by the poet in simple habitual formulas. "Transitory grammar" and anagrams may also be used. The Formalist demands that this is considered as an aspect of the poetic text in its own right. Formalist analysis is therefore clearly not about the meaning of the text but the structure, and does not necessarily seek to go beyond this. This characteristic of Formalist analysis does not render the meaning irrelevant; it is a profound exploration of the use of poetic language and, in itself, holds much that is both fascinating and revealing about a language and, of course, in the end about the poet who uses it.

In her third chapter (1976: 17–21) Brooke-Rose discusses the use of shifters. Her analysis includes a numerical listing of the different forms, I, you etc. She also includes analysis of the possessive adjectives – his, her etc. She establishes a patterning of these forms within the two parts of the poem and also considers the linkage of the patterning with different verb tenses. From her detailed study she concludes: "In its use of the 3$^{rd}$ person and of the past, therefore, the Canto has the tone of impersonal historical narrative rather than that of a rhetorical litany which is its overt form but otherwise it steps into discourse" (1976: 21). The Appendices to her analysis provide tables of usage of words and parts of speech. This is exhaustive Formalist analysis. In her conclusion, as mentioned above, she stated "I think that the essential function of literary discourse is to perform what it says rather than to prove it" (1976: 67).

It is her stated prerogative of selecting that which the text itself specifically reveals, which governs her approach to Formalist technique. Her analysis is therefore not necessarily a complete Formalist analysis of a text, although it is very extensive and possibly exhaustive. The present author has chosen this route for development of Formalist analysis, of which there are examples in the following chapter. Brooke-Rose has provided the platform for using the system, which in a useful way, is governed by the text itself, at least in part. It would seem obvious, for example, that to employ a Formalist analysis based strongly on rhyme and metrics, would not be useful when confronted by a poem which apparently contains neither form.

Formalist Praxis may seem daunting, but there is a simple over-arching requirement to examine what the text itself says and therefore reveals, rather than concentrating on an interpretation which derives from outside the text. It is the components of the structure which are examined. Formalism is the technique, and literariness is revealed through its use. Literariness may manifest itself through a range of techniques but not all of Jakobson's areas of interest may be present in analysis of any one poem. When applying Jakobson's Formalist techniques to a poem, the poem itself will require certain aspects of the system to be highlighted. The poem itself will suggest certain priorities with regards to what is selected in terms of analysis – which parts of grammar, linguistics, syntax and semiotics. In the chapter that follows, suggestions on how to use Jakobson's system of poetic analysis and a summary of some of the semantic, syntactical and semiotic patterns to look for, provides Formalist Praxis of city poetry.

All of these individual characteristics can be analysed as providing crosscurrents within the poem – so that lines can be drawn as diagonals, parallels or other shapes for example, linking certain features of the text. These can be factual iconicity (as, for example, in the Fisher poem and the grasshopper poem by e e cummings, quoted above) or imputed iconicity (as in the Fisher poem above, Baudelaire, Pound). There is also the interpreted and developed diagrammatic representation which includes attributes, some of which Jakobson did not identify – as in the cubist representation of the "Spleen" poem above. It is essential to start with the poem, not with a formula of what must be covered and analysed –

for example the use of verb tenses or rhyme may be important and the use of deictics minimal – or vice versa. The poem itself yields up its fruits, if its structure is closely examined, and this is "literariness".

In order to expand the use of Formalist analysis, the following chapter examines three works in progress by the present author: "The Poet Listens in on the Eidometropolis"; "Arches" and "Centrifuge at Play". It is suggested that these poems are "works in progress" because the Formalist analysis may lead to alterations in the text. These three poems were all included in the PhD thesis version of the poem, but only two were finally published in the subsequent published book *Shades of Light* (2012). However, as suggested, the Formalist analysis may conclude that, after close examination, alterations might improve the poems. This leads to a development of Formalist techniques as a tool, not only for the critic or theoretician, but also for the poet.

# Chapter 12
# Formalist praxis of city poetry: Poems from "Shades of Light"

Rather than concentrating on the interpretation, Jakobson concentrates on the components of the structure of a text. Formalist analysis may manifest itself through a range of techniques, but not all of Jakobson's areas of interest may be present in a particular poem. Based on Jakobson's own analyses, here is a summary of some of the grammar and patterns to observe when analysing a text:

> verbs – transitive/intransitive – with object/without
> > tense, passive/active/conditional
> > participles
> > qualifiers to participles
> adjectives
> prevalent features
> vowel sounds (onomatopoeia) and consonant juxtaposition (assonance)
> beginning of lines/endings – patterns of similarity or difference
> deictics
> shifters
> subject/object – animate/inanimate
> pivot/balance point of development of the poem
> stanzas/sections/comparison/balance
> repetition and lacuna
> typography and font
> prevalent features or omissions of certain characteristics
> punctuation
> sections
> parallels
> transitory grammar

All of these can be analysed as providing crosscurrents within the poem, even to the extent, as has been shown, that lines can be drawn as diagonals, for example, linking certain features of the text. There are a number of other interpreted and developed diagrammatic representations which can be constructed and which include other attributes. It is important to start with the poem, not with a formula of what must be covered and analysed – for example, the use of tenses or rhyme may be important and the use of deictics minimal – or vice versa. In this way, the poem reveals its structure – its "literariness".

The selection of poems below, by the present author, is an attempt to show that the poet may be influenced by Formalist analysis as well as the theorist. The discussion of the poem, "The Poet Listens in on the Eidometropolis", includes

## Chapter 12 Formalist praxis of city poetry: Poems from "Shades of Light"

suggestions of how it might be improved with use of ideas taken from outside the text itself. The analysis of the poem "Arches", explores how Peircean semiotics can be used to write a poem and is a test of Jakobson's own theory of communication. The examination of "Centrifuge at Play", resulted in the final deletion of the poem from the published version of *Shades of Light* (2012) [*SOL*]. All of these analyses provide indications of how Jakobson's use of Formalist analysis can change the final version of a poem.

What is the "eidometropolis"? For the purposes of this chapter, an exploration and definition of the term refers to Chandler and Gilmartin (2005: 1–41). The "Eidometropolis" was a panoramic painting of London by Thomas Girtin displayed in 1802. Chandler and Gilmartin argue that there is a romantic artistic and poetic linkage between the countryside and the city; they analyse Wordsworth's sonnet "Composed Upon Westminster Bridge" in order to illustrate these connections. Historically, the term was specific to the description of the Girtin's very large painting. The painting no longer survives. The original was 18 feet high and 108 feet in circumference. There is a watercolour which gives some idea of its scope available at the British Museum. The term describes how a city is perceived, deriving from the Greek "eidos" meaning idea – how the city is culturally explored as an idea, the city as ideated. It is, by nature, a panoramic view of the city. There are two drafts of the "Eidometropolis" poem reproduced below, the final version submitted as part of a PhD, and the published version. These will be followed by an exploration of possible changes to the poem suggested by the Formalist analysis.

The deictics of place and time have been highlighted as a first point of discussion. The deictics of place are in **bold** and the deictics of time are in ***bold italics***. There is double the number of deictics of place as compared to the number of deictics of time. At a first glance, using this method of identification, it emerges that there are other variants which are important to the poem. For example, in line 8 there is a deictic "time phrase". In lines 50 and 51 there is a cluster of time deictics. And in line 65, there seems to be a form which can only be described as an interrogatory deictic – "in what garden". Using the most basic of Jakobson's Formalist techniques, the frequency and clustering of these forms is noted. Secondly, using Brooke-Rose's suggestion, the most obvious forms of grammar and structure should be noted when analysing any particular poem (see Chapter Eleven, above). Another suggestion is to find a centering of the poem. Is there some kind of central – or even off-centre – core to the poem? Lastly, the early draft can be compared with the next one to discover how the poem has (or indeed has not) become a tighter more densely structured poetic form. Indeed, the poem contains the story of meeting a friend in the first half, then, in the central 9 lines (lines 34–42), there is a switch to the story of the nightingale. The sense of frustration builds to a climax of a standstill (line 40: "stop dead") leading to the outset of hearing the nightingale set in a sense of brackets: "I am sure I hear the most beautiful recording ever" (line 42).

The following paragraph is taken from the commentary submitted with the PhD thesis:

> *this is a poem developing city theory* – **The Poet Listens in on the Eidometropolis** The sense of self within the city dictates, the eidoself perhaps, and what governs this. This poem also develops the sense of place and reality by exploring how the very unexpected sound of the nightingale singing is understood within the city environment. Also **Meronymy** about the interaction of space and time, opposites existing within one space or experience.
>
> (2012: 178)

The language in the poem embellishes both reality and the not-so-real, the reality and what is imagined, what is expected and unexpected, how levels of acceptance enable or disable appropriation of meaning. The prefix "eido", which creates neologisms, indicates that there is a level which exists above and beyond the specific and the real, which is counterbalanced by the language of strong doubt about what is actually heard in the poem. But the "eido" prefix contains the panoramic sense of its original use in the Girtin painting. How is this interpreted?

The lines are of unequal length, although there is a predominance of lines with 4 and 8 syllables. The beginning and end of the poem have an increased number of lines with unequal syllables in them (for example 3,7,11). Using Jakobson's techniques, it is one thing to note certain characteristics, but it is a synthesis of that information that provides an understanding of the patterns – this is, in effect, a reference to parallels. This is not the same as interpreting the text in terms of its content and meaning. The analysis of structure may release meanings and implications but Jakobson's methods do not encourage the release of meanings through paraphrase of the content or reader-oriented connections and personal allusions.

This is a fine line. As evidenced in Brooke-Rose's analysis of Pound's "Usura Canto" (1976), her understanding of the Eleusinian mysteries is perhaps not as extensive as it could be. She understands the Eleusinian Mysteries as fertility rituals rather than in their more complex interpretation as a mystical celebration of re-birthing of all life forms – the symbol of corn as the cyclical rebirth of life – the heart of the mysteries taking place in complete darkness and then sudden light. Perhaps, there is an incomplete analysis of the *Canto*. Content and personal understanding are, ultimately, linked (1976: 54 *et seq.*). The later celebration of the Eleusinian Mysteries was less mystical and more earthy in their interpretation of fertility symbols (for further analysis and references see Coghill 1980: 34–39).

With reference to Saussure, Brooke-Rose wrote: "Whenever I analyse a poem phonically I find that the sounds of the opening (title if any and the first line) recur more frequently than subsequent ones, paragramming the first motif" (1976: 59). A paragram is a form of play upon words, consisting in the alteration of one letter or group of letters of a word (*OED* 1968). This is a form of punning which often occurs in advertising and branding of goods – a putative form of pun. But, here, the term is used to understand the serious intent of the poet. For example, in the first draft of the poem, "Eidometropolis . . . ", the "a" vowel is omitted until line 4, "taking me by surprise" (the "a" in "was" in line 3 is an "o" sound). This is a neat double revelation, a paragram – the surprise with the first "a" sound occurring in the line. This feature has, however, been removed from the final published version of the poem.

The poem reproduced below is the PhD version. Deictics of place are typed in **bold** and deictics of time typed in ***bold italics***. The verbs have also been identified and categorised; pronouns underlined; verb **"to be"** underlined in bold. The number of syllables in each line has been counted and the number is placed at the beginning of each line. The lines are numbered for convenience and in blocks of five lines. This number is placed in **bold** at the start of the appropriate lines before the syllable count number.

The Poet Listens in on the Eidometropolis (PhD version)

8 **this** friend not used to the city          negative passive
4 getting in touch          active participle
6 the cue was not given          negative passive past
6 taking me by surprise          passive participle
5/10 asking me to do the unexpected passive participle/infinitive
6 the unacceptable
11 drive **into** and **out of** the city centre          active/imperative
9 ***twice*** **in** ***one*** day taking instructions:          passive participle
10 you will not take the trouble more than ***once***          negative active future
10/8 you will not do the same thing ***twice***          negative active future
11 not notice your immediate surroundings          negative implied future
6 eidoindividual
4 who **is** female          active verb to be/boundary of section
4 born **here** by chance          passive
                              negative active          don't visit galleries 6/**15**
          negative active          don't travel **on** the tube for years 8
                    negative active          shut **down** the options 5
future active verb to be/boundary of section          become home based **it's** safer 7
active verb to be/boundary of section          except the neighbours turned out to be . . .well 11
**20**/4 eidosequence
5 all the things seen ***once***          passive
6 must I repeat myself          negative active
10 I arrange to meet you **at** the V&A          active/infinitive
6 and ***when*** we meet we talk active x 2
**25**/7 "I've got your birthday present"          active
6 and ***later*** you told me          active

6 "what a lovely present"
6 I remembered the seat          past active
5 the sunlight **through** glass
30/6 this **is** nothing special     verb 'to be'/boundary section
4 eidoevent
12 and in *any event* I didn't see you *again*          negative active
8 falling **in and** out of favour
sequence of participles     taking the thoughts to their logical conclusions 12
          participle     dropping them like hot cakes when frustration
          present                  reigns 11/**35**
                leave house for work but never getting **there** 10
present acting as participle sequencetake the bus and it's **out of** service after 10 minutes14
                    walk to the shops with the wrong credit card 10
          drive to the superstore (marked on the map) **there's** no room to park 15
          present active stop dead **in** the street **by** the petrol station 11/**40**
                **under** the plane tree 5
          I am sure I hear the most beautiful recording *ever* 15 active x 2/subjunctive
                **a** bird singing 4 present participle
11 startling beauty that falls like honey **on** air     active
                                thrill **on** soul 3/**45**
7 *where* can I really hear this?          conditional
                             unbelievable **in** NW4 9
7 looking harder and harder          participle
                       participle     forgetting my errand 6
**50**/9 *gradually* the *late* summer evening
7 city night air *dawns* **on** me  metaphoric active
               active/to be/boundary section     **is *this*** the nightingale 6
                             high **up** in the street lining plane tree 9
6 undertowed **by** cars past active
**55**/5 sound falling through dust     participle
          **this is** what Keats would have died 7 to be/present + conditional
                would have lived for 4     conditional
  the quality of the sound empowering **a** moment 14     participle
of madness and **this** is inappropriate 11     to be/boundary section
   no-one else stopped **on** the pavement 9/**60**     active negative
       looking **up** I was stared **at** 7 active negated by passive
5 so the meaning changes          active
2 creak crack
5 one word of warning
**65**/7 slight invasion **in what** garden
3 blackbird cries          active
3          break break break (18)          active
5 one step *further* and
8 start **up** and look there's nothing but     active x 2
**70**/4 the silence breaks          active
3          creak crack creak (18)          active x 3
5 crack the interface     active

9 poet **among** the speakers **between**
5 password: **ay2zed** (19)
**75**/3 speak speak speak    active x 3
3 break break break    active x 3

There are 130 "a's" in the poem and 156 "i's" and including the "y's". The title has 4 "i" sounds and 5 "o's". There are 125 "o's" in the text. So, the expression of the paragram is not completely borne out – that the prevalence of a sound from the title is reflected in the poem as a whole. However, there is a paragram which emerges in the first five lines in the earlier version, as mentioned above. There are three terms which include "eido" – these are: eidoindividual, eidosequence, eidoevent. There are more in the final version and each term designates a portion of text, the exploration of an eido-idea in context. The verb "to be" tends to occur only at the boundary of different sections of the poem lines: "who is female"; "become home based it's safer"; "this is nothing special"; "there's no room to park"; "is this the nightingale"; "this is what Keats . . . ". There are two interrogatory deictics "where can I really hear this" and "in what garden". There are twenty-three pronouns. These are underlined: line 4: me; line 5: me; line 9: you; line 10: you; line 11: I; line 22: I, myself; line 23: I, you; line 24: we, we; line 25: I, your; line 26: you, me; line 28: I; line 32: I; line 42: I, I; line 46: 1; line 49: my; line 51: me; line 61: I. It is important to note that possessive pronouns (see lines 25 and 49) can be classed as adjectival, where the deictic quality is stronger than the adjectival, then they can be classed as pronouns. They appear to be pronouns within the context of their use in the poem, the sense of possession is not highlighted within the sense of their use. The reflexive pronoun in line 22 neatly echoes the repetition expressed in "repeat" within this same line.

The line 37 needs some explanation: "present acting as participle sequence **take** the bus **and** it's **out of** service **after** 10 minutes14". It appears to be a present tense but it seems to be acting as a participle, as in taking. The present imperative "take" is a single action but its meaning is that of taking the bus many times. As such it is an "eidoaction" in effect. The action described as taking place once, represents or stands in for a universal action – taking the bus every day to work for example. This is an example of "transitory grammar". The predominance of tense usage in the first half of the poem is similar to this (lines 1–19). The story of the meeting and birthday present (lines 21–30) includes the simple past tense – the single past action denoting a single event. Lines 33–49 include a number of present participles and then the present tense, denoting repeated action, takes over again. The line "stop dead" (line 40) provides a shock just after the centre of the poem. After this, there is a cluster of conditional tenses around the nightingale singing and the reference to Keats. Within the framework of English grammar, the final section of the poem contains a number of words "creak", "crack", "break", which can be either verb or noun. Once again, this is an example of Jakobson's "transitory grammar". These words colour the word "speak" in the penultimate line. It is clearly a verb but the nouns surrounding it affect it. The earlier version is much looser in format and the number of "eido" words and their placing has no structure to them. However, as previously noted, the opening paragram is interesting. The centre of poem is "**wa**lk to the shops with the wrong credit c**a**rd/drive to the superstore (m**a**rked on the m**a**p) **there's** no room to p**a**rk" (lines 38, 39). These are lines which denote frustration and stasis. They are also longer lines than the rest of the poem.

The final published version (*SOL* 2012:15,16) has been cut by one third. Please see below for the text. Unfortunately, the poet has seen fit to remove the paragraph in the first few lines of the PhD version. There are 85 "a's" in the poem. This ceases to be significant as the introductory paragram is now removed. The sequence of "eido" words now clearly occurs at the end of each section: "eidoindividual" line 8; "eidosequence" line 15; "eidoevent" line 23; "eidodawns" line 30; "eidoquality" 36; "eidocreak" line 42. Again, the deictics of place are in **bold** and the deictics of time in ***bold italics.*** The verb "to be" is no longer significantly placed at the boundary of each section. There are fourteen pronouns. These are underlined: line 2: me; line 5: you; line 6: your; line 16: I, you; line 17: I, your; line18: you; line 20: I; line 22: I, you; line 25: I; line 26: I; line 28: my; line 39 I. There is a significant cluster in the third section of the poem (lines16–23). The deictics of time have now been reduced to approximately one third of the deictics of place. The deictic "further" (line 68 in PhD version and line 45 in the published version) is a deictic which can be either a deictic of place or time. The number of syllables in each line has been counted and the number is placed at the beginning of each line. The lines are numbered for convenience and in blocks of five lines. Again, this number is placed at the start of the appropriate lines before the syllable count number. The poem is reproduced below first without annotations, and secondly with the variant format. This is the final published version (*SOL* 2012: 15,16).

**The Poet Listens in on the Eidometropolis**
this friend not used to the city                                1
asking me to do the unacceptable
drive into and out of the city centre
twice in one day taking instructions:
you will not do the same thing twice                            5
not notice your immediate
        surroundings –
eidoindividual
          who is female born here by chance
            don't visit galleries                    10
         don't travel on the tube for years
           shut down the options

## Chapter 12 Formalist praxis of city poetry: Poems from "Shades of Light"

```
                    become home based it's safer
              except neighbours turned out to be –
                              eidosequence                        15
I arrange to meet you at the V&A
'I've got your birthday present'
and later you said
'what a lovely present'
I remembered the seat                                             20
the sunlight though glass
I didn't see you again –
eidoevent
                    stop dead by the petrol station
                    under the plane tree I am sure                25
              I hear the most beautiful recording ever
              a bird sings falling like honey on soul
                              forgetting my errand
                    gradually the late summer evening
                              city night air eidodawns            30
this is the nightingale
high up in the street lining plane tree
undertowed by cars
sound falling though dust
Keats would have died for this                                    35
the eidoquality sound
                    madness inappropriately
                    no-one stopping looking up
                              I was stared at
                    so the meaning changes                        40
                    slight invasion in what garden
              eidocreak crack one word of warning
a blackbird cries
              break break break
one step further and                                              45
the silence breaks
              creak crack creak
interface between speakers
password: ay2zed
speak speak speak                                                 50
break break break
```

And secondly, with the annotations:

**The Poet Listens in on the Eidometropolis** (published version – annotated)
8**this** friend not used to the city    negative passive                 1
11asking **me** to do the unacceptable   passive participle/infinitive
11drive **into** and **out of** the city centre   active/imperative
9***twice* in *one*** day taking instructions:   passive participle
8**you** will not do the same thing ***twice***   negative active future  5

8not notice your immediate          negative implied future
3            surroundings –
7eidoindividual
active verb to be/boundary of section/passive who **is** female born **here** by chance 8
                negative active   don't visit galleries6
negative active      don't travel **on** the tube for years8
         negative active     shut **down** the options5
future active verb to be/boundary of section become home based it's safer8
active verb to be/boundary of section except neighbours turned out **to be** –8
                                eidosequence4
11I arrange to meet you **at** the V&A   active/infinitive
7'I've got your birthday present'         active
5and *later* you said           active
6'what a lovely present'
6I remembered the seat      past active
5the sunlight **through** glass
7I didn't see you *again* – negative past
4eidoevent
present active    stop **dead** by the petrol station8
active subjunctive   **under** the plane tree I am sure8
present   I hear the most beautiful recording *ever*12
present/participle a bird sings falling like honey **on** soul10
participle                 forgetting my errand6
           gradually the *late* summer evening10
metaphoric active       city night air eidodawns7
6this is the nightingale active/to be/boundary section
9high **up in** the street lining plane tree
6undertowed **by** cars   past passive
5sound falling though dust   participle
6Keats would have died for **this**   conditional
7the eidoquality sound
                    madness inappropriately8
  negative participle    no-one stopping looking **up**7
active negated by passive        I was stared **at**5
active                  so the meaning changes6
                slight invasion **in what** garden8
      eidocreak crack one word of warning9
4a blackbird cries     active
              3break break break active x 3
5one step **further**   and
4the silence breaks   active
            3creak crack creak active x 3
7interface **between** speakers
5password: ay2zed
3speak speak speak        active x 3
3break break break         active x 3

In the published version, the paragram is omitted; yet it could be usefully re-inserted. The strophic format is regularised (6 or 7 lines) the form of the poem breaks up after "eidocreak crack" – this is appropriate to the meaning. Each "eido" term can be defined as describing both the previous strophe and the following one and as such might be better placed as centred on their own line rather than placed on the same side as the strophe above. But the "eido" terms are accompanied by other words (lines 30, 36, 42); does this mean that the whole line should be centred? But then this shortens strophes 5 and 6 which are already only 6 lines but this can be solved in strophe 6 by switching two lines round so that the poem reads "slight invasion in what garden/a blackbird cries/crack one word of warning/ eidocreak [centred] /break break break"/. But in strophe 5 there is no such option unless line 57 of the earlier version were re-inserted "would have lived for". But in any event, there are other strophes with varying numbers of lines – in this order: 7 (or 6 with the small change listed above); 7; 8; 7; 6; 6 (or 7 with the change listed above) and then in the final fragmented coda, the poem is broken into by the literal environment, the password is placed where an "eido" word would normally occur, following the pattern of the poem so far.

The centre (lines 26, 27: 12 and 10 syllables respectively) is "I hear the most beautiful recording ever/a bird sings falling like honey on soul". These are both still longer lines than the rest of the poem apart from line 29 which also has 10 syllables. But lines 6/7 should really be one line "not notice your immediate/ surroundings". This is an editorial/printer's error. This makes line 5, 11 syllables long and expresses an antithetical idea to the central heard event in the centre of the poem. This highlights the tension between the unperceptive individual and the surroundings which provide the material for the poem. The poet/speaker is forced to register his/her environment by the events that follow.

Overall, the "eido" neologisms define the sections and this makes the ideation of the poem very explicit. The neologisms define the overall poetic quality of the poem rather than other poetic tropes. Poetic tropes are rare in the poem. There are two metaphors: the use of the neologism "eidodawns" when in fact the day is drawing to a close ("late summer evening") and therefore refers to an awakening of understanding by the poet/speaker; and "undertowed" which is a word that is usually applied to the movement of water – "A sea-current below the surface of the water, moving in a contrary direction to that of the surface current." (*OED online 2022*). Within the context of the poem the word indicates the traffic flow pulling against what is happening higher up in the plane tree – the more fragile experience of the bird song.

Given the subject matter of the poem – the enormous size of a city, its multiplicity of environments and sensations felt by the individual – it seems hard to then subject a city poem to Formalist analysis, when chaos or irregularity lies at the heart of its subject. Is there perhaps an "eido" neologism that has been left out – eidochaos? The verb tenses in the poem are largely present repeated tense (as opposed to present specific tense – see strophe 2 where the tenses are also in the past), strophes 3 and 4 are present specific and then the sense of the present repeated tense re-emerges in strophe 6 before the break down of the poem's structure and the present tenses (which seem almost to be nouns) – creak, crack, break – are repeated. Is this a verb tense usage which has extra relevance to the city?

There are a number of vertical and horizontal lines in the poem which form paths of comprehension. Their recognition enables implied iconicity. For example, the nightingale is "high up in the street lining plane tree", this is a vertical line and horizontal line. A horizontal line is created by the movement of the cars ("undertowed") travelling contrary to the sound of the song falling ("vertical"). The trees line (horizontal line), the sound falls (vertical line), cars move (horizontal line), poet looks up (vertical line), "I was stared at" (horizontal line), "invasion of what garden" (horizontal and vertical) provide a sense of the combined forces at work).

The suggestions above, have implications for the poetic skill in the poem. Has the above analysis helped in any way? Has shortening the poem helped its cohesion? Is it sufficient to employ Jakobson's often used analysis of balancing of the strophes: how does the poem balance outer and inner strophes? Has such a balance been examined and proved? The most noticeable balancing is, that after the central lines ("I hear . . . on soul" lines 26/27), if the "my" in line 28 is understood as an adjective rather than a pronoun (it is also part of a negated expression "forgetting"), and the "I was" (line 39) is a negated action because of its use within the passive tense, then the second half of the poem does not contain any personally reinforcing pronouns. It is as if the doubted reality of the nightingale's song leads to the removal of the individual from the poem. The disputed interpretation of the "Spleen" poem, between Jakobson and Culler (see Chapter Eleven, above), influences this suggested interpretation. In poetry, especially, the linguistic categorization of words leads to a central debate concerning how poets constantly break rules in their use of language (Culler 1967: 53–66; Jakobson 1973: 420–435 and 496–497).

The second poem "Arches" is now discussed. No argument is complete without recorded efforts to refute it. Formalist analysis is the province of Jakobson, but here the work of Charles Sanders Peirce is used to construct a poem. This is an attempt to sidestep Jakobson's theory of poetic function by using a different model of poetic language construction. Can Peirce's decalogue of signs be developed and applied to a textual entity – a poem – with useful results? The use of Peirce's theory provides open-ended results rather than conclusive either/or conclusions. Jakobson acknowledged Peirce's contribution to semiotics but did not develop his contribution with regard to his theory of poetic function. The poem "Arches", taken from *SOL* (2012) was deliberately constructed using the theory of Peirce's decalogue, as interpreted by Merrell (2000). Each line of "Arches" fulfils a classification on Peirce's diagrammatic representation of his system of signs (Merrell 2000). The steps are closely analysed as an exercise in praxis. Merrell first indicated this possibility with his footnote: "Peirce himself suggests that a poem is a form of argument, and indeed, that the entire universe itself is like a poem – an argument" (2000: 37). Merrell does not give a source for the quotation but Peirce himself wrote the following:

> The Universe as an argument is necessarily a great work of art, a great poem – for every fine argument is a poem and a symphony – just as every true poem is a sound argument. But let us compare it rather with a painting – with an impressionist seashore piece – then every Quality in a Premiss is one of the elementary colored particles of the Painting; they are all meant to go together to make up the intended Quality that belongs to the whole as whole. That total effect is beyond our ken; but we can appreciate in some measure the resultant Quality of parts of the whole . . . (CP 1.315: 1903)

Peirce was a logician and semiotician. It should be noted here, that the word "argument" is a Peircean theoretical term with a particular meaning. Here is not, unfortunately, the place to further examine his definitions and frames of reference.

The text of the poem below is taken from the "Discipline" section of *SOL* (2012: 48–50). It is important to note that the lines in grey are taken from the top of each of the pages and represent the sequence of a second poem which is read continuously through the "Discipline" section. The lines in bold or italics at the bottom of each page are third and fourth poems which are read throughout this section in the same way. This constructs pages, each of which reveal parts of four poems at the same time. The poem "Arches", in itself, is presented on the page in a more conventional way, as are the other main text poems of the section. The line: "Memo: Mr Eliot can you calculate our annual leave?" is a reference to the newsletter *Red Tape*, (1923.138: 198). The full quotation taken from the journal is an example of the kind of problems that women civil servants had to solve in the workplace:

> For instance, if one-eighth of the staff are allowed away at once, and leave is divided into eight periods of three weeks each from April 23$^{rd}$ to October 15$^{th}$, then where there is, say, a total staff of 1,600, 200 of the staff would be away at the same time. The first year this scheme is put into force the senior women choose the period they want, but the next year they automatically have to take their leave three periods on. Thus, it works out that all the staff in due course get a decent leave period.

*Red Tape* was the newsletter of Women civil servant secretarial staff. There was also a second contemporaneous journal, "AWK", which was produced by The Association of Women Clerks. The quotations have been chosen as their publication in these newsletters coincided with the dates that T.S. Eliot originally wrote "The Waste Land"1974 [1922]). They refer to section: "III: The Fire Sermon", where the following lines describe the typist in an unsympathetic and objectified manner: "The typist home at teatime, clears her breakfast, lights Her stove, and lays out food in tins." Et seq. (lines 222–256; 1974: 59–60).

Returning to the poem by the present author, Coghill, the lines in bold are the repetition of an automated announcement at a supermarket and those that are italicized at the bottom of each page are explorations of St Augustine's understanding of time from his "Confessions". The following quotation is his examination of the nature of poetry in relation to time:

> I could not *measure the movement of a body* [current author's italics], its period of transit and how long it takes to go from A to B, unless I were measuring the time in which this movement occurs. How then do I measure time itself? Or do we use a shorter time to measure a longer time, as when, for example, we measure a transom by using a cubit length? So we can be seen to use the length of a short syllable as a measure when we say that a long syllable is twice its length. By this method we measure poems by the number of lines, lines by the number of feet, feet by the number of syllables, and long vowels by short, not by the number of pages *(for that would give us a measure of space, not of time)* [current author's italics]. The criterion is the time words occupy in recitation, so that we say "That is a long poem, for it consists of so many lines. The lines are long, for they consist of so many feet. The feet are long for they extend over so many syllables, the syllable is long, for it is double the length of a short one. (1998: 239/40)

This description of the passage of time uses the relativity between perceived short and long poetic text events. In part it provides the context for that perception of time which, as highlighted in the "Eidometropolis" poem, is explicated through the prevalent use of the present continuous tense throughout most of the poem. The present continuous tense enables the combined perception of a single action and a repeated action. This condensed perception of time can be used by the poet to interpret multiple events as happening both once and often. Just such perception is used in the "Arches" poem reproduced below. The lines of text which are the words of the automatic announcement at the supermarket, reiterate this multiple tense perception – that the warning is heard once and many times. Where St Augustine was using the length of lines and syllables to measure brevity and length in poetry. Here it is the use of different verb tenses which provide a sense of the elongation of present time.

The published text of the poem is reproduced below. The poems which run along the text at the top and bottom of each page are not included in the subsequent analysis.

## Chapter 12 Formalist praxis of city poetry: Poems from "Shades of Light"

**Memo: we invite you to debate comptometers**

**Arches**
To B C

some kind of
and there
from within and without
I walk in shaded triangles
and into light
(I think this is a God given place)
and palaver and paloma
and imprint
turning
just to see the shadows
of arches shifting
I walk past pillars

something
and that
above and below
I am shaded haptic
into past
(I think this is a God given place)
and maelstrom and mayhem
and breath
living
in time to see the light
of arches shifting
I walk under arches

**please take care please hold the handrail while travelling   Caution moving conveyer**
*measuring a not knowing hope or*

Memo: Mr Eliot can you calculate our annual leave?

somewhere
and this
beside and within
I am light chiralled
and swept
(I think this is a God given place)
and is and is not is
and glints
throwing
off the sunbaked air
of time shifting
I walk past roses

and some
and those
around and outer
I walk through scents
and then dark
(I think this is a God given place)
and ease and embrace
and touchstone
walking
towards home
into darkness shifting
I walk past pillars

**care please hold the handrail while travelling Caution moving conveyer please take**
*within itself takes twice as long*

Memo: as we are gravely underpaid

some errors
and these
under and beneath
albescent and umbrescent
and tear touched
(I think this is a God given place)
and torment and adamantine
and face up
laying
from radiant tombstone
how does she
I walk past grace

and shadows. . .

**hold the handrail while travelling Caution
moving conveyer please take care please**
*please use the lift*

SOL (2012: 48–50).

Before proceeding further with analysis of the poem, it is necessary to discuss some aspects of the work of Peirce. As mentioned above, "Arches" was specifically written using Peirce's system as detailed by Merrell (2000: 37–54). Each line fulfils a box in the diagrammatic representation of Peirce. This is found in Merrell's Chapter Three (2000: 37–54). It should be noted that Peircean semiotics is in a constant state of development and interpretation. It is accepted by the current author that using Merrell's interpretation of Peirce is a limiting framework for the definition of Peirce's lifelong and intricate theorisation of the nature and use of language. Nevertheless, the use of Merrell's practical analysis has produced poetry.

# Chapter 12 Formalist praxis of city poetry: Poems from "Shades of Light" — 293

Merrell admits the problem of Peirce's complexity: "if we want to get a fairly good grip on Peirce's semiotics, in addition to icons, indices and symbols, we must at least take in what he calls *qualisigns, sinsigns and legisigns,* and *terms (or words), propositions,* (or *sentences*) and *arguments* (or *texts* or *narratives*)" (2000: 37). Merrell's diagram (see Figure 15) is a starting point for his analysis:

| Qualisign | Icon   | Term<br>Word                 |
|-----------|--------|------------------------------|
| Sinsign   | Index  | Proposition<br>Sentence      |
| Legisign  | Symbol | Argument<br>Text<br>Narrative |

**Figure 15:** from Merrell Figure 10 (2000: 37).

In the pages following the diagram, Merrell explains each of these categories with reference to Peirce's system of numbering. It is this system of combination and explication which inspired the lines of the poem "Arches". The Icon, Index and Symbol are terms which Jakobson used (see Chapter Eleven, above) and which Merrell similarly interprets (2000: 12). With regards to Merrell's diagram, Merrell adds:

> Notice that as we move from the upper left-hand corner of Figure 10 [see figure 15 in this text above] to the lower right-hand corner, the signs increase in degree of complexity, and the makers and takers of these signs are required greater sophistication in order to process them. This ... does not imply a one way path from simple signs to complex signs. Rather the path is two-way. Signs of relative complexity can sink into consciousness, ... in such a manner that their making and their taking becomes relatively nonconscious. (2000: 38)

He systematically explores each category of the diagram, each "box". The Merrell diagram, above, is supplemented with additional information with reference to Peirce's system of terminology and numerology, as provided by Merrell, abbreviated and simplified by the current author (2000: 37–54):

Sign 111: *a qualisign*: a sign with possibility, not defined
211: *an iconic sinsign*: a defined diagram, map as yet not compared with others, an individual copy of a map
221: *an indexical sinsign*: a sign which is interpreted and understood
222: *a dicent sinsign*: an index which relays information
311: *an iconic legisign*: an interpreted diagram
321: *a rhematic indexical legisign:* a sign which includes deferred signification
322: *a dicent indexical legisign:* words which are commonplace expressions

331: *a term or a word:* words which denote single ideas
332: *a proposition or a sentence*
333: *an argument, text or narrative*

Merrell (2000: 193) provides a list of Peirce's decalogue categories, with his own brief interpretation of the combinations. The chart reproduced below is a simplified version. In short:

111: Feeling of blue
211: Vague sense of form
221: Recognition of something still indefinite
222: Awareness of indication of something
311: Consciousness of something interelated with something else
321: Personal Pronoun
322: Commonplace expression
331: Word
332: Sentence
333: Argument, text

It is immediately clear (Peirce was a logician after all) that there are combinations which are missing. Where are the variables: 112; 122; 123; 132; 133; 223; 323, for example, and how might they be designated? Merrell's clear and cogent definitions of Peirce and how to understand his terminology cannot be bettered by the current author. In the poem "Arches", each stanza describes a combination of Peirce's categories with reference to the above designation. They are used in a sequence that almost replicates Merrell's listing of classification but not quite. To reiterate the diagrammatic schema: Peirce describes nine signs (three rows of three) which can be combined with qualities of firstness, secondness, and thirdness – respectively:

Qualisign, Icon, Term/Word (111/211/311);
Sinsign, Index, Proposition/Sentence (211/221/222);
Legisign, Symbol, Argument/Text/Narrative (311/321/322);

Additional categorisations listed by Merrell in his defining chapter are: 331/332/333 (2000: 37–54). The theory is demonstrated by using 3 numbers to define the nature of the communication on each of the lines of the poem. Accordingly, using as an example, the first stanza of the poem, reproduced below, demonstrates this construction. The same construction is used for each of the stanzas:

Arches

| | |
|---|---|
| some kind of | 111 |
| and there | 211 |
| from within and without | 221 |
| I walk in shaded triangles | 222 |

# Chapter 12 Formalist praxis of city poetry: Poems from "Shades of Light" — 295

| | |
|---|---|
| and into light | 311 |
| (I think this is a God given place) | 333 |
| and palaver and paloma | 321 |
| and imprint | 322 |
| turning | 211 |
| just to see the shadows | 331 |
| of arches shifting | 322 |
| I walk past pillars | 332 |

The stanza is reproduced again below using Merrell's interpretation of Peircean terminology in order to explain how the words and Peircean categories are demonstrated. Please also see the list reproduced above (taken from Merrell: 193). For ease of reference the actual text of the poem is reproduced in **bold:**

Arches

**some kind of** 111 *Qualisign:* a feeling that is not conscious;
**and there** 211 *Iconic sinsign*: a self-contained diagram – here indicated by the use of the deictic of placing:
**from within and without** 221 *Indexical sinsign*: first consciousness that the sign has a meaning
**I walk in shaded triangles** 222 *Dicent sinsign:* first indication of the other than our self
**and into light** 311 *Iconic legisign:* separate signs begin to combine and produce secondary meaning
**(I think this is a God given place)** 333 *Argument, text or narrative:* a complete sentence which contains a perceivable meaning
**and palaver and paloma** 321 *Rhematic indexical legisign:* delayed, deferred signification – here the poetic elaboration means that the full meaning of the stanza is not yet
**and imprint** 322 *Dicent indexical legisign:*
**turning** 211 *Iconic sinsign:* a self-contained diagram – the loss of context is indicated through the present participle which has no apparent subject or object
**just to see the shadows** 331*Term or word:* word(s) which do not indicate specific cause or effect
**of arches shifting** 322 *Dicent indexical sinsign:* short, clear groups of words which have a particular meaning
**I walk past pillars** 332 *Proposition or sentence:* complete sentence with clear meaning

Within the poem, the line "(I think this is a God given place)" lies centrally within the text of each stanza. It jumps out of Peircean sequence to "333". This is why it is in brackets; it has arrived before its place in the sequence and requires the reader to read all the stanza and then back to the "333" line in order to understand the full impact of each stanza and provide a sense of completion to the meaning. For

Peirce, the category of sign "333", is the numerical designation for a complete text. The whole poem therefore expresses, within each stanza, not only its own completeness but, as the text sign sequence is completed before it logically should be, it contains its own interpreted uncertainty or error. The logical development is not there. And furthermore, the conclusion is open-ended: "and shadows . . . ". This fulfils the Peircean category of the *Iconic sinsign* (211). This throws the poem backwards in meaning towards a more elementary state of understanding. The Peircean numbers for each line are only suggestions. These may not be seen as correct by another critic or another reader may interpret them differently. But the conclusion is that Peirce, although not interested in poetic form himself, constructed a semiotic system which can be used to both construct and interpret poetry.

Tyler James Bennett in his chapter: "Incompatibility, unlimited semiosis, aesthetic function" (in 2021: 149–163), observes that there are links between Jakobson's theory of poetic function and Peirce's unlimited semiosis:

> Using the theories of Jakobson and Lotman it has been shown that the creative or aesthetic moment of semiosis features the intersection of at least two incompatible codes, which can be described in terms of the interaction of the syntagmatic and paradigmatic axes, and discrete and continuously coded chain structures. The uncanny experience of aesthetic meaning, the paradox of that sublimity, this unreality is for Jakobson and Lotman demonstrably the register of contact with the real world. //But there is no reason Peirce's system should not also inform aesthetic theory. (2021: 159)

Bennett's suggestion concerning Peirce's contribution to poetics opens up the possibility of a new area of poetic expression and analysis. There is not space here, unfortunately, to consider this in any detail. The above discussion is a starting point, referring, as it does, more to Peirce's categories of function, rather than to his complex theories of perception. With Peirce's categories of icon in mind, the chapter continues with the Formalist examination of a poem which includes a discussion of the function of punctuation, and which is an iconic contribution to poetic form.

The following poem was included in the PhD version of *SOL* (2012), but was omitted in the published version. The poet's reasoning was that the content of the poem had been covered elsewhere in the book-length poem. As explained in the analysis of "Arches" above, the text above and below the poem on each page was part of two separate poems read continuously through the "Discipline" section of the book. The full text of the poem "Centrifuge at Play" is reproduced below. As it is unpublished, there are no page references. The Formalist analysis includes the use, or not, of punctuation. There are therefore two versions of the poem here. The question asked is "does the use of full punctuation change, enhance or reduce the meaning and/or impact of the poem?" The first drafted version is even less punctuated than the submitted PhD version:

Memo: though you may laugh 'where cattish Sups. hold sway'

**Centrifuge at Play**

I tell you I control the throughput
removing the focus of control
each layer of security doors
each task on the shopping list each day
I recognise or exclude order                                5
negotiate the words *mores* print
the balance of power meaning I
am content double entendre right
serve up death by natural causes
headache the poets temperature                              10
or blood pressure rising with effort
overdrive deals with Thursday Friday
invocation muse boss brain take out
character slash plot energetic
diegetic recorder witness                                   15
passage of time the alarm bells warn
impending atmosphere immediate
concluding quotation cold calling
reserves the right controls have gone down
no phone back option she is distant                         20
despite the intimate close distress
so recently divulged and why does
she wish to study and take drugs and
overcome her husband's shouting at
the same time life crashing repelling                       25
involved in a pattern of words that
salvaging combining each minute
but you will do it compelling hope
then tortured by external demands
and is that involved enough for you                         30
I do not see events as either
a construction of consecutive
affections contrive to cross line breaks
we accept the interference we
do not involve ourselves face to face                       35
nothing to do with intimacy

please take care please hold the handrail while travelling Caution moving
        *not by the number of times willing*
        Memo: as we are gravely underpaid

out to the periphery bare bones
driven out to the edge scrutinise
take measurements reconfiguring
we think they looked like this evidence                     40

I use words like plunge without despair
or severe height or far flung vistas
are not available or measured
how can I feel the force of the depths
unsought by levels feel strongly how                    45
the heights are shabby or mundane feel
future between buildings one road and
another one day and another
plot cross-hatched crossed lines forward slash
acting layers one another seek                          50
reflection that brings cursor closer
unskilled undersigned return to
deposited words remaining tied
the functions of this space are used for
objectification by object                               55
recording recent experience
contains no ulterior message
               spun out
conveyor please take care please hold the handrail while travelling  Caution
*time drags out distress*

This version is followed by a punctuated version with some comments on tropes involving time in **bold**. The use of simile and metaphor have also been highlighted. The lines with square brackets are the suggested centre of the poem. The PhD version has the same punctuation but not as much, and it is not divided into stanzas of eight lines, with a coda. The lines are numbered (the gaps between lines and the header and footer poems are not included in the numbering).

Memo: though you may laugh "where cattish Sups. hold sway"

**Centrifuge at Play**

I tell you, I control the throughput
removing the focus of control
each layer of security doors,
each task on the shopping list, each day **time x 2**
I recognise or exclude order,                           5
negotiate the words, *mores,* print;
the balance of power meaning – I
am content – double entendre, right?

*Serve up death by natural causes?
Headache – the poet's temperature                       10
(or blood pressure) rising with effort;
overdrive deals with Thursday, Friday – **time**
invocation – muse? boss? brain? Take out
character, slash plot, energetic,

diegetic, recorder, witness.                                    15
Passage of time: the alarm bells warn;  **time**

*impending atmosphere, immediate,
concluding quotation, cold calling
reserves the right, controls have gone down,
no phone back option, she is distant             20
despite the intimate, close distress,
so recently divulged and why does  **time**
she wish to study and take drugs and
overcome her husband's shouting at

*the same time – life crashing, repelling, **simul.time**    25
involved in a pattern of words that
salvaging, combining, each minute **units of time**
but you will do it – compelling hope,
then tortured by external demands -
and is that involved enough for you?             30
[I do not see events as either
[a construction of consecutive **time**

[affections. . . . contrive to cross line breaks. . . .
We accept the interference, we
do not involve ourselves face to face,            35
nothing to do with intimacy

      please take care please hold the handrail while travelling Caution moving
                  *not by the number of times willing*
             Memo: as we are gravely underpaid

out to the periphery bare bones –
driven out to the edge. Scrutinise,
take measurements, reconfiguring,
we think they looked like this – evidence. **simile**     40

*I use words like "plunge without despair"
or "(severe) height" or "(far) flung vistas"-
are not available or measured.
How can I feel the force of the depths,
unsought by levels, feel strongly how             45
the heights are shabby, or mundane, feel
future between buildings, one road and **time**
another, one day and another, **time passing**

plot cross-hatched crossed lines, forward slash, **condensed metaphor**
acting layers, one another, seek                  50
reflection that brings cursor closer, **condensed metaphor**
unskilled, undersigned, return to, **place**
deposited words remaining tied –
the functions of this space are used for

objectification by object,  55
recording recent experience:

contains no ulterior message,

                spun out.

conveyor please take care please hold the handrail while travelling  Caution
              *time drags out distress*

It is suggested that the poem, especially the unpunctuated version, represents context-deficient aphasia (Jakobson 1987: 106). It is an agrammatical "word-heap". Jakobson is here quoting the words of an earlier researcher, Hughlings Jackson, from 1866 (see Chapter Four, above). But in the poem, the words, subjected to a centrifuge, portray a "life-heap" which is "spun out". This is a construction based on contiguity – association. The properties of contiguity are discussed in Chapters Two and Four above. Here it is understood as demonstrating a disorder. With reference to Jakobson's analysis of aphasia (1987: 95–114 [1956]) "contiguity disorder" means that similarity (metaphor) holds the central meaning of the text. Metaphor becomes the important axis of meaning. Jakobson also explains that there is an analogous disorder, that of "similarity disorder", meaning that contiguity holds the central meaning of the text. Metonymy becomes the important axis of meaning or, indeed lack of it, the words can seem to be simply a jumble. In the poem above, the agrammaticism appears to indicate metonymy (a property of contiguity) but in fact the lack of grammar pushes the complete text towards the metaphorical pole/axis. Both grammar and meaning are subjected to torque (see Chapter Two, above) and fragmentation. However, the poem as a whole can still be identified as a metaphor: "An entire poem, if it is organically unified, can therefore be called a metaphor." (*NPEPP*: 1993: 761b). The second version reproduced above, with punctuation, would seem to over-ride this analysis – an imposition of order over the "word-heap".

What, then, is the function of punctuation in poetry? If the author reads aloud his/her own text, there is almost no need for punctuation: their own words and "voice" are well known to themselves and they will interpret as they read. Once words were written and understood to be read silently it became necessary for the author to tell the reader where to pause or stop. St Augustine described the shock of seeing St Ambrose reading and absorbing knowledge in silence. In his *Confessions* St Augustine wrote:

> And when he was not engaged with them – which was never for long at a time – he was either refreshing his body with necessary food or his mind with reading//Now, as he read, his eyes glanced over the pages and his heart searched out the sense, but his voice and tongue were silent. Often when we came to his room – for no one was forbidden to enter, nor was it his custom that the arrival of visitors should be announced to him – we would see him thus reading to himself. After we had sat for a long time in silence – for who would

dare interrupt one so intent? –we would then depart, realizing that he was unwilling to be distracted in the little time he could gain for the recruiting of his mind, free from the clamor of other men's business.  (*Confessions* (2002) p86 [400])

This is a reminder of how silent reading is now taken for granted without examining the implications. Petrarch was meticulous in his use of punctuation when he copied out his own work. Whilst his use of punctuation is not a modern one, he used it to promote comprehension of his argument. He wanted "a system which could indicate subtle logical and semantic relationships between constituent parts of the period" (Parkes, 1992: 83). The interest in punctuation led to an interest in the layout of the text, including, for example, paragraphs (in prose) and stanzas (in poetry). It is a form of factual iconicity in poetry, and the particular form is extant today in the use, or lack of it, in free verse, concrete poetry, or any poetry that uses shapes of lines to indicate an added layer of meaning to the text (see Parkes, 1992: 101). The use of the colon has, for example, highlighted the use of the parallel in poetic text, something which Jakobson develops from Hopkins' theory. As poetry is a denser use of language than prose, punctuation, which can include the use of layout, rhyme and meter, is more important in poetry. The complexity of poetry benefits from the extra guidance of punctuation (see Parkes, 1992: 114).

Cuddon (1977) categorises punctuation as: elocutionary (indicating breathing places); syntactic (indicating logic); and deictic (indicating emphasis). It is a mistake to think of punctuation as merely syntactic; that is, for the promotion of meaning and precise grammar. Its elocutionary attribute informs how the text is to be read aloud – where the pauses are, which phrase belongs to which. The deictic attribute assists in how to emphasise the text and includes space to separate words – the space between words, the use of paragraphs, text breaks to indicate a shift in time, place or narrator in a text. Cuddon (1977) devised an eight-point scale of the functions of punctuation, which has been developed by Lennard (2005) to include two examples of new forms of punctuation marks which give structure to transcribed conversations between people who cannot see each other (as in phone calls) (see Lennard (2005:108–111 and: 141/2). It is Lennard's analysis of T.S. Eliot's use of punctuation which is more relevant here. Modernist writers sought to move away from traditional use of punctuation. For Eliot, this arose from his interest in Petrarch – who was an innovator in his day. In "The Waste Land" Eliot specifically decided to minimise the use of full stops and in *Four Quartets* omitted them where the reader might expect them to be (see Lennard 2005: 110 and 114).

The punctuation in *SOL* (2012) is sometimes absolutely traditional, as in the poem "Caravanserai" (2013: 152–154), for example. One poem: "Peroration by Punctuation" deliberately misuses punctuation. The poem becomes almost impossible to read (*SOL* 2012: 74). Other poems omit almost all punctuation so that the reader of the text is not guided by the usual indicators, resulting in a faster reading of the text and a tendency to a breakdown in absolute logical meaning. This is appropriate for the poem "Centrifuge at Play", and can be a textual reflection of city existence. Any minimal use of punctuation in *SOL* is not modernist in the sense of trying to break with tradition, but it is minimised in order to highlight control (or lack of control) of the meanings of the text. It is also the author's intention to emphasise how patterns and rhythms arising from the words themselves, both within and across the lines contributes to a possible absence of logic. Many poems have lines which are constructed on the basis of a syllable count – as is the case with "Centrifuge at Play". It was very interesting to discover how easy it was to read these lines when the counted pattern was consistently maintained throughout a poem. If the number fluctuated, the rhythm of the poem broke down. This has been noted with reference to the poem by Sarah Wardle, "Commuter's Pentameter", analysed in Chapter Four, above, and can be a deliberate device of the author. The version of "Centrifuge at Play" with the punctuation included, removes much of the sensation of the "word-heap" which it was specifically intended to portray. It also removes some of the ambiguity of the content – which is a planned purpose of the unpunctuated version.

Formalist analysis does not have to begin with a formula or list, it can begin with the poem itself. The Formalist tools enable the structure of the poem to be closely examined, its "literariness" reveals the poetics of the poem. The analysis of "Centrifuge at Play" begins with the observation that there is no rhyme in the poem. The lines are all nine syllables long – this results in steady movement and little change of speed. Are there any components in the poem which alter the speed – the use of spondees for example? "serve up death" (line 9), "muse? boss? brain?" (line 13), "but you will do it" (line 28), (this is combined with the only use of the future tense in the poem) and two passive tenses in lines 43 and 54. So the first half of the poem is slightly slower than the second half, and the second half is less active than the first half – it balances out.

The poem seems, in fact, to be roughly divided up into sections of 8 lines each with a pivot in the poem around the almost central lines 31–33 (see lines with square brackets) – these lines end and begin the 4$^{th}$ and 5$^{th}$ sections (cf. Jakobson's 1970 analysis of Shakespeare's sonnet "Th'expence of Spirit"). Each section of 8 lines tends to have a different shifter. Each section also seems to deal with a different method of distancing: "words *mores* print; . . . – double entendre" (lines 6 and 8); "slash plot . . . .diegetic recorder witness" (lines 14 and 15); "no phone back option . . . distant . . . intimate" (lines 20 and 21); "is that involved enough for you?" (line 30); "cross line breaks . . . . nothing to do with intimacy" (lines

33 and 36); "feel . . . heights are shabby or mundane" (lines 45 and 46), "acting layers" (line 50).

Punctuation is scanty and reading the text is difficult – where does one breathe? Using punctuation removes some of the ambiguity: e.g.: "each task on the shopping list each day" (line 4); "witness/passage of time" (lines 15/16); the lines around the pivot of the poem (lines 29–34); and "we think they looked like this evidence" (line 40). The poem contains a lot of hard "c" sounds (30). There are also a large number of "s" sounds – "sh", "sl", "ss", "st", The shifters tend to be on the left. The verbs are largely present tense – one future and some past tense, three of which are passive "are not available or measured" (line 43) and "are used for" (line 54)

The poem starts with "I tell you I control" but moves to "she" and "you" and "we" (choric), and back to "I", but "contains no ulterior message" – this is betrayal – first the distancing throughout the poem though use of terms such as: "slash plot" and "diegetic recorder witness" (line 15), and later the use of negatives: "I do not see" (line 31) and "do not involve" (line 35), "nothing to do with intimacy" (line 36), and a negative question: "how can I feel" (line 44), and lastly "contains no ulterior message" (line 57). Qualifiers tend to be attached to verb participles rather than to nouns – e.g. "life crashing, repelling/involved in a pattern of words that/salvaging combining" (lines 25/26).

Deictics of place (but perhaps line 52 "undersigned") are almost absent. Deictics of time are more frequent (lines: 4, 12, 16, 22, 25, 27, 32, 48). Deictics as part of the verb is a repeated feature, that is, verbs with prepositions attached: "serve up" (line 9)", "take out" (line 13), "gone down" (line 19), "phone back" (line 20), "driven out" (line 38), "spun out" (line 58). What are the pervasive features of the poem: the syllable count of each line; the use of the present tense; shifters tending to be on the left-hand side of the poem: see lines 1, 5, 23, 31, 34, 40, 41. But see also: mid-line shifters; see lines 1, 20, 28, 44; right hand side: see lines 7, 30.

The grammar is "torqued": see lines 7/8 where there is a self-reflexive question – not expecting an answer; line 13 where there are three questions without sentence construction – 3 in 1; lines 16–30 – ending in a question, although it does not start as one; and there is an apparent question that does not lead to a question at the end of the poem – the question becomes rhetorical and useless: "spun out" (lines 44–58). Parallels – apart from some use of torqued questioning – do not seem to occur in the poem. It is a continuous action of the centrifuge being represented and interpreted. It is perhaps possible to correlate the loosely defined sections of 8 lines with different shifter positions by the poet and the dialogue with his/her environment. It was an intention of the poet to write a poem containing development of narrative theory – how separation of parts of persona and/or their distillation is represented by construction of different viewpoints.

How does the above analysis connect to the axial diagram constructed by Coghill as a development of Jakobson's axial diagram (see Chapter Two, above)? Some of the words: repetition, torque, fragmented, random are used in the analysis of the poem. Repetition is not a function of the poem; fragmentation is manifested through lack of punctuation and open-ended grammatical construction; the phrases are strongly contiguous metonymically because of the imperfect grammar and also contain the element of randomness because of this imperfection. The whole poem is a metaphor – life is controlled by the movement of the centrifuge – and one that has no serious motivation either. This, interestingly, suggests that the poem is a metonymic metaphor of a particular kind. The deictics indicate time rather than place; the title and constant motion – the syllable count of nine syllables per line – both indicate a passage of time rather than simultaneity. The lack of grammar indicates similarity disorder i.e. indicates a primary metonymic structure. The accumulation of descriptive phrases, delineating certain kinds of events and a distancing from these events, without any capacity to process them, or the information arising from them – despite the subjection to centrifugal force – ensures that the poem therefore has "no ulterior message". The poem does not, therefore interpret Jakobson's metonymic and metaphoric disorders in a true sense – it may be evidence of the poet's similarity disorder (it is a poem comprised of mainly metonymic construction) but the poem itself is a metaphor and it also contains some condensed metaphors – "alarm bells warn" (16), impending atmosphere" (17), "cursor closer" (51) and "ulterior message" (57). As a final observation, the poem starts with a strong assertion of control: "I tell you I control the throughput" and ends with this focus spun out of control – "no ulterior message/spun out".

Formalist analysis is a malleable tool. The above examples of Formalist Praxis demonstrate that semantic, syntactic and semiotic terms are all needed to analyse the complexity of the words that the poetic text provides. It has never been the intention of the current author to supersede or in any way disprove the Formalist theory of Roman Jakobson. But the rigours of free verse, long poems, dislocative techniques in poetry and the constant pushing of boundaries of form and meaning which many poets construct, all need a system of critical analysis which include development and adaptations of method to cope with the greater and changing demands made of that method. It is also hoped that by subjecting the current author's own poetry to the rigours of Formalist analysis, the above examples provide some useful ideas on how the poet, him or herself, may also use the techniques to inform how they write city poetry and provide reasons as to why they might consider changing their text to provide greater precision of observation, form and impact on the reader/listener.

# Conclusion

Throughout the book it is argued that only close reading of the text can reveal both the detailed art and craft of the poet and poem, and provide the key to understanding how a particular genre of poetry might be established. Jakobson's Formalist theories and praxis, have been used to provide the basis for a definition of a city poetic genre. His Formalist analysis of poetry was both linguistic and semiotic. Re-examination and development of his work is something which the present author believes Jakobson himself would have wanted. His central theory of "Poetic Function" has responded well to the pressure of close examination and provides hitherto unexplored theoretical ideas. The results are not a ratification of well-worn and simple references to Jakobson's theories. A detailed discussion has opened up the wider possibilities of Jakobson's frames of reference of "equivalence" and "projection". These construct a sense of movement within his model which, in turn, is expressed as a semiotic structure. Understanding movement as inherent in "Poetic Function" is an important development of the Formalist contribution to poetics. The construction of an axial model further extends and interprets function. Here, metaphor forms the paradigm and metonymy the syntagm. The model enables a diagrammatic space between the axes. Because city poetry interprets how humans inhabit a particular space delineated by structures – buildings, maps of streets, transport networks – city poetry is enabled by this theoretical space. The argument of this book is that it is further expressed with the help of particular poetic tropes.

Why try to establish a genre of a city poetic? The majority or people live in cities and the events of our city lives are under-represented. Poetry of the city exists, but all too often the city is not recognized as important in poetic interpretation. Living in the city has a strong impact, on how we live, what we do and how we are affected by the environment. It would therefore seem important to establish how these events and surroundings can be understood. How they can be adequately, artfully, even beautifully, interpreted by a poetic that is enabled by the city space. City poetry also expresses how humans perform the balancing act that is required to survive the impacts arising from the structure of the city.

The present author argues, that the demands the city makes of us, foreground not only the use of deictics of both time and place, but also the use of shifters, which provide the sense of place, identity and identification with the city. Examples of city poetry are analysed with specific reference to the use of various tropes and structures, including metonymy, shifters, deixis, parallels, iconicity and even anagrams. The Jakobsonian, Formalist function of communication is used as a fundamental process of communication for the city poet (the addresser), the city poem (the message), and the reader/listener (the addressee). Women have indicated that there is a particular problem of placing and identity within the city environment and, because of this difficulty, separating the shifter from the deictic has provided a new theoretical basis for the analysis of poetry, especially women's poetry. A newly defined function of the city narrator for women in city poetry arises from this. As praxis to illustrate the argument, poetry by Bartlett, Duffy, Guro, and the present author, Coghill, has been analysed to demonstrate the importance of the separation of the two categories.

Establishing a city poetic genre was the impetus for reviewing Jakobson's theory, understanding new insights arising from it and then using the tropes which emerged on the axial diagram to understand the city poetic. Throughout the book there is praxis to support – or even detract from – the attributes, the tropes, the factual and imputed similarities – the sum of all the parts – which are identified as city poetics. This not only provides proof for the suggested theories of the book, it also provides information for poets to understand, use and develop their range of interpretive verse of the city. The book is memorable, not only on account of the new insights into Jakobson's theories of communication and poetic function, but also on account of the development of a city poetic theory and praxis through categorization of relevant tropes and patterns of structure.

The book has also covered other contributions to the impetus of constructing a city poetic. Semiotic poetic theory uses parallels to assist in the analysis of poetic form. Hopkins' analysis of parallels provides a particular knowledge of poetic construction and effect, although his theoretical roots lie more with rhetoric than Jakobson's linguistic and semiotic categorisations. The parallels, which Hopkins understood in detail, include diagonal lines – something which Jakobson also understood. Jakobson used the terms "factual similarity" and "imputed similarity" to describe how the patterning of words creates structures – not the words singly or even in small groups but in relation to each other – providing a whole poetic structure. As a development of the theory, "factual iconicity" and "imputed iconicity" are new terms which are explored and defined with reference to city poetry. How have these categories emerged? Jakobson's lifelong interest in art enabled his theory of how a poem can be "visualised" as a structure, revealing more poetic meaning than if just the linguistic parts are examined. This approach works particularly well with the comparison made between Crane's and Mayakovsky's poems about Brooklyn Bridge. A number of catenaries are observed in these poems. Lines can be drawn, in complex and revealing ways, which enhance the connections the poet makes within a poem. The lines produce a structure which iconically reflects the bridge and the city space. Discussion of Crane's work also reveals the use of the "idiom" as a poetic trope, with particular reference to city poetry. Blake's poetry is also understood more clearly with the use of the visual analytical method of ekphrasis. Jakobson's own interest in art, which informed his communication theory and his Formalist analysis, foregrounds the importance of art as a part of the semiotic analysis of poetry.

Allan Fisher, poet and artist, emphasises location in his London poetry. He has used a variety of theories and techniques to explore his city life. His methods of interpretation of the city provide the basis for developing both factual and imputed iconicity. His poetry also contains material which establishes a strong sense of movement of both time and place in the city, and which, as explored by the present author, reinforces the Russian Formalist focus on movement as an important aspect of poetic function. Iconicity readily becomes one of the "primary devices for representing a practical and spatially productive knowledge of the city" (quoted from the Introduction above – Roberts, 1999: 50). Through both factual iconicity and imputed iconicity, city poetry can be expressed through its own iconic idioms.

The examples given throughout the book indicate that the process of Formalist analysis adapts to suit the poem considered. Jakobson did not attempt a Formalist analysis of a long poem. A discussion of a short section of the book length London poem by David Jones, *The Anathémata* (1972 [1952]), provides knowledge of Jones' overall techniques. Jones' theory of "layering", includes a diachronic presentation of historic events which results in the complex text of the poem, and produces a new source for a city poetic form. It further enhances understanding of the use of metonymy in city poetry. Fisher has also made a major contribution through the development of his theories, the "Processual" and "Procedural" techniques of writing poetry. These methods add to particular forms of the layering of information, through which to interpret the city. A city has a multiplicity of constructed spaces. All city dwellers know this and respond to it. A process which constructs forms and patterns of city space from this knowledge is of central importance in writing city poetry.

The axial diagram, derived from Jakobson's theories of communication develops the theory for this space through the placing of tropes on the syntagm and on the paradigm. It has been suggested that these axes do not stop at the intersection of the positive side of the graph. There is, perhaps, also a negative poetic space on the left-hand side of the axial space. One suggestion for the interpretation of such a space is that the "zero sign" has relevance to a city poetic, partly because it can add a new dimension to the shifter. It can construct a poetics of the self which nearly disappears through the neutralising of personal characteristics. The use of gender in Russian language nouns shows this to be relevant to an understanding of Mayakovsky's city poetics. It is also important when considering poems which are constructed with "words" that do not carry meaning – neologisms or words that simply denote city sounds, as in the train poem analysed by Ferreiro, discussed by Conley (2014). The development of this "zero space" goes beyond Jakobson's own explorations of poetic form and function.

Because Jakobson regarded metonymy as a trope which belonged more to prose than poetry, it is interesting to discover that metonymy is, in fact, a significant trope in city poetry. The investigation is especially relevant because Jakobson himself is not detailed in his analysis. Metonymy expresses the contiguity, not the simultaneity, of the relationship between the person and the city. The "as" of the metonymic form gives rise to a greater complexity of juxtaposition of content than the "is" of the metaphor. The city provides so much stimulus that poetic forms have to be constructed which are able to interpret this plethora. The praxis for the theoretical exploration in the present volume has been made with reference to specific city poems, and includes examples by Coghill, Jones, Lopez, Tonks and Wardle. A process of assimilation is a metaphoric quality and metaphor may therefore be more difficult to use as a trope to express life in the city. In whatever way it is done, humans within the city need to communicate the reality of their lives within the location. The suggestion is that metonymy is particularly useful in enabling poets to interpret the city in their work.

Throughout the book, the use of deictics and shifters has been strongly highlighted in several chapters as providing a combined sense of place and identity, a balancing point for some kind of control of the multi-directional forces which a city generates and which humans adapt and interpret. The axial model provides for the establishment of various forms of metonymy, which include several new tropes, including "cohesion", "repetition" and "torque". Their role in a city poetic genre is discussed. The use of Jakobson's term "projection" has particular relevance in establishing communication and movement between the human and city structure. It has been suggested that there is a very important play of forces constructed – a "relational equivalence" in the axial model – which is dependent on accepting that there is a control of the city poetic by the poet – an encoder-orientation within the text or poetic message. Without this balance, the city would overpower human expression.

As an integral aspect of a city poetic, the viewpoint used by the poet – how she/he presents the city from an upstairs window or from eye-level on the street, for example - establishes a register or idiom of a city poetic genre. Guro's city poetry reveals her use of the window as a proscenium arch, providing an additional complexity of viewpoint. Guro's work also contributes to the discovery of the trope of "analogy" in poetry. The existence of this structure which indicates a complex interaction between the poet (encoder) and the reader/audience (decoder/recoder) is an area for future research and poetic expression. The nature and function of punctuation, has also been shown to be pivotal as an iconic aspect of city poetry. The speed of life and change within the city environment has enabled new insight into its function – even when it is absent. In the final chapters of the book the work of Charles Sanders Peirce was suggested as a theoretician who could contribute theory for a city poetic genre. There has not been the space to examine his work in full but, in terms of the city, Merrell's (2000) interpretation of Peirce's work offers some very interesting theories which can be further explored when writing city poetry.

The intentions of the book, then, have been twofold: to re-examine and develop the Formalist "Poetic Function" of Roman Jakobson; and to prove the existence of a city poetic genre, through both the theory and praxis of city poetry. In the view of the present author, a city poetic genre is now established and, within this genre, women are particularly enabled by a theory which separates shifters from deictics. The separation enables women to place themselves in the city environment (with all its viewpoints, shapes and lines) and then to speak (give personal voice) to their intersection with the environment. With the help of metonymic analysis, personal pronouns or shifters delineate specific malleable relationships between people, women, and the city, making such relationships both more clearly expressed and more fully understood.

The book has gone beyond a simplistic re-iteration of Jakobson's theory of "Poetic Function"; instead, it has presented a development of his Formalist theories. In the face of the neglect of Jakobson's work, in the time since the emergence of reader theory in the latter part of the twentieth century, this volume has shown how misplaced that neglect has been. Arguably the doyen of reader theory, Culler's criticism of Jakobson's analysis of "Les Chats" has been specifically explored and rebutted. Jakobson's Formalist analysis, through this example, reveals that the complexity of poetic structure can be enhanced by reference to paintings and provides clarity for Jakobson's closely wrought analysis. Jakobson's acknowledgement of poets' use of "transitory grammatical forms" (1975: 71) in this particular example of his Formalist analysis is decisive in establishing the supremacy of his theoretical insight.

Jakobson tested his theories through praxis many times throughout his career. In his later book *The Sound Shape of Language* (1979c) he analyses a poem by e e cummings which experiments with neologisms of grammar and meaning (1979: 222–231). There can be no better summing up than to quote his own words here, on "Language and Poetry":

> A dynamized tension between *signans* and *signatum* – and in particular the direct interplay of the speech sound with meaning – is superimposed by cummings on his poem and in general by poets upon their creations destined:
>   to overcome the palling flatness and univocity of verbal messages,
>   to curb the futile and impoverishing attempts aimed at 'disambiguation',
>   and to affirm the creativity of language liberated from all infusion of banality.
> (1979c: 230, 231)

Jakobson spent his life trying to understand how we all use words. The desire to explain, in words, what the process is, whereby we express meaning, is complex and continuing. Jakobson's own love of poetry led him, later in his life, to accept that linguistics holds many of the keys but the semiotician and the poet are often the ones who keep opening the doors. With reference to poets' use of language he mentions Saussure's phrase, the: "fureur du jeu phonique" (literally: a passion for gambling) with which poets express their elasticity of language usage (1967: 434). Furthermore, in his Afterword to *The Sound Shape of Language* (1979), Jakobson adds: "The Saussurean vision of linguistic dust (*poussière linguistique*) far from disintegrating linguistics, widens its vistas in the search for general laws." (1979: 237). Jakobson has provided sophisticated tools for the analysis of poetry, and poets are continually providing not only further material for analysis, but further puzzles for interpretation.

The structure of poetry has become increasingly varied in form and content, especially over the last century or more, and, as such, demands an ever-increasing range of analytical methods to interpret it. However, there are still theories which need to be explored. For example, Hopkins' nineteenth century theory of parallels in poetry, has still not been fully discussed as a system of analysis of poetic structure. This book originated with the questions: is Jakobson's theory of "Poetic Function" fully understood?, and: is there a city poetic genre? These questions have been answered with "no" and "yes" respectively. The development of Jakobson's Formalist theory, as explored in the chapters above, provides a rich mine for the definition and exploration of a city poetic genre. The genre is led by the poet who is always finding new ways to communicate the city with the use of particular tropes and forms, and which construct the genre of a city poetic. Any theorist or poet interested in exploring theory and praxis of how to express life in the city will find many indications in the preceding pages which will assist their expression. It is conclusively stated that the city dictates that certain things be said in certain ways and that pastoral or purely reflective poetics do not provide the tools with which to interpret the city experience. The genre of a city poetic does indeed exist, its full range of tropes and forms will, of course, be constantly experimented with and developed by poets (and theorists) who have already written and who are yet to write about their city lives. Jakobson's theories of "Poetic Function" and communication will always make an important contribution to the theoretical discussion of the genre.

# Appendix: Jakobson on Mayakovsky and Dostoyevsky

Two essays by Roman Jakobson are here published in English Translation for the first time. The English titles of these essays are: "About Mayakovsky's Later Lyrical Poems" and "Dostoyevsky Echoed In Mayakovsky's Work". Edited by Dr Mary Coghill: Visiting Research Fellow Institute of English Studies (2013–2015), School of Advanced Studies, University of London Fellow London Metropolitan University. Translators: Elena Richard and Paul Jude Richard.

The two essays are published as the conclusion of research undertaken for a Visiting Research Fellowship. They are an Addendum to The Roman Jakobson Fellowship Colloquium Presentation, 23rd October 2015, held at The School of Advanced Studies, Senate House, University of London, entitled: "The Development of Roman Jakobson's semiotic interpretation of poetic form and function with special reference to his axial model of the poles of language: metaphor and metonymy; and the application of this developed model to the construction of city poetics with reference to Vladimir Mayakovsky's poetry."

The copyright of these translations, with the kind permission of Professor Linda Waugh, Executive Director, Roman Jakobson Intellectual Trust, and the translators, Elena and Paul Jude Richard, rests with the editor, Dr Mary Coghill. The right of Dr Mary Coghill to be identified as the editor of this work has been asserted by her in accordance with the Copyrights, Designs and Patents Act 1988. All rights reserved. Reproduction of any part of the translations, by permission of the Editor.

The two essays by Roman Jakobson which are now presented in English translation for the first time were originally published in Russian, in one of the nine volumes (a tenth volume is under preparation, edited by Professor Linda Waugh) of Jakobson's Selected Writings. In keeping with a number of his other essays in various languages, it was published in Russian, in the English edition: *Selected Writings, Vol 5, On Verse, Its Masters and Explorers* (1979) The Hague, Mouton (382–412). The title details of the essays are: К ПОЗДНЕЙ ЛИРИКЕ МАЯКОВСКОГО (382–405), translated as: "About Mayakovsky's Later Lyrical Poems"; and ДОСТОЕВСКИЙ В ОТГОЛОСКАХ МАЯКОВСКОГО (1979: 406–412), translated as: "Dostoyevsky Echoed In Mayakovsky's Work". These essays were originally written as a commentary to previously unpublished texts by the Russian poet Vladimir Mayakovsky for an edition of his work *Russkij literaturnyi arkhiv* (1956) New York, Harvard University Press.

Roman Jakobson wrote about Mayakovsky in his essay: 'On a Generation That Squandered Its Poets' in 1931. It was re-published in English in *Language in Literature* (1987) Cambridge MA, Harvard University Press (1987: 273–300). These two newly translated essays reveal insights, not only into Mayakovsky but into Roman Jakobson himself, both as a theoretician and as a person. Known for his commitment to, and exploration of Formalism, the essays also reveal the more personal biographical response of a close friend. However, Jakobson clearly states his Formalist analytical position in the opening sentence of the first essay (see below): "In Mayakovsky's literary works, love poems and lyrical cycles befittingly alternate with lyrical epic poems about world events". As is indicated in the Colloquium essay to which these translations originally provided an addendum (see Chapter Two), this alternation of composition is also evident within individual poems. After providing details of Mayakovsky's personal life events, Jakobson returns to Formalist analysis, in the penultimate paragraph of the second essay stating, that Mayakovsky often made: "declarations about the alternation of genres and their dramatic collisions; about the fight between the lyrical and anti-lyrical inspiration. This is not a fight that was imposed upon the poet. No one could have imposed anything upon such a stubborn poet." The English translation of these essays provides fresh knowledge of Roman Jakobson the theorist, by revealing how he uses personal biographical details to provide material for his Formalist analysis.

## Acknowledgements

My very grateful thanks are due to Professor Linda Waugh for giving permission for the translation and publication of these essays. Professor Linda Waugh is Professor Emerita of French; English; Anthropology; Linguistics; Language, Reading & Culture; and Second Language Acquisition & Teaching (SLAT); Member, Advisory Board, Center for Educational Resources in Culture, Language and Literacy (CERCLL); Executive Director, Roman Jakobson Intellectual Trust. My grateful thanks go also to the translators of the essays. Their diligence and expertise have rendered two very complex theoretical essays into readable and cogent English. They have been kind enough to allow me to make suggestions during the final drafting. This is a privilege, the rewards of which, I hope, outweigh any faults and criticism which might arise.

## About Mayakovsky's later lyrical poems

[Translator's note (T.N.) the use of triple asterisks in the translations indicates text which the translators know to have been published elsewhere in English translation, though the choice of words may be different. Where, in the text, Mayakovsky's poetry is quoted, the sign: / – indicates a line break and: // – a space and a line break].

In Mayakovsky's literary works, love poems and lyrical cycles are appropriately alternated with lyrical epic poems about world events. David Burlyuk, always very meticulous in his poetry evaluations, accurately remarked that Mayakovsky's pre-war poems gravitated towards city still life scenes, where women entered only as decorative motifs. Later, women make an appearance "adorned with a name". Burlyuk names this type of lyrical genre "a bedpan diary", where nothing is made up and life is written with indelible letters.[1]

Between June 1914 and July 1915, Mayakovsky wrote the tetraptych "A Cloud in Trousers". And by the end of the year, he completed the poem "The Backbone Flute". Later, in the spring of 1916, he wrote the poems from the same cycle: "To All" and "In Place of a Letter", and finally the poem "Don Juan", which he later destroyed after Lilya Brik "became upset that it was once again about love." This is his first wave of love poetry, which was followed by a social poem, "War and Peace," finished towards the end of 1916. "'War and Peace' is going round and round in my head, and 'A Man' in my heart,'" remembered the author.[2] The lyrical side was once again dominating Mayakovsky.

This poem about "inconceivable love", *a thing* in which the poet, according to his own words, "lifted his heart like a flag," was already thought out by the end of 1916 and written, with periods of interruption, by October 1917.[3] Then again

---

[1] D. Burlyuk. Three Chapters from the Book *Mayakovsky and His Contemporaries*, Red Arrow, New York, 1932, 11.
[2] "I Myself", *Vladimir Mayakovsky*, I (1928: 23).
[3] In *Mayakovsky's Complete Collected Works*, I (1939: 466), the period of work on "A Man" is wrongly attributed to the year 1916 and the beginning of 1917. In February of 1917, Mayakovsky told me about "A Man" as a new concept: see "About a Generation"***, above mentioned, p. 358. When he read the poem to several writers at the end of January 1918, he spoke about it as if it were newly finished. This is a quote from his autobiography: "Year 1916. 'War and Peace' is finished. A little later, 'A Man'". This is an illustration of the author's warnings: "I swim freely in my own chronology". Some of these inconsistencies in dating are intentionally done by the poet. Compare Pertsov, V. *Mayakovsky* (Moscow, 1951:153). It's interesting that Mayakovsky recreates the title hero of his previous poem in the draft of the poem "About This", when he worked on it at the end of 1922 and the beginning of 1923: "a man is standing chained before me" and he is imploring the poet: "For five years I have stood / and have gazed at these waters, // Tied to the handrails by the verse ropes, // For five years this abyss didn't take its eyes off me". Consequently, while working on the poem, Mayakovsky substitutes the correct number with the fictitious "seven years": "Complete Collected Works", V (1934:135). It is true that the events of 1917 were not reflected in "A Man". Regarding the question about the inhabitants of our world: "What should they do, / water the fields with their blood?" Mayakovsky answers from the sky [T.N. with scorn],

"the lyrics of the heart" are replaced by poetry ruled by reason. In 1919, the poet declares that "'150,000,000' is dominating my head".[4] He began working on the poem in the summer, and by the end of the year it was already completely drafted. In January of 1920, he read it at the Moscow Linguistic Circle.[5] In the spring of the same year, Mayakovsky conceived a new social-political poem later entitled "The Fifth International". He worked on it until 1922, but abandoned it when he "thought of love".

He was drawn again to personal poetry, and in November of 1921 he started working on his only idyllic poem "I Love." "I started writing and I would be glad to be in such a state."[6] "Is this my heart / I admire mine," proclaimed these lines finished in February of 1922. The following winter, Mayakovsky wrote the tragic poem entitled "About This": "a thing of the grandest and best works", as the author himself boasts.[7]

> This angry theme came to me,
> ordered:
> 	Give me
> 		the rod of the day!
> It looked, twisted at my every day,
> and dumped a storm on people and things.
> This theme came,
> 	erased the rest
> and alone
> 	became inseparably close.
> This theme put a knife to my throat.
> Hammer-fighter!
> 	From my heart to the temples.

In the above-quoted introduction to the poem, Mayakovsky answers the question regarding "about what, about this," but the name of the theme itself, *love*, was replaced with an ellipsis by the author, out of superstition.

There is an internal connection between the three cycles of Mayakovsky's love poems, and the poet accentuates it through direct references in verses from

---

laughing: "I don't give a damn! / They can, / I don't care!" (lines: 537–538, and 540–542). In a similar manner, reflections of the current events are almost totally absent from "A Cloud", which was written at the beginning of WWI.

**4** "I Myself", p 24.

**5** V. Katanyan, *Mayakovsky. Literary Chronicle* (Leningrad, 1948: 124), he guesses the poem was finished in February or March of 1920.

**6** Mayakovsky's letter to Lilya Brik 5 XII 21: Katanyan,. *Mayakovsky*, p. 159.

**7** *Complete Collected Poems*, II (1939: 507).

the preceding cycle to the subsequent one. In "A Man": "Bowed before the hand / The lips whisper / to the little hairs underneath, // One calls it 'Little flute', / 'Little cloud' calls it the other\*\*\*" (lines 352–356). "About This" purposefully continues the theme of the 1917 poem "A Man That I Twisted Around Stands Before Me". (line: 486) "Remember till your grave the over-splash // that splashed around in 'A Man'" (lines 566–567). "The way it used to be – // to grow up // and fly out the window like a verse// No,/ to grow weak in the wall's dampness // the verse / and days have changed" (lines 1120–1126). In the initial draft of the poem "About This", the thread points to the first period of Mayakovsky's poetic creation: "The second cloud writes in trousers".[8]

For the third time a political poem would follow a personal one. It was finalized in October of 1924 and was entitled "Vladimir Ilyich Lenin". "I feared this poem very much," noted Mayakovsky in his autobiography, "since it was very easy to fall into a simple political retelling (of the story)".[9] A new outburst of lyrical poems followed. Mayakovsky expressed repentance to Lilya Brik in a letter dated December 6, 1924: "Unfortunately I am drawn again to writing lyrical poems!"[10] In a poem written in the summer of that year, "I am / now / free / of love," Mayakovsky confessed:

```
No,
        I'm not going to wrap myself in black melancholy,
and plus I don't feel like talking
                                    to anyone.
Only
in people like us
                the rhymes' gills
                                    flap quickly
on the poetic sand.
To dream is harmful
                and it's useless to desire.
We have to
        continue
            the boring job.
But sometimes it happens that
                                life
                                    arises in a different shape,
and you
        understand the big picture
                                    through nonsense.
```

---

**8** *Complete Collected Works*, V (1934), 145.
**9** "I Myself", 26.
**10** Katanyan, *Mayakovsky*, p.214.

> We repeatedly attack
> 
>         lyrical verses
> 
>                 with bayonets,
> 
> We seek
> 
>     the precise
> 
>         and naked speech.
> 
> But poetry is the worst scum:
> 
>             it exists and it's clueless.[11]

This sand without love, which was only glimpsed in "Jubilee," will grow into the theme of the fatal shoal in Mayakovsky's farewell lines: "the sea goes backwards".

The period of work required by social commission was extended, and in the spring of 1926, Mayakovsky conceived a poem and finished it in the summer of the following year. It was dedicated to the 10th anniversary of the October revolution. If the title "One Hundred and Fifty Millions" was a polemical answer to Blok's "Twelve", the same poet also suggested to Mayakovsky the title of the second poem about revolution: "Good".[12]

One evening in April of 1927, in the restaurant Nezdara in Prague, famous for its vintage Tokay wine, Mayakovsky assured me that his rhythm of alternating genres was unchanged, and real lyrical poems are going to follow the October poem. At that time, he had just barely finished the screenplay "How Are You?", the theme of which "is 24 hours in the life of a person". In the last draft, the character openly receives the surname "Mayakovsky", and along this secondary track, and under the guise of a cinematic experiment, the author keeps and further develops the symbolism of his previous lyrical poems. He wanted to meet the unconquerable resistance of the administrative types with a decisive voice. In a short article published in the April edition of a magazine, he gave notice, in his usual manner of anticipating events, that he was preparing "a poem about a woman".[13] Maybe it was about this woman that he spoke about in parodical contrast to his programmatic "Good", in his autobiography, captioned "Year 1928": "I am writing the poem 'Bad'".[14]

"It's bad," he told his closest friends at the time, and "only a great and good love might still be able to save me". His appetite for changing places is accompanied by the inescapable leitmotif of Onegin's wanderings. After only five days in France he writes to Lilya Brik on October 20th, 1928: "Unfortunately I am in Paris,

---

[11] "Jubilee", 47–79, *Complete Collected Works*, II (1939) p. 333.
[12] "The Death of Alexander Blok", *Complete Collected Works*, II (1939), p 474.
[13] "What Am I Doing?", *Complete Collected Works*, X (1941), p 267).
[14] "I Myself", p. 28.

and it bores me senseless; it nauseates and repulses me". More news followed on November 12th: "My life is somewhat strange, uneventful, with numerous details, but this is no letter material***".¹⁵ Soon these "details" would be conveyed to the readers in verses from "A Letter to Comrade Kostrov".

> Imagine:
>                 enters the hall
>                               a beauty,
> decked out
>         in furs and bead strands.
> And I
>     took this girl
>                and told her:
> - Am I right
>         or am I wrong? -

At the end of October, Mayakovsky meets a Russian girl in the hall of a doctor's office in Paris. The fashion at the time, furs and beads, describes her very well.

The first book sent by Mayakovsky to Tatyana Yakovleva, Volume I of his Works, begins with the introductory lines of his autobiography: "I am a poet. This is the interesting part about me. This is what I write about – if I love, or if I'm a gambler; or about the beauty of nature in the Caucasus, but only if it's defensible in words". The strange life with multiple details was "defensible in words" in Mayakovsky's poems from Paris. He says in a banal, prosaic phrase, "I took this girl and told her". The linguists explain that the verb "to take" loses its lexical meaning here, and simply becomes an auxiliary verb. In Mayakovsky's prosody: "Four. / Heavy like a blow. // To Caesar the things that are Caesar's and to God the things that are God's" – this verse, is made of fully stressed words conferred upon each of them equal importance.¹⁶ He returns to the Devil the things that are the Devil's by breaking up monolithic utterances into a formula-ridden way and making the Devil into a kind of indefinite pronoun.

---

15 V. Katanyan, *Mayakovsky*, p. 361; same, *Tales About Mayakovsky* (Moscow, 1940), p., 298.
16 "The author dedicates these lines to his beloved self", the poem was written not in the beginning of 1916, as the editor wrote in the *Complete Collected Works*, I (1939), p. 447, but in fact a year later. Mayakovsky read it to me in February of 1917 as if it were just written. In Mayakovsky's works, other chronological inaccuracies sneaked in as well. For example, in the *Complete Collected Works*, II (1939), p. 550, "Ode to the Revolution" was attributed to the beginning of 1918, but Elsa Triolet and I heard it when the author read it with "Our March" in December of 1917 on the stage at the Poet's Cafe.

> If it's not
> > a day of human birth,
> star,
> > should we celebrate
> > > the Devil, then!?[17]

If, in the allocution "I took her and told her", the word "took" is a full-fledged verb, it means that it requires a nearby and direct object, not a far away, indirect one: it's not "I took and told / the girl", but "I took the girl / and told her". Both the poet's life and poetics demanded this. And the question "was I right or wrong?" is transformed into a simple coda.

People's stories about this "human, simple" love are told by Viktor Shklovsky: "They resembled each other so much, they fit each other so well, that people in the cafe smiled with gratitude when they saw them. It was pleasant to see two good looking people together".[18]

"You are the only one / as tall as I am // so stand next to me", he writes in a "Letter to Tatyana". Mayakovsky resonates with this classic example in both title and content, something he does more than just once. He was always under the spell of Onegin's lines (T.N. this is in reference to Pushkin's poem "Evgeny Onegin"), which lines, according to him, he would remember "even at the very moment when death will impose upon me***with a noose around my neck". Reformulated by him, the lines sounded like this:

> My days are numbered, yet it's true,
> My life in order to prolong
> I have to know each morning
> That every day I may see you.

On December 3rd, 1928, Mayakovsky left Paris for Moscow to finalize his work on the magical comedy "The Bedbug", and in order to prepare its stage production, intending to return to Paris. He mails letters and numerous telegrams to Paris. A part of this correspondence still exists: 7 letters from December 27th, 1928 through October 5th, 1929, and 25 telegrams from December 3rd through August 3rd.

He writes the following, and the same words find an echo in his farewell lines: "Letters are so slow, and every minute, I so need to know about the things you do and what you think. That's why I send telegrams. Send me telegrams and letters, piles of both" (28.XII.28). In response to her reproaches for days without receiving mail, he says, "You are my one and only letter-master". "You keep saying that I don't write, but what are my telegrams?". And in awaiting letters from her, he

---
[17] "A Man" (1939, 57–62).
[18] V. Shklovsky, V. *About Mayakovsky* (Moscow, 1940), p. 215; Katanyan, V. Mayakovsky, p. 207.

states: "Your lines are at least a half of my life in general, and the entirety of my personal life" (3.I.29).

Mid-January of 1929, Mayakovsky begins a lecture tour in Ukraine, but after two days of presentations in Kharkhov, he cancels the remaining seven scheduled performances "due to throat problems", and returns to Moscow.[19] "I quit traveling", he writes to Tatyana in Paris, "I remain sitting here in the fear that I'll be late in reading your letters, even if only by an hour. To work, and to wait for you, is my *only* joy." These are the two themes of Mayakovsky's letters at this time.

On December 28th, the very day of the actors' reading of the comedy "The Bedbug", the author writes again to Paris: "What news do you have? We (your Waterman and I) wrote a new play. We read it to Meyerhold. We wrote about 20 hours a day without food or drink. My head is all puffy from this kind of labor (even my cap doesn't fit). I can't judge for myself whether it came out well or not, and I'm not sending other opinions to avoid reproaches about self-advertising and having a hyper-inflated sense of inborn modesty. (Does it seem like I brag too much? It's all right. I deserve it.). I work like an ox, with my head down and my eyes red from staring at the desk. Even my eyes betrayed me and I have to wear glasses! I am also using some cold compresses for my eyes. It's okay. By the time we meet it will be okay. I can work with glasses. And I don't need my eyes anyway before we get together, because except for you, I don't have anyone to look at. And I have heaps and piles of work. I'll finish and I'll dash to see you. If we collapse from all this work (in the most unhappy case), you'll come to me. Right? Right? . . . What are you writing about, the New Year? Crazy woman! What kind of celebration can I have without you? I'm working. This is my *one and only* pleasure." The next letter is about the same thing: "I am working until I can't see straight and my shoulders ache. In addition to writing now, I have daily play readings and rehearsals. I hope to finish all the work in a month. I'll rest afterwards. When I get completely tired, I say to myself "Tatyana" and then I entrust myself to paper again" (3.I.29).

The play "Bedbug", the most anti-lyrical of all Mayakovsky's works, is close to being finalized, and meanwhile, the lyrical tendency starts dominating the poet again: "I don't spill all over the paper (professional hate towards writing), but if I would write down all my conversations with myself about you, the unwritten letters, the unsaid affectionate words, then my collected works would swell to three times their usual size, and would be all lyrical" (3.I.29).

Even before his trip to Kharkov, Mayakovsky sent telegrams to Paris: "In the beginning of February I hope to go somewhere and rest. I need the Riviera \*\*\*",

---

[19] V. Katanyan, *Mayakovsky*, p. 367.

and Katanyan's literary chronicle also notes: "The last few days in March – beginning of April (?), there was a trip to Nice and Monte-Carlo". According to this chronicle, he went abroad the day after the Moscow stage premiere of the "Bedbug", which took place February 13th,[20] but according to T. Yakovleva, he left the day before the premiere. On February 15th Mayakovsky send a telegram to Negorelyi: "Leaving today will stop Prague Berlin few days". He went to Berlin to sign a contract with a publisher for a translation of his prose and spent a day at my place in Prague. I called the critic Kodichka, who at the time ran the programming for Vinogradsky Theater to listen to "The Bedbug" read by the author. The critic was thrilled with Mayakovsky's dramatic courage and his masterful reading, but he doubted he'd be able to get the director's approval for staging the play. All of this, I have to say, didn't affect the poet much in his hurry to go West. A telegram was sent to Paris: "I arrive tomorrow twenty second two o'clock blue express". He did not go to Nice, but just stayed in Paris and went to the Paris Plage (beach).

While developing the motifs of his November poems, he warned, while still in Moscow: "Please gather your thoughts (and then your things) and look into your heart to see what you think about my hope to take you into my paws and bring you to us, here in Moscow. Let's think about it and then let's discuss it. We'll turn our separation into a test. If you love me, is it good to waste our hearts and time in exhausting leaps from one telegraph post to another? 'Am I right or am I wrong?'".

In Paris they [he and Tatyana] were always together, but sometimes he was overcome by his unending passion for gambling. Those who saw them together remember that he was very protective of, and shy with her, and carefully avoided any trace of rudeness or ambiguity. He was in awe of her "absolute ear" for poetry, as he called it, and recited to her Pasternak's, Esenin's and more often than not, his own, poems. He sought her support for his own belief that he "beats Pushkin".

However, he couldn't remain in France beyond the end of April due to the expiration of his visa. Moreover, his presence was required in Moscow in order to receive money that was an absolute necessity for both himself and all those who depended on him at home.

His words to Pushkin, "I am now free", were now absolutely true, but the past burdened him. "The calendar and the map hinder me" – was Mayakovsky aware of the secret tragedy of this dedication to Tatyana in a book of his poems? Were time, with its past of "hundred pound weights", and space, with its deep chasm of no return across the border, standing in the way? On May $2^{nd}$, Mayakovsky returned to Moscow, alone again and hoping to go back to Paris soon.

---

**20** Katanyan, *Mayakovsky*, p. 370.

"I'll try to see you as soon as possible", he writes in a telegram on May 25th. He laments the slow pace of his writing. "I am just starting to write; I will finish my 'Bathhouse'" (15.V.29). "I started to write The Bathhouse (after a damned delay!), and so far, I don't even have all the surnames of the characters" (8.VI.29). Immediately he complains that he "didn't write one poetic line. After your poems, all the others seem bland". By *your poems* he means both of his lyrical letters in November, as for *the others,* it's enough to mention the poem "Thrust in Self-criticism", published a few days before the above-quoted letter and characterized in Mayakovsky's *Complete Collected Works,* X (1941: 392), as a "poetical paraphrase of Stalin's words".

"I am throwing myself into my work", continues Mayakovsky, "bearing in mind that there isn't long until October, but work is terribly hard and I retreat from it with bumps on my forehead from perplexity and respect for the theme". The reference to October is explained in the letter dated July 12th: "Beyond October (like we decided) I can't imagine anything without you. Starting in September, I'll begin making myself little wings to fly to you". This is an allusion to the lines in "Letter to Comrade Kostrov": "Here even / bears / would grow little wings" (134–136). The letter further develops the image of the bear: "I'm such a tall splayfooted and unsympathetic bear. On top of everything today I'm also very gloomy." He laments again: "I write very little. My head doesn't work. I have to do nothing for a while". He writes in a telegram: "Miss you hope to see soon" (25.VI), repeating the same complaint in each and every way: "miss you very much", "unbelievably miss you", "miss you endlessly", "absolutely long for you", "miss you like never before", "I long for you regularly, and lately more than regularly, I miss you even more often."

"It cannot be" – Mayakovsky wants to believe this and yet knows that as long as he lives, it cannot really be – "the case that we wouldn't be able to be together for all time." (8,.VI). He exhorts her to go as an "engineer-woman" somewhere in Altay: "Won't you?" (12.VII). But the tragedy advances "heavily, rudely, and visibly". If, during the fall of 1928, life in Paris was full of "numerous details", now, in answer to a question from Paris about details of his life in Moscow, he replies abruptly: "There are no details".

The Ukrainian poet Tychina, who visited Moscow in the beginning of 1929, remembers how fashionable the attacks on Mayakovsky were at the time.[21] Sending the "Letter to Comrade Kostrov" to the printing press, the author entirely understood that, in the environment created by the Russian Association of Proletarian Writers (RAPP), it would be akin to a bomb. And in fact, they did not

---

21 Katanyan, *Mayakovsky*, p. 368.

forgive him for it. Enmity towards the poet continued to grow, while both overt and covert hounding took place.

Only two weeks after returning to Moscow, Mayakovsky begs: "please don't repine and don't reproach me, I dealt with so many unpleasant things, from fly-size to elephant-size, truly you shouldn't be mad at me" (15.V.29).

"The Bathhouse" was finished in time, during the second half of September, but "it's impossible to retell and rewrite all the sad things that make me even more silent than usual", as the author relates in his clear style in one of his last surviving letters dated October 5th. The month arrived that Mayakovsky had previously mentioned as being the "limit," beyond which their reunion could not be delayed, but Mayakovsky is stubbornly silent. In Paris she feels that the earth is moving under her feet and the relationship is going nowhere. That same month Mayakovsky receives a letter from Paris that unequivocally bids him farewell. Within few months the poet's life would end, even before the woman in Paris finds out from Moscow acquaintances that in September Mayakovsky was irrevocably denied any further trips abroad.

"Another horse is done for," he says receiving the letter. This is both an expression from horse racing, but also from "A Good Attitude Towards Horses". Soon after, friends organized a merry name-day celebration at his apartment. Later that night they asked him to recite some of his older poetry. According to an eyewitness,[22] he refuses repeatedly, complaining that his voice has disappeared. He is asked by everyone, begged, and ultimately convinced – *** He stood up and grabbed the corner of the wardrobe with his hand, scanning us with a slow, memorable look that we would always remember and began reciting in a low voice and a sudden surliness:

[T.N. Alliteration that is impossible to convey in English with similar effect and meaning.]

> The hooves trotted.
> They seem to sing:
> "Grib (Mushroom).
> Grab' (Plunder).
> Grob (Coffin).
> Grub (Rude)"

He continued reciting, gradually becoming gentler, lowering his tone line after line.*** And everybody around became more serious. It wasn't a joke anymore, a poet's merry celebration, a friendly get together. We were all suddenly grabbed by the thought, like a draft going through all the circumvolutions of our brains, that

---

[22] Kassil, L. *Mayakovsky – Himself* (Moscow 1940) p. 144.

we had to remember this moment. *** And he continued reciting while glancing somewhere along the wall:

> Horse, don't.
> Horse, listen,
> why do you think that you are worse than them?
> My little one.
> We all are part horse,
> Each of us is a horse in our own way[23]

and then he turned his back towards us with his broad shoulders hunched over as if he deeply understood something, as if he was strapped in some enormous harness, as if trekking up the mountain.*** He moved softly as if he was afraid to hurt somebody. He went to the room next door and stayed there for a long time, his elbows on the desk, holding a glass with unfinished cold tea tight in his hands. There was something helpless, lonely, and plaintive seeping from him, something not understood by anyone at the time.

Everything is known ahead of time, but everything happens suddenly. "And the giant will stand for a second and will collapse, // entombing himself under a ripple of notes"[24] "They tear me apart, cut me into pieces, they rip me up, these fleshy people,", says Mayakovsky on New Year's Eve.[25] "He is horribly tired", writes Lilya Brik about him in February. He read his new poem "At the Top of My Voice", in contrast to his former habit of reciting, "from a piece of paper and with no energy".[26] "Something is wrong", noticed Mayakovsky's driver in March: "his mood rarely improves".[27] By the beginning of April, the illness "was given a name – a nervous breakdown"[28] in the Kremlin's hospital.

Mayakovsky's fate was sealed by the same inseparability of life and creative work that thrilled the poet in regards to his teacher, Khlebnikov. On April 1st, 1923, amidst feverish work on his poem "About This", Mayakovsky reveals in a letter to Lilya Brik: "Love is life, it's the most important. All poetry, life affairs, and everything else stems from it. Love is at the heart of everything. If it stops beating, everything else dies, becomes extraneous, useless. But if the heart beats it cannot help but make itself known in everything *** But if I don't have any 'activity', I'm dead".[29] In Mayakovsky's lyrical work from Paris, he loudly affirmed that his new

---

23 "A Good Attitude Towards Horses" (1918), 1–6 and 35–40.
24 "About This" (1923), 31–34.
25 Kassil, *Mayakovsky – Himself*. cited work, p. 146.
26 Brik, L."From Memoires about Mayakovsky's Poems", *Znamja*, 1941, No. 4, p. 235.
27 Katanyan, Mayakovsky, p. 367, 379.
28 V. Shklovsky, *About Mayakovsky* (Moscow, 1940), p. 216.
29 Brik, L. cited work, p. 232.

love "heart's cold engine / was turned on again", and the break in the heart's activity symbolized on this occasion, was not a metaphorical death but an actual one; no matter how much the poet tried to find a "tiny" replacement for the great love destroyed in his life.

On the eve of his last trip to Paris, Mayakovsky signed an agreement with the theater for a "Comedy with Suicides". The theme of the comedy, according to the author is "the head-to-head collision between the European and the Soviet cultures". On September 2nd, 1929, three days after his last letter to Tatyana he tells representatives of the Artistic Theater about the content of the play, outlining the main plot as "a profound dialogue about love between two characters". According to the Pravda newspaper dated April 14th, 1930, Mayakovsky's suicide prevented him and the theater from finalizing the Comedy with Suicides.[30]

One morning in 1919, while walking with Lilya Brik on Okhotny Ryad, I said for some reason: "I can't imagine Volodya being old". A sudden and surprising reply followed: "Volodya, old? Never! He had already fired the gun twice, leaving a single bullet in the revolver. In the end the bullet will find its aim". In America this method is called "Russian roulette". On April 14th the lone bullet, which had remained in the cylinder as before, went through his heart. Mayakovsky lived and died as a gambler. Kassil was right when he said: "Whether falling in love or having a fight, writing a poem or playing pool, poker or mahjong, he embarked on each activity with his sizzling hot innards. \*\*\* He loves the very ardor of the game, its heat, nerves and risk".[31]

The first few lines of Mayakovsky's debut in print showed how he perceived the world through the gambling metaphor:

> The red and white are thrown and crumpled,
> the ducats are dumped on the green,
> and the black hands of the gathered windows
> were dealing the yellow burning cards.[32]

In the poem "About This" the same "gambling" symbolism grows into a "jeu suprême":

> My entire life
>       lay on the cards of the windows -
> The point belongs to the glass -
>             and I am losing.

---

30 Katanyan, *Mayakovsky*, p. 367, 379.
31 Kassil, L. cited work, p. 119).
32 "Night" (1912).

> The blackamoor -
> cardsharper of mirages -
> he marked
> on windows the impudent ticking of merriness.
> The deck of the glass
> is glowing with victorious
> bareknuckle brightness
> in the paws of the night.[33]

The characteristic title of this part of the poem, "Nowhere to Hide", repeats the verse from "A Cloud", "there is nowhere to hide now," and pre-figured the words in the letter written before his death: "there is no way out". The stake is life "Either, or // all or nothing":[34] In this lies the essence of Mayakovsky's hypnotic, irrepressible and smashing will to win, to "discover a different country", to "wrest joy from the coming days"; here is the key to his passion for asceticism and martyrdom, and the continuous recognition of final despair: "there is no way out". He grabbed life in a lethal embrace. Low-minded people leading banal lives maliciously called this *wishful thinking*. "The flinging Mayakovsky", as he described himself in a screenplay,[35] developed into the belief that "armies of ascetics are condemned to be volunteers / there is no mercy from people".[36]

Mayakovsky opened his first volume of collected poems, initially entitled "Five Crucifixions,"[37] with an anathema:

> Now
> I swear with all my pagan power!
> give me
> any
> beautiful
> young woman
> I won't waste my soul,
> I'll rape her
> and I'll spit in her heart with disdain!
> Eye for an eye![38]

He met someone "beautiful and young," but instead of curses for two days before dying, he carried his final letter in his pocket from April 12th through April 14th, which was dedicated "to everyone" and which ended with the lines:

---

33 "About This": 1109–1119.
34 "150 000.000", 447–448.
35 "How Do You Do", *Complete Collected Works*, XI (1947), p. 168.
36 "To Everything" (1916), 54, 55).
37 Katanyan, *Рассказы о Маяковском* ["Conversations about Mayakovsky"], p. 29.
38 "To Everything", initially published with the title "Anathema", 57–66.

> Like they say,
> > "the incident is over",
>
> the love boat
> > broke on the impact of everyday life.
>
> I don't owe life anything
> > there is no point to list
>
> reciprocal pains,
> > misfortunes
> > > and wrongs.

This stanza, with its remarkable replacement of the words "I and you" with the words "I don't owe life," is taken by Mayakovsky from his last poem. In January he finished his farewell monologue to his "comrade-descendants," entitled "At the Top of My Voice," and reputed to be as an introduction to a future poem. According to the words of a biographer "nothing is known"[39] about the concept of this future poem. This civilian, anti-lyrical introduction was to be followed by another, purely lyrical one. Fragmented drafts of this other lyrical poem were found in the poet's notebooks. Almost all of them combine into one consolidated text with slight variations.[40]

> Loves me? Loves me not? I am breaking my hands
> and my fingers
> > I'm throwing them after breaking
>
> That's how you tear up road side chamomile coronets
> after making a wish and
> you let them loose in the month of May
> May gray hair be uncovered by haircuts and shaving
> May the silver of passing years make plenty of noise
> I hope, I believe the shameful reasonableness
> will never come to me
> It's one o'clock already
> > you probably went to sleep
>
> Or maybe
> > you are going through this too
>
> [*var.* In the night the Milky Way looks on with a silver eye]
> > I am not in a hurry
> > > and I don't have a reason
> > > > to wake you up and disturb you
> > > > with lightning-like telegrams

---

**39** Katanyan, *Mayakovsky*, p. 387.
**40** See *Complete Collected Poems*, X (1941) p. 187–190 and 419–420; and photos of the four fragments before p. 189 and 421).

> the sea goes backwards
> the sea goes to sleep
> [*the last two lines are omitted in a different version*]
> like they say,
> the incident is over,
> the love boat
> broke on the impact of everyday life.
> I don't owe life anything
> there is no point to list
> reciprocal pains,
> misfortunes
> and wrongs.
> Look how quiet the world is
> The night gifted the sky with stars
> In hours like this you wake up and say
> [*var.* When you wake up grow up and say]
> to the centuries of history and creation

These verses conclude the fourth and last lyrical cycle of Mayakovsky's creation, which began with the Parisian dedications of 1928 and are connected through a common heroine.[41] He was used to "giving a farewell concert just in case".[42] The theme of a lyrical epilogue is repeated in his poetry: "Let me at least / lie down my last affection // for you to step on when you leave".[43] In general the succession of symbols connects all four cycles in one inseparable tetraptych.

Two opposite forces – the oppression and revival of lyricism constantly coexist in Mayakovsky's work. Lines like "Love me? Loves me not?" contrast strikingly with its contemporary presentation during his exhibit entitled "20 years of work": "Why should I write about Manya's love for Petya, instead of considering myself a part of that governmental organization which constructs life? *** The poet is not one who walks around like a curly lamb and bleats about lyrical love themes ***" (25.III.30).[44]

At the same time, when the "Letters" to Tatyana and Kostrov were written in Paris, the poet was composing "The Bedbug". Very soon afterwards he finished it in Moscow, while at the same time trying to get back to Paris. The poem represents the cruelest satire of the lyrical genre in general, and Mayakovsky's own

---

[41] In spite of the editor's prejudiced suggestion in *Complete Collected Works*, X (1941), p. 412, 419.
[42] "The Backbone Flute" (1915), 10–11.
[43] "Instead of a Letter" (1916), 64–66, *Complete Collected Works*, I, p. 116.
[44] *Complete Collected Works*, X, p. 373.

lyrical works in particular. "The Bedbug", affirms its author, "is a theatrical variation of the main theme about which I wrote in my poems \*\*\*"[45]

The final part of the poem "About This" was the author's request, addressed to the future "workshop of human resurrections", to a comrade chemist from the thirtieth century. Anticipating his possible doubts about resurrecting Mayakovsky, the poet swears: "I did not finish living my earthly life // on earth / I did not finish loving" \*\*\* "Resurrect me, I want to finish living!" \*\*\* "I'll do anything you want for free, // \*\*\* Do you / have // pets? / Let me be a guard for the animals. // I love animals. / If you see a little dog // \*\*\* I'm ready / to take my liver out. // I won't spare it, dear, eat it!"

The hero of the "Bedbug", Prisypkin, is an "extreme example of bourgeoisie", his engagement is an "escape from the trenches of working-class lifestyle". He undertakes exactly what the poem "About This" had reproached the poet himself, with a voice from his suffering past: "You may be adhered to their caste? // You kiss them? / Eat? / You grow a belly? // You / intend to enter / their lifestyle / their family happiness / the back way". The erotic grotesque elements of the magical comedy resemble Gogol's "Marriage". The fire during the wedding banquet "destroys all characters". Prisypkin, who does not get to marry, is "frozen in a cascade of water by the firemen",[46] and he is discovered fifty years later, in 1979. After a discussion, "the earth federation" decides to resurrect him. The "Institute of Human Resurrections" performs an experiment. Along with the man from the past mysterious ailments are also resurrected and the "ancient illness" of love becomes widespread again. On the other hand, "all attempts to turn Prisypkin into a man of the future are doomed.\*\*\* The human being protests against the fact that he was defrosted in order to be dried out" into the rational lifestyle of the new world. The bedbug, the helpful creature defrosted by happenstance together with Prisypkin, saves the day. Prisypkin is brought to his "joyful senses" when he is sent to the zoo and put in a cage for "daily bites" and for keeping the freshly acquired bedbug in "normal animal conditions".

Young Mayakovsky's constant dream about the future is derided. If in "150,000,000" he believed that "in the new world will be uncovered / the roses and dreams that were desecrated by the poet, // all / to the joy / of our / big children eyes!," in the "Bedbug" the resurrected Prisypkin is told: "The things that you talked about don't exist and nobody knows about them. There is something about roses in gardening manuals, and dreams are mentioned only in medicine

---

[45] Note published in January 1929: *Complete Collected Works*, XI (1947), 423.
[46] In the screenplay "Forget About the Fireplace", the first version of the "Bedbug", "the husband with a guitar, executing a salto-mortale [T.N. daring deadly leap] in the air, is crushed in the hole of a cellar" and snow covers him: *Complete Collected Works*, XI (1947), p. 225.

books in the chapter about dreaming in one's sleep". The defrosted Prisypkin adopts the slogan "I am for the heart," the same slogan used in the poem "A Man," but it receives an adamant answer from a female-citizen: "I don't know what that means".

Mayakovsky's comedy completes that polemic commenced in the autumn of 1927, with the love lyrics of the Komsomol poet Molchanov, and with the satyrical verses "Letter to Molchanov's lover, who was left by him" and further, with the "Meditations about Molchanov Ivan and his poetry", but also in the screenplay "Forget about the Fireplace" which was the initial version of "The "Bedbug". In "The Bedbug", he's making fun of Molchanov's own writings in the following lines: "My dear, I love another // She is more beautiful and shapely",[47] Mayakovsky paraphrases them in a "Letter to Comrade Kostrov": "I've seen / more beautiful girls, // I loved / more shapely girls", but then weakens the resemblance in the published version by replacing the initial word "loved" with "seen".[48] Mayakovsky's answer to Molchanov is "Love / Masha / and her tails, / this is your / family affair",[49] and, in "The Bedbug", the reportage about the future generation, he makes fun of the "ancient illness that becomes manifest when the human sexual energy rationally allocated to each living being for its entire lifespan suddenly condenses, within a week, into a single infectious process and thus leads to irrational and unbelievable acts". At the same time in "Letter to Comrade Kostrov" the same "infectious process" is described in terms of an ode:

> Hurricane,
>         fire,
>                 water
> are coming near in a rumble.
> Who
>       will be able
>               to reign them in?
> Can you?
>       Try.

The theme of steaming, widening humidity, a powerful water mass, is closely connected with erotic motifs, and its presence is spread throughout Mayakovsky's poetry. At the end of the tragedy "Vladimir Mayakovsky" (1913), the "children-kisses" bring a heap of tears, and the poet wanders away with his back-breaking burden of tears "to the place where / in the tight squeeze of the

---

[47] I. Molchanov, "Date", *Komsomolskaya pravda*, 21 IX 27, comp. "Bedbug", reply 58.
[48] The text is similar to Mayakovsky's note to T. and in his Moscow diary, see *Complete Collected Works*, VII, p. 450.
[49] "Meditations about Molchanov Ivan and his poetry", (1927), 15–20.

endless longing / the waves' fingers / of the ocean-bigot / eternally / tear apart his chest". In the first part of "A Cloud in Trousers" Gioconda-Maria is stolen from him: "mama! / he has a fire in his heart". He doesn't want the firemen: "Large boots are forbidden! / *** I'll do it myself. / My eyes filled with tears I'll roll away like barrels". In the lyrical lines "Aside from your love / I don't have / the sea,"[50] the images from both planes are obviously fused.

Vasili Kamensky, when remembering his Black Sea tour with Mayakovsky in January of 1914, talks about his infatuation with Maria in Odessa: "(Volodya) was pacing nervously around the room, not knowing what to do, how to act and where to go with this sudden outpouring of love. For the first time in life, he had experienced this immense feeling; he paced from corner to corner and kept saying in a low voice: What to do? What now? Write a letter? But isn't it stupid? *** "I love you. What else can I say? ***" Should I tell her everything right away? She'll get scared *** And everyone will be terrified *** They'll say, a yellow jacket and suddenly . . . ***" And he gently, *childlike*, almost helplessly told us: 'I am very restless for some reason *** Let's walk to the sea ***'"[51]

"Mayakovsky played with the waves in the sea like a little boy", remembers Viktor Shklovsky about his meeting with the poet in Norderney in the summer of 1923.[52] In the poem "About This", published at that time,[53] the image of the wet bed (in the draft he described his own infantilism with childish expressions, but erased them from the final text): "Where is this water from? / Why so much? // I cried it out myself. / Cry-baby. / Slush // Untrue / one cannot cry so much". The leaking room turns into a river, "the storm makes bass sounds, it can't ever be conquered" (compare this with "Letter to Comrade Kostrov" "Who'll be able to conquer it?"). "The river ended / the sea rose. // The ocean / is so big it hurts". An increasing procession of water symbols will merge with the "love that was not-to-be";[54] an unfinished, endless love motif.

"The thunder of the worldwide surf" will be replaced only once in Mayakovsky's poetry by the image of an ebbing tide. "The sea goes backwards // the sea goes to sleep". This theme of recession frames the image of a broken love boat in Mayakovsky's poetic epilogue, the second introduction to an unwritten poem.

The first introduction is an emotional answer given to "comrade-descendants" after they pass a plausible historical sentence on Mayakovsky – "once upon a time lived / a singer who lauded boiled water / and was the sworn enemy of

---

50 "Instead of a Letter" (1916), 34–36.
51 V. Kamensky, *Life with Mayakovsky* (Moscow, 1940), p. 89.
52 V. Shklovsky, cited work, p. 177).
53 "About This", 390–396, *Complete Collected Works*, V (1934), compare N. Aseev's note: 41.
54 See "About This", versions and drafts, p 165, 176.

uncooked water."[55] The imaginary conclusion of the professor from the future was based on the lines of a health campaign slogan written by Mayakovsky in 1928: "Uncooked water / replace with boiled! // *** One of the most important / benefits of evolved life // is a tub filled with boiled water".[56]

These slogans and advertisements are a complete antithesis to Mayakovsky's poetic work. His own words and images, but also those of others, continued to survive in Mayakovsky with amazing persistence.[57] In the spring of 1924 when he wrote for the Department of Tea: "Our right / is in our power. // Where is the power? In this *cacao*",[58] he was undoubtedly remembering his lines from "A Cloud in Trousers": "It's good to shout / when thrown to the fangs of the scaffold // Drink Van-Guten's cocoa!". The pages in the poem "About This," about a poet on a scaffold, belonged to this recent past. "The themes of his verses were almost always his own feelings", L. Brik notes correctly, and this "refers to all his poems", including his advertising texts.[59]

In addition to composing slogans for the Department of Tea, Mayakovsky also writes some bitter verses dedicated to Pushkin, which contain a jocular proposal to work also for the Fat and Bone Factory and GUM: "Everything happened: / I stood under the windows, // wrote letters, / my nerves were like jelly. // See / when / one cannot even grieve // this / Aleksandr Sergeich / is more difficult. // Come on, Mayakovsky! / go South! // Torment / your heart with rhymes // look! / the skiff of love is here, // dear Vladim Vladimich".[60] These lines, just like his slogans for the Department of Tea, mark the end to his lyrical poem "About This" from the previous year.

In the tragedy "Vladimir Mayakovsky" the author talks about how he "searched for / her / unseen soul" and when he found it: "she came out / in a blue robe, // 'Take a seat! / I've been waiting for you for a long time. / Would you like a cup of tea?'"[61] As a symbol, drinking tea signifies for Mayakovsky an emblem of ritualized ordinariness. "What is interesting in the life of a writer", he said, "we get up in the morning, drink tea".[62] But "stupid historians" incited by contemporaries, will be wrong again if this "boring and uninteresting life" with its eternal

---

55 "At the Top of My Voice" (1930), 14–16.
56 *Complete Collected Works*, IV, part 2 (1936), p. 436.
57 Brik, L. gives interesting examples, cited work, p. 282.
58 *Complete Collected Works*, IV: part 2 (1936), p. 406.
59 Brik, L. "Mayakovsky and the poetry of others", *Znamya*, 1940, no. 3, p. 161.
60 "Jubilee" (1924), 121–136.
61 "Vladimir Mayakovsky", 185–187, 915–202.
62 Katanyan, *Mayakovsky*, p. 3; "A Man", Mayakovsky's Christmas.

"morning coffee"; this ordinary appearance of the "wonderful poet" masks the wonders and passions of his true existence.

In the fantasy reality of the poem "About This", Mayakovsky is in the throes of animal suffering in the shape of a bear, and he wanders along rivers and seas, and swims off to some "Gren / lap / liub-landia?" covered in snow. [T.N. *liub* = root of the word *love*]. His relatives, scared, call on him to calm down. "But I told them // in answer to this high-pitched family choir: // So what then? You'll replace love with tea?" Mayakovsky describes the nightmare of a worldwide family tea time: "Paris, / America, / Brooklyn bridge, // Sahara, / and here / a black man drinks tea with his family / with his curly hair". A faceless parade of ordinary, stale life: "Everything stays as is, for centuries, / as it was. // They don't hit her / and the mare of everyday life doesn't move". The animal-helpers of the musty everyday life "from mattresses / lifting the rag linens, // the bedbugs raised their paws in a salute. // The samovar lit up in rays of light // and wants to give a hug with its handles". In the initial draft, "huge tea roses from wallpaper" are associated in a play on words with the samovar. Jesus, Marx, and in the draft, Lenin as well, are forced to "tug the strap of philistinism". In this tea-related context the writer recognizes with horror his own, everyday, bedbug twin.[63]

A year later, when the poet is "free of love" and the "clawed bear / lies down like a skin of jealousy", the two-lined slogans of Mayakovsky sound like a mean parody of this victorious symbolism: "Eskimo, / a bear / and a reindeer herd // drink / *the teas / from the Department of Tea*. / To the very Pole // use them / and warm yourselves up". Or see the answer given by the author of "About This" to his everyday twin: "My dear, / throw away your words, // what am I to do / with these songs?! // Send / me tea as a gift // from the Department of Tea".[64] The bear changes from an unhappy sea traveler into a rug underfoot, or into an earnest tea drinker, until he is given wings with the new wave of lyrical work in "Letter to Comrade Kostrov". By the way, the short distance to this very Department of Tea (to pay off the advance) was that very "sharp and necessary contrast", which Mayakovsky needed to be inspired with to write his poem at Esenin's death: "You passed, / like they say, / into the other world. // Emptiness ⋯ Fly away, / crushing into stars. // No need for an advance anymore" and so on.[65]

The first part of "A Cloud in Trousers" is connected to Maria from Odessa, and to "The Backbone Flute," as well as the other poems that followed it ending with "About This", all of which are addressed to Lilya Brik. "But where, my love, /

---

[63] "About This", 772–777, 790–796, 886–889, 898, 908, 915–921. Comp. versions and drafts, p.151.
[64] *Complete Collected Works*, IV: part 2, 403–404.
[65] "How do you create poems?" *Complete Collected Works*, X (1941), p. 230; "To Sergey Esenin", VIII (1936).

where, my darling, // where / in a song! / I betrayed my love? // Here / every sound / is for admitting, / for calling. // But only from the song, don't throw one word". Mayakovsky wrote this in the poem "About This",[66] and from this moment on, the lyrical poems are sidelined for years, even up to the "Letters to Tatyana" and the poems from that new cycle.

There's a fourth woman in Mayakovsky's poetry, who is from Moscow and is the main character from the last part of his tetraptych "A Cloud", who borrows the name of the girl acclaimed in the first part: "Maria! Maria! Maria! / Let me go Maria!" This figure seems to disappear from the poet's life and work when the tetraptych, recently finished, received a new dedication: "To you, Lilya". The paintings by Moscow Maria, whose real name was Antonina Gumilina, have a direct connection to Mayakovsky, as well as her unpublished poetical prose "Two in One Heart". The artistic works, exhibited in the spring of 1919 in a posthumous show that took place soon after the painter had ended her own life, closely resembled, in motifs and treatment, the main part of the autobiographical screenplay "How Are You", and the hero is the same. The screenplay, written at the end of 1926, at a time when Mayakovsky the poet was silent, was filled with his poetical motifs.[67] This "film detail" entitled "Natural Love" begins with the image of stagnant, swampy water, similar to the departure of young Mayakovsky from city still-life scenes. In his poem "Love" from 1913, "scared, the girl enveloped herself in the swamp".[68] The "regular circles of the swamp" spread on the screen after a stone is thrown into the water. There is a circle of people around the wedding, and another circle of people around the fire. The girl is part of the first circle, and Mayakovsky is part of the second circle. The circles merge, the girl and Mayakovsky exit their circles. There is a joyful love scene, built on Russian folklore images and the first, magical part of "A Man". The relevant line of the magical part: "a room, that looks like an ordinary, dirty one. *** The man takes his watch out. Nine twenty-two. The hands of the watch point in different directions. The man shows the watch hands to the girl, and says goodbye. They leave in opposite directions".

The screenplay reveals the end ahead of time: Mayakovsky reads the news section; from a dark corner of the newspaper, a girl's figure emerges, a revolver to her temple. She pulls the trigger. The poet tries to catch and divert the arm holding the revolver, but it's too late and the girl falls to the ground. He "squeezes the newspaper, pushes the tea away with disdain and falls in the chair". Mayak-

---

[66] "About This", 1238–1247.
[67] *Complete Collected Works*, XI (1947), p. 146–168, 452–479. The images used in the screenplay in opposition to Mayakovsky's poetic symbols, are extensively analyzed in W. Rudy's dissertation, *Mayakovsky and the Art of Film* (Harvard University, 1955).
[68] *Complete Collected Works*, I, p. 48).

ovsky talked about Gumilina's death (the Moscow Maria) with unexpected and unnaturally cruel disdain both in Pushkin [T.N. town near St. Petersburg] in the summer of 1919 and in Paris almost ten years later, during the time of the "Letter to Comrade Kostrov".

The screenplay contrasts, with deep disdain, the grotesque figures of tea drinking performed by the watery people, the image of the predawn sea, frames the film and the tense work of the central water pipe. Under the title "The Water Destroyers" he creates the image of "a water faucet of incredible feebleness" from which "Mayakovsky fills the samovar with water". There is also the pig-like family with a father who "grows a beard and fur on his paw holding the cup of tea" and a toddler son who brags about his dog who "doesn't pee when it wants, but when I want". There is the kettle that whistles, shakes, and then rises ridiculously "imitating" an erupting volcano. The sordid poverty of divided, distributed slime, like in the screenplay "Forget About the Fireplace", where the "melancholy yardman tries hard to splash" the wedding fire with a handheld hose. The tiny puddle of water as motif merges with the theme of self-satisfied everyman and matrimonial well-being in the poem "Vladimir Ilyich Lenin": "We / sleep / at night. // We do deeds / during the day. // We love / to crush water / in our mortar *** [T.N. to crush water in the mortar = to do something pointless] We are liked by our wife / and we are extremely / satisfied".[69]

In November of 1926, Mayakovsky was on a tour in Rostov and had a conversation in a hospital with a young woman poet who was seriously injured in an attempt to kill herself.[70] Obviously influenced by the encounter, his memory of Maria will appear in the screenplay, which was started right after the return to Moscow.

In Mayakovsky's last poems, the central motif from "A Cloud" resurfaces in the lines addressed to the Moscow Maria: "The bird / begs through its song, / sings, / is hungry and loud, // but Maria, I'm a man / ordinary, / coughed up by a night sick with tuberculosis in the dirty hand of Presnya. // Maria, do you want someone like me? / Release me, Maria! / I'll tightly squeeze the iron throat of the bell with twitchy fingers!"[71] In the poem "At the Top of My Voice" the poet appears again directly associated with "sputum producing cough" but disassociated with the song, and his actions are presented again in terms of metaphorical suffocation: "But I / tamed myself, / standing // on the throat / of my own song".[72] It's true, the theme of the twitchy spasm towards unrealizable love is apparently

---

[69] "Vladimir Ilych Lenin" *Complete Collected Works*, VI: 114–122, 135–138, (1934).
[70] Shklovsky mentioned the encounter, cited work, p. 202–203.
[71] "A Cloud in Trousers", 567–585.
[72] "At the Top of My Voice", 62–64, 209–210.

replaced with the theme of decimated lyrical work, but it's not by chance that, in the drafts of the text, these lines appear next to the gambling words of lyrical despair:

> Where to seek love in such a neper
> it would be like trying to seek amidst car-filled New-York
> a good-luck horseshoe. ***[73]

[T.N. Like the decibel, the neper is a unit in a logarithmic scale.]

The theme of female suicide plays a role in Mayakovsky's lyrical work only under cover of the screenplay, while being treated in a satiric way in newspaper-published verses such as "Marusya Took Poison" (1927), and the comedy "Bedbug". In the poem "About This" "in the silky / hands / steel" a sudden boyish suicide, which Mayakovsky is unable to stop, echoes the "event" in the screenplay.

The first of the three parts of the poem "About This" is entitled "The Ballad of the Reading Gaol": "Why jail? / Christmas. / Mess. // The windows of the little house don't have bars! // This is none of your business. / I'm telling you: jail". The draft sounds even sharper and wholehearted: "This is absolutely / none of anybody's business / other than mine. / This is my / private affair".[74] The commentators have referred to circumstances that surrounded the writing of the poem: his separation from the people closest to him and a voluntary two-month seclusion.[75] These comments might explain the jail reference, but the connection with the Reading Gaol remains unclear.

In Oscar Wilde's ballad of the same name, the focus is not as much the jail, in which, and about which, the ballad was written, as the story of the condemned and his punishment: "For he who lives more lives than one / More deaths than one must die" (Mayakovsky read the ballad in Bryusov's Russian translation). The tragic outcome of the poem "About This" is the "last death", the poet's execution: "after all / everything comes to an end. // Trembling ends too". Standing above both of the executed persons, the executioner's "merriness bubbled over". In Mayakovsky's poem, in the depths of its complex thematic elements, where "the day turned dark", there lies the allusion to the Reading ballad:

> He killed the one he loved,
>     And he'll die for it.
> Everybody kills the ones they love,
>     It's been like this across centuries,

---

[73] *Complete Collected Works*, X (1941), p. 414.
[74] "About This", 104–109; Versions and drafts, p. 121.
[75] N. Aseev, "Mayakovsky's Work on the Poem 'About This'", *Mayakovsky's Complete Collected Works*, V (1934), p. 31). Comp. L. Brik, *Znamya*, 1941, p. 232).

> That one, with mean wild eyes,
> > That one with flattering words,
> The coward, with a treacherous kiss,
> > The brave, with a blade in hand!

[Written in Cambridge, Mass. (1955), as a commentary to previously unpublished texts by Mayakovsky: *Russkij literaturnyi arxiv* of Harvard University (New York, 1956), 180–206.

## Dostoyevsky echoed in Mayakovsky's work

The eloquent title of Viktor Shklovsky's book *Pro and Contra* (Moscow, Sovetskij pisatel', 1957, 260 p.) is borrowed by the author from Book Five of *The Brothers Karamazov*. The volume was given an explanatory subtitle: "Notes about Dostoyevsky". The work is filled with accurate, witty, and sometimes unexpected intimations, oppositions, guesses and findings that enrich Dostoyevsky's literary biography in multiple directions, and is tightly connected to questions about his poetics.

The new study captivates the reader with the author's familiar sharp-sighted observations both about the role of continuity in Dostoyevsky's creative work, about artistic repetitions and their diverse functions, and "repetitive messages" within the same work. For example, in *Notes from the House of the Dead*, we find a repetition of that which has passed before, in particular, that which is rehashed from *Poor Folk* in *The Insulted and Humiliated* and from *White Nights* in *Notes from the Underground*. "Actually nothing is repeated: as always in art, there was a return to search for new artistic meanings and expression" (108). With reference to this, even more representative are "repeating quotes", brilliant examples of conversation between Dostoyevsky and Gogol, Dostoyevsky and Tolstoy, and *The Hero of Our Time*. The researcher, Shklovsky, discovered a remarkable connection between the landscape of *Crime and Punishment* and "The Bronze Horseman".

The literary dynamics of paraphrased quotes [T.N. inexact quotes from other writers' works, used as a type of literary conversation] is masterfully described by Shklovsky, as in, for example, the distinctive deflection of Lermontov's *Masquerade* and its hero, mentioned by Dostoyevsky "often and inexactly as his entire life" (157). The foreword to *Diary of a Writer* begins with a reference to the speech addressed to the Big Dipper by Werther, the suicide, and the opposition between the vastness of the starry universe and his personal fate. The image of the Big Dipper frames Shklovsky's book. He starts with a quote from Dostoyevsky, who foresees his own symbolism in Werther's farewell lines, and in his turn, ends the book with a free interpretation and treatment of the Big Dipper motif in the tragic culmination of Mayakovsky's poem "About This". Dostoyevsky's foreword somewhat anticipates Mayakovsky's star leitmotif, which previously surfaced in his earlier poems ("Listen!"), then in "Our March," with its direct address ("Hey, Big Dipper, request that we are taken to the skies alive!"). Mayakovsky's lyrical poems closely connect the image of a star with the poet's death. In the final lines of "A Cloud", "the universe sleeps, lying down with enormous ears on its paws, the stars as ticks.". In the epilogue of "A Man", which is called "Some Star", the poet, having severed his ties with the earth, lies down for centuries to come. Meanwhile, "the world attracts and tugs at him, peace is with the saints" and the requiem theme also migrates to the epilogues of Mayakovsky's social poems: "150,000,000", "V.I. Lenin", and "Good". In the poem "About This," the guiding star is given a name: in answer to the execution of the bear-poet, "the Big Dipper started singing" in the mood of the entire "starry sky" ("Big, carry along centuries-Ararats."). Even the poet himself, torn apart by bullets "the bear brother throatily recites poems to the creation amidst the noise". The same ending is repeated in Mayakovsky's farewell lyrical verses: "The night gifted the sky with stars. In hours like this you wake up and talk to the centuries of history and creation".

The poem "About This", which its author considered "one of his grandest and best works", was the most literary, most filled with quotes among his creations. Besides including references to his previous work, e.g., "A Man", "A Cloud", "Mystery-Bouffe", the themes of the new poem include parallels with Pushkin's and Lermontov's biographies, a parodic allusion to Blok's *Inadvertent Joy*, an imitation of a gypsy romance, echoes of biblical motifs, and images from Beklin's *Island of the Dead*. The title to the first part of the poem echoes Wilde's "The Ballad of Reading Gaol", and the second part of the poem echoes Gogol's "Night Before Christmas". The hero, exhausted by love and jealousy, plans to commit suicide, and his fantastic flight from, and back to Petersburg is transformed from an amusing grotesque about the adventures of the merchant Vakula, into a tragic story about Mayakovsky's passions in the second, more central part of this, his most personal of poems.

Shklovsky pauses to examine Raskolnikov's "return" to the apartment where he killed the woman as being "one of the most emotional examples of '"returns' to the crime scene" in world literature. Comparing the poem "About This", and more precisely, its second part, with Dostoyevsky's themes, he quotes Mayakovsky's fascinating comparison: "That's how, having killed, Raskolnikov came to ring the doorbell" (line: 1135). At first glance it seems that the poet doesn't compare *himself* to Raskolnikov, he only compares "his return to the house of his lover with the returns of Dostoyevsky's character". Meanwhile, the entire context is filled with allusions to *Crime and Punishment*. The segment's title, "There is Nowhere to Hide", echoes Marmeladov's words, "there is nowhere to go", words that Raskolnikov remembers when he is overcome by the thought of killing (I/IV). To be more precise, the persistent motif from "A Cloud in Trousers" as in "he doesn't have anywhere to go anymore," merges with the recollections of Marmeladov's and Raskolnikov's diatribes. The above mentioned title is followed by the poetic lines (lines: 1093): "That's how they enter your dream with an axe, measuring the foreheads of the ones who are asleep, and suddenly everything vanishes, and you can only see the axe butt". In the novel, at exactly the same time mentioned above, "Raskolnikov had a horrible nightmare", a nightmare dominated by the shouting of "Kill her with an axe. Finish her at once ***" and the awakened character exclaims: "Well, knock me down with a feather, would I really take an axe and hit her in the head, break her skull . . . " (I/IV). The theme continues: "The deed is to be done with an axe ***" (I/IV). "He pulled the axe out, *** and hit her head with the axe butt *** Now he hit with his entire strength, again and again, and just with the axe butt ***" (I/VII). In the poem, another dream follows immediately (line: 1098). "In this way, the street drums enter the dream and it is suddenly remembered, that melancholy is in that corner, and there she is behind it, the guilty one." In Raskolnikov's delirious nightmare, in which the murder is re-enacted, "he thought it was strange that he didn't remember how all of a sudden he was on the street *** The apartment is wide open to the staircase; he considered it and went in *** In the corner, between a small wardrobe and the window, he noticed an overcoat that seemed to hang on the wall *** Carefully he pulled the overcoat aside and right there saw a chair, and on the chair in the corner sat an old lady, hunched over, head bent, so that he couldn't see her face at all, but it was her" (III/VI). In draft versions of the poem, we discover the motive for the murder after the second nightmare: "*** she's wringing her hands, wringing them and crying, quieted, but if this is forever *** Having killed love, not having time to escape, I am trying to run ***". Therefore, the initial comparison with Raskolnikov's bell received a complex motivation, which offers the key to the gaol ballad in the title and verses of the first part, since the prisoner at Reading "had killed the thing he loved / And so he had to die". The formula "he executes himself", heard in the poetic lines of "War and Peace," becomes the leitmotif of the poem "About This". During the time of Mayakovsky's voluntary imprisonment, he continued working on the poem – yet, do we know who was part of his reading circle at the time? In any case, the poem keeps the memory of *Crime and Punishment* fresh by including "the unpleasant encounter" between Raskolnikov and the coachman, which in turn connects the chapter "There was pain" in Mayakovsky's poem with the lines about the coachman's whips, the ones that lashed Evgeny in "The Bronze Horseman".

Viktor Shklovsky especially thoroughly examines that period of Dostoyevsky's life and work right after the writer's return from hard labor, i.e., the time of the

*Notes.* The editing technique used in *Notes from the House of the Dead* is shown and explained in an innovative and convincing way, for example, the story about the fate of the faux criminal, where two hundred pages expressly separate the documented denial from the initial declaration of patricide. The polemic between the publications *Iskra* and *Vremya* forms a clear background for the researcher in his characterization of *Notes from the Underground*. The episode about F. Berg's poem "The Birds Flew in from Across the Sea***", published in 1863 in *Vremya* magazine, with various parodies of these birds from Berg's poem and the derisive nickname "swifts" given to Dostoyevsky and his collaborators, is subjected to additional clarification. Berg's poem was not only a recasting of an oral epic narrative poem about birds, but at the same time, was also a polemic answer to an older paraphrase of this epic poem, "Choir to the Fickle World" (1763), probably in connection with its [the poem's] one hundredth anniversary. Berg does not use the rhythm variations of the "Choir" and its folkloric prototype, but instead uses the strict frame of the regular trochaic pentameter for his birds. If Sumarokov's poem "the titmouse landed on the shore" exposed local customs and lauded the overseas lifestyle, then a hundred years hence "the gentle birds" don't search for anything except the quiet "in the thick fog". The same year in which the gentle birds poem was published, the magazine *Vremya* also published *Winter Notes about Summer Impressions* with a harsh condemnation of overseas habits and morality.

The magazine *Epokha* published *Notes from the Underground* replacing the magazine *Vremya*, which had earlier published *Winter Notes*. Dostoyevsky's friend Suslova, who, during those years, was connected with Russian political émigrés and who tried to preserve Dostoyevsky's connection to his revolutionary past, was revolted by the "scandalous story". "I don't like it when you write cynical things. They don't fit you somehow, the person I imagined you to be". The scandalous character of the piece consisted in the author's refusal to remove the contradictions he revealed.

The polyphonic quality of Dostoyevsky's work, discovered by the literary experts of the 1920's and especially by the talented Bakhtin, is defined by Shklovsky as an unending conflict between "pro and contra", which permeates his entire life and work: "Not only characters fight in Dostoyevsky's work. Separate elements of the developed subject contradict each other: the facts are elucidated in different ways, the character's psychology is self-contradicting ***" (223). Dostoyevsky's "pro and contra" conflict was inexactly understood by Saltykov-Schedrin in his polemic about *Notes from the Underground* as "a *mix* of contradictory declarations" (147). Meanwhile, a non-organic, haphazard mix can only destroy the unity of an artistic creation, but not a polyphonic conflict of declarations. Instead of a unilateral "polemic against Dostoyevsky" and his similarly flat dithyramb, Shklovsky's book demonstrates Dostoyevsky's "pro and contra" internal conflict and, succumbing to the writer's charm, transforms them into a congenial internal "pro and contra" conflict for Dostoyevsky, influenced by his typical methodology, including his "intonation breaks".

The self-contradictory psychology of the character, the irreconcilability of internal dialogue finds a better expression in the literary motif of "the double." In his comprehensive chapter about "Doubles and about *The Double*", despite its sketchiness, Shklovsky comments on Dostoyevsky's persistent attempts to conquer the idea of *The Double*. In Dostoyevsky's *Diary of a Writer* he confesses he "never created anything in literature" more serious than this. Shklovsky compares Dostoyevsky's "Petersburg Poem" and the new treatment given the same theme in Mayakovsky's Moscow poem "About This", endowing the poet with "several doubles". The "pro and contra" dispute is between the first person of the poem and the Christ-like figure of the Komsomol member who is interspersed in the poem and later commits suicide. The verses describe him: "It's amazing how much he resembles me". In predictable fashion, even after this young double dies, the poet's dispute with himself about "a walk in life after death" continues both in and after the poem. The other double of the autobiographical hero of the poem "About This" is a "man from seven years ago" – the autobiographical hero of the older poem "A Man", who calls from the past to "stop the suffering", while the younger double doesn't find a premise for an exchange in the "time being." Furthermore, the lyrical 'I' of the poem "About This" has a third and insufferable, bedbug double: "*** I ran and saw *** I'm coming towards myself with gifts under my arms". It continues with the same double "*** the most terrifying: height, skin, clothes, even the gait is mine! In a word, in him I recognized myself, we are like twins, me and myself". This is the same double in whom the hero of "A Man" tries to identify the hero of "About This": "You may be adhered to their caste? You kiss them? Eat with them? You grow a belly? You intend to enter their lifestyle, their family happiness the back way?". This is the same double, Prisypkin, described in a comedic way in the "Bedbug". The author talked to us about the "Bedbug" as being a caricature of his poem right after he finished it and it was performed. It wasn't a coincidence that the actor Ilyinsky, who according to his own admission, used a parody of Mayakovsky's gait for his role, and who delighted Mayakovsky with his interpretation of Prisypkin.

In 1930,[76] in the article "About a Generation Who Wasted Its Poets" ['On a Generation that Squandered Its Poets' by Jakobson, *Language in Literature* (1987)], I

---

[76] This quotation is translated in *Language in Literature* (1987: 275/6) is as follows:
"The poetry of Majakovskij from his first verses, in "A Slap in the Face of Public Taste", to his last lines is one and indivisible. It represents the dialectical development of a single theme. It is an extraordinarily unified symbolic system. A symbol one thrown out only as a kind of hint will later

tried to demonstrate that "Mayakovsky's poetic creation, from his first poems \*\*\* to his last lines is unitary and indivisible. There is a dialectic development of a unitary theme. There is an unusual unity of symbols. A symbol that was alluded to in passing is developed and offered from a different angle. \*\*\* An image that was initially humorously presented is shown in a different way, or vice versa, a sad motif is repeated in a parodical way. This is not contemptuous of yesterday's belief, as these are two sides of a unitary symbolism, the tragic and the comic, like in medieval theatre." In a note to "Mayakovsky's Unknown Poems" (*Novosel'ie*, nr. 2, New York, 1942), I declared, and I continue to declare to this day, that although "not too long ago there were very serious discussions whether or not Mayakovsky is a poet, and if he is a poet, is he only a poet of the lyrical pieces 'A Cloud', 'The Flute' and so on; or is he only a poet in regard to his social satire and odes". "All of these attempts to disregard some things from Mayakovsky's work \*\*\* are recently abandoned to the distant past of the archives. Everything that Mayakovsky wrote is unitary, inseparable and inextricable". Therefore, I wholly agree with G. Cheremin's words that it is impossible to examine the political, agitational poetry as "something alien in regards to Mayakovsky's original work" (*Voprosy literatury*, nr. 8, 1957: 250).

The love poems, or the poetry of the heart, as Mayakovsky referred to it in an old-fashioned way, and the lyrical-epical poems on social themes are equally essential and lively genres in his work. We will not negate the distinct fundamental differences between the genres. It is true that often Mayakovsky's love poetry, from "A Cloud in Trousers" to the "Letters" from Paris in 1928, is sometimes closely tied with social problems, but, on the other hand, personal, love motifs (e.g. "War and Peace": "Hello, my love!"; "Good": "eyes like the sky, the eyes of my beloved") sometimes surface in his epic poems. It is, however, true that common characteristics bring the themes of both genres closer to each other. For example, regardless of the genre, all major things that young Mayakovsky wrote before in "About This" and "The Fifth International," end in the future. However, the major world events (war and peace, revolution and the world) which are characteristic of Mayakovsky's social poems, are opposed in his lyrical

---

be developed and presented in a totally new perspective. He himself underlines these links in his verse by alluding to earlier works. In the poem "About That" ("Pro èto"), for instance, he recalls certain lines from the poem "Man" ("Čelovek"), written several years earlier, and in the latter poem he refers to lyrics of an even earlier period. An image at first offered humorously may later and in a different context lose its comic effect, or conversely, a motif developed solemnly may be repeated in a parodistic vein. Yet this does not mean that the beliefs of yesterday are necessarily held up to scorn; rather, we have here two levels, the tragic and the comic, of a single symbolic system as in the medieval theater".

poems, by tragedy in personal love, inescapable loneliness, and martyrdom. The polyphonic character of Mayakovsky's poetry consists in the interruption of both unmerged genres. This is not a theory imposed from the outside and backdated about the literary inheritance of a dead poet. Mayakovsky wrote many times in his poems and letters, and made oral declarations about the alternation of genres and their dramatic collisions; about the fight between the lyrical and anti-lyrical inspiration. This is not a fight that was imposed upon the poet. No one could have imposed anything upon such a stubborn poet. "I have to write from a sense of mandatory obligation", indicated his poetic line about poetry in answer to the upcoming "social order". He creates these poems, although they will be met with censorship, as happened before the revolution with "War and Peace", or lengthy negotiations around the permission to publish "One Hundred and Fifty Millions", which faced many obstacles and was disparaged in the beginning. The dispute of pro and contra and the pressure of writing lyrical poems, drove him again to write "about that and about this." The attacks by others in response to his lyrical poems – became the internal law of Mayakovsky's life and literary path. According to the prologue to the poem "About This," the lyrical theme dominated the poet, but he talks about overcoming the lyrical inspiration in metaphoric terms, as in. suffocation, in the prologue "At the Top of My Voice", as if to an unwritten poem: "But I tamed myself, standing on the throat of my own song".

It is not coincidental that the notes about Mayakovsky's poetry serve as a background for the notes about Dostoyevsky in Shklovsky's book *Pro and Contra*. The researcher calls upon us not to confuse the polyphonic structure of confrontational lines [T.N. i.e.form] and the discord and gibberish of contradictory declarations [T.N. i.e.content], rather he prompts us to meditate about the polyphonic character of the opposing genres [T.N. i.e.forms], which shouldn't be confused with the silly chaos of discordant dissonance [T.N. i.e.content].

[Notes originally published in *International Journal of Slavic Linguistics and Poetics*, I (1959: 305–310).]

# References

Aizlewood, Robin. 2000. *Two Essays on Maiakovskii's Verse*. London: School of Slavonic and East European Studies, University College London.
Aizlewood, Robin. 1989. *Verse Form and Meaning in the Poetry of Vladimir Maiakovskii*. London: The Modern Humanities Research Association.
Allen, Kathryn. 2008. *Metaphor and Metonymy: A Diachronic Approach*. Chichester: Wiley Blackwell.
Almereyda, Michael. 2008. *Night Wraps up the Sky: Writings by and About Mayakovsky*. New York: Farrar, Straus and Giroux.
Andersen, Henning. 1991. On the Projection of Equivalence Relations into Syntagms. In Linda Waugh & Stephen Rudy (eds.), *New Vistas in Grammar: Invariance and Variation*; 287–311. Amsterdam: Benjamins.
Anon. 1910–1913. *Sadok Sudei I and II*. Peterburg: Zhuravl.
Anon. 1953. *Pearl*. Edited by Eric Valentine Gordon. Oxford: Clarendon Press.
Aristotle. 2006. *The Art of Rhetoric*. Translated by John Henry Freese. Cambridge MA: Harvard University Press.
Armstrong, Daniel & Cornelis Hendrick van Schooneveld. 1977. Roman Jakobson and Avant Garde Art. In Daniel Armstrong & Cornelis Hendrick van Schooneveld (eds.), *Roman Jakobson: Echoes of His Scholarship*, 503–514. Lisse: Netherlands: The Peter de Ridder Press.
Attridge, Derek. 1995. *Poetic Rhythm: An Introduction*. Cambridge: Cambridge University Press.
Augst, Bertrand. 1981. Metz's Move. *Camera Obscura: A Journal of Feminism and Film Theory* 7 (Spring). 31–41.
Augustine. 1998. *Confessions*. Edited by Henry Chadwick. Oxford: Oxford University Press.
Augustine. 1975. *De Dialectica*. With an introduction and translated by Darrell Jackson. Dordrecht: Reidel.
Austen, Jane. 2006. Barbara Benedict & Deidre Le Faye (eds.), *The Cambridge Edition of the Works of Jane Austen: Northanger Abbey*. 261. Cambridge. Cambridge University Press.
Balzer, Wolfgang & Heide Göttner. 1983. A Theory of Literature Logically Reconstructed: Reconsideration of the Example: Roman Jakobson. *Poetics: International Review for the Theory of Literature* 12, (6). 489–510.
Banjanin, Milica. 1993. Between Symbolism and Futurism: Impressions by Day and by Night in Elena Guro's City Series. *Slavic and East European Journal* 37 (1). 67–84.
Banjanin, Milica. 2000. The City as Framed Spectacle. In Karen Ryan & Barry Scherr (eds.), *Twentieth-century Russian Literature: selected papers from the fifth world congress of Central and East European Studies*, 42–57. Basingstoke, New York. Macmillan.
Banjanin, Mladen & Elena Guro. 1986. Nature and the City in the Works of Elena Guro. *The Slavic and East European Journal* 30 (2). 230–246.
Barry, Peter. 2000. *Contemporary British Poetry and the City*. Manchester: Manchester University Press.
Barsch, Achim & Helmut Hauptmeier. 1983. Speculations about Jakobson: Logical Reconstruction from a Literary Point of View. *Poetics: International Review for the Theory of Literature* 12 (6). 537–565.
Barthes, Roland. 1977. *Image-Music-Text*. Translated by Stephen Heath. Glasgow: Fontana/Collins.
Barthes, Roland. 2000. *Mythologies*. Translated by Annette Lavers. London: Vintage.

Bartlett, Elizabeth. 1995. *Two Women Dancing: New and Selected Poems*. Northumberland: Bloodaxe Books.
Baudelaire, Charles. 1993. *The Flowers of Evil*. Oxford: Oxford University Press.
Baum, Paull Franklin.1963. *Anglo-Saxon Riddles of the Exeter Book*. Durham, North Carolina: Duke University Press.
Bennett, Jamie. L. 2008. *Elena Guro: and the Holy Fool as Prophet, Performer and Poet* Columbia University. Partial fulfilment of PhD Dissertation. ProQuest Dissertations Publishing. 3299246. (last accessed 1 October 2019).
Bennett, James Tyler. 2021. Incompatibility, unlimited semiosis, aesthetic function. In Elin Sütiste, Remo Gramigna, Jonathan Griffin & Silvi Salupere (eds.), *(Re)considering Roman Jakobson*, 149–163. Tartu, Estonia: University of Tartu Press.
Bergman, Denise (ed.). 1992. *City River of Voices*. Albuquerque, New Mexico: West End Press.
Bertram, Vicki. 2005. *Gendering Poetry: Contemporary Women and Men Poets*. London: Pandora.
Blake, William. 1923. *Songs of Experience* London https://www.bl.uk/collection-items/william-blakes-songs-of-innocence-and-experience Slide 44: 48. A facsimile of a coloured and gilded copy of the first edition. Liverpool [1794]. (last accessed 3 October 2019).
Bohn, Willard. 1981. Metaphor and Metonymy in Apollinaire's Calligrams. *Romanic Review* 72 (2). 166–181.
Boym, Svetlana. 1994. *Common Places: Mythologies of Everyday Life in Russia*. Cambridge. Mass and London: Harvard University Press.
Bradford, Richard. 1994. *Roman Jakobson: Life, Language, Art*. London: Routledge.
Bredin, Hugh. 1984a. Metonymy. *Poetics Today* 5 (1). 45–58.
Bredin, Hugh. 1984b. Roman Jakobson on Metaphor and Metonymy. *Philosophy and Literature* 8 (1). 89–103.
Brooke-Rose, Christine. 1954. *Gold*. Ashford, Kent: The Hand and Flower Press.
Brooke-Rose, Christine. 1958. *A Grammar of Metaphor*. London: Martin Secker and Warburg.
Brooke-Rose, Christine. 1976. *A Structural Analysis of Pound's Usura Canto: Jakobson's Method Extended and Applied to Free Verse*. The Hague: Mouton.
Bruhn, Mark. 2006. Cognition and Representation in Wordsworth's London. *Studies in Romanticism*. 45 (2). 157–177.
Bühler, Karl. 2011. *Theory of Language: The Representational Function of Language*. Translated by Donald Fraser Goodwin. Amsterdam/Philadelphia: John Benjamins Publishing Company.
Burke, Kenneth. 1969. *A Grammar of Motives*. Berkeley, London: University of California Press.
Cameron, Michael. 2012. *Christ Meets Me Everywhere: Augustine's Early Figurative Exegesis*. New York: Oxford University Press.
Carrick, Rosie. 2017. *Vladimir Mayakovsky: The Language of Revolution*. Brighton: University of Sussex. PhD thesis. http://sro.sussex.ac.uk/id/eprint/66949/.
Cassedy, Steven. 1985. *Selected Essays of Andrey Belyj*. Berkeley: University of California Press.
Chandler, James & Kevin Gilmartin (eds.). 2005. *Romantic Metropolis: the urban scene of British culture, 1780–1840*, 1–41. Cambridge: Cambridge University Press.
Chatman, Seymour. 1973. *Approaches to Poetics: Selected Papers from the English Institute*. New York: Columbia University Press.
Chatman, Seymour. 1978. *Story and Discourse: Narrative Structure in Fiction and Film*. Ithaca: Cornell University Press.

Cicero. 1942. *De Oratore Books I-III*. Translated by Edward William Sutton & Harris Rackham). Cambridge MA: Heinemann and Harvard University Press.
Cicero. 1954. *Rhetorica ad Herennium*. Translated by Harry Caplan. Cambridge, MA. London: Harvard University Press: Heinemann.
Cobley, Paul. 2001a. Analysing Narrative Genres *Signs Systems Studies* 29 (2). 479–502.
Cobley, Paul. 2001b. *Narrative*. London: Routledge.
Cobley, Paul (ed.). 2001c. *The Routledge Companion to Semiotics and Linguistics*. London: Routledge.
Cobley, Paul (ed.). 2010. *The Routledge Companion to Semiotics and Linguistics*. Abingdon: Routledge.
Cobley, Paul. 2019. Peirce in Contemporary Semiotics. In Tony Jappy (ed.) *The Bloomsbury Companion to Contemporary Peircean Semiotics*. London. Bloomsbury Publishing.
Coghill Mary. 1980. *The Politics of Matriarchy*. London: Matriarchy Study Group.
Coghill, Mary. 2006. *Designed to Fade*. Exeter: Shearsman Books.
Coghill, Mary. 2011. *A Theory and Praxis of a City Poetic: Jakobson, Poetic Function and City Space; Women, Deixis and the Narrator: A City Poem: "Shades of Light: A Triumph of City"*. London: London Metropolitan University PhD thesis. Available https://ethos.co.uk.
Coghill, Mary. 2012. *Shades of Light: A Triumph of City*. London: www.cityofpoetry.co.uk.
Coghill, Mary. 2017. *Assay of Blood and Gold: London Poems*: www.cityofpoetry.co.uk.
Conley, Tim. 2014. City Transit Gloria: Mass Movements and Metropolitan Poetics. *Journal of Modern Literature*. 37 (4). 91–108.
Crane, Hart. 2001. *The Complete Poems of Hart Crane*. Liveright: New York and London.
Cronan, Dennis. 2016. The Poetics of Poetic Words in Old English. In Leonard Neidorf, Rafael J. Pascuel et al. (eds.), *Old English Philology: Studies in Honour of R.D. Fulk*. 256–275. Boydell and Brewer. Woodbridge: Suffolk.
Crowther, Claire. 2006. *Stretch of Closures*. Exeter: Shearsman Books.
Cuddon, John Anthony. 1999. *The Penguin Dictionary of Literary Terms and Literary Theory*. London: Penguin Books.
Culler, Jonathan. 1971. Jakobson and the Linguistic Analysis of Literary Texts. *Language and Style* 5. 53–66.
Culler, Jonathan. 2001. ACLA Presidential Address [Online] *Comparative Literature* 53 (3). vii. 12 pages.
Culler, Jonathan. 2002. *Structuralist Poetics: Structuralism, Linguistics and the Study of Literature*. London: Routledge [1975].
Culler, Jonathan. 2002a. *The Pursuit of Signs: Semiotics, Literature, Deconstruction*. London: Routledge [Cornell University Press. 1981].
Cureton, Richard. 2000. Jakobson Revisited. *Journal of English Linguistics*. 28 (4). 354–392.
Daalder, Saskia & Andreas Musolff. 2011. Foundations of Pragmatics in Functional Linguistics. In Wolfram Bublitz & Neal Norrick (eds.), *Foundations of Pragmatics*, 229–260. Berlin: De Gruyter.
Daintith, John & Elizabeth Martin (eds.). 2005. *Oxford Dictionary of Science*. Oxford: Oxford University Press.
Dalgard, Per. 1987. The City as Symbol and Metaphor: Analyses of Selected Urbanistic Poems by Brjusov, Blok and Majakovskij. *Slavica Othiniensia* 9. 3–22.
Dancygier, Barbara & Eve Sweetser (eds.). 2014. *Figurative Language*. Cambridge: Cambridge University Press.

Daniel, Julia. 2017. Carl Sandberg and the Living American City. In *Modern American Poetry, Landscape Architecture, and City Planning*. 19–49. Charlottesville VA. University of Virginia Press.
Data Shadow. www.techopedia.com. (last accessed 16. 8.21).
Daylight, Russell. 2017. Saussure and the Model of Communication. *Semiotica* 2017 (217). 173–194.
Deely, John. 2002. The Absence of Analogy. *The Review of Metaphysics* 55 (March). 521–550.
Deely, John. 2006. On 'Semiotics' as Naming the Doctrine of Signs. *Semiotica* 158 (1–4). 1–33.
Deignan, Alice. 2005. *Metaphor and Corpus Linguistics*. Amsterdam: John Benjamins.
Denroche, Charles. 2015. *Metonymy and Language: A New Theory of Linguistic Processing*. New York: Routledge.
Denroche, Charles. 2018. Text Metaphtonomy: The Interplay of metonymy and metaphor in Discourse. *Metaphor and the Social World*. 8(1). 1–24.
Dirven, René. 1993. Metonymy and Metaphor: Different Mental Strategies of Conceptualisation. *Leuvense Bijdragen: Leuven Contributions in Linguistics and Philology* 82 (1). 1–28.
Dirven, René & Ralf Pörings (eds.). 2003. *Metaphor and Metonymy in Comparison and Contrast*. Berlin: Mouton de Gruyter.
Drake, James. 1998. The Naming of the Disease: How Jakobson's Essay on Aphasia Initiated Postmodernist Deceits. *Times Literary Supplement*. 4 Sept. 14/15.
Drake, James. 2002. The academic Brand of Aphasia: Where Postmodernism and the Science Wars Came From. *Knowledge, Technology, & Policy*. 15. (1 & 2). 13–175.
Duffy, Carol Ann. 2004. *New and Selected Poems*. London: Picador.
Durst-Andersen, Per. 2008. Linguistics as Semiotics. Saussure and Bühler Revisited. *Signs* (2). 1–29.
Durst-Andersen, Per & Paul Cobley. 2018. The Communicative Wheel: Symptom, Signal and Model in Multimodal Communication. *Semiotica*. 225. 77–102.
Eco, Umberto. 1977. *A Theory of Semiotics*. London: Macmillan.
Èikenbaum (Eichenbaum), Boris. 1924. Ann Shukman & Michael O'Toole (eds.). *Formalist Theory (Russian Poetics in Translation* Book 4*)*. Kindle Locations. 612–617.
Eliot, Thomas Stearns. 1948. *Selected Essays*. London: Faber.
Eliot, Thomas Stearns. 1974. *Collected Poems: 1909–1962*. London: Faber.
Elleström, Lars. 2016. A Medium Centred Model of Communication. *Semiotica*. 224. 269–293.
Engler, Rudolf & Carol Sanders. 2008. *Ferdinand de Saussure: Writings in General Linguistics*. Oxford: Oxford University Press [2006].
Erlich, Victor. 1981. *Russian Formalism: History – Doctrine*. New Haven: Yale University Press [1965].
Esh, Sylvan. 1993. Pound, and Jakobson: The Metaphorical Principle in The Cantos. *Paideuma: A Journal Devoted to Ezra Pound Scholarship*. 22 (1–2). 129–43.
Fauconnier, Gilles & Mark Turner. 2002. *The Way We Think*. New York: Basic Books.
Federov, Andrei. 2021. *Federov's Introduction to Translation*. Edited by Brian James Baer. London. Routledge [1953].
Feinstein, Elaine. 2010. *Cities*. Manchester: Carcanet.
Ferreiro, Alfredo Marrio. 2015. *El hombre que se comió un autobús: poesía y prosa de vanguardia completas*. Sevilla: Grupo Renacimiento, Ediciones Ulises.
Firth, John R. 1957. *Papers in Linguistics (1934–1951)*. Oxford: Oxford University Press.
Fisher, Allen. 2004. *Gravity*. Cambridge: Salt Publishing.
Fisher, Allen. 2005. *Place*. Hastings: Reality Street Editions.

Fisher, Allen. 2007. *Leans*. Cambridge: Salt Publishing.
Fisher, Roy. 1996. *The Dow Low Drop: New and Selected Poems*. Newcastle: Bloodaxe.
Fludernik, Monica. 1989/90. Jesperson's Shifters: Reflections on Deixis and Subjectivity in Language. *Beiträge zur Sprachwissenschaft* 15/16. 97–116.
Fludernik, Monica. 1991. Shifters and Deixis: Some Reflections on Jakobson, Jesperson and Reference. *Semiotica* 86 (3/4). 193–230.
Forrest-Thomson, Veronica. 1978. *Poetic Artifice: A Theory of Twentieth-Century Poetry*. Manchester: Manchester University Press.
Fowler, Henry Watson. 2004. *Fowler's Modern English Usage*. Oxford: Oxford University Press.
Gallo, Ernest. (ed.). 1971. *The Poetria Nova and its sources in early rhetorical doctrine*. The Hague: Mouton.
Garnett, Richard. 1893. *Poems*. London: Mathews and Lane; Boston, Copeland and Day.
Gasparov, Boris. 2014. Futurism and Phonology: The Futurist Roots of Jakobson's Approach to Language. *Ulbandus Review*.16. 84–112.
Geeraerts, Dick. 2010. *Theories of Lexical Semantics*. Oxford: Oxford University Press.
Genette, Gérard. 1980. *Narrative Discourse: An Essay in Method*. Translated by Jane Lewin. Ithaca: Cornell University Press.
Genette, Gerard Thais Morgan. 1989. Modern Mimology: The Dream of a Poetic Language. *PMLA*. 104 (2). 202–214.
Goodman, Ann. 1981. *The Communicative Nature of Poetic Metaphor: A Study Based on the Work of Roman Jakobson and Kenneth Burke*. Chicago: University of Chicago PhD Thesis.
Goossens, Louis. 1990. Metaphtonymy: The Interaction of metaphor and Metonymy n expressions for linguistic action. *Cognitive Linguistics*. I.3. 323–340.
Gorlée, Dinda. 2008. Jakobson and Peirce: Translational Intersemiosis and Symbiosis in Opera. *Sign Systems Studies* 36 (2). 341–374.
Gozzi, Raymond Jr. 1999. *The Power of Metaphor in the Age of Electronic Media*. New Jersey: Hampton Press Inc.
Green, Keith. 1992a. *A Study of Deixis in Relation to Lyric Poetry*. Sheffield: University of Sheffield PhD thesis. Available https://ethos.bl.uk. (last accessed 3 September 2010).
Green, Keith. 1992b. Deixis and the Poetic Persona. *Language and Literature* 1 (2). 121–134.
Green, Keith (ed). 1995. *New Essays in Deixis: Discourse, Narrative, Literature*. Amsterdam: Rodopi.
Guro, Elena. 1983. *The Little Camels of the Sky*. Translated by Kevin O'Brien. Ann Arbor: Ardis.
Guro, Elena. Nina Gourianova & Anna Lunggren (eds.). 1995. *Elena Guro: Writings from the archives*. Stockholm: Stockholm University Press.
Hamacher, Werner. 2019. What Remains to be Said: On Twelve Ways of Looking at Philology. In Gerhard Richter & Ann Smock, *Give the Word: Responses to Werner Hamacher's "95 Theses on Philology"*, 217–354. Lincoln: University of Nebraska Press.
Harris, Roy. 1987. *Reading Saussure: A Critical Commentary on the Cours de Linguistique Générale*. London: Duckworth.
Harris, Roy. 2001. *Saussure and His Interpreters*. Edinburgh: Edinburgh University Press. *JSTOR*, www.jstor.org/stable/10.3366/j.ctv125jrcw.1. (last accessed 8 July 2021).
Head, Henry. 1915. Hughlings-Jackson on Aphasia and Kindred Affections of Speech. Parts I and II *Brain* 38 (July). 1–27.

Heffernan, Margaret. 3 November 2014: 20.30. *Analysis: Just Culture* BBC. https://www.bbc.co.uk/programmes/b04n31d2 includes Interview with Bill McAleer of General Motors. (last accessed 28 September 2018).
Helle, Lillian. 1994. Metaphor and Metonymy: a Theme with Variations. *Scando-Slavica* 40: 37–52.
Holenstein, Elmar. 1976. *Roman Jakobson's Approach to Language: Phenomenological Structuralism*. Translated C Schelbert & T Schelbert. Bloomington: Indiana University Press.
Holenstein, Elmar. 1983. Five Jakobsonian Principles of Poetics. *American Journal of Semiotics*. 2 (3). 23–34.
Hopkins, Gerard Manley. Humphrey House & Graham Storey (eds.). 1959. *The Journals and Papers of Gerard Manley Hopkins*. London: Oxford University Press.
Hopkins, Gerard Manley. Katherine Phillips (ed.). 2009. *The Major Works including all the poems and selected prose*. Oxford: Oxford University Press.
Howard, Jeremy.1992. *The Union of Youth*. Manchester: Manchester University Press.
Jackson, John Hughlings.1866. Notes on the Physiology and Pathology of Language. *Brain* (1915 reprint) 38. 48–58.
Jackson, John Hughlings. 1868. Notes on the physiology and pathology of the nervous system. *Medical Times and Gazette* (vol. ii). 65–71.
Jackson, John Hughlings. 1879. On affections of speech from disease of the brain. *Brain* (vol. i). 107–129.
Jackson, John Hughlings. 1893. Words and other symbols in mentation. *Medical Press and Circular*. 30.8 (vol. ii). 107–129.
Jakobson, Roman. 1959. Dostoyevsky Echoed in Mayakovsky's Work. *International Journal of Slavic Linguistics and Poetics*. 1/2: 305–10.
Jakobson, Roman. 1967. "Une Microscopie du dernier "Spleen" dans les Fleurs du mal. *Tel Quel* 29. 12–24 (also: *Selected Writings III*. Stephen Rudy (ed.). 1981. The Hague: Mouton. 465–481).
Jakobson, Roman & Lawrence G. Jones. 1970. *Shakespeare's Verbal Art in "Th'Expence of Spirit"*. The Hague: Mouton.
Jakobson, Roman. 1971a. *Selected Writings, Vol. II Word and Language*. The Hague: Mouton.
Jakobson, Roman. 1971b. *Fundamentals of Language*. Edited by Morris Halle. The Hague: Mouton.
Jakobson, Roman. 1971c. Toward a linguistic classification of aphasic impairments. In *Selected Writings II: Word and Language*. The Hague, Paris: Mouton, 289–306. [1963].
Jakobson, Roman, [1977 (sic)] (1972) (eds.). Verbal Communication. *Scientific American* 227 (3). 72–80. Also: 1962. *Selected Writings Vol. 10*: Stephen Rudy (ed.). 81–92. S'-Gravenhage. Mouton.
Jakobson, Roman. 1973. Modern Russian Poetry: Velimir Khlebnikov. In Edward James Brown (ed.). *Major Soviet Writers: Essays in Criticism*, 55–82. Oxford: Oxford University Press.
Jakobson Roman (with Tzvetan Todorov). 1973. *Questions de Poétique*. Éditions Du Seuil: Paris.
Jakobson, Roman. 1977. *Yeats "Sorrow of Love" Through the Years*. Lisse: Peter de Ridder Press.
Jakobson, Roman. 1978. *Six Lectures on Sound and Meaning*. Translated by John Mepham. Hassocks: Harvester Press. [1942].
Jakobson, Roman. 1979a. *Selected Writings, Vol 5, On Verse, Its Masters and Explorers*. Кпоздней Лирике Маяковского: 382–405. translated as: About Mayakovsky's Later Lyrical Poems; and Достоевский В Отголосках Маяковского: 406–412. translated as: Dostoyevsky Echoed In Mayakovsky's Work; 382–412: The Hague, Mouton.

Jakobson, Roman. Stephen Rudy & Linda Waugh (eds.). 1979b. *Selected Writings, Vol V: On Verse, its Masters and Explorers*. The Hague: Mouton.
Jakobson, Roman & Linda Waugh. 1979c. *The Sound Shape of Language*. Brighton: Harvester Press.
Jakobson, Roman & Jurij Tynjanov. 1980. Problems in the Study of Language and Literature. Translated by Herbert Eagle. *Poetics Today* 2 (1a). 29–31.
Jakobson, Roman & Susan Kitron. 1980b. On Poetic Intentions and Linguistic Devices in Poetry: A Discussion with Professors and Students at the University of Cologne *Poetics Today* 2 (1a). 87–89.
Jakobson, Roman. 1980c. *The Framework of Language*. Ann Arbor: University of Michigan.
Jakobson, Roman. 1980d. Sign and System of Language: A Reassessment of Saussure's Doctrine. Translated by Benjamin Hrushovski. *Poetics Today* 2 (1a). 33–38.
Jakobson, Roman. Stephen Rudy (ed.). 1981. *Selected Writings III: The Poetry of Grammar and Grammar of Poetry*. The Hague, Paris, New York. Mouton.
Jakobson, Roman & Krystyna Pomorska. 1983. *Dialogues* Cambridge: Cambridge University Press.
Jakobson, Roman. 1984. Shifters, Verbal Categories and The Russian Verb. In Roman Jakobson, Linda Waugh & Morris Halle (eds.), *Russian and Slavic Grammar: Studies 1931–1981*, 41–58. Berlin: Mouton.
Jakobson, Roman. Krystyna Pomorska & Stephen Rudy (eds.). 1985a. *Verbal Art, Verbal Sign, Verbal Time*. Oxford: Basil Blackwell.
Jakobson, Roman. Stephen Rudy (ed.). 1985b. *Selected Writings, Vol. VII Contributions to Comparative Mythology, Studies in Linguistics and Philology*. Berlin: Mouton.
Jakobson, Roman. Stephen Rudy (ed.). 1985c. From Jaljagrov's Letters. *Selected Writings, Vol. VII Contributions to Comparative Mythology, Studies in Linguistics and Philology*. Berlin: Mouton. 357–361.
Jakobson, Roman. Krystyna Pomorska & Stephen Rudy (eds.). 1987. *Language in Literature*. Cambridge MA: Belknap Press of Harvard University Press.
Jakobson, Roman. Stephen Rudy (ed. and trans.). 1992. *My Futurist Years*. New York: Marsilio Publishers.
Jaljagrov. pseudonym: Roman Jakobson. Stephen Rudy (ed. and trans. ). 1992. *My Futurist Years*. New York: Marsilio Publishers.
Jangfeldt, Bengt. 2014. *Mayakovsky: A Biography*. Chicago: Chicago University Press.
Jeffries, Lesley. 2008. The Role of Style in Reader-involvement: Deictic shifting in Contemporary Poems. *Journal of Literary Semantics* 35. 69–85.
Jeffries, Lesley & Peter Sansom (eds.). 2000. *Contemporary Poems: Some Critical Approaches*. Huddersfield: Smith/Doorstep Books.
Jeffries, Lesley & Dan McIntyre. 2010. *Stylistics*. Cambridge: Cambridge University Press.
Jensen, Kjeld Bjørnager. 1977. *Russian Futurism, Urbanism and Elena Guro*. Aarhus: Arkona.
Jespersen, Otto. 1923. *Language: Its Nature, Development, and Origin*. New York: Holt, Allen & Unwin.
Jones, David. 1972. *Anathémata*. London: Faber and Faber.
Joseph, John. 2001. *Landmarks in Linguistic Thought II*. London: Routledge.
Jusdanis, Gregory. 1985. The Poetics of Roman Jakobson: Aesthetics or Semiotics? In John Deely (ed.), *Semiotics 1984*, 267–275. Lanham MD: University Press of America.
Khlebnikov, Velimir. Paul Schmidt & Charlotte Douglas (trans.). 1985. *The King of Time: Selected Writings of the Russian Futurian*. Cambridge, MA: Harvard University Press.

Kiparsky, Paul. 1983. The Grammar of Poetry. *International Journal of Slavic Linguistics and Poetics* 27. 20–29 (Suppl.).

Kruchenykh, Aleksei, Ivan Kliun, & Kazmir Malevich. 1916. *Tainye poroki akademikov (The Secret Vices of Academicians)*. Moscow: no publisher.

Kruchenykh, Aleksei & Olga Rozanova. 1916. *Zaumnaia gniga*. Moscow: no publisher. https://rosettaapp.getty.edu/delivery/DeliveryManagerServlet?dps_pid=IE538403.

Kursell, Julia. 2010. First Person Plural: Roman Jakobson's Grammatical Fictions. *Studies in East European Thought*. 62. 217–236.

Lakoff, George & Mark Turner. 1989. *More Than Cool Reason: A Field Guide to Poetic Metaphor*. Chicago: University of Chicago Press.

Lakoff, George & Mark Johnson. 2003. *Metaphors We Live By*. Chicago: University of Chicago Press.

Lass, Andrew. 2006. Poetry and reality: Roman O. Jakobson and Claude Lévi-Strauss. In Christopher Benfey & Karen Remmler (eds.), *Artists, Intellectuals and World War II: The Pontigny Encounters at Mount Holyoke College, 1942–1944*, 173–184. Amherst: University of Massachusetts Press.

Lenin, Vladimir. Written: October 2, 1920 Source: Collected Works, Volume 31 First Published: Pravda Nos. 221, 222 and 223, October 5, 6 and 7, 1920 Online Version: marx.org in 1997, marxists.org 1999 Transcribed: Colin S. Cavell HTML Markup: Brian Baggins and David Walters http://www.marxists.org/archive/lenin/works/1920/oct/02.htm (last accessed 13 February 2013: 12.15).

Lennard, John. 2005. *The Poetry Handbook*. Oxford: Oxford University Press.

Levertov, Denise. 1979. *Collected Earlier Poems 1940–1969*. New York: New Directions Books.

Littlemore, Jeannette. 2015. *Metonymy: Hidden Shortcuts in Language, Thought and Communication*. Cambridge: Cambridge University Press.

Ljunggren, Anna & Nils Åke Nilssen (eds.). 1988. *Elena Guro: Selected Prose and Poetry*. Stockholm: Almqvist &Wiksell International.

Ljunggren, Anna & Nils Åke Nilssen (eds.). 1995. *Elena Guro: Selected Writings from the Archives*. Stockholm: Almqvist &Wiksell International.

Llewelyn, John. 2019. *Gerard Manley Hopkins and the Spell of John Duns Scotus*. Edinburgh. Edinburgh University Press.

Lodge, David. 1979. *The Modes of Modern Writing*. London: Edward Arnold.

Lopez, Tony. 2000. *Data Shadow*. London: Reality Street Editions.

Lopez, Tony. 2012. *False Memory*. Bristol. Shearsman.

Lorde, Audre. 1997. *The Collected Poems of Audre Lorde*. New York: W W Norton & Co.

Lowth, Robert. 1799. *Isaiah: A New Translation, with a Preliminary Dissertation and Notes, Critical, Philological and Explanatory*. Isaiah: A New Translation, with a Preliminary Dissertation and Notes ... – Robert Lowth – Google Books. (last accessed 6 January 2022).

Loy, Mina. 1997. *The Lost Lunar Baedeker*. Manchester: Carcanet.

McCullough, David. 1972. *The Great Bridge: The Epic Story of the Building of the Brooklyn Bridge*. New York. Simon & Schuster.

McIntosh, Colin. 2020. *The Oxford Collocations Dictionary*. Oxford. Oxford University Press.

Mclean, Hugh. 1983. A Linguist among the Poets. *International Journal of Slavic Linguistics and Poetics*. 27. (Suppl.) 7–19.

McLean, Hugh. 1987. Majakovskij's "How to Make Verses" and Jakobson's Theory of Verse. In Krystyna Pomorska, Elzbieta Chodakowska, Hugh McLean, Brent Vine. *Language, Poetry and Poetics: The Generation of the 1890's: Jakobson, Trubetzkoy, Majakovskij*. Paper

presented at the Proceedings of the First Roman Jakobson Colloquium. MIT 10.1984: 33–48. Berlin. Mouton de Gruyter.
Macey, David. 2000. *The Penguin Dictionary of Critical Theory*. London: Penguin Books.
Magorian, Michelle. 1983. *Goodnight Mr Tom*. London: Puffin Books.
Mariani, Paul. 1999. *The Broken Tower*. New York, London: W W Norton & Co.
Marshall, Herbert. 194-? [n.d.] *Mayakovsky and His Poetry*. London: The Pilot Press.
Matejka, Ladislav.1997. Jakobson's Response to Saussure's Cours Cahiers de l'ILSL 9. 169–176.
Matejka, Ladislav & Krystyna Pomorska (eds.). 1978. *Readings in Russian Poetics: Formalist and Structuralist Views*. Michigan: University of Michigan Press.
Matthews, Peter Hugoe. 2005. *The Oxford Concise Dictionary of Linguistics*. Oxford: Oxford University Press.
Mayakovsky, Vladimir. 1982. *Three Views: Essays and a Biography specially to coincide with the British showings of the "Vladimir Mayakovsky: Twenty Years Work" Exhibition*. 275/377 High Street Stratford London E15 4QZ: Scorpion Press Ltd.
Mayakovsky, Vladimir. Victor Christyakov (trans.). 1985. *Selected Verse Vol. I*. USSR: Raduga Publishers.
Mayakovsky, Vladimir. Dorian Rottenberg (trans.). 1986. *Selected Verse Vol. II*. USSR: Raduga Publishers.
Mayakovsky, Vladimir. George Malcolm Hyde (trans.). 1990. *How Are Verses Made?* Bristol: The Bristol Press.
Menezes, Philadelpho. 1993. Brazilian Visual Poetry. *Visible Language* 27.4. Autumn. 394–409.
Merquior, José Guiherme. 1986. *From Prague to Paris*. London: Verso.
Merrell, Floyd. 2000. *Signs for Everybody or, Chaos, Quandaries, and Communication*. New York: Legas.
Metz, Christian. Celia Britton, Annwyl Williams, Ben Brewster and Alfred Guzzetti (trans.). 1982. *Psychoanalysis and the Cinema: the Imaginary Signifier*. London: Macmillan.
Morgan, Edwin. 1982. *Vladimir Mayakovsky: Three Views: Essays and a Biography specially to coincide with the British showings of the "Vladimir Mayakovsky: Twenty Years Work" Exhibition*. Oxford: Prometheus Press.
Morgan, Edwin. 1996. *Collected Translations*. Manchester: Carcanet.
Nänny, Max. 1985. Iconic Dimensions in Poetry. In Richard Waswo. (ed.), *On Poetry and Poetics*, 111–135. Zürich: Swiss Association of University Teachers of English.
Nöth, Winfried. 1990. *Handbook of Semiotics*. Bloomington: Indiana University Press.
Notley, Alice. 1992. *The Descent of Alette*. Harmondsworth: Penguin Books.
O'Brien, Sean (ed.). 1998. *The Deregulated Muse*: Essays on Contemporary British and Irish Poetry. Hexham, Northumberland: Bloodaxe Books.
Oxford English Dictionary. (ed.). 1968. Charles Talbot Onions. *Shorter Oxford English Dictionary*. Oxford: Oxford University Press.
*Oxford English Dictionary: OED Online Resource*. 2022. Oxford. Oxford University Press.
Osimo, Bruno. 2008. Jakobson: Translation as imputed Similarity. *Sign Systems Studies*. 36 (2). 315–339.
Osterwalder, Hans. 1978. *T. S. Eliot: Between Metaphor and Metonymy: a Study of his Essays and Plays in Terms of Roman Jakobson's Typology*. Bern: A. Francke.
Osterwalder, Hans. 1984. Metonymic Ways of Sympathizing with the Underdog: Philip Larkin's 'Mr Bleaney' and Anthony Thwaite's 'Mr. Cooper'. *English Studies* 65 (5). 426–33.
Parkes, Malcolm Beckwith. 1992. *Pause and Effect*. Aldershot: Scolar Press.

Pavel, Antipov - Форум по искусству и инвестициям в искусство (artinvestment.ru) (last accessed30 December 2021).
Peirce, Charles Sanders. (1931–1935 and 1958) *Editorial Introduction to Electronic Edition Membra Ficte Disjecta (A Disordered Array of Severed Limbs)*. Editorial Introduction by John Deely to the electronic edition of The Collected Papers of Charles Sanders Peirce reproducing Vols. I-VI. Edited by Charles Hartshorne & Paul Weiss. Cambridge MA. Harvard University Press 1931–1935. Vols. VII-VIII ed. Arthur W. Burks. 1958. Cambridge, MA: Harvard University Press. Available at: https://colorysemiotica.files.wordpress.com/2014/08/peirce-collectedpapers.pdf (last accessed 26 June 2022).
Petrilli, Susan. 2007. Interpretive Trajectories in Translation Semiotics. *Semiotica* 163 (1–4). 311–345.
Plato. Harold Fowler (trans.). 1963. *Cratylus, Parmenides, Greater Hippias, Lesser Hippias*. London: Heinemann [1926].
Plato. Paul Shorey (trans.). 1999. *The Republic; Books I-V*. Cambridge MA: Harvard University Press.
Plato. Paul Shorey (trans.). 2000. *The Republic; Books VI-X*. Cambridge MA: Harvard University Press.
Pollard, Clare. 2005. *Look! Clare! Look!* Northumberland: Bloodaxe Books.
Pomorska, Krystyna. 1983. A Semiotic Approach to the "Literature of Fact": Majakovskij's Poem "To Comrade Nette" *American Journal of Semiotics*. 2 (3) 71–87.
Pomorska, Krystyna. 1985. Majakovskij and the Myth of Immortality. In the Russian Avant-garde. In Nils Nilsson (ed.), *The Slavic Literatures and Modernism* Paper presented at The Slavic Literatures and Modernism Conference no.16. A Nobel Symposium 5–8th August 1985. 49–70.
Pomorska, Krystyna, Elzbieta Chodakowska, Hugh Maclean, Brent Vine. (eds.). 1987. *Language, Poetry and Poetics: The Generation of the 1890's: Jakobson, Trubetzkoy, Majakovskij*. Proceedings of the First Roman Jakobson Colloquium, Massachusetts Institute of Technology 5–6th October 1984. Berlin: Mouton de Gruyter. 157–173 and 277–290.
Pomorska, Krystyna & Stephen Rudy (eds.). 1987a. *Language in Literature*. Cambridge, Mass: Belknap Press.
Preminger, Alex & Terry V.F. Brogan. 1993. *The New Princeton Encyclopedia of Poetry and Poetics*. Princeton: Princeton University Press.
Propp, Vladimir. Laurence Scott (trans.). 2003. *Morphology of the Folktale*. Austin: University of Texas Press.
Propp, Vladimir (ed.). Adriana Martin & Richard P Martin (trans.). 1984. A Liberman. *Theory and History of Folklore*. Manchester: Manchester University Press.
Quintillian. 2001. *The Orator's Education Books 6–8*. Translated and edited by Donald A Russell. Cambridge MA: Harvard University Press.
Ransom, John Crowe. 1941. *The New Criticism*. Norfolk, CT. New Directions. *Red Tape*. 1923. Vol. XII. 138.
Rees-Jones, Deryn. 2004. *Quiver* Bridgend: Seren Books.
Riffaterre, Michael. 1966. Describing Poetic Structures: Two Approaches to Baudelaire's "Les Chats". *Yale French Studies*. 36/37. 200–242.
Riffaterre, Michael. 1971. *Essais de Stylistique Structurale*. Paris. Flammarion.
Roberts, Gary. 1999. London Here and Now: Walking, Streets, and Urban Environments in English Poetry from Donne to Gay. In Michael Bennett & David Teague (eds.), *The Nature of Cities: Ecocriticism and Urban Environments*, 33–54. Tucson AZ, University of Arizona Press.

Robinson, Anna. 2010. *The Finders of London*. London: Enitharmon.
Robinson, Anna. 2014. *Into the Woods*. London: Enitharmon.
Rose, Gillian.1993. *Feminism & Geography: The Limits of Geographical Knowledge*. Minneapolis: University of Minnesota Press.
Rowell, Margit & Deborah Wye (eds.). 2002. *The Russian Avant-Garde Book 1910–1934*. New York: The Museum of Modern Art.
Rudy, Stephen. 1987. Jakobson-Jaljagrov and Futurism. In Krystyna Pomorska, Elzbieta Chodakowska, Hugh Maclean, Brent Vine (eds.). *Language, Poetry and Poetics: The Generation of the 1890's: Jakobson, Trubetzkoy, Majakovskij*. Proceedings of the First Roman Jakobson Colloquium, Massachusetts Institute of Technology 5–6th October 1984, 277–290. Berlin: Mouton de Gruyter.
Rumens, Carol. 2004. *Poems 1968–2004*. Northumberland: Bloodaxe Books.
Ryan, Karen L. & Barry P. Scherr (eds.). 2000. *Twentieth-Century Russian Literature*. Basingstoke: Macmillan.
Saussure, Ferdinand de. Wade Baskin (trans.). 1966. *Course in General Linguistics*. New York: McGraw-Hill.
Saussure, Ferdinand de. Jean Starobinski Ed. and trans.). 1979. *Words upon Words*. New Haven and London: Yale University Press.
Saussure, Ferdinand de. 2008. *Writings in General Linguistics*. Simon Bouquet & Rudolf Engler with the assistance of Antoinette Weil (eds. and trans.); translated into English by Carol Sanders & Matthew Pires with the assistance of Peter Figueroa (trans.); Carol Sanders (introd.). Oxford: Oxford University Press, Basingstoke and Hampshire, NY: Macmillan Press & St Martin's Press.
Schneider, Myra. 2008. *Encircling the Core*. London: Enitharmon.
Schooneveld, Cornelis H van & Daniel Armstrong (eds.). 1977. *Roman Jakobson: Echoes of His Scholarship*. Lisse: Peter de Ridder Press.
Schorer, Mark. 1949. Fiction and the "Matrix of Analogy". *The Kenyon Review* 11 (4). 539–560.
Semino, Elena. 1995: Deixis and the dynamics of poetic voice. In Keith Green (ed.), *New Essays in Deixis: discourse, narrative, literature*. 103, 145–160. Amsterdam: Rodopi.
Shelley, Percy Bysshe. 1824. *Posthumous Poems*. London: John and Henry Hunt.
Sheppard, Robert. 2011. *When Bad Times Made for Good Poetry: epistoles in the history of the poetics of innovation*, 81–93. Exeter: Shearsman Books.
Sheppard, Robert. 2011. Allen Fisher's Apocalypse Then. In *When Bad Times Made for Good Poetry: epistoles in the history of the poetics of innovation*, 31–54. Exeter: Shearsman Books.
Shukman, Ann, L. & Michael O'Toole (eds.). 1977. *Russian Poetics in Translation Vol 4: Formalist Theory*. Oxford: Holdan Books; and Kindle: Ann Shukman & Michael O'Toole. 2013-12-05. *Formalist Theory* (Russian Poetics in Translation Book 4).
Sidney, Sir Philip and Shelley, Percy Bysshe. 1959. Harold Alfred Needham. (ed.). *Sidney: An Apology for Poetry; Shelley: A Defence of Poetry*. London: Ginn & Co. also: https://www.poetryfoundation.org/articles/69375/the-defence-of-poesy (last accessed 10 October 2019).
Silliman, Ron. 1995. *The New Sentence*. New York: Roof Books.
Spicer, Jack. (2009) *My Vocabulary Did This to Me: The Collected Works of Jack Spicer*. Wesleyan University Press: Connecticut.
Stapanian Apkarian, Juliette. 1999. In Christine Tomei (ed.), *Russian Women Writers: vol 1 and 2*. New York and London: Garland Publishing.
Starobinski, Jean. Olivia Emmet (trans.). 1979. *Words upon Words: The Anagrams of Ferdinand de Saussure*. New Haven & London: Yale University Press.

Steiner, Peter. 1984. *Russian Formalism: A Metapoetics*. Ithaca: Cornell University Press.
Surette, Leon. 1987. Metaphor and Metonymy: Jakobson Reconsidered *University of Toronto Quarterly*. 56 (4). 557–573.
Sütiste, Elin. 2008. Roman Jakobson and the Topic of Translation: Reception in Academic Reference Works. *Sign Systems Studies* 36 (2). 271–314.
Sütiste, Elin, Remo Grampigna, Jonathan Griffin & Silvi Salupere (eds.). 2022. *(Re)considering Roman Jakobson*. Tartu: University of Tartu Press.
Swann, Janet & Joan Maybin. 2007. Everyday Creativity in Language: Textuality, Contextuality, and Critique *Applied Linguistics*. 28 (4). 497–517.
Tate, Bronwen. 2016. The Day and the Life: Gender and the Quotidian in Long Poems by Bernadette Mayer and Lyn Hejinian. *Journal of Modern Literature* 40 (1). 42–64.
Tesnière, Lucien. 2015. *Elements of Structural Syntax* Amsterdam/Philadelphia: John Benjamins.
Thesing, William. 1990. Gerard Manley Hopkins's Response to the City: The "Composition of the Crowd". In Alison Sulloway (ed.), *Critical Essays on Gerard Manley Hopkins*, 132–154. Hall & Co. Boston.
Thomson, James.1932. *The City of Dreadful Night and Other Poems; Being a Selection from the Poetical Works of James Thomson*. Edited by John Richard Watson. London: Watts & Co.
Thurston, Scott. 2001. *Rescale: Method and Technique in Contemporary British Linguistically Innovative Poetry and Poetics*. Lancaster: University of Lancaster PhD thesis. https://ethos.bl.uk.
Todorov, Tzvetan. 1985. Three Conceptions of Poetic Language. In Roman Jackson & Stephen Rudy (eds.). *Russian Formalism: A Retrospective Glance; A Festschrift in Honor of Victor Erlich*, 130–147. New Haven: Yale Center for International and Area Studies, Yale Russian and East European Publications 6.
Tomei, Christine. D. 1999. *Russian Women Writers: vol. 1 and 2*. New York and London: Garland Publishing.
Tonks, Rosemary. 2014. *Bedouin of the London Evening: Collected Poems*. Hexham: Bloodaxe Books.
Trench, Richard. 1850. *The Parables of Our Lord*. New York. D. Appleton & Co.
Triolet, Elsa. Susan de Muth (trans.). 2002. *Mayakovsky, Russian Poet: a Memoir*. London: Hearing Eye.
Trubetzkoy, Nikolai. Christiane Baltaxe (trans.). 1939. *Principles of Phonology*. Berkeley: University of California Press. [1969].
Turner, Terence. 1977. Narrative Structure and Mythopoesis: A Critique and Reformulation of Structuralist concepts of Myth, Narrative and Poetics. *Arethusa* 10 (1). 103–163.
Unterecker, John. 1969. *Voyager: A Life of Hart Crane*. New York: Farrar, Straus and Giroux.
Uspensky, Boris. Valentina Zavarin & Susan Wittig (trans.). 1973. *A Poetics of Composition: The Structure of the Artistic Text and Typology of a Compositional Form*. Berkeley: University of California Press.
Vallier, Dora.1987. Intimations of a Linguist: Jakobson as a Poet. In Krystyna Pomorska, Elzbieta Chodakowska, Hugh McLean, Brent Vine (eds.). *Language, Poetry and Poetics: The Generation of the 1890's: Jakobson, Trubetzkoy, Majakovskij*. Paper presented at the proceedings of the First Roman Jakobson Colloquium, Massachusetts Institute of Technology 5/6th October 1984, 291–304. Berlin: Mouton de Gruyter.
Vickers, Brian. 1988. *In Defence of Rhetoric*. ebook. Oxford: Clarendon.

Vico, Giambattista. 1982. On the Ancient Wisdom of the Italians. In Leon Pompa (ed. and trans.). *Selected Writings*, 48–79. Cambridge: Cambridge University Press.
Vico, Giambattista. Thomas Bergin & Max F. Fisch (trans.). 1984. *The New Science*. Ithaca, NY: Cornell UP [1725; 3rd edition 1744] https://www.jstor.org/stable/10.7591/j.ctt20d89gr.16 (last accessed 1 November 2018).
Vico, Giambattista. 1996. *The Art of Rhetoric*. Translated by Giorgio Pinton & Arthur Shippee Amsterdam: Rodopi.
Wales, Katie.1996. *Personal Pronouns in Present-day English*. Cambridge: Cambridge University Press.
Wales, Katie. 2001. *A Dictionary of Stylistics*. Harlow: Longman.
Wardle, Sarah. 2014. *Beyond*. Hexham: Bloodaxe Books.
Wardle, Sarah. 2005. *Score!* Northumberland: Bloodaxe Books.
Warner, Val. 1998. *Tooting Idyll*. Manchester: Carcanet.
Warren, Beatrice. 2006. *Referential Metonymy Scripta Minora* Regiae Societatis Humaniorum Litterarum Lundensis. Stockholm: Almqvist and Wiksell International.
Waswo, Richard (ed.). 1985. *On Poetry and Poetics*. Zürich: Swiss Assn. of Univ. Teachers of English Gunter: Narr Verlag Tübingen.
Waugh, Linda. 1976. *Roman Jakobson's Science of Language*. Lisse: Peter de Ridder Press.
Waugh, Linda. 1980. The Poetic Function in the Theory of Roman Jakobson. *Poetics Today* 2 (1a). 57–82.
Waugh, Linda. 1983. Illuminating the Grammar of Poetry and the Poetry of Grammar, an Essay Commemorating the Publication of 'Russian and Slavic Grammar' By R Jakobson. *American Journal of Semiotics* 2 (3). 131–139.
Waugh, Linda. 1984. Some Remarks on the Nature of the Linguistic Sign. In Edward Stankiewicz, Jerzy Pelc, Thomas A Sebeok, Thomas Winner (eds.), *Sign, System and Function: papers of the first and second Polish-American Semiotics Colloquia 1978*, 389–438. Berlin: Mouton Publishers.
Waugh, Linda. 1985. The Poetic Function of Language. In Krystyna Pomorska & Stephen Rudy (eds.), 143–168. *Verbal Art, Verbal Sign, Verbal Time*. Oxford: Basil Blackwell.
Waugh, Linda. 1998. Semiotics and Language: The Work of Roman Jakobson. In Roberta Kevelson (ed.), *Hi-Fives: A Trip to Semiotics*. New York: Peter Lang. 85–102.
Waugh, Linda & Morris Halle (eds.). 1984. *Russian and Slavic Grammar Studies 1931–1981*. Berlin, New York: Mouton Publishers.
Waugh, Linda & Monique Monville-Burston (eds.). 1990. *On Language*. Cambridge MA London: Harvard University Press.
Waugh, Linda and Stephen Rudy (eds.). 1991. *New Vistas in Grammar: Invariance and Variation*. Amsterdam: John Benjamins.
Weber, Brom. 1965. *The Letters of Hart Crane 1916–1932*. Berkeley & Los Angeles: University of California Press.
Weber, Brom. 1968 (ed.). *The Complete Poems and Selected Letters and Prose of Hart Crane*. London: Oxford University Press.
Weststeijn, Willem. 1983. Poets Are not Aphasics: Some Notes on Roman Jakobson's Concept of the Metaphoric and Metonymic Poles of Language. In A Van Holk (ed.) *Dutch Contributions to the Ninth International Congress of Slavists*. Kiev. September 6–14. 198, 125–146. Amsterdam: Rodopi.

Widdowson, Henry. 2008. Language Creativity and the Poetic Function: A Response to Swann and Maybin. 2007. *Applied Linguistics*. 29 (3) 503–508.

Wilson, Raymond. 1994. Metaphoric and Metonymic Allegory: Ricoeur, Jakobson, and the Poetry of W B Yeats *Analecta Husserliana* 42. 219–228.

Winner, Thomas G. 1977. Roman Jakobson and Avantgarde Art. In Daniel Armstrong & Cornelis. H. Van Schooneveld (eds.). *Roman Jakobson: Echoes of His Scholarship*, 503–514.Lisse: Peter de Ridder Press.

Wordsworth, William 1807. *Poems in Two Volumes*. London: Longman.

Wordsworth, William. 1969. *Poetical Works*. Edited by Thomas Hutchinson. London: Oxford University Press. writingroma (wordpress.com) The True Story of the Leonine Walls: Dedicated June 27, 852 (last accessed 29 December 21).

Yeats, William Butler. 2008. *The Collected Poems of W.B. Yeats*. Ware, Herefordshire: Wordsworth Editions.

# Name and subject index

abstractum pro concreto 195–197
addressee 4, 11, 12, 20, 27, 34, 46, 71, 113–116, 136, 138–139, 140–142, 168, 176, 179, 182, 184, 245, 252–254, 305
addresser 11, 12, 20, 27, 34, 113–115, 136, 138–142, 168, 176, 179, 182, 184, 245, 252–254, 305
Aizlewood, Robin 183, 184
allegory 45, 80, 219, 243, 263
anagram 262, 266, 267, 273, 275, 305
analogy 7, 79, 82, 101, 109, 163, 182, 210, 223, 224, 242–248, 268, 269, 308
Andersen, Henning 18, 21, 30–32
angle 81, 98, 140, 215, 225
antithesis 13, 29, 159, 160, 170, 190, 229, 231, 233, 255, 331
antonymy 12, 15, 44, 46, 49, 67, 68, 132
aphasia, aphasic 38, 39, 67, 76, 83, 85, 91–94, 104, 300
Aristotle 31, 85, 244, 245
art 1, 3, 9–11, 15, 19, 20, 42, 74, 79, 81, 87, 88, 91, 157–159, 161, 163, 165, 173, 182, 185, 215, 232, 234, 241, 262, 267–269, 289, 305–307
artifice 25, 26, 51, 52, 84, 88, 89, 96, 99, 101, 102, 104, 111, 116, 134, 141, 156–159, 161, 163, 163, 169–174, 250–252, 275
assimilation 104, 308
asymmetry 157, 215
audience 27, 50, 139, 156, 177, 179, 181, 188, 190, 196, 206, 240–243, 246–248, 308
Augst, Bertrand 93–95
Augustine, Saint 23, 70–74, 171, 290, 300
Austen, Jane 156, 247
axes 1, 6, 18–20, 22, 27, 28, 32, 33, 35, 37, 39–43, 47, 49, 50, 52, 62, 66, 67, 85–88, 95–97, 125, 128, 130, 132, 133, 159, 196, 296, 305, 307
axial model 6, 14, 15, 27, 29, 37, 38, 40, 43–45, 52, 69, 82, 86, 87, 133, 153, 191, 192, 249, 304, 307, 311

axial space 50, 66, 307
axis 9, 13, 14, 16, 18, 19, 22, 24, 27, 35, 36, 37, 38–40, 43–39, 62, 86, 87, 100, 111, 122, 125, 132, 148, 266, 300
axis of combination 9, 13, 14, 16, 18, 19, 24, 27, 35–37, 38, 39, 132, 260, 266
axis of contiguity 22
axis of selection 9, 13, 14, 16, 18, 19, 22, 24, 35–37, 38, 39, 266
axis of simultaneity 14, 39, 40

balance 14, 23, 28, 31, 37, 67, 68, 128, 132, 143, 149–152, 154, 175, 270, 274, 278, 288, 308
Balzer, Wolfgang 16, 21
Banjanin, Milica 235, 236
Banjanin, Mladen 235, 236
Barry, Peter 254
Barthes, Roland 21, 96, 172, 271, 272
Bartlett, Elizabeth 136–138
Baudelaire, Charles 62, 129, 132, 134, 228, 262–267, 268, 272, 309
– "Les Chats", and Formalist analysis 62, 129, 134, 228, 262–269, 272, 309
Baum, Paull 77, 78
Belyj, Andrej 42, 43, 74, 76, 77
Bennett, James Tyler 295
Bennett, Jamie 235, 240–242
Bergman, Denise 144
Bertram, Vicki 146
Blake, William 119, 158, 170, 224–228, 257, 269
Boym, Svetlana 186, 187, 193
Bradford, Richard 13, 21, 32–35
Bredin, Hugh 21, 72–76, 80, 94, 111, 196
Brogan, Terry 13, 14, 18
Brooke-Rose, Christine 87, 88, 267, 270, 271, 273–275, 280
Bruhn, Mark 255
Bühler, Hans 114, 115, 124, 141
Burke, Kenneth 73, 74
"byt", 184–189, 193, 197, 233, 234, 255

Cameron, Michael 73, 80
Carrick, Rosie, and "byt", and Mayakovsky 185–188, 255
Cassedy, Steven 43
catenary 214–220, 222, 306
catharsis 248
centrifuge 106, 277, 279, 296–298, 300, 302–304
Chandler, James 21, 279
Chatman, Seymour 21
Cicero and metonymy 70, 73, 74, 77
city poetic genre 1, 4, 7, 9, 10, 15, 16, 19, 20, 24, 26–29, 31, 36, 37, 39, 44, 47, 49, 52, 89, 99, 112, 143, 146, 155, 197, 198, 223, 227, 248, 249, 250–255, 257, 260, 304, 305, 306, 308–310
city poetry 1, 7, 28, 47–49, 52, 80, 90, 97, 116, 118, 123, 125, 134, 144, 147, 154, 164, 191, 231, 232, 234, 236–237, 248, 251, 254, 255, 261, 276, 305–309, *see* various chapters
city structure 23, 28, 30, 31, 33, 52, 154, 308
city dweller 4, 5, 102, 125, 143, 153, 231, 307
Cobley, Paul 4, 16, 20, 21, 22, 36, 42, 173, 251, 253
code 2, 11, 12, 19, 20, 25, 27, 30, 45, 46, 103, 113–115, 140, 172, 173, 245, 296
Coghill, Mary, *Shades of Light* 32, 36, 125, 144, 147, 149, 154, 191, 237, 278–304
cohesion 44, 46, 47, 67, 68, 82, 128, 165, 288, 308
collocation 48, 71, 72, 80, 154
combination zone 44, 46, 48
communication 1, 6–8, 9–12, 16, 20–22, 25, 27, 29, 34, 38, 39, 82, 84, 98, 104, 113, 114, 135, 136, 138, 140, 155, 158, 172, 175–178, 181, 184, 191, 194, 216, 218, 234, 245, 252, 253, 271, 279, 294, 305–308, 310
conative 12, 20
concatenation 41, 46, 213, 215, 219
condensation 71, 72, 80, 84, 87, 94, 99–102, 109, 110, 218
Conley, Tim 192, 306
contact 11, 12
context 11, 12, 15, 18, 24, 34, 35, 42, 44, 46, 48, 49, 54, 71, 83, 86, 94, 97, 104, 108, 109–111, 113–115, 119–121, 139, 169, 171, 172, 183, 184, 186, 219, 220, 224, 231, 240, 252, 254, 259, 264, 283, 287, 290, 295, 300, 332, 337, 341
contiguity 13, 16–20, 22, 24, 25, 30, 32, 36, 39, 41, 42–44, 46, 48–51, 67, 68, 75, 77, 79, 82, 84–86, 90, 94, 95, 102, 110, 134, 191, 192, 227, 228, 230, 250–253, 300, 308
contiguity disorder 110, 300
Crane, Hart 198, 199, 211–223, 306
Cronan, Dennis 21, 48
crowd 97, 98, 117, 154, 163–165, 174, 192, 197, 216, 236, 241, 242, 255
Crowther, Claire 144
cubism 20, 78–80, 234, 269, 276
Cuddon, John 3, 4, 13, 59, 66, 301
Culler, Jonathan 11, 21, 29, 30, 49, 62, 157, 262–266, 288, 309
cummings, e.e., 251, 261, 262, 276

Daintith, John 46
Dalgård, Per 21, 234
Dancygier, Barbara 50
Daylight, Russell 21
decoder 30, 119, 123, 179, 181, 245, 252, 253, 254, 273
Deely, John 172, 243–245
deictics 4, 5, 7, 44, 45, 80, 113–116, 118, 120, 123, 124, 125, 128, 133, 135–143, 146–149, 152–155, 167, 169, 197, 199, 206–210, 213, 214, 221–223, 254–256, 259, 276, 278–284, 295, 301, 303, 304, 305–308, and time 123, 128, 169, 206, 208–211, 214, 254, 257, 259, 279, 281, 284, 303–305
Deignan, Alice 50
Denroche, Charles 21, 22, 50, 81–84, 95, 105
diagonals 33, 122, 126, 130, 132, 134, 166, 225, 255, 276, 278, 306
Dirven, René, 21, 32, 45, 50, 86, 87, 96, 102
discourse theory 105
dissimilarity 2, 12, 15, 17, 44, 46, 48, 49, 67, 68, 82, 132, 134
dominant 3, 12, 24, 35, 36, 83, 207
Donne, John 4, 5

Dostoyevsky, Fyodor  6, 53, 54, 55, 337–342
Drake, James  21, 93
Duffy, Carol Ann  139, 142, 145, 306
Durst-Andersen, Per  21, 22

Eco, Umberto  20
eidometropolis  4, 237, 278–281, 284–290
Èikenbaum, Eichenbaum, Boris  38, 42
Eleusinian mysteries  280
Eliot, Thomas Stearns  27, 29, 38, 50, 72, 83, 116, 156, 168, 217, 218, 289, 290, 301
Elleström, Lars  21, 22
emotive  12, 20, 26, 34, 35, 48, 117, 136
encoder  20, 27, 29, 30, 35, 37, 121, 123, 173, 179, 181, 245, 253, 308
Engler, Rudolf  18, 40
epic  53–55, 59–64, 66, 67, 105, 184, 230, 231, 312, 313, 339, 341
equilibrium  147, 214
equivalence  9, 12–16, 20, 22, 24–28, 30, 31, 35, 37, 39, 44, 46, 50, 52, 130, 132, 133, 166, 222, 266, 305, 308
equivalent  2, 12, 14, 15, 22, 30, 171, 268
Erlich, Victor and Formalism  10, 33, 34
Esenin, Sergey  175–179, 183, 184, 188, 189, 320, 332
estrangement  154, 192
exophoric references  105, 111, 273

factual iconicity  147, 250–252, 257, 259–262, 274, 276, 301, 306, 307
factual similarity  25, 28, 51, 52, 84, 96, 97, 101, 104, 105, 111, 133, 163, 250–252, 262, 306
Fauconnier, Gilles  88
Federov, Andrei  180
Feinstein, Elaine  144
feminist  146
Ferreiro, Alfredo  192, 193, 307
figurative  19, 45, 46, 70, 75, 79, 80, 82, 86, 87, 96, 97, 102, 137, 147, 217, 243
Firth, John  72
Fisher, Allen  32, 123, 124, 239, 254, 256–258, 260, 276, 307
flaneur  5
Fludernik, Monica  114, 136

Formalism  2, 3, 6, 7, 10, 31, 33, 34, 36, 54, 62, 89, 157, 224, 231, 232, 237, 252, 276, 312
Formalist praxis  1, 116, 197, 222, 266, 276, 304, "Les Chats", 62, 129, 134, 228, 262–269, 272, 309
Formalists  10–12, 33, 34, 38, 41, 42, 74, 182, 192, 232, 234, 248, 252, 255, 258
Formalist theory  8, 39, 66, 123, 175, 179, 194, 196, 198, 304, 310
 – "byt"  233, 234, 255
Formalist technique  1, 5, 7, 51–53, 225, 263, 270, 276, 279
Forrest-Thomson, Veronica  116, 135, 141, 250
fractioned idiom  213, 218–220
fragmented  44, 46–49, 67, 68, 91, 103, 104, 118, 119, 124, 128, 131, 234, 236, 255–258, 287, 304
futurism  33, 88, 116–118, 123, 124, 178, 179, 180, 191, 192, 194, 231–237, 240, 248

Gallo, Ernest  196
Garnett, Richard  160, 161
Gasparov, Boris  21, 117
Geeraerts, Dick  50
Genette, Gerard  16, 17, 21
genre  4, 7, 11, 54, 55, 134, 146, 147, 240, 241, 248, 252, 254, 255, 257, 260, 261, 269, 270, 305, 309, 310, 312–314, 316, 327, 341, 342
Goossens, Louis  83, 96, 105
Gorlée, Dinda  15, 21
grammar of poetry  9, 20, 26, 28, 37, 52, 64, 156, 159, 170, 195, 198, 229, 250, 269
Green, Keith  114, 135, 139–141
Guro, Elena  7, 117, 191, 224, 231–233, 235–237, 239, 240–243, 246, 248, 306, 308

habit  47, 53, 61, 191, 250, 251, 252
Harris, Roy  15, 21
Helle, Lillian  42, 77
Holenstein, Elmar  21, 33–35
Hopkins, Gerard Manley  2, 7, 13, 88, 98, 156–166, 168, 169–171, 173, 174, 217, 218, 220, 225, 250, 251, 301, 306, 310
hyperbole  78, 157

icon  17, 25, 51, 52, 171–173, 250–252, 254, 293–296
iconic  1, 17, 23–25, 27, 42, 50, 122, 123, 125, 128, 149, 155, 215, 222, 250, 251, 258, 260, 261, 273, 274, 293–296, 307, 308
iconic space  36
iconicity  9, 16, 17, 25–28, 32, 222, 249, 250–252, 260–262, 270, 305, 306
idiom  4, 5, 7, 71, 72, 76, 80, 212, 213, 217–220, 223, 306, 308
imbalance  23, 28, 52, 147
implied iconicity  147, 288
imputed  99, 100–102, 104, 132, 133, 158, 172, 251, 253, 259, 262
imputed iconicity  250–252, 258–262, 273, 276, 306, 307
imputed similarity  25, 26–28, 51, 52, 84, 88, 89, 96, 97, 99, 100, 104, 105, 111, 133, 134, 161, 163, 171, 172, 250, 251, 262, 270, 273, 306
index, indexical  51, 52, 114, 171–173, 250, 251, 254, 293–295
inscape  98, 161–165, 174, 217
instress  161–163
interpretant  253
irony  70, 157, 178

Jackson, John Hughlings  91–93, 300
Jaljagrov  167, 113–122, 191, 232
Jangfeldt, Bengt  177
Jeffries, Lesley  135, 139, 140, 142
Jensen, Kjeld  239
Jespersen, Otto  114, 135, 139, 140
Jones, David  90, 106–112, 167–169, 307, 308

Khlebnikov, Velimir  2, 26, 117, 180, 188, 323
Kiparsky, Paul  21, 22, 23, 28
Kruchenykh, Aleksei  191, 233

Lakoff, George  47, 82, 88
Lass, Andrew  232
Layer, layering  15, 50, 66, 109, 110, 111, 169, 220, 258, 260, 301, 307
legisign  293–295
Lenin, Vladimir  121, 315, 332, 334, 337
Lennard, John  301
Levertov, Denise  144

Lévi-Strauss, Claude  35, 134, 232
– "Les Chats", and Formalist analysis  62, 129, 134, 228, 262–269, 272, 309
likeness  13, 77, 85, 159, 166, 254
linguistics  1–5, 7, 9, 10–17, 20–26, 28–31, 33–36, 38–45, 48–52, 62, 64, 65, 67, 70, 72, 77, 81–89, 91–95, 100, 102, 111, 112, 113, 115, 118, 119, 123, 124, 134, 140, 142, 156, 161, 165, 166, 170, 172–175, 180, 182, 197, 224, 229, 252, 262, 265, 267, 272, 276, 310
linked  1, 11, 20, 40, 42, 44, 46, 48, 49, 67, 68, 79, 94, 99–103, 128, 153, 161, 163, 184, 218, 280
literariness  2, 5, 10, 29, 31, 32, 34, 38, 118, 134, 173, 182, 198, 232, 276, 277, 278, 302
Littlemore, Jeannette  81, 82, 84, 104, 105, 111
Ljunggren, Anna  241
Llewelyn, John, and Hopkins  162
Lodge, David, poetry and metonymy  83, 105
Lopez, Tony  48, 90, 102–106, 308
Lorde, Audre  144
Lowth, Robert  166
Loy, Mina  144

Marshall, Herbert  64
masculine grammar  62, 66, 129, 134, 263
Matejka, Ladislav  9, 41, 46
mathematics  1, 42, 43, 77, 215
Matthews, Peter  3, 4, 15, 36, 84
Mayakovsky, Vladimir  5, 6, 11, 52–69, 116, 117, 174, 175–197, 198–215, 221, 222, 233–235, 306, 307, 311–342
– "byt"  184–189, 197
McAleer, Bill  76
McIntosh, Colin  71
McLean, Hugh  21, 175
Menezes, Philadelpho  191, 181, 182
Merrell, Floyd  52, 251, 289–295, 309
message  4, 11, 12, 20, 24, 26–31, 34, 35, 37, 38, 46, 52, 60, 63, 85, 99, 102, 113–115, 140, 145, 172, 173, 176–179, 181, 219, 245, 252, 271–273, 303–305, 308
metalingual  12

metaphor  7, 13, 15, 16–19, 22, 24, 25, 28, 31, 35, 36, 38, 42–47, 49–52, 62–64, 67, 70, 75–77, 79–88, 90, 91, 93–96, 98–100, 103–105, 108, 110–112, 120, 132, 134, 153, 157, 159, 165, 217, 219, 223, 224, 227–231, 234, 242, 248, 298–300, 304, 305, 308, 324
metaphoric  6, 17–19, 22, 25–29, 39, 41–43, 45–49, 51, 59, 62–69, 71, 72, 76–79, 81–83, 85–87, 90, 95, 97, 101–105, 108–111, 128, 129, 132–134, 137, 139, 143, 218–220, 227, 228–231, 250, 260, 282, 286, 304, 308, 342
metaphoric axis, pole  19, 39, 41, 45–47, 78, 79, 86
metaphoricity  45, 96
metonymic pole, axis  6, 19, 22, 26–29, 39, 41, 42, 45, 48, 49, 78, 79, 86, 95, 100, 110
metonymy  7, 16, 18, 19, 22, 28, 32, 35, 36, 38, 42–46, 49, 50–52, 67, 69, 70–89, 90, 91, 93–105, 108–112, 134, 156, 157, 196, 228, 236, 245, 248, 300, 305, 307, 308
metonymic  18, 35, 36, 39, 41, 42, 43, 44, 45, 46, 49, 51, 62–68, 70–88, 90, 95–106, 108–112, 129, 132, 134, 143, 195–197, 218–220, 227–230, 245, 250, 255, 257, 260, 261, 304, 308, 309
metre  1, 13, 14, 16, 22, 32, 43, 46, 50, 52, 98, 158, 159, 165, 166, 178, 183, 184, 189, 190, 270
Metz, Christian  93–96, 102, 111
Morgan, Edwin  177, 178
Moscow Linguistic Circle  2, 314
multiplicity  108, 287, 307

Nänny, Max  21, 26, 27, 261, 262
narrative  9, 32, 35, 44, 48, 59, 60, 89, 94, 95, 99, 100, 102, 104, 140–142, 151, 227, 228, 231, 276, 293–295, 303, 339
narrator  1, 53, 60, 62, 98, 99, 101, 135, 139–141, 145, 146, 154, 157, 209, 210, 227, 239, 240, 242, 243, 301, 306
negative  49, 62, 66, 100, 102, 104, 130–133, 165, 171, 192, 195–197, 281, 282, 285, 286, 303, 307

neologism  5, 177–179, 187, 191, 216, 234, 248, 280, 287, 288, 307, 309
Nöth, Winfried  14, 25
Notley, Alice  144

O'Brien, Sean  145
origo-deixis  114, 115, 141, 213
Osimo, Bruno  21, 26
Osterwalder, Hans  20, 21, 27, 29, 38, 83
*ostranenie*  19

parable  13, 243, 246
paradigm  14, 15, 18, 31, 32, 39–41, 43–45, 48, 49, 79, 94, 96, 125, 128–134, 159, 192, 196, 305, 307
paradigmatic axis, pole  22, 32, 39, 44, 48, 62, 86, 87, 125, 130, 296
paradox, 117, 157, 296
parallelism  13, 14, 20, 22, 24, 32, 41, 50, 51, 134, 158–161, 165, 166, 169–171, 173, 192, 251, 270, 272
parallels  7, 16, 24, 26, 31, 50, 51, 67, 78, 84, 88, 89, 94, 96, 97, 99, 100, 102, 111, 124, 132–134, 155, 156, 158–163, 165–167, 169–174, 197, 246, 250, 258, 270, 278, 280, 301, 303, 305, 306, 310, 337
Parkes, Malcolm  301
Peirce, Charles Sanders  1, 4, 17, 23, 25, 26, 36, 51, 52, 88, 114, 171–174, 250–254, 273, 279, 288, 289, 292–296, 308, 309
Petrilli, Susan  15, 36, 251
phatic  12
phonology  91
place  5, 45, 46, 48, 73, 110, 112, 115, 118, 119–121, 123, 124, 130, 131, 133, 134, 135, 140, 142, 144–148, 153, 154, 167–169, 176, 182, 192, 208–210, 214, 221, 230, 231, 250, 254–259, 275, 279–281, 284, 287, 301, 305–304, 305, 307–309
Plato  17, 19, 25, 163
poetic artifice  52, 88, 101, 141, 156, 159, 163, 169, 171, 174, 250
poetic function  1, 6–8, 9–37, 38–39, 41, 48, 49, 51, 52, 79, 82–85, 87–89, 97, 99, 102, 111, 112, 156, 163, 165, 171, 175–177, 181, 232, 250, 252, 254, 255, 258, 266, 269, 288, 289, 296, 305, 306, 309, 310

poetic space  28, 29, 38, 49, 50, 184, 307
poetic theory  9, 22, 85, 143, 155, 156, 174, 195, 232, 266, 306
poetics  1, 4, 7, 10, 12–16, 18, 22, 26, 29, 35, 38, 48, 51, 67, 80, 83–85, 87, 88, 90, 90–112, 119, 134, 147, 154, 155, 156, 157, 159, 165, 169, 171–174, 179, 182–184, 188, 196, 197, 231, 232, 241, 242, 247, 263, 265, 267, 296, 302, 305–307, 310, 318, 336
poles – *see* metaphoric, metonymic, syntagm, paradigm
Pollard, Clare  144
Pomorska, Krystyna  7, 10, 11, 21, 88, 185, 232, 263
positional  93–96, 102, 131, 214
Prague Linguistic Circle  10, 12, 41, 54
praxis  1, 6, 7, 38, 69, 78, 83, 89, 90–112, 113, 116, 135, 147, 167, 174, 197, 198, 222, 232, 250, 266, 276, 278, 289, 304, 305, 305, 308–310
procedural  257, 258, 307
processual  257, 258, 307
projection  1, 9, 10, 15–20, 23, 24, 26–28, 30–32, 35–37, 39, 133, 137, 250, 252, 258, 266, 305, 308
pronouns – *see* shifters and deictics
proscenium arch  236, 247, 308, and stage  236, 241, 246, 247
punctuation  6, 27, 47, 69, 104, 121, 134, 152, 190, 261, 270, 278, 296, 298, 300–304, 308

qualisign  293–295
Quintillian  73, 74

random  44, 46–49, 67, 68, 99, 100, 104, 110, 124, 128, 149, 164, 304
Ransom, John Crowe  156, 157
realism  9, 19, 33, 78, 79, 158, 165, 232
recoder  252–254, 273, 308
Rees-Jones, Deryn  144, 254
referential  12, 25, 26, 83, 103, 105, 197, 209
repetition  44, 46, 48–50, 67–69, 102, 128, 156, 158, 166, 170, 228, 278, 283, 290, 304, 308

revolution  9, 33, 53, 59, 63–66, 117, 174, 175–197, 231–233, 235, 316, 317, 339, 341, 342
rheme  119, 125, 129–134
rhetoric  2, 14, 22, 46, 50, 72, 77, 79, 80, 84, 85, 91, 93, 94, 98, 100, 111, 112, 156, 157, 161, 163, 174, 196, 209, 210, 213, 214, 222, 239, 276, 303, 306
riddle  77, 78
Riffaterre, Michael  21, 271, 272
Roberts, Gary  4, 5, 307
Robinson, Anna  145
Rose, Gillian  146
Rudy, Stephen  7, 21, 116–118, 191, 192, 232–234, 274, 333
Rumens, Carol  145
Russian Formalism  2, 10, 31, 224
Russian Formalist  5, 9, 38, 39, 74, 77, 173, 175, 176, 182, 191, 192, 231, 232, 258, 307

Saussure, Ferdinand de  1, 4, 10, 12, 19, 21–23, 34, 39–43, 46, 51, 82, 85–88, 108, 109, 171, 172, 245, 246, 252, 266, 267, 280, 310
Schneider, Myra  145
Schooneveld, Cornelis  21
Schorer, Mark  246
science of poetics  10, 38, 134, 182
selection zone  44
semantic, semantics  2, 3, 13, 16, 17, 34, 42, 49–51, 70, 77, 80, 84, 85, 89, 93–97, 99, 102, 104, 156, 157, 161, 166, 169, 174, 178, 180, 206, 241, 263, 270, 272, 275, 276, 301, 304
Semino, Elena, and deixis  136–138
semeiosis, semiosis  6, 23, 163, 172, 173, 296
semiology  4, 23, 172, 267
semiotic theory  6, 111, 165, 174, 232
semiotician  51, 88, 119, 134, 171, 232, 251, 271, 289, 310
semiotic, semiotics  1, 3–7, 9, 10, 12, 14–18, 20, 22–26, 28, 30, 31, 36, 37, 38, 38–69, 41, 42, 47, 49, 51, 52, 62, 64, 70, 71, 77, 78, 80, 83–85, 88, 89, 91, 92, 97, 99,

100, 102, 104, 111, 112, 118, 119, 123, 134, 139, 141, 142, 154, 158, 159, 161, 163, 165, 166, 169, 170–174, 175, 182, 197, 198, 206, 217, 224, 225, 230, 232, 241, 247, 250–253, 262, 265, 268, 272–276, 279, 289, 292, 293, 296, 304, 305–307, 311
Shelley, Percy Bysshe 160
Sheppard, Robert 255
shifter, shifters 5, 7, 44, 45, 53, 68, 109, 112, 113–120, 123–125, 130, 131, 134, 135–141, 143, 146, 147, 151–155, 167–169, 197, 199, 206, 208, 209, 211–214, 221–223, 240, 264, 270, 272, 275, 278, 302, 303, 305–309
Shukman, Ann 2, 53
Sidney, Philip 266
signans, signatum 23–25, 172, 173, 250–253
Silliman, Ron 21, 45–48
similarity 2, 4, 9, 12, 14–19, 22, 24–28, 30, 36, 37, 41–44, 46, 48–52, 67, 68, 75, 79, 82, 84–86, 88, 89, 94–97, 100–102, 104, 105, 110, 111, 132–134, 159, 161, 163, 166, 171–173, 222, 228, 250–253, 258, 262, 270, 273, 278, 300, 304, 306
similarity disorder 110, 300, 304
simile, similes 13, 18, 36, 40, 41, 44, 46, 48, 51, 55, 60, 63, 64, 67, 69, 82, 85, 100, 101, 128, 152, 153, 159, 190, 210, 211, 216, 217, 229, 243, 298, 299
simultaneity 14, 18, 31, 38–41, 43–45, 47, 50, 65, 77, 79, 84, 87, 88, 90, 110, 128, 159, 217, 234, 304, 308
sinsign 293–296
space 5, 6, 16, 19, 23, 26, 28, 29, 32, 36, 38, 39, 42, 49, 50, 52, 62, 66, 89, 90, 108, 125, 128–134, 135, 141, 143–148, 154, 171, 184, 187, 192, 196, 197, 198, 213, 231, 235, 241, 245, 260, 268, 269, 280, 290, 296, 301, 305–307, 309
Spicer, Jack 48
Stapanian-Apkarian, Juliette 236
Starobinksi, Jean 266, 270
Steiner, Peter 10, 21, 33–35
stimulus 5, 94, 95, 103–105, 110, 181, 255, 260, 308
structural 1, 6, 11, 15, 23, 28, 38, 42, 77, 80, 90, 136, 159, 180, 247, 252

structuralism 29
structuralist 9, 11, 29, 41, 91, 136, 157, 262, 263, 265
stylistics 9, 50, 135, 139, 141, 142, 161, 174
supraconscious 33, 185, 232
Sütiste, Elin 3, 21
syllable, syllables 13, 24, 125, 129, 133, 158, 171, 183, 225, 227, 261, 267, 280, 281, 284, 287, 290, 302–4
symbolism 43, 90, 233, 243, 316, 324, 332, 336, 341
symbol, symbols, symbolic 11, 16, 17, 27, 36, 42, 43, 51, 52, 54, 55, 79, 85, 92, 93, 114, 171–173, 197, 218, 230, 234, 243, 247, 250–252, 254, 267, 280, 293, 294, 327, 330, 331, 333, 340, 341
symmetry, asymmetry 157, 169, 225, 263, 265, 270, 327
synecdoche 14, 43, 49, 63, 64, 70, 73–75, 79, 84, 91, 98, 99, 131, 134, 157, 219, 220, 228, 245
synonym, synonymy 12, 15, 36, 44, 46, 48, 49, 67, 68, 94, 128, 132
syntagm, syntagmatic 14, 15, 18, 22, 30–32, 39–41, 43–46, 48, 49, 62, 79, 86, 87, 94, 96, 97, 111, 125, 130–133, 148, 153, 159, 192, 196, 305, 296, 307
syntagmatic poles, axis, axes 14, 15, 22, 30, 32, 40, 41, 46, 79, 86, 87, 96, 97, 111, 125, 130, 296
syntax 3, 22, 31, 49, 77, 102, 120, 123, 134, 138, 166, 167, 17348, 62, 178, 269, 272, 276

Tate, Bronwen 235, 236
Tesnière, Lucien 263–266
theme, themes 4, 5, 119, 124, 125, 129–134, 231, 240, 254, 267
theory of communication 6, 8, 12, 27, 34, 140, 245, 279
Thesing, William 164, 165, 174
Thurston, Scott 123, 239, 257
time 5, 13–15, 17, 32, 33, 38–46, 48, 50, 73, 79, 84, 85, 87–89, 90, 99, 102, 109, 110–112, 115, 123–125, 128, 133, 135, 137, 139, 140–143, 146, 147, 148, 153, 167, 169, 171, 172, 176, 185, 187, 206,

208–215, 221, 223, 230, 231, 239, 245, 254, 257, 259, 279, 280, 281, 284, 290, 300, 301, 304, 305, 307, 309
Todorov, Tzvetan 10, 263
Tomei, Christine 236
Tonks, Rosemary 90, 99, 100, 112, 145, 171, 308
torque 44, 46–50, 67–69, 128, 300, 304, 308
train 192, 193, 229, 230, 307
transitory grammar 228, 264, 275, 278, 283, 284, 309
translation theory 7
Trench, Richard 243
Triolet, Elsa 181, 318
trope, tropes 4, 17, 19, 20, 25, 33, 43, 46, 48, 50–52, 62, 64, 66–69, 70, 74, 75, 77, 79–81, 84, 88, 90, 91, 93, 97, 103, 105, 111, 131, 156–159, 163, 165, 166, 169, 170, 174, 197, 223, 224, 231, 236, 237, 245, 246, 248, 249, 255, 256, 258, 261, 287, 298, 305–308, 310
Trubetzkoy, Nikolai 1, 91
Turner, Terence 21, 35, 36, 133

unfractioned idiom 212, 217–219
unlikeness 13, 159, 166
Unterecker, John 217
urbanism 4, 5, 23, 104, 105, 117, 145, 154, 234, 254
Uspensky, Boris 242, 247

Vallier, Dora 21, 116
value 3, 10, 11, 14, 15, 31, 39–43, 84, 85, 87, 92, 112, 169, 182, 187, 266
verb tense, tenses 116, 120, 123, 125, 136, 140, 168, 210, 211, 221, 247, 276, 277, 288, 290

verbal art 12, 34, 41, 83, 119, 158, 178, 224
Vickers, Brian 21, 91
Vico, Giambattista 91
viewpoint 98, 99, 106, 109, 130, 131, 137, 139, 146, 154, 164, 214, 219, 220, 228–231, 234, 237, 240, 247, 249, 255, 268, 303, 308, 309
vocabulary 4, 5, 111, 177, 178, 183, 184, 264, 269

Wales, Katie 4, 14, 16, 49, 72, 113, 135, 141, 148, 152, 169, 191
Wardle, Sarah 90, 97, 98, 112, 145, 164, 224, 229–231, 302, 308
Warner, Val 145
Warren, Beatrice 82
Waswo, Richard 261
Waugh, Linda 3, 15, 21, 22–26, 28, 31, 34, 311
Weber, Brom 217, 218
Wilson, Raymond 21, 45, 80, 83, 97
window 72, 77, 131, 147, 164, 235–237, 240, 259, 308
Winner, Thomas 235
woman narrator 1, 135–155
women 134, 142–146, 154, 232, 235, 236, 240, 241, 248, 254, 289, 290, 305, 306, 309, 313
Wordsworth, William 224, 228, 229, 231, 254, 255, 279

Yeats, William Butler 80, 83, 97, 119, 141, 274

zero sign 45, 61, 62, 66, 67, 132, 139, 191, 192, 307, and feminine endings 129, 194, 195
zero space 307

www.ingramcontent.com/pod-product-compliance
Lightning Source LLC
Chambersburg PA
CBHW061930220426
43662CB00012B/1853